Mac OS X Developer's Guide

Jesse Feiler

Morgan Kaufmann

AN IMPRINT OF ACADEMIC PRESS
A Division of Harcourt, Inc.

San Diego San Francisco New York Boston
London Sydney Tokyo

Acquisitions Editor	Tim Cox
Publishing Services Manager	Victor Curran
Senior Production Editor	Julie Bolduc
Production Coordinator	Mei Levenson
Editorial Coordinator	Stacie Pierce
Cover Design	Laurie Anderson
Copyeditor	Jill Hobbs
Printer	Graphic Services

This book was typeset by the author using FrameMaker.

Designations used by companies to distinguish their products are often claimed as trademarks or registered trademarks. In all instances in which Morgan Kaufmann Publishers is aware of a claim, the product names appear in initial capital or all capital letters. Readers, however, should contact the appropriate companies for more complete information regarding trademarks and registration.

Morgan Kaufmann Publishers
340 Pine Street, Sixth Floor, San Francisco, CA 94104-3205, USA
http://www.mkp.com

ACADEMIC PRESS
A Division of Harcourt, Inc.
525 B Street, Suite 1900, San Diego, CA 92101-4495, USA
http://www.academicpress.com

Academic Press
Harcourt Place, 32 Jamestown Road, London, NW1 7BY, United Kingdom
http://www.academicpress.com

06 05 04 03 02   5 4 3 2 1

Library of Congress Control Number: 2001095851
ISBN: 0-12-251341-X

This book is printed on acid-free paper. (∞)

Mac OS X Developer's Guide

Contents

Part I
Introducing Mac OS X

2. Architecture Overview 21

3. Frameworks and Object-Oriented Programming 49

Part II
Designing for Mac OS X

10. Planning Your Project 193

11. The Tools of Mac OS X: Project Builder 207

Part III
Writing for Mac OS X

29. Writing Reusable Components 573

Index 581

Preface

When the first Mac OS shipped with the first Macintosh computer in 1984, the development environment was a Lisa computer. No compilers existed on the first Macintosh computers when they shipped. Much has changed in the almost two decades since then. The first copies of Mac OS X shipped in the spring of 2001 with compilers for C, C++, Objective-C, and Java. Apple's integrated development environment featuring Project Builder and Interface Builder was also on the CD, and third party products such as CodeWarrior were also available from the first day.

Born into a mature development environment, Mac OS X provides new and exciting opportunities for developers of all sorts to explore the possibilities of personal computing. This book provides an introduction to those possibilities.

You will find the background of Mac OS X in Part I, including the architectural features of Mac OS X along with introductions to its various languages and frameworks. Part II focuses on developing projects: It explores Project Builder, Interface Builder, development techniques, and issues related to providing help and packing your software. Part III looks closely at code: It hones in on particular tasks that you need to do and provides line-by-line analysis of the code you will use.

The book looks primarily at the Cocoa framework using its two languages (Java and Objective-C) equally in the examples. A lot of space is also given to Carbon, the other major development framework that is unique to Mac OS X. Examples for Carbon are provided in C++.

There are two other significant development environments that matter on Mac OS X: Java and UNIX. Both are covered extensively in other books, as they are not unique to Mac OS X. It is important to note how easy it is to use both of them. In particular, integration of UNIX command line processing is a great opportunity for developers. Using the `system()` function, you can add calls to the command line to any C-based application (Objective-C, C++, or C). Thus, you can use the sophisticated interface development tools such as Interface Builder to create a spiffy front-end to these critical UNIX-based tools: That, in large part, is what Apple expects many developers to do. The opportunities there are enormous, and the amount of work involved for each one is low.

Major features of the new Aqua interface are dealt with: You will find drawers and toolbars described, and the implementation code for them is provided. Services, too, are given a lot of space, in view of the fact that they represent yet another area in which individual developers can significantly leverage their own work and that of others.

Diary

This book refers to an actual program written using Cocoa in both Java and Objective-C. Called Diary, it implements a basic journal that can contain various entries and images. You can download the application and the source code from http://www.philmontmill.com (go to the Mac OS X area). The full code is not repeated in this book, but major sections of it are presented and annotated. These sections implement the functionality that many Mac OS X applications use.

For common features that are not used in Diary (drawing, for example), code from the Mac OS X Developer CD is used—Sketch, in most cases.

Other Documentation and Developer Resources

Apple provides a great deal of documentation on its Web site, on the Developer CD, and as printed materials that you can purchase. Of particular interest are the Project Builder examples that are installed with Project Builder. The step-by-step tutorials for Interface Builder and Project Builder walk you through many of the processes described here.

In addition to the step-by-step tutorials that Apple provides in several media, there also is definitive and encyclopedic documentation of Mac OS X APIs available online and with the Developer CD. As new features are added to the Mac OS X APIs, sometimes the documentation lags behind the code a little bit: If you do not find what you are looking for, check back later.

Rather than duplicate Apple's documentation, this book attempts to provide alternative perspectives in order to provide a well-rounded view of the technology.

Apple's Web site is an essential resource for all developers. Located at http://developer.apple.com, it provides sample code, technical documentation in a variety of formats, and information about Apple and third-party resources including training, consulting, and publications.

In addition to the developer site, the support discussions at http://www.apple.com/support can be of help to developers. Sections devoted to developers contain exchanges that may provide you with information and tips; you can also post your comments and questions there.

Mailing lists are available through http://www.lists.apple.com. These lists include announcements as well as discussion lists of interest to developers, including lists devoted to Project Builder, Cocoa, Carbon, and Java. Most of the lists are managed by Apple, but some third-party lists are also included.

Finally, the author's Web site at http://www.philmont-mill.com contains a section devoted to Mac OS X. It provides a question and answer forum as well as a section with postings of information relevant to Mac OS X.

Acknowledgments

Many people have contributed to this book. At Morgan Kaufmann in San Francisco, Tim Cox and Stacie Pierce provided strong editorial guidance, while Mei Levenson and Laurie Anderson did great work on designing the cover. Sheri Dean's help on marketing is always terrific. In Boston at Academic Press, Julie Bolduc, production editor, and Jill Hobbs, copy editor, worked wonders with a very complex manuscript and a very tight deadline.

Notwithstanding the assistance of all of these people, any errors that remain are the author's handiwork alone.

Part I
Introducing Mac OS X

Mac OS X, the new operating system from Apple Computer, is built on firm foundations. These include the principles of modern operating systems (including multithreading, multiprocessing, a UNIX-based kernel, and memory protection) as well as object-oriented programming and component software.

This part of the book provides a summary of the Mac OS X architecture, as well as the principles of modern operating systems and object-oriented programming.

Chapter 1
Introduction

Mac OS X is a departure from previous operating systems both on mainframes and on personal computers. Its structure is thoroughly modern—it is based on a small kernel that isolates the most critical aspects of the operating system, and it is object oriented to a degree that has not been seen in a mainstream operating system. Its user experience has been developed based not only on Apple's years of research and development in this area, but also on the powerful processors of today and tomorrow that can provide a rich, sophisticated, and delightful user experience of greater elegance and power than their earlier incarnations could provide.

This book is for Mac OS X developers—for people who are starting to explore Mac OS X to find out what's there and what the opportu-

nities are. It is about writing software and about how Mac OS X makes the developer's job much easier—and very different.

Writing computer software can be very rewarding—both intellectually and financially. Yet it requires scrupulous attention to detail and often consists of continuing repetitions of nearly similar tasks—tasks that must be carried out with attention and accuracy, despite their likenesses. Errors can cause immediate problems, or they can lie in wait until a particular combination of circumstances conspires to loose their destructive forces on unsuspecting people.

The work is extraordinarily labor intensive, consuming large amounts of the lives of often highly paid people while requiring them to repeat (not mindlessly but mindfully*) the same tasks over and over, at the same time exacting high prices for even the slightest flaws or inattention to these complex, repetitive processes.*

For nearly 50 years, people have looked at the process of programming computers and tried to improve it. The impetus for these attempts comes from programmers themselves as well as from their managers. Management, of course, would like to reduce costs, improve the reliability of code, and produce software more quickly. These incentives are nothing compared to the goals of programmers—people who find themselves writing sort routines, natural language parsers, report formatters, and mouse-tracking procedures over and over and over again. Each version is almost like the last one—similar enough to pose little imaginative challenge, yet different enough to be riddled with snares for the inattentive.

Meanwhile, the nature of computer software has been changing, with the focus moving from mainframes to personal computers and then to networks of machines. As the nature of software has changed, enormous advances in hardware (processing speed, memory, and storage) coupled with dramatic decreases in their costs have allowed developers to experiment with new techniques that previously would have been impractical to implement.

This chapter addresses three basic issues that are at the core of Mac OS X development:

- *Who is a programmer?*

- *The search for better ways to write software*

- *The evolution of software*

Far from being abstract historical issues, these are at the core of the developer tools and experience in Mac OS X.

Who Is a Programmer?

Traditionally, there has been an enormous barrier between programmers and software users. With Mac OS X, that barrier is being broken down; in fact, it has been wobbling for some time now. The concept of power users or advanced users has been around for ages: Macros, Visual Basic scripts, Apple-Script scripts, and the like are typically written by these people. Programs that need compilation, however, have been the province of programmers. True, some power users have experimented with them, but by and large, they have stayed away.

With Mac OS X, the range of programming tools is vast: it ranges from the command line that is available in Terminal, through scripting technologies such as AppleScript and Perl, and on to services (which allow for the construction of very customized programs and processes). Also, the development tools—compilers, Project Builder, and Interface Builder—are distributed with shrink-wrapped copies of Mac OS X and are easily downloadable from Apple's developer site located at (http://developer.apple.com). Apple is making it easier to program, and it is making those tools more widely available.

The bulk of programming is done not for shrink-wrapped products but for custom applications. Some of these are extremely tailored: one person writing code for private use. Others are written for a particular environment (one school or office) or for vertical markets (libraries, veterinarians, or graphic artists).

If you are wondering if you could possibly write a program, worry no more: You can with Mac OS X. This book helps you understand the concepts behind developing for Mac OS X. The development tools that are on the Developer CD as well as the tools and sample code on Apple's developer site (www.apple.com/developer) are thorough and informative: their information is not repeated here to any great extent.

The Search for Better Ways to Write Software

Perhaps more than the economic motives of management, the sense among many programmers that they are wasting enormous amounts of time repeating and repeating the same old code has inspired a decades-long search for better ways to develop software.

This search for better ways to write software has centered on three primary areas:

- The process of producing code

- The reuse of existing code

- The abstraction of code

Improving the Production of Code

In this strategy to improve the production of software, the focus is on the actual production of code. Compilers and code generators automate its production while techniques of coding such as structured programming improve the quality of the code. Nontextual programmer tools bring the power of graphical user interfaces to programmers (at last!).

Compilers and High-Level Languages   Strange as it may seem today, the possibility of writing a compiler was not widely accepted in the early 1950s. Compilers and high-level languages (starting with Fortran, Algol, and Cobol in the late 1950s) have grown far beyond their early implementations.

The idea of compilers is to allow people to program in ways that are more natural to them than the peculiar instructions of individual computers. In 1978, Dr. Grace Hopper, one of the most important early compiler developers (she led the group that developed A-0 for the UNIVAC), recalled in an address on the origins of compilers:

> [T]he primary purposes [of building compilers] were not to develop a programming language, and we didn't give a hoot about commas and colons.... We were trying to solve problems and get answers....
>
> We were also endeavoring to provide a means that people could use, not that programmers or programming language designers could use. But rather, plain, ordinary people, who had problems they wanted to solve. Some were engineers; some were business people. And we tried to meet the needs of the various communities. I think we somewhat lost track of that, too. I'm hoping that the development of the microcomputer will bring us back to reality and to recognizing that we have a large variety of people out there who want to solve problems, some of whom are symbol-oriented, some of whom are word-oriented, and that they are going to need different kinds of languages rather than trying to force them all into the pattern of the mathematical logician.[1]

The "tough-guy" early programmers who struggled with machine code and then with assembly language often looked down on the softies who used compilers and high-level languages. The code generated by compilers was never so effi-

---

1. *History of Programming Languages*, Richard L. Wexelblat, editor. Academic Press, 1981, p. 11. The address was given as the keynote speech at the ACM SIGPLAN History of Programming Languages Conference, June 1–3, 1978.

cient as that written directly in assembler or machine code (or so they said). With today's highly optimized compilers and blazingly fast processors, such arguments surely have little basis in practical reality. (But a reminder such as this is always welcome in some quarters.)

Code Generators Code generators represent another approach to the problem of improving the production of software. Code generators—which in fact antedate compilers—let you specify the nature of the problem you want to solve (a file to be sorted, a report to be produced, etc.) and they then produce the code to do the job. This code can be low- or high-level code, depending on the particular code generator. Some generators are quite complex—Burroughs Corporation's LINC system in the 1980s allowed users to specify screen layouts, report formats, and database designs, and it generated Cobol code as output. The code that is produced can often be modified manually to fine-tune the end product.

Code generators are a very efficient means of producing basic code with little customization. Mac OS X's Project Builder and Interface Builder allow you to create the basic files of an application automatically; stubs for classes and methods are generated automatically as you specify them graphically.

Structured Programming and Other Techniques In addition to compilers and code generators, a third technique for improving the production of code was developed early on. It is in essence the "good faith" efforts of programmers to police themselves and to write understandable code. Whereas computers and compilers are quite persnickety about the code they read and are intolerant of even the smallest faux pas, they have infinite patience when it comes to deciphering the complexity of the code. People, however, are just the reverse. In reading code (or any text, for that matter), the eye and brain often correct minor errors without your noticing it. (That is why you can so often not find a compiler error that consists of a single misplaced letter.) By the same token, following a convoluted logical process quickly taxes the poor human brain.

Realizing that the challenge is often to produce code that can easily be read and understood by people (who are modifying it at some time in the future), programming styles and techniques have been developed to make it easier for people to read code.

These techniques include the notion of structured programming (from which `goto` statements are banished) and more recently the development of object-oriented programming (from which conditional statements are largely excluded). The results of these two stylistic decisions are programs that consist largely of declarative statements that are executed sequentially in the same way each time. Such programs are much easier to write and debug than they would otherwise be.

Graphical Tools for Programmers   Programmers often do not get to use the fruits of their own labors. Recognized productivity improvements for end users such as databases and graphical user interfaces have been slow in coming to the programmer's environment. With Mac OS X, developers will find an environment that is heavily graphically oriented. Other environments have provided more or less successful interfaces to text-based tools; with Interface Builder, you will find a true graphical programming tool. And because its primary purpose is to build graphical interfaces, that focus is totally appropriate.

In fact, experienced programmers who used Interface Builder when it was a product of NeXT, refer to "ASCII code"—the text-based code that is written to augment their graphically written code. No longer is it assumed that "code" means text.

Reusing Code

The advantage of reusing code has been obvious to programmers for decades. Every programmer has reused code, whether from a previous project, from a colleague, from code samples, or from books and magazines.

Reusing code provides obvious and immediate benefits, albeit at a cost. For code to be reused, it must be directly applicable to the problem at hand. Routines that calculate mathematical functions (sines, cosines, etc.) are fairly easy to reuse. As soon as the code starts to be customized for a specific purpose, however, its reuse becomes problematic. Of course, it is precisely such customized code that people want to reuse. Unfortunately, in doing so, all too often the advantage of reusing old code outweighs the disadvantage of its not being quite right for the job. More often than not, it is the user who suffers with an interface that just isn't quite right.

To deal with the problem of reusing code that isn't exactly right, three approaches have been developed to make the situation better: parameter-driven code, object-oriented programming, and moving commonly-used code into system software.

Parameter-Driven Code   For many years now, code has been factored into functionally separate parts. The interface including variables that change from time to time is divorced as much as possible from the operational side of the program. As needed, the program queries the interface (or a file) for the parameters it needs to carry out its work.

The use of resources with the Mac OS is a prime example of parameter-driven code. The appearance of windows is specified in resources that can be changed without recompiling the program itself. Text can be changed from one language to another without touching source code. Over time, even fairly complex issues such as centering of windows on monitors have been moved into resources rather than application-specific code.

In Mac OS X, the parameters and data are located in files of their own. Whereas on the Mac OS resources often are placed in the program file, customization and localization in Mac OS X requires no change at all in the application file.

Object-Oriented Programming   Some people consider object-oriented programming as an issue of programming style as well as a strategy for reusing code. It allows the reuse of existing code while allowing its modification (overriding). The modification of preexisting code can be done at compile time as well as at run time with dynamic linking.

Frameworks extend the benefits of object-oriented programming into a more generalized sphere. Until recently, frameworks were viewed much as high-level languages, databases, and compilers were seen by assembly-language programmers. They were considered inefficient tools for sissies who didn't want to do "real" programming. Of course, nothing could be further from the truth, and programmers (and managers) gradually became aware that there were large sections of critical pieces of software that duplicated one another and that were so patched up that it was almost suicidal to make any changes to them. The issue today with regard to frameworks is which one to use, not whether to use one.

System Software   One final approach to reusing code is the gradual incorporation of common functionality into the operating system. Originally, operating systems provided the minimal functionality necessary to run application programs on a computer. Gradually, functions that were written—over and over—by application programmers have migrated to the system software level.

Thus, in mature operating systems, programmers can expect to find utility routines that manage arithmetic, trigonometric, and date functions. Communications between and among programs and computers are managed increasingly by the system software and not by the programs themselves.

Abstraction

The last main approach to improving the development of software has been the increasing use of abstraction. Initially, computer code had to be written for the specific computer on which it was to be run. Even as late as the 1960s, programmers needed to know the identifying number of the tape drive used for standard input on their computer and the number of the tape drive used for standard output. Programs written for a computer whose tape drives were numbered differently would not run.

From the earliest days of computing, people realized that by providing an abstract concept of a "virtual machine" or a "pseudo-machine," code could be written to interact with these imaginary machines—and at run time an operating system could concretize the code to the machine on which it was running. This abstraction meant that programmers needed to learn how to write for the abstract machine (a general concept) rather than for individual machines.

The cost of abstraction lies in the additional work that the operating system must do at run time to concretize the code. As the power of computers has dramatically increased, this cost has been worth bearing—particularly when weighed against the advantages derived from allowing programmers to write in a more general way. In Mac OS X, the architecture of the system (which incorporates an abstraction away from the hardware layer) is based on the notion of hardware-independent abstractions; no additional run-time cost is incurred.

The Evolution of Software

While people have been dealing with the issues surrounding improvements in the production of software, the nature of software has changed. In response to the development of personal computers and the rise of networking (including the use of the Internet), the nature of software has changed substantially.

Increasing Complexity of Software

Along with the increasing power of computers, the complexity of commonly used software has increased. The increasing complexity of software is not merely a problem for users; for developers it has become a nightmare. As many applications have encompassed more and more functionality (often far beyond what their original designs considered), the code has become more fragile with each additional modification.

Software for the Twenty-first Century

The computer revolution is just about over. Ninety-two percent of Americans under age 60 have used a computer; 75% percent of them have used the Internet; and 67% have sent at least one email message. A whopping 81% regularly use a computer at home or at work.[2]

The survey cited in footnote 2 explored a variety of demographic issues. The only one that was very significant was age: People over 60 are much less likely to use computers. As this book goes to press, that statistic needs revision. Now, it is safe to say that the results refer to people over and under age 63, since nearly 3 years have passed since the data was collected.

Many of these people use computers only sporadically—for periodic word processing, to access the Internet, or to do bookkeeping. Only a relatively few people actually use computers routinely and regularly throughout the day. Most computers today are woefully underutilized, yet few of their users would willingly increase their use of the machines.

It has been suggested that all the major software that needs to be written has already been produced. Word processing, spreadsheets, communications, bookkeeping, databases, desktop publishing, etc.—sometimes it seems as if only relatively minor enhancements (and simplifications!) are needed in these categories. From this point of view, new software will follow along in these molds, customizing data structures, being applied to specific markets, and otherwise being refined—but staying the way that it is.

---

2. *The National Public Radio/Kaiser Family Foundation/Kennedy School of Government Survey of Americans on Technology.* Survey conducted in November and December, 1999. http://www.kff.org/content/2000/20000228a.

On the other hand, many people see an industry just waiting to take off. It is hard to underestimate the deleterious effects of the crisis in development of the mid-1990s. Software is just too complicated to produce in anything like a timely, efficient, and cost-effective manner—at least using the old techniques.

With a solution on the horizon for the difficulties of developing software, and with the dramatically increased power of computers, the software industry could indeed take off... but to where?

Software and the Internet   The Internet is everyone's favorite destination these days, and its effects on the world of software can scarcely be overestimated. Internet protocols are relatively simple, yet they allow people to communicate and to share information with little difficulty. The computer industry has seen in the Internet a way to disseminate information about its products quickly and to provide technical support to bewildered users (who are not quite so bewildered that they can't get to the Internet).

The Internet is also seen by many as a marketplace—a tool that can deliver digital products almost instantaneously anywhere in the world. Not surprisingly, one of the first digital products to be sold over the Internet was software.

Perhaps the Internet's greatest influence is, in a perverse way, due to its simplicity. People stymied by their word processors are finally getting up the nerve to say, "If I can connect to a computer halfway around the world, why can't I get a header to print on my report?"

Empowered by their connections to remote computers, they are starting to realize that the problem with printing headers might actually not be their fault—the software might be too complex. How few programmers realized that empowering the masses to surf the Net with a click of a mouse would turn people into demanding users, no longer content to adjust their activities to the arbitrary restrictions of computer software.

Activity-Centered Computing   Increasingly, the focus of software developers is on people and the activities that they are carrying out with the aid (and occasionally the hindrance) of their computers. As computer software addresses more and more routine and mundane aspects of people's lives, the reluctance to invest substantial amounts of time and money in learning how to use the software grows.

The meadows of pastel notes taped to the sides of monitors around the world testify to the fact that it remains simpler to write a memorandum on a scrap of paper than to use a computer as an *aide-mémoire*. Any hope of expanding the market for computers and software must rely on increasing the simplicity of software products. It is true that the big things are done (probably), but the myriad pesky details of life with which a computer could assist with remain. And until they are easier to handle using a computer, people will continue to save scraps of annotated paper, tape notes to doors, and keep an extra sum in their checking account to avoid having to strike a balance once a month.

Software for Work and Play   One of the biggest areas of growth in the software industry for the twenty-first century is in all of those domains that remain relatively untouched by today's software products. Computers and software have found a place in offices and workplaces; in homes, they have become established in the office-like activities of a home (everything from a home business, to personal accounting, to the office-like activities of students preparing research papers).

A relatively small market does exist for computer games and diversions—but often these remain in the office mode. The vast range of activities that could use an assist from computers but that are carried on in places too noisy or dirty for computers (garages and workshops), or in places too dignified and quiet for computers, represent a vast untapped market for computers and their software.

The computer industry has learned how to put computers on desktops and on the laps of business travelers. It is taking the first few baby steps toward putting computers in briefcases, backpacks, and purses. The software that will help the industry break out of its relatively confined mold (and will provide fame and fortune for its developers and promoters) must also break out of the office model.

The U.S. Federal Communications Commission has estimated that two-thirds of the people alive today have never placed a telephone call. When considering the opportunities for computers, remember this point. You may be looking at a market that is close to being saturated in a very few areas of relative wealth and sophistication, but there is an almost unimaginable market out there for software that does the things the vast majority of the Earth's population want to do.

Chronology versus Complexity Most people today have grown up to a certain extent with the growing up of the computer industry. In its evolution and development, the industry has provided ever-richer data types and more powerful processors. For people who have experienced this process, it is easy to fall into the trap of thinking that software has become more complex. In fact, it hasn't; the chronology is being confused with complexity.

Half a century ago, the popular impression of what a computer would be (as seen in the press and movies) included video, speech recognition and synthesis, and near-instantaneous communication among people around the world. The available products, constrained by limitations of existing hardware and software, have fallen far short of those expectations. Despite having lived through advances of hardware (and the concomitant reductions in the compromises that users had to make to deal with the machines), you should remember that it is the current data types that are natural. Communicating with anything (person or machine) by typing in only capital letters (and expressing a gloss on the content by typing marks of punctuation sideways [:)]) is unnatural and confusing. The so-called advanced technologies are the basic ones.

Graphics aren't decoration; multimedia isn't optional. They are parts of our lives—and have been for millennia. Anyone who feels that all the basic software has been written is living in a two-dimensional, text-based world that is very quiet and still. Adventuresome people and those whose jobs have required assistance from computers have adapted to live in that world. These people constitute only one-third of the population of the United States (and for many of them, their patience is wearing thin). In fact, there is a grain of truth to the notion that all the major software has already been written. It is highly likely that all the major software of the old kind has been written. The software for the vast majority of people in the world has yet to be written. It requires new ways of thinking about software and its development, and it requires a new tool.

Cocoa Cocoa is the basic framework that provides a robust, powerful, development environment with the tools needed to develop for Mac OS X. You use Objective-C or Java (or both) to program in Cocoa.

For some, it will be your first experience with using an object-oriented framework. Still others will be exploring the world of object-oriented programming for the first time.

Object-oriented programming and reusable frameworks are sophisticated concepts that ultimately make the job of developing—and maintaining—software easier. Remember, however, that the more new concepts you have to learn with Cocoa, the longer it may take.

The biggest challenge most programmers have in learning to use a framework such as Cocoa is learning to trust it. It's there to be used—and while at first it may seem easier to go off and write some code of your own, in the long run it makes great sense to take a moment and see if Cocoa already has code to do what you want to do.

Almost all experienced programmers taking a one-week introductory course in MacApp exhibit similar behavior. On the first two days, they roll their eyes and complain about having to use the "complicated" framework. Instead of being allowed to write a dozen lines of code, they complain, they are forced to look through the framework to find the classes to use and the methods to override. All of this is woefully inefficient (they say).

Sometime during the third day of most introductory MacApp classes, the experienced programmers get very quiet. As the examples get more complex and the lab exercises become closer to real-life situations, a hush generally descends on the class. And then things start to get noisy again. The programmers who were complaining about having to use an "awkward clumsy framework" to do something they could have done in "a few lines of code" are now excited that by overriding only one method they are able to implement drag-and-drop, multiple selections, or undoable commands. It is that moment—the moment when the power of the framework is unlocked—that convinces people that they are on the right track.

If you are new to frameworks, remember this idea. It will take a little while for you to get to the point where you trust the framework. Once you do, you'll be on the road to a powerful way to develop the exciting software that is part of the Mac OS X world.

Carbon   Carbon is a shared library that lets you program for Mac OS X as well as for Mac OS 9 and earlier. You can use C, C++, or Java to program for Carbon.

If you are starting from scratch, you will normally use Cocoa unless your application must run on pre-Mac OS X systems. If you are modifying existing code, modifying it to use the Carbon libraries is often easier than rewriting it in Cocoa. On Mac OS 9, Carbon is not a framework, although there are frameworks that take advantage of it (such as PowerPlant and MacApp). On Mac OS X, Carbon is a framework—in the sense of that word in the Mac OS X environment (a bundle containing a shared library and all the headers needed to use it). You need not write object-oriented code to take advantage of Carbon; in fact, you can write perfectly awful spaghetti-code circa 1970 to run against the Carbon libraries (although why you would want to is unclear).

In this book, Carbon is presented most frequently as a comparison to Cocoa. This dual presentation will help you read and understand Carbon code as you modify it or use it as a template for Cocoa code.

What matters most about code compiled with the Carbon libraries is that they run natively on Mac OS X. Unlike Classic applications that were written for Mac OS 9 and earlier, they do not run in the Classic environment. They adopt the Aqua interface automatically, and they can take advantage of memory management and stability in Mac OS X.

Summary

Mac OS X provides an extraordinary computing experience for users. Its highly reliable performance is unfortunately a rarity on the desktop; it is as robust as many high-end mainframe systems. Its integrated graphics and networking make a strong statement to users and developers alike: This is a serious, twenty-first century computer.

But there is something else.

The process of developing applications for Mac OS X is unlike anything else. Developers and programmers get the same treatment that early users of the Macintosh got: intuitive, simple, highly productive tools. If you are old enough to remember typewriters, remember how liberating it was to use a word processor—no longer did you slow down at the bottom of a page, living in dread of a typo on the last line that would cause you to have to retype the whole page. As you start to develop for Mac OS X, you will experience the same sort of liberation.

The system embodies the contemporary ideas about software development that have been touched on in this chapter. It is not Cobol or Assembler hidden under a mask of trendy buzzwords—it is new and exciting, and it can help you to remember that programming can be fun.

Whether your emphasis is on the act of programming or on the results that you deliver to your users, you will find the power of the Mac OS X environment invigorating. You may choose to use that power to drastically shorten your development and maintenance cycles—or you may choose to use it to tackle projects that you never would have dreamed of doing before.

Programmers have been among the last to profit from the new technologies that they themselves develop for others. There may be a silver lining to that cloud. If you look at the development of programs as a generic task, the tools that developers have for that task are now at least as good as—if not better than—the tools anyone has to do anything on a computer.

Chapter 2
Architecture Overview

This chapter covers the Mac OS X architecture. You can find the day-to-day record of how Apple arrived at this architecture in old magazine and newspaper clippings; there were many false leads and turns in the road at Apple and NeXT as well as throughout the computer industry and academe over the last half-century. At times, the direction in which the computer world was headed was not clear; in retrospect, it is possible to trace the evolution of the architecture of Mac OS X without the digressions and distractions that in fact occurred on the way here.

This coherent story is what actually happened—although few people realized at the time where the adventure would end up.

The Story So Far...

Operating systems shouldn't be of any concern to end users and should be of only minimal concern to developers and programmers. They should just go about their business, keeping the hardware running smoothly and trafficking among the needs of software.

Of course, the computer world is far from this happy picture. Operating systems do matter. They not only influence developers in what and how they develop, but also impinge on users' consciousness when they get in the way (often by misbehaving). Precisely because operating systems are not yet highly developed enough to be invisible (or at least transparent) to developers and users, it does matter what is down there gurgling at the bottom of your computer.

By the time of the first personal computers, computer operating systems were highly developed and quite sophisticated. They were able to manage computers with enormous banks of disks, endless rows of tape drives, large amounts of memory (at least for those days), and many simultaneous (or almost simultaneous) tasks running under the control of scores of users—many of whom sat at remote terminals connected via phone lines from distant locations.

Personal Computer Operating Systems

Precious little of this sophistication in operating systems carried over into the early personal computer operating systems. Personal computers, of course, were an inherently different type of computer from mainframe time-sharing computers. Personal computers had no banks of disks—two diskette drives were a luxury; they had small amounts of memory; they ran single tasks under the control of one person—hence the term "personal computer." Their operating systems, therefore, had different characteristics, and they were implemented to fulfill the needs of the single-processing, unnetworked, desktop world.

As happens with so many things (particularly in the computer industry), time brought change and improvement. The desktop operating systems evolved just as the computers they were running on evolved and grew. Today, the desktop personal computer is likely to be more powerful than the mainframe of yore, with more memory, more disk storage, and even faster processors. Like the mainframe of yore, however—and unlike the personal computer of yore—it is likely to have several processors, be called upon to carry out several tasks at once, and communicate over a telecommunications network that is more complex than the mainframe-centric network of two decades ago.

Sharing

Today's personal computing environment may be more familiar to the 1980s corporate mainframe programmer than to a colleague who has grown up totally in the personal computer world. One characteristic of today's environment (and of the time-sharing environment in the past) is that the computer resources are shared among many processes and potentially among many users.

When the computer and its resources are shared, its problems are also shared. There are times when the computer crashes or finds itself wandering along some dark and dangerous byway. When the computer is not shared, restarting it means that your unsaved spreadsheet may be lost or that your Internet connection may be broken. In a shared mainframe environment, many users' spreadsheets, transactions, databases, and calculations may be lost; if the computer is serving as a telecommunications hub (as many mainframes did and do), hundreds, if not thousands, of network connections may be broken—and with them scores more spreadsheets, transactions, databases, and calculations may be lost. Restarting a shared computer is a Very Big Deal.

You can appreciate this fact when you read on the front page of your local paper that an Internet access provider's system has crashed. Programmers from the mainframe era can also recall the consequences of computer crashes: meetings, retributions, memos, and even dismissals. Restarting a mainframe computer was not taken lightly.

On a personal computer where many programs may be running, restarting the computer after it crashes or hangs is equally disturbing. A user may easily not know what was running, and an unsaved spreadsheet may not be noticed for weeks, if not months.

More than anything else, modern operating systems address the issues involved in sharing a computer's resources among many users and many programs. Almost everything that makes an operating system "modern"—at least in the formulation given here—can be seen to stem from these needs. As personal computers get bigger and faster, as people demand more and more functionality and responsiveness, and as communications among computers become more intricate, the need for a modern operating system becomes ever greater.

Some programmers remain reluctant to give up their proprietary ownership and management of system resources. You will find many cases where developers have grabbed the event loop to "optimize" part of their code; writing to memory directly, patching traps on the Mac OS, and a myriad other examples show how easy it is to justify the "need" to avoid sharing critical resources at certain times. To the programmer who is reluctant to give up this control, remember that you are giving this control up not to another programmer, but to the user. Sometimes that makes a seemingly bitter pill easier to swallow.

Modern Operating Systems

Modern operating systems don't start (or end) with UNIX, but UNIX certainly is on the scene of a lot of modern operating systems. Virtually all modern operating systems have their roots in the great time-sharing operating systems developed or perfected in the 1970s: IBM's System/360, the Burroughs 5000 mainframe series (and successors), Digital's VAX computers, and UNIX.

The amount of raw computing power devoted to the operating system on those computers was relatively large. A heavily loaded mainframe computer could easily use over half of its processing power in running its operating system.

In those days, sharing computer resources was necessary because they were so expensive and scarce. The advent of personal computers made these resources relatively inexpensive and plentiful, so the early personal computer operating systems didn't need to worry about the sharing aspects of their predecessors. Before long, however, sharing once again became necessary as users' demands for processing power made even these plentiful resources once again relatively scarce. (Why shouldn't you be able to surf the Net, move files back and forth from a local server, print out a 50-page report, and check your calendar all at the same time?)

You can view the role of an operating system in a shared environment as being that of an agent of transition: almost any programmer of modest skills can develop a simple operating system that runs one program at a time and manages a limited amount of memory (for example, 640K). The operating system that shares processing power and other resources may have this appearance at any given moment, but in fact its power and innovation must lie in its management of the transitions between allowing one program access to its resources at one moment and allowing another program access to those resources at another time.

Thus, the modern operating system needs to provide the basics of all operating systems (access to hardware and other system resources) as well as tools for managing transitions that involve the sharing of:

- Processing power
- Memory
- Communications channels
- Disks and other storage devices

The sharing of these resources is done in the simplest way, although it is relatively expensive in terms of computer power. Rather than placing a burden on users, operators, or programmers to determine what programs can fit together, the computer's operating system gives each program total access to all resources for finite periods of time. Each program (and user) can then function as if it were running with no other programs or users, and the resources are shared by being allocated *in toto* to a constantly changing collection of programs and users.[1]

The maid to a touring tragedian playing one-night stands could turn hotel room and dressing room into "homes" in five minutes—and disassemble them equally rapidly, leaving nothing but the shell of the room while all the makeup, mementos, clothes, hot plates, and ashtrays found their places in the nooks, crannies, drawers, compartments, and shelves of the touring trunk. The star entered hotel rooms and dressing rooms that were always fully furnished and looked as if they had been that way for years. This is basically what an operating system does as it shares its resources. The operating system is responsible for the packing and unpacking of not one, but every process that is running. The programs, like the vaudevillians of the past, never see anything but the complete environment.

---

1. Some operating systems—particularly on well-endowed mainframes—actually support a combination of these techniques. The total pool of resources is subdivided into partitions with programs and users being assigned to specified partitions within which the rotational sharing is carried out.

To accomplish this goal, a modern operating system needs to implement functionality in the following areas:

- User-level security must be provided so that data from one program or user can be identified and restored to its rightful owner; in addition, the operating system generally plays favorites. Once it can identify users (and classes of users) reliably, it can modify its rotation of resources to favor certain ones. Thus, scheduling is intimately connected to security in a modern operating system.

- Process management is needed to enable a process to be encapsulated in some manner, stored temporarily, and then restored to the appropriate registers and storage locations when it is next given the opportunity to run.

- Memory management must be able to handle the relatively large amounts of memory that the system and process management may require to be allocated and then periodically stored temporarily on less valuable devices than memory (such as virtual memory disks).

- Some communication mechanism is needed between and among processes that are "running" on the same computer but that may be temporarily inactive and not in memory.

- Exception and fault handling techniques complete the basic list of modern operating system essentials by limiting damage to the smallest possible area so that shared resources are unaffected by a single process's failure.

As noted previously, there are many other services that any operating system must perform. The functions mentioned here are the most critical ones that a modern operating system must perform—usually over and above the services found in other types of operating systems. Experience (often painful!) has shown that these features must be built into an operating system at its most basic level; attempts to retrofit existing operating systems have proven costly failures.

If you read some of the accounts of the development of modern operating systems—or if you were there as the process unfolded—you will note that these five areas of functionality did not always assume such importance. Their importance today is based on hindsight and on the differences that they strike with traditional personal computer operating systems.

Security

It is hard to overemphasize the importance of security in making a time-sharing system work. Because all operating systems are responsible for managing input and output to and from files, terminals, and other devices, they in fact can intercept every single byte or character that is read or written. Moreover, because a time-sharing operating system must periodically pack up each program's entire operating environment—including values stored in memory that are never read or written to disk —it has access to absolutely everything that a program touches.

Thus, a modern operating system has a concept of security that involves individual users with passwords as well as at least a superuser with access to everything. (There may be intermediate levels of privileged users with increasing access.) Implementing security on personal computers has always been a problem, because it has traditionally been done as an add-on. The fact that you can boot most computers from a diskette means that almost all security mechanisms can be bypassed if you have the appropriate diskette and access to the drive itself.

The ability to know who is using the computer is important for more than just security reasons: Many computers are shared in classrooms, offices, and homes. As users are increasingly able to customize their computing environments, it becomes essential to be able to tell who the current user is so that the appropriate interface can be presented. Without the concept of logging into a computer (and its parallel notion of the ability to automatically log out a user after a specified period of inactivity), no practical security exists. A glimpse at the monitors of computers in almost any computer store will demonstrate the problems involved in not providing log in and automatic log out mechanisms.

Why It Matters   Security is important not just to identify the current user of the computer, but to prepare the computer (and its current user) for access to networked resources.

Process Management	Process management is the heart of a modern operating system—it is the core of the packing and unpacking mentioned previously. A computer program that is running on a modern operating system should not be aware that it is doing anything but running alone on a single-user computer.

In Mac OS (as in many operating systems), programs can be suspended whenever they temporarily pause—usually by calling `WaitNextEvent` or `GetNextEvent` in their main event loop. At such a moment, the operating system is able to service other processes. However, if a program does not call `WaitNextEvent` or `GetNextEvent`, the operating system never has a chance to intervene. Thus, lengthy procedures in which the program does not need to poll for mouse, keyboard, or menu events can grab hold of the processor and not let it go—sometimes for very long periods of time. Examples of such programs are disk utilities that may be checking every sector of a hard disk for quite some time, installers and compression/decompression utilities, and major calculation beasts. The damage (that is, the problem of not letting other applications use the processor) can be mitigated by not letting other applications run at the same time. In fact, many installers and some disk utilities enforce this restriction before starting their work.

Furthermore, Mac OS supports only multithreading rather than full-fledged multitasking. In a multithreaded environment, memory is not moved and the individual threads have access at times to other threads' data. (Threads are sometimes processes but may be smaller units of a single process that legitimately should share data.)

Thus, on traditional operating systems, the sharing of the processor requires that programs be written in certain ways (by calling `WaitNextEvent` or `GetNextEvent` periodically so that the operating system can intervene). In a modern operating system, this strategy—cooperative multitasking—is replaced by symmetrical multitasking in which the operating system is not thwarted in its sharing mission by the way in which a program is written. The operating system is capable of starting and stopping any running process at any moment, moving its entire environment somewhere, and restoring and restarting it at will.

Nomenclature In this chapter, "program," "application," and "process" have loosely been used interchangeably. From here on, the specific term "process" is used to mean a single executable software environment with its own code, registers, memory, and other resources (files, communications channels, etc.). A simple program is always at least one process.

Later in this chapter, "process" will be redefined and narrowed to mean a Mach task that contains one or more threads. At this stage, "process" is used in the more general sense that applies to UNIX and most other operating systems.

"Multitasking" and "multiprocessing" are used interchangeably at this point; "multitasking" is the preferred term.

Why It Matters Multitasking allows a computer's resources to be shared among more tasks than one. If all tasks were busy at all times, there would be little, if any, saving. However, because most tasks periodically wait on external events (keyboard input, network or disk communications, etc.), that time can be given to other tasks.

Much more important, however, is the fact that the mechanism by which a task can be stopped, packed up, restored, and then restarted can be used for more than just sharing a single set of resources. Nothing says that the task has to be restored to the same environment from which it was removed (although the environment must be quite similar). In a computer with multiple processors and significant amounts of memory, the task can be restored to a different processor and to a different area of memory—provided that its internal pointers are undisturbed. This provides additional opportunities for optimization and for using increasingly powerful computers.

Memory Management

The single-process computer (whether an old batch-mode mainframe or a traditional personal computer) allows the process that is running to access memory at will. The advent of virtual memory allowed programs to access more memory than was physically available with the operating system by using disk to store the additional memory. However, even under virtual memory, the process has access to all of the computer's memory—both real and virtual.

Some programs took advantage of this fact. Quite a few early Mac OS programs (as well as those for other operating systems) relied on the fact that certain memory addresses contained certain operating system variables—screen size, for example. Programmers who needed to get this information simply read it from the appropriate memory location despite the fact that that memory location logically "belonged" to the operating system, not to the application program.

Modern memory management involves several features, the two most important of which are virtual memory and protected memory (also known as memory protection). Virtual memory is the same technique that has been around for some time now (although it is continuously enhanced); memory protection is the ability to divide the computer's memory into areas that belong to certain processes (or to the operating system) and to prevent other processes from accessing those memory locations.

Why It Matters Virtual memory is used to support large memory demands of programs and of the operating system. Memory protection obviously increases the stability of the entire computer because a single process cannot inadvertently or otherwise access other processes' memory locations.

Communication between and among Processes

In many traditional personal computer operating systems, applications can read and write from and to memory locations that are owned by other applications. Some programs take advantage of this fact to communicate with one another. Clearly this approach is risky, as changes in memory layouts for one application program can cause another to behave erratically.

But it is necessary for processes to communicate with one another from time to time. For example, if a single process is divided into multiple subprocesses (threads) to take advantage of a system's multiprocessing capabilities, the threads need to be able to share data, status, etc.—particularly if the process is going to use any mechanism at all to allow semi-concurrent access to data. For threads within a single process, the solution is to access shared data locations that legitimately are visible to all threads. For processes that do not share memory locations—and that are prevented from looking into one another's memory locations by a memory protection mechanism—it is necessary for them to be able to communicate by sending messages to one another.

A modern messaging system allows processes to find one another, identify one another, and to acknowledge, receive, and send messages according to their own internal formats.

Why It Matters In addition to providing solutions to the problems posed in this section, modern interprocess messaging lays the groundwork for messaging between and among processes on different computers (e.g., over the Internet).

Failure and Exception Handling

Failure and exception handling returns full circle to the issue of security, which started this section on modern operating system attributes. Like security, robust failure and exception handling makes everything else possible. Having memory protection is all well and good, but if a process attempts to access another process's memory, is rebuffed, and then causes the operating system to crash, you are no better off than if it had been able to access the off-limits memory, proceeded to corrupt it, and caused a crash at some point in the future.

Modern operating systems manage failure and exceptions both within their processes and for themselves. They should not crash (as indeed no operating system should).

Why It Matters To deliver an operating system as immune as possible from its own failures, modern operating system architectures take advantage of all of these features in a design called a kernel.

Kernel Architecture

When you have an operating system that can run multiple processes at more or less the same time, where the processes can have their own memory spaces, and where they can communicate reliably among one another, you can take many system services and run them as separate processes. Modern operating system architecture splits out functions such as file management, sophisticated message processing, and user access into separate processes that can run either as necessary or as permanently resident processes that respond to messages as needed.

In such an architecture, the operating system is first divided into separate entities that can run in this manner. What is left is the kernel—that part of the operating system that is needed to enable the others to run. Typically, the kernel provides process and memory management as well as basic communication and input/output services. Everything else can be run as processes taking advantage of these tools.

Most operating systems themselves are allowed to play by different rules than applications or user processes. (Operating systems, for example, are not restricted from reading or writing memory because they must manage virtual memory and enforce memory protection.) The kernel is no exception.

The other parts of the operating system, however, can usually safely run as processes in user space (as opposed to the fewer-holds-barred kernel space). By placing these processes in user space with its restrictions, they are less likely to cause system-wide problems. The strategy is as simple as that of the bank president's giving the vault combination only to the branch manager rather than to all employees of the branch. In both cases, customers would not know the vault combination; however, by giving only the manager the combination, the bank is reasonably well protected against employee misbehavior and need worry only about the manager.

Mach

The preceding part of this chapter outlined the idea of a modern operating system in general terms. It is safe to say that no actual operating system exactly implements all of those concepts. Mach—the kernel that is at the heart of Mac OS X—implements most of them.

Mach moves beyond some of the general principles, refining them and enhancing them to provide even more flexible, robust, and efficient performance.

Tasks and Threads

The concept of processes (described on page 30) is refined and extended in Mach. The modern operating system's process is split into a single task and one or more threads within that task. Tasks do not run: Their threads run, with each thread containing its own execution state. The task owns the common resources that are available to all threads, including a single address space in virtual memory. Registers, stack pointers, program counters, and other elements that control and record the execution state of a thread belong to the individual threads of a task.

Mach's design builds in multiprocessor support from the start. Threads can run on different processors more or less simultaneously: Mach contains the mechanisms to provide synchronism and to prevent threads from running ahead of or behind others. The design also allows for control (even down to the task level) of which processor specific threads will run on and what area of memory will be used for the task's memory.

As increasingly powerful and numerous processors show up in computers, these capabilities become more and more important.

Memory Management

In addition to Mach's support for sophisticated thread management, it contains a very flexible memory management model based on memory objects. The management of logical memory (as opposed to physical memory) is designed to run in user space—not in the kernel space. By running in user space, the virtual memory module does not have access to system-level calls and is therefore more robust and less likely to have adverse effects on anything else that might be running.

As a developer, you are unlikely to worry about memory management in Mach; its architecture allows for sharing of memory objects among tasks and indeed for sophisticated distribution of memory resources. These capabilities are among those that are difficult to retrofit, and as you find your-self needing them it is reassuring to know that they are there.

Communication between and among Tasks

As software evolves away from the single-processor/single-process model, communications between and among tasks on individual computers and across networks become increasingly important. It is hard to overemphasize the value of powerful communication technologies and protocols (the Internet being perhaps the best example to date). In fact, many would argue that the greatest benefits that have been derived from computers in the last 50 years have been due to their networking and communications technologies rather than their computational technologies.

Communications in the world of Mach are managed by ports and messages. You may be familiar with UNIX pipes, which are byte streams that can link two processes together; the Mach mechanism supports message streams, not pipe streams. As with the task/thread structure and the memory structure, Mach provides a more structured environment than some other modern operating systems.

Ports are created inside the kernel; they are owned by individual tasks and, like all task resources, are available to all of the threads within that task. A thread can communicate with a thread in another task through the port that they both can see. Just as with process (task/thread) management and memory management, the communications infrastructure is designed to work in an environment of multiple processors and equally well within a single computer or over a network.

Mach and Other Operating Systems

The Mach kernel is designed to manage multiprocessor and distributed operations. Wherever possible, operating system functions have been moved into tasks that run in user space (rather than in the fewer-holds-barred kernel space). This provides increased stability for the system.

Among user space tasks, Mach has always been planned to be able to support UNIX, MS-DOS, and other operating systems running as user tasks. This ability to be able to run a number of operating systems on top of the kernel was one of Mach's original goals.

The Evolution of Mac OS X

The first computers had no operating systems. They were rooms full of electronic components that were programmed with circuit boards and switches, many of which had to be set by hand. Management of the computer and its resources was done by someone armed with a sign-up sheet; bills for the use of the machine were sent out by a secretary. A single application program ran the computer and did whatever it wanted to do, as shown schematically in Figure 2-1. The functionality delivered to the user consisted of the application and the hardware—the total area within the two boxes.

Figure 2-1. The Beginning: Program and Hardware

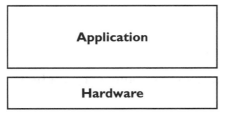

The Beginnings of Operating Systems

Operating systems evolved for a number of reasons—scheduling and billing for computer resources being among the primary ones. As it became possible for computers to run more than one job at a time, this feat of time-sharing was accomplished with operating systems. And so, by the end of the 1960s, operating systems were born out of the necessities to schedule, share, and bill for computer resources.

Figure 2-2 presents a schematic of the computer environment at this time: the computer hardware, an operating system, and, within the operating system, an individual application program.

Figure 2-2. A Basic OS

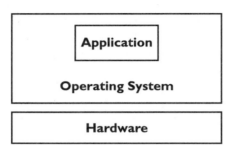

Increasing Functionality Figures 2-1 and 2-2 are drawn to a similar conceptual scale. Note that the application shown in Figure 2-2 is smaller than the single application in Figure 2-1, which had to do everything. Notice also in Figure 2-2 that the total functionality that could be provided to users is larger than that in Figure 2-1. The OS itself provides functionality (albeit in the early days limited); that functionality falls into three general areas:

1. The OS can take advantage of economies of scale in development and deployment; code that otherwise would have had to be written inside individual applications (if it had been written at all) can now be written once and shared by various applications. For example, starting in very early times, application programmers left the mechanics of positioning tape and disk drives to the operating system. For this reason, the individual applications are smaller.

2. The OS itself can provide direct services to the user: billing and scheduling of time-sharing jobs were some

of the first. Thus, the total box of services encompassing both application programs and OS suggests more functionality than was provided by the single application program shown in Figure 2-1.

3. The OS provides services to itself that only it needs. This is usually a significant chunk of the processing of the OS. Operating systems are voracious consumers of computer resources in many environments. Mainframe systems running time-sharing often spend well over 50% of their processing power managing the OS itself.

With operating systems such as these, it was possible to run several application programs at the same time, as shown in Figure 2-3.

Figure 2-3. Multiple Application Programs in an Operating System

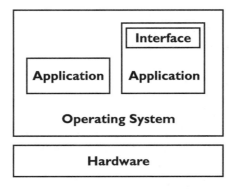

The operating system has grown compared with the early one shown in Figure 2-2. Note also that the application program on the right has grown in size. Adding functionality is not confined to operating systems—users of programs want and need new features, too. Here a specific type of new functionality has been added—a sophisticated interface to the program.

Added processing power made it possible to write more sophisticated user interfaces; the increasing numbers of people using computers made such interfaces necessary. With the advent of graphical user interfaces and the widespread deployment of the Macintosh computer, people began to appreciate not only the advantages of a graphical user interface, but also the benefits of a consistent graphical user interface across many applications. Standards for interfaces were promulgated and programmers (more or less) tried to adhere to them.

Isolation and Dependencies of System Components The first operating systems were relatively unconcerned with the internals of the applications that they ran. They started and stopped the jobs, then sent the bills, and that was that.

Operating systems performed another valuable service. Without an operating system, the application program itself had to interact directly with the hardware. Any change to the hardware—even so slight a change as the renumbering of tape drives to accommodate a new device—required changing the programs.

In Figures 2-2 and 2-3, the application programs are removed from the hardware; under normal circumstances, application programs communicate with their operating system, which in turn deals with the hardware. Relatively large changes to the hardware can be made without having to change the application programs.

The boundaries between the objects in these diagrams are like the Earth's great tectonic plates: There is tremendous pressure and friction at these points. Two plates in the Earth's crust may fit together more because of the pressures holding them in place than because of any simple fit. Geologic events that are relatively contained within a single plate can be magnified to catastrophic proportions when they occur at the boundary between two plates.

Similarly, the boundaries in these diagrams are fraught with danger. Whereas the application running within an OS may be relatively immune to changes in the hardware level, the OS itself, which abuts the hardware level, must change constantly in response to hardware changes. (On very rare occasions the hardware changes in response to software requirements.)

Thus, although the OS itself normally shields the application program's structure and code from hardware changes, the fact that the OS itself must change in response to hardware changes does mean that the application's environment is at least potentially disrupted by changes in hardware.

Common Interfaces

In 1984, the Macintosh presented developers with an environment like that shown in Figure 2-4.

The interface design and implementation, which in the Figure 2-3 design were done by individual applications if they were done at all, are now basic parts of the system architecture. By not relying on individual applications to implement the interface, each application can become smaller (note the relative decrease in size from the previous diagram). Furthermore, because the interface itself is a system service, it should be more consistent. The notion of a single type of interface for the entire environment carries with it significant benefits for end users in the areas of training, software evaluation, and general usability.

Remember that every dividing line in Figure 2-4 represents the computer equivalent of a fault line in the Earth. That is, pressures build up, and there are periodic cataclysmic shifts as one or the other side of the line shifts. Compared with Figure 2-1, there are far more fault lines in Figure 2-4. Changes in hardware can affect the operating system; changes in the operating system can affect application programs; and changes in the application programs can affect the interfaces. And just to make life more interesting, remember that the changes can move in the other direction: Advances in interface design can require changes in the operating system, which then require changes to applications—and sometimes even to hardware.

Figure 2-4. Operating System with a Graphical User Interface

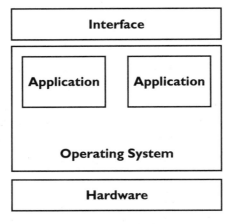

Managing Changes

Changes to application programs come from two primary sources:

1. Many changes come from changes in user requirements or additions to the application's functionality.

2. A significant number of changes come from external forces in the program's environment—changes in the operating system are one of the most common causes of application program changes.

Managing these changes has been a challenge for developers and managers for many years. Two strategies have been used repeatedly (and successfully) to address these issues:

1. Libraries of common code have been made available to applications. They let separate programs use and reuse code that has been developed, tested, and documented for both programmers and users.

2. Object-oriented programming and reusable frameworks have allowed applications to be developed as more manageable collections of objects that can often be reused. More important, individual objects within an application can often be replaced with fewer side effects.

Figure 2-5 displays the applications from Figure 2-4, schematically showing the one on the left taking advantage of a reusable library and the one on the right taking advantage of an object-oriented framework.

Figure 2-5. Libraries and Object-Oriented Frameworks at Work

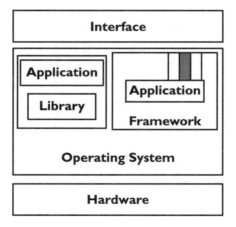

As is common throughout this saga, the application programs themselves provide greater functionality when they incorporate either a library or a framework; the specifically written code, however, is smaller. (This is not a necessary condition, as nothing prevents you from using a library or a framework and coming up with a less functional application than you could otherwise have done. However, this is the most common scenario.)

If you consider the boundaries between application, operating system, library, and framework together, there are many, many fault lines in this diagram. However, although they are theoretically more prone to disruption, the smaller size of each of the components suggests that these disruptions may be less severe than in the earlier diagrams. Certainly in Figure 2-1 (with simply hardware and an application) almost any change to the hardware is likely to cause some change in the software.

In the object-oriented world of a framework, there should exist individual components (such the gray shaded box in Figure 2-5) that should be relatively easily replaced. Although a two-dimensional schematic suggests far fewer boundaries than actually exist, it still stands to reason that a change requiring a modification only to the shaded box should have a limited effect on the rest of the system.

This has been the popular theory of the past few years. It does make sense, and people who have used frameworks and libraries (particularly shared libraries that can be used by several applications at run time) can testify to a very real sense that they are saving programming effort in the development and maintenance of their applications.

But the payoff isn't as big as it should be. Something's not quite right.

The Object-Oriented/Flat World Boundary

Part of the problem with frameworks is that while they do an excellent job at shielding the custom-written application code from changes in the operating system and beyond, and although their object-oriented modularity interacts well with the object-oriented modularity of applications built using them, the boundary between the world of the objects and the outside world (the traditional operating system) is a major obstacle. Most operating systems deal with procedure calls and data structures rather than objects. Frameworks, on the other hand, live in a world of objects. Every call across that boundary needs to move from one world to the other. And while there is a reasonable amount of control of changes within the object-oriented world of a framework and object-oriented applications, as soon as this boundary to the flat world is reached, the efficiencies are greatly reduced.

As a result, it is almost impossible for an application framework to keep pace even with one moderately sophisticated operating system and interface—the flat, native, non-object-oriented code of the operating system is updated before the frameworks.

In fact, it is quite rare for a framework to incorporate all of an operating system's application programming interface (API) in its classes and methods, much less to keep pace with its changes. The task is enormous, and it is always faster in any individual case to code directly to changed platform APIs than to change the framework—or to wait for a third-party vendor to do so.

The solution, of course, is to make the operating system object oriented itself. Then there would be no need to synchronize the API changes in the operating system's flat world with changes to an object-oriented framework: They would be one and the same.

The fly in this particular ointment, however, is that there is a certain degree of inefficiency in object-oriented systems. Normally this is not significant, but an operating system's tasks are often extremely time critical. This is a risk that few would be willing to take.

Splitting the Operating System

Meanwhile, the notion of a "modern OS" began to take shape in the minds of many. (See the next chapter for more details.) One of the notions behind a modern OS is that of a kernel—a very small, fast section of code that does the direct hardware interaction; the rest of the OS is implemented as services above the level of the kernel.

If you combine this notion with the issues in the previous section, you might see a way out—as did the people at NeXT. The operating system itself can be split into two parts: one can be the critical kernel running as fast as it can, and the other can be an object-oriented OS.

Figure 2-6 presents a schematic of this stage of evolution: the splitting of the OS into two parts.

Figure 2-6. A Two-Part OS

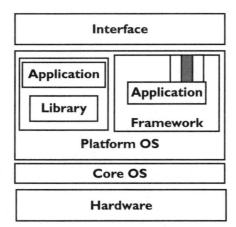

Figure 2-7 depicts the basic design of Mac OS X. The core OS is Darwin, based on Mach 4—a kernel-based modern operating system that is not object oriented and on the Berkeley Standard Distribution (BSD) of UNIX.

The platform OS consists of most of Mac OS X. In Apple's diagrams, the emphasis is on the presentation technologies, Quartz, OpenGL, and QuickTime, but a wide variety of other services are provided here, too.

Figure 2-7. The Mac OS X Nomenclature

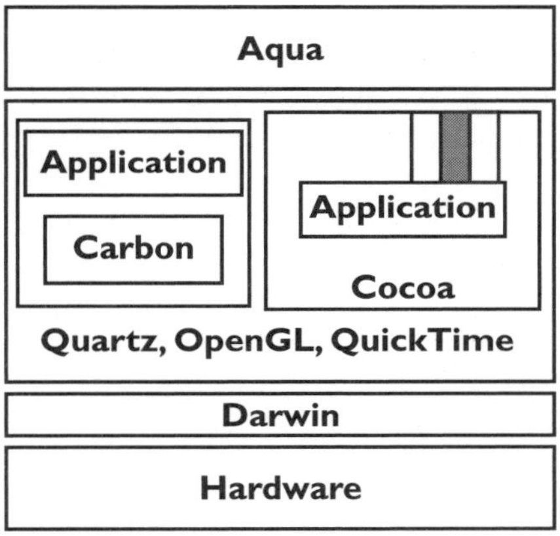

The Carbon libraries allow applications that may or may not be object oriented to run within what is basically not an object-oriented world. Cocoa is totally object oriented, and its applications run alongside Carbon applications in Mac OS X.

One other aspect of Mac OS X needs to be added to this diagram: Java. Java occupies a special place because it functions both as a programming language (you can write Cocoa applications in Java) and as a self-contained, object-oriented world (the Java Virtual Machine). Thus, you can add Java as a second high-level framework (next to Cocoa); you can also add it as a Cocoa programming language.

Summary

With all the commotion over the importance of a modern operating system, sometimes the jargon gets overpowering and developers (much less users) are to be forgiven if they react to these discussions with a modern attack of the vapors.

At its heart, the notion of a modern operating system isn't some esoteric litmus test as to whether feature A is or is not supported. The ideas behind modern operating systems fall into two major categories: ways to improve the performance, stability, and reliability of today's computers; and ways to be positioned to exploit the computers of tomorrow, which, with multiple processors and persistent network connections (wired and otherwise), offer opportunities and challenges never seen before.

Chapter 3
Frameworks and
Object-Oriented
Programming

A firm foundation on a modern operating system is not enough to make most people confident about putting their development (and production) money into a programming environment. Half a century of software development experience has shown that programs last much longer than anyone ever predicted. (Much of the problem with the year 2000 bug came from software written in the 1960s and 1970s that is still in regular use today. When you consider that few automobiles from that time are still on the road, the longevity of software is alternately awe-inspiring and depressing.)

Object-oriented programming is at the heart of Mac OS X. Cocoa itself is an object-oriented framework; MacApp, Apple's C++ framework, is a comfortable fixture in the Carbon environment. Cocoa offers the developer a choice of two object-oriented languages: Objective-C and Java. This chapter provides a very brief overview of object-oriented programming from a language-neutral point of view. It highlights some of the implementational issues that need to be addressed and which the three languages address in different ways.

Object-Oriented Programming

Object-oriented programming is one of the technologies that has been proposed—and adopted—so as to make the process of creating software easier, faster, and more efficient. (The other major technologies that have been proposed and adopted to these ends are structured programming and databases.) In contrast, some technologies have been proposed and *not* adopted widely. Why have CASE (computer-aided software engineering) tools not been more successful despite a relentless flood of promotion? Why have code generators had limited acceptance? And perhaps the biggest question of all, Whatever happened to the 1980s grand design methodologies that promised to take only a few years to completely model an organization's data needs (during which time, of course, nothing would change)?

The difference is quite clear, but you must promise not to tell anyone (because some people might get a little upset). The tools and techniques that have succeeded are those that programmers have perceived as making their lives easier. The tools and techniques that have failed have been those that management embraced and that programmers didn't particularly understand, appreciate, enjoy, or use.

There is a little-noted measure of a technology's viability in the programming world: weekend projects. Most programmers love to program and to design software. Some augment their working lives with volunteer work for community organizations; others steal away on evenings and weekends to come up with a shareware or freeware product—or even to work on what just might be the next "killer app." In these projects, structured programming, databases, and object-oriented programming abound.

To be sure, object-oriented programming and the other major technologies are found in the largest corporations, and the most horrible unstructured spaghetti code messes can also be found in private skunkworks projects. But by and large, these are the tools that programmers use when they're working for the most demanding (yet understanding) bosses of all—themselves.

Why Is It Liked?   Despite a steep learning curve, object-oriented programming is easier than traditional procedural programming. An application is divided into objects that have the characteristics described further in this chapter but that have one critically important feature: They can be totally self-contained.

Totally self-contained entities can be combined into various combinations in ways that can produce larger and complex systems that would be prohibitively expensive to produce on their own. An example from the 1960s was a combination clothes washer and dryer. Combining the two products into a single cabinet seemed like an efficiency; in practice, the two products constantly managed to interfere with one another and the combination product ended up saving floor space at the expense of being constantly in need of repair.

From a practical point of view in the world of object-oriented programming, an object can be left untouched once it has been developed. Its functionality and interfaces can be frozen, and it can be used without worrying about its internals. Procedural languages—even with shared libraries and utility routines—rarely can provide this degree of isolation.

Of course, these write-once-use-many objects need to be carefully designed. You can do many things to break down the ramparts of self-containment (you can use globals, refer to other objects about which you make certain assumptions, etc.). Nevertheless, many object-oriented programmers have a bag of objects that they drag along from project to project. Each object can be reused because it is self-contained and adheres to strict programming standards (the programmer's internalized set of standards). The reality of object-oriented programming leans toward programmers saving a day here and a day there by reusing objects that they have written or used before. The enthusiasm for object-oriented programming comes from programmers having experienced this process and being able to testify that it does indeed work.

Where Are the Benefits?

What has remained elusive, however, is the large-scale payoff for using object-oriented programming on large systems. On a daily basis, programmers experience firsthand the benefits of object-oriented design as they reuse objects. There is also an almost tangible feeling that the objects that are written anew will be easier to maintain in place (even if they are never reused).

The benefits of object-oriented programming in large systems depend on the ability to integrate objects written by different people with vastly different programming standards as well as on the ability to combine these objects dynamically.

Using Other People's Objects   Despite the fact that an object designed for reuse can (and should) be designed to make as few assumptions as possible about its environment, many do make quite a few assumptions. There is not a significant market in off-the-shelf objects because they often don't fit together well. Even the recent enthusiasm over Java applets has not been able to cover the fact that most Java applets are reusable only in the contexts for which they have been designed. (Of course, for those applets that have been designed as buttons or other controls on Web pages, that context is so widely available that some reuse is possible.)

Developers and designers pay a great deal of attention to the inside of objects, but the big payoff in reusability comes when attention is paid to the outside of the objects—that is, to their interfaces and to their functional scope. And that is one of the most important elements of Cocoa.

Run-Time Object Combinations   When it comes to actually combining objects, the details often scuttle the ship. Unless some binary standard is available, objects in different languages and from different compilers will likely be unable to be used together. Standards such as CORBA (Common Object Request Broker Architecture) are available, but in a classic chicken and egg syndrome, few developers see the need to adhere to these standards because no one is combining objects dynamically across machines—and no one is bothering to try combining such objects because the standards are not widely supported.

Part of the attraction of Java is its promise to simplify this combination of objects at run time across networks. The crunch is only now coming where it will be seen whether the full power that can be delivered is demanded by consumers.

Thus, object-oriented programming is liked by programmers, is supported anecdotally as saving development and maintenance time, and has at least the potential to provide significant savings in large system development if some standards-related issues can be solved.

The Learning Curve

Many people find object-oriented programming hard to learn; for others, it's not at all complicated. One of the factors that contributes to this discrepancy is the fact that some programmers can be comfortable only if they understand the entire program on which they are working. Others are comfortable working on a part of a program and relying on others to do the rest.

For programmers who aren't comfortable until they see the big picture, object-oriented programming may be difficult to accept. There is always a faster and more efficient way to do something procedurally—but it is a way that breaks the object-oriented design and that requires all future programmers to also have the big-picture outlook.

Unfortunately, many computer science courses and programs emphasize the big-picture outlook and encourage students to develop large applications on their own. The fact that they are training their students to solve yesterday's problems using yesterday's technologies should not surprise those who were themselves taught to solve day-before-yesterday's problems using day-before-yesterday's technologies.

If you're not interested in learning new technologies and re-thinking the way you work, object-oriented programming may not be for you. The demand for programmers is so enormous that there is room for everyone. There's plenty of Cobol code that needs maintenance, and there's a whole bunch of PL/1 applications that need to be converted into something—anything—else.

Objects

What, then, is object-oriented programming, in a language-neutral sense? This section is a brief overview of this concept.

Objects are entities that in some ways are like small programs. They have their own data and their own functionality—just as a solitaire or payroll program does.

Data An object can contain data of any kind—integers, floating point numbers, arrays, strings, etc. The data can even consist of other objects. In the strictest (and best) object-oriented programming, an object never presents its data directly to the world. You always have to call one of its functions or methods to get the data.

In other words, even if the object has a data field called "time started," you access it by calling a routine like GetTime-

`Started` rather than accessing the variable directly. This is good programming practice even in non-object-oriented programs.

Data fields may be called fields or values; they may also be called member values. Some objects have no data fields of their own.

Functionality Alongside its data, an object has routines—methods or functions—that it can run. You can call these routines just as you would call routines (methods, functions, subroutines, or procedures) in any programming language. You may also invoke them by sending messages to the object that cause the appropriate routines to be run.

The distinctions between methods and functions as well as those between calling routines and sending messages that invoke them are semantic in the various object-oriented programming languages.

Instances Each specific object that is created is called an instance. For example, you may have 500 instances of the employee object—one instance corresponding to each employee in a company.

Each instance shares the names of the data fields and routines of the object itself, but each instance has its own data values.

Classes The most common usage holds that the class is the abstract object that is instantiated in instances. The relationship between classes and noninstantiated objects is different in the different object-oriented programming languages (but is quite close).

Programmers often talk interchangeably about instances and objects (when they mean an object that has been created and has its own data) as well as about classes and objects (when they mean the abstract, noninstantiated thing). This imprecision is a minor point because the context is almost always clear.

Object-Oriented Design Issues

You define an object with a class definition that specifies its variables and methods. You create a specific instantiation of that object to contain a single set of data.

In a nutshell, that's it. However, there are a few design issues that are important in all object-oriented programming languages and that are particularly relevant to Cocoa and Mac OS X.

Inheritance

An object may be based on another object—may in fact "descend" from that other object. Typically, the descendant inherits all of the data fields and member functions of its ancestor. Thus, if an employee object has an employee ID field, a descendant of the employee object (hourly employee) automatically has an employee ID field, just as another descendant (salaried employee) will also have an employee ID field.

Any instance of the employee object, the hourly employee object, or the salaried employee object may use the employee ID field (subject to some language and scoping constraints).

Similarly, if the employee object has a method called CalculatePayCheck, each of the descendant objects automatically has access to that method and may call it (again, subject to some language and scoping constraints).

Polymorphism

An object may reimplement any method that it inherits from an ancestor. Thus, the salaried employee object may reimplement CalculatePayCheck (the method of employee) to return a value equal to the annual salary divided by 52 (in the case of weekly pay).

The hourly employee object may reimplement `Calculate-PayCheck` to return a value equal to the product of its own data fields, hourly rate and hours worked.

In fact, the `CalculatePayCheck` method of the employee object may do nothing whatsoever, relying on its descendants to perform the appropriate calculations.

In such a scenario, you can instantiate objects of hourly employee and salaried employee as necessary. As both are descendants of the employee class, they both have a `CalculatePayCheck` method (although their methods are different). You can therefore call `CalculatePayCheck` and rely on each object to carry out the correct behavior.

This is polymorphism—the ability of disparate objects to respond appropriately to messages or function calls that call a common ancestor's routine.

This scenario also demonstrates the use of an abstract superclass. The employee object may be designed never to be instantiated; only its descendants are actually to be instantiated. Such an abstract superclass contains common routines that are either stubs (where the subclasses provide their own polymorphic implementations) or common routines that need no overrides in the subclasses.

As you can see from this discussion, the terms *ancestor* and *descendant* are used interchangeably with *superclass* and *subclass*.

Data Hiding and Encapsulation

An object can contain data in its instance variables. This data is available subject to certain scoping and language restrictions, as previously noted. The most basic restriction is in the class definition: You may declare variables as being public, private, or protected. Public variables are visible to anyone who uses the object instance and may be referred to directly according to the appropriate language syntax. Public variables are second only to global variables in their inappropriateness for use in good code.

Private variables are visible only to instances of this particular class. Thus a method of class X may refer to a variable of class X, but no other method of any other object may do so. Private variables are as good as public variables are bad.

Also good are protected variables. They may be referenced by methods of their own class as well as by classes that descend from it.

Accessors   Typically, variables are referenced by accessors—functions whose duty is simply to return a value, as in the following code:

```
short GetEmployeeID (void)
{
   return employeeID;
}
```

Accessors typically come in pairs. The complement to the code above would set the value:

```
void SetEmployeeID (short theNewID)
{
   employeeID = theNewID;
}
```

Accessors generically describe the types of routines shown here; you may refer to them more specifically as getters and putters, but that is poor English.

Accessors are a good idea in all code—even traditional procedural programming.

What It Means: No if Statements

At a fairly high level, object-oriented programming is a way for programmers to be more productive. They can feel more in control of their code because it is broken up into sturdy chunks, and the opportunities for reuse—not fully realized yet—are very attractive.

At a low level, object-oriented programming means the end of `if` statements and their `switch/case` statement cousins. In traditional procedural programming, the employee example used previously would probably have been written in this fashion:

```
fixed CalculatePayCheck (employeeID)
{
  short employeeType;
  employeeType = GetEmployeeTypeFromEmployeeID
  (employeeID);

  switch employeeType {
    case 1: //salaried employee
      ...
      break;

    case 2: //hourly employee
      ...
      break;

  ...
```

Or, if only two cases can occur, it could be written as follows:

```
  if (employeeType == 1)
    ...
  else if (employeeType ==2)
    ...
```

Code with conditions (such as `if` and `switch` statements) is very hard to debug. The number of possible execution paths quickly becomes enormous. In object-oriented programming, the conditions are normally moved outside the objects. A specific type of employee object is created and within its processing (salaried or hourly) everything proceeds in a clear and straightforward manner with very few branches.

The benefits of sequential processing are enormous—particularly in debugging and maintaining code.

An Example

Accessors allow you to easily add all types of filters to data. For example, if an accessor returns the coordinate of a point at which to draw an interface element, the accessor can take into account a scale factor for the view in which it is drawn and adjust the point accordingly.

Here are a few examples of how that could be done, following on from the accessors discussed previously. Together they give you an idea of some object-oriented design issues.

These examples should all be considered pseudocode.

```
point GetLocationWithScaleFactor (
  real theScaleFactor)
{
   return instancePoint * theScaleFactor;
}
```

This is fairly straightforward, but it is quite specific. What if your interface allows you not only to scale the view, but also to relocate it within a larger context? You could create a `Get-LocationWithScaleFactorAndOffset` method and allow either the scale factor or the offset to be zero, but the need to do this would surely alert you to the possibility that other changes may come down the road.

A more general way is to construct a new object that can encapsulate all possible adjustments. The new object could be called something like CoordinateAdjuster; its instance variables would include a scale factor, an offset, and any other possible modifiers. The accessor then becomes

```
point GetLocation (
  CoordinateAdjuster* the Adjuster)
{
   point localPoint = instancePoint;
```

```
localPoint =
  localPoint * theAdjuster.GetScaleFactor ();
localPoint =
  localPoint + theAdjuster.GetOffset ();

return localPoint;
}
```

A change to the imaging algorithms would entail only a modification to the CoordinateAdjuster object (addition or deletion of an instance variable and accessors) and a possible modification to the GetLocation code. No calls to GetLocation would have to change and anyone who uses it would likely be shielded from the changes.

A final structure provides an even more sophisticated methodology:

```
point GetLocation (View* theView)
{
  point localPoint = instancePoint;

  localPoint = theView.ConvertPointToDisplay
    (localPoint);

  return localPoint;
}
```

The ConvertPointToDisplay method of the View object might look something like this:

```
point View::ConvertPointToDisplay (point thePoint)
{
  CoordinateAdjuster*the Adjuster =
    GetCoordinateAdjuster ();
  return theAdjuster.AdjustPoint (thePoint);
}
```

In this final version, you can see a number of object-oriented programming techniques and issues coming into play. The most interesting one is the decision as to where to place variables and functionality. In the first case, the scale factor and offset were simply passed in as parameters. With the creation of the CoordinateAdjuster object, that—and other—data could be encapsulated in an object that could itself be shared. This object can be passed around by other objects that have no knowledge or interest in its internals.

Finally, you see the CoordinateAdjuster object being used as a data member of the View object. Someone who is interested in finding a point at which to draw something need not even know if there is a CoordinateAdjuster involved: It is totally the View's business.

The ultimate decisions on where to locate data and functionality often take much trial and error. Fortunately, with object-oriented programming the revisions are usually fairly easy to make.

Performance   When object-oriented programming began to become widely used in the mid-1980s, a number of people went ballistic over this hiding of data. They passed around detailed analyses of the "wasted" processor cycles spent in getting to data through method calls.

Suffice it to say that 50 years of experience with computers shows that they get faster and cheaper—wasted cycles are of less and less importance. On the other hand, programmers get scarcer and more expensive. A technology that optimizes a programmer's time at the expense of a computer's time is right on the mark.

Run-Time Issues

You can design an object-oriented programming language whose "object-ness" disappears at run time. For example, the initial C++ used a preprocessor that turned everything into C for compilation; strictly speaking, no object-oriented language constructs remained, although some object-oriented structures were created in the process.

Two major run-time issues affect all object-oriented programming projects to a greater or lesser extent: dynamism and management of objects in memory.

Dynamism

Dynamism (which is discussed more fully in the chapters on Objective-C and Java) refers to the general notion of allowing objects to be assembled and connected at run time rather than at compile time. The general concern is larger than an arcane compiler issue: It involves the ad hoc combination of objects over a network that may have been written in various languages.

Dynamism is a very important concept; with the advent of the Internet as a pervasive connectivity tool, the ability to combine objects over networks is becoming increasingly important. Mac OS X and Cocoa specifically address these issues in many ways, and much of Part III is devoted to these concerns.

Managing Objects in Memory

Instances of objects are created from some big glob of memory (not to be too technical about it). In this sense, they are very different from the variables that are created on the stack in traditional methods. If you declare an integer i inside a block, its memory is deallocated when you leave that block and the compiler will not recognize references to it beyond that scope.

By their very nature, objects exist in another dimension than the scopes of blocks and functions. While some small objects are created on the stack in C++ (and automatically are deleted when control passes out of their block), most objects need to be kept around.

Two issues need to be addressed. The first is the decision of how to create these objects. Most commonly, chunks of memory are allocated for object creation; as objects are created and therefore use up memory, other chunks are created. Years of experience with much object-oriented software (particularly MacApp) showed that memory usage for objects is very different from memory usage for other purposes. Object-specific memory managers have been developed and will continue to be developed.

The flip side of the memory allocation issue is the problem of knowing when to delete objects. Cocoa relies on a reference-counting mechanism to automatically delete objects when it is safe to do so. In all cases, for automatic deletion (garbage collection) to work, the programmer must take a few modest steps to enable the functionality.

Frameworks

Frameworks like MacApp and Cocoa are collections of objects that are designed to work together. You use many of the objects directly; others are subclassed or used with various extensions such as delegates (Cocoa), or behaviors and adorners (MacApp). Together, the framework objects, your subclasses of them, and your totally customized objects allow you to easily create an object-oriented application.

Summary

This chapter has presented some of the high points of object-oriented programming and noted some of the issues that come into play as you start to use object-oriented tools. Mac OS X is thoroughly object oriented, and it allows you to use its framework with several languages.

The languages of Mac OS X—Objective-C, C++, and Java—are described in the following chapters.

Chapter 4
The Languages of
Mac OS X: Java

Java caught the imagination of the programming world in the mid-1990s. It seemed to promise one of the long-sought objectives of object-oriented programming—the ability to write objects that could be used and reused in different contexts without having to recompile and relink them. In fact, Java does do this to a large extent.

Java was designed originally as a language to use for embedded microprocessors in consumer appliances. Issues such as stability, reliability, and compatibility with network communications were paramount. On the World Wide Web, these issues turned out to be very important, and the ability to write and compile Java applets once and to deploy them via Web pages is very important.

Java can be used to create applets—small programs that can be distributed over the Web and embedded in HTML. It can also be used as a traditional programming language. In Mac OS X, a Java Virtual Machine is included as part of the overall architecture so that applets can run. Furthermore, you can use Java as a programming language for Cocoa.

This chapter provides a high-level look at Java, emphasizing some of its similarities to and differences from other object-oriented programming languages. As with the other chapters in this section, it is no substitute for a complete language reference. However, if you are an experienced object-oriented programmer, you may well find that the sample code from Apple is sufficient to get you going with Java (or Objective-C or C++) as you start to experiment with Cocoa.

The Look of Java

If you look at Java code, two things may strike you immediately:

1. Java allows Unicode characters.

2. Java looks a lot like C and C++.

Unicode

Most programming languages limit the characters that their compilers will process to standard ASCII characters. This eliminates such useful symbols as π and $\sum$ as well as all non-Roman characters and a number of non-English characters. Java accepts any Unicode character, which makes it possible to write readable code in any language. (Unicode characters are 16-bit characters; you can represent not only the standard ASCII upper- and lowercase letters in Unicode, but also the double-byte characters from non-Roman alphabets.)

The choice of a character set for a language has long been a matter of some debate. One of the original criticisms of Algol by the Cobol language team was that the Algol replacement operator could not be represented by a single keystroke on the IBM 026 keypunch machine. While Algol syntax required x←y to indicate that x was to receive the value of y, keypunch operators had to use the two-character symbol := to achieve that result— x:=y. You may note the great pride that the Cobol team expressed in proclaiming that their language didn't require any such rigmarole. (And who would have thought that the IBM 026 keypunch would not remain the programmer's primary input device forever?)

Java Isn't C

Java looks like C and C++. However, there is one critically important difference: Java is not built on top of C. Both C++ and Objective-C were designed to expand, enhance, and (in the case of C++) improve C. They started with the assumption that they would do not violence to the original language. C code should compile without error in a C++ or Objective-C compiler.

Java, on the other hand, is not built on top of C and is free to reimplement C constructs. For example, C defines a basic type called float to be a floating point number. Both Objective-C and C++ therefore recognize the float type.

In Java, float is not a floating point type. Although it serves the same purpose, float in Java is in fact a floating point class (as opposed to a type). In fact, everything in Java is an object, and that is one of the most significant differences between it and the other object-oriented languages.

This line of code has identical meanings in C, Objective-C, and C++:

```
float taxRate;
```

Its meaning in Java is similar, and you can write it and use taxRate more or less as you would in the other languages, but in fact taxRate will be an object in Java.

Everything Is an Object

As you will see in Chapter 5, which covers Objective-C, classes in that language are themselves objects, and you can use class methods and class variables as well as instance methods and variables. Class objects are commonly capitalized, while their instances are not. Thus in Objective-C

```
[Triangle alloc] //Objective-C
```

calls the Triangle class's `alloc` method, while

```
[aTriangle draw] //Objective-C
```

calls a specific triangle instance's `draw` method.

Java uses a C++-like syntax in which classes can have static fields and methods; those fields and methods belong to the class, not to particular instances.

In Objective-C, classes are members of the Class class, and they inherit some utility methods from it. Java approaches the issue somewhat differently.

Object Class

In Java, all objects are descendants of the Object class, and they therefore inherit the utility methods from it. Object has 12 methods; therefore all Java objects have at least these 12 methods—either by inheritance or through overrides. Because everything is a descendant of Object, every element of the language—every Boolean, every array, every string, and every floating point number—can do any of the things listed in Table 4-1.

TABLE 4-1. Java Object Methods

Method	Use
`Object`	constructor
`clone`	provides a copy of itself with all fields set to the same values as in the original
`equals`	returns true if another object is the same as this one (i.e., refers to the same object in memory)
`finalize`	does nothing; similar to a C++ destructor; designed to be overridden in subclasses
`getClass`	returns the run-time class of an object (run-time classes are described later in this chapter)
`hashCode`	returns an integer value that uniquely identifies this object at run time; different values may be returned during different executions
`notify`	wakes up a thread waiting on this object's monitor
`notifyAll`	wakes up all threads waiting on this object's monitor
`toString`	returns a textual representation of this object; it is meaningful (to people) and concise but usually is not the entire object's data
`wait`	waits for a thread to notify it of a change
`wait (long timeout)`	waits with a timeout in milliseconds
`wait (long timeout, int nanos)`	waits with a timeout in milliseconds plus nanoseconds

A glance at the methods will show several important aspects of Java:

- Java is designed for a multithreaded environment (`notify`, `notifyall`, and `wait` methods).

- Java defines a run-time object (Class) that interacts with the descendants of Object that you describe in your code.

- The `hashCode` method demonstrates Java's implementation of a mechanism for locating and identifying objects on the fly at run time.

- The `finalize` method is called when an object is being automatically destroyed by Java's garbage collection mechanism. You don't have to do anything to have automatic memory management with Java.

Some Java Syntax

The actual Object API shows several language features that distinguish Java from other languages. Here is the API:

```
public class java.lang.Object
{
  //Constructors
  public Object ();

  //Methods
  protected Object clone ();
  public boolean equals (Object obj);
  protected void finalize ();
  public final Class getClass ();
  public int hashCode ();
  public final void notify ();
  public final void notifyAll ();
  public String toString ();
  public final void wait ();
  public final void wait (long timeout);
  public final void wait (long timeout, int nanos);
}
```

These are some of the syntactical elements that distinguish Java from other languages:

- Names in Java can be qualified to make them unique, as in java.lang.Object. You can create your own name space; the convention is to reverse your Internet domain to provide a unique identifier. Thus, Apple's Internet address is apple.com; a unique Java identifier for Apple Java objects is com.apple. (Because the Internet domains are unique, the reversed-order identifiers are also unique.)

- The `clone` and `getClass` methods return objects. In C++, they would return pointers to objects—Object* and Class*. Because everything in Java is an object, it is unnecessary to distinguish between references and objects. As there are no pointers in Java, that distinction would be irrelevant.

- Methods can be marked as final, which means that subclasses cannot override them. This is in contrast to the approach in C++, where methods are marked as virtual to indicate that where a like-named method exists for a subclass, that method should be used instead. C++ asks you to specify when a method will be overridden; Java asks you to specify when it *cannot* be overridden. Classes and fields can also be marked as final.

  In the case of Object, only `clone`, `equals`, `finalize`, `hashCode`, and `toString` can be overridden. As they all obviously need to use the fields of a specific descendant of Object, this makes sense. You cannot override the thread-management and run-time class management methods.

Inheritance and Organization in Java

Organizing the parts of an object-oriented system is always a challenge. C++ provides for organization primarily through the use of inheritance (including multiple inheritance). Objective-C supports not only inheritance, but also the concept of protocols—sets of methods that as a unit can be adopted by an object.

Java addresses the issue in a somewhat similar manner to Objective-C. Any class can be a descendant of any other class. In Java terms, a subclass extends its superclass, as in

```
public final class java.lang.Boolean
    extends java.lang.Object
```

This Boolean class wraps the primitive Boolean value that corresponds to the Boolean type in C. It uses fully qualified names for itself and its superclass (java.lang.Object); by being declared as final, the class cannot be overridden.

You can also declare an interface that looks like a class declaration, complete with methods and fields. A specific class can extend a given superclass and may implement any number of interfaces in a manner somewhat similar to Objective-C's adoption of protocols.

You can query the Class object at run time to find what (if any) interfaces it implements.

Packages

You can assemble classes into a package in a single source file and import the package as a whole. You identify the package with a fully qualified name using the convention cited previously of starting with your reversed Internet domain name (as in com.apple).

You can then import a package into any other Java file. Names are unique within packages and—if you are using the reverse

Internet naming convention—package identifiers will be unique. You can refer to items within a package either by using fully qualified names or by having imported the package.

Frameworks and Java

From the start of object-oriented programming, there has been uncertainty over what features should be part of the languages and what should be part of a framework. C++ is very pure in this sense—it has no framework-type constructs (such as a common object from which all others descend).

Objective-C has some framework-type syntax; when used with Cocoa, it, of course, is tightly bound to that framework. For example, NSObject is the common ancestor of most Cocoa objects and has many common utility functions that Cocoa objects can use.

In Java, the use of a common ancestor (Object) in the language itself means that some of the framework-type functionality moves into the language. This includes object inspection at run time (what type of object is this, does this object support X, etc.) as well as extensive exception handling.

Exception Handling

Java uses the `try/catch/finally` mechanism that is familiar to most programmers today. Method declarations explicitly specify the exceptions that may be thrown with a throws clause:

```
public int read (byte b[], int off, int len) throws
    IOException
```

Exceptions themselves are objects. Using the principle of polymorphism, you may actually throw a descendant of the exception type specified in your declaration.

The Java Bridge

Cocoa is written in Objective-C. A mechanism called the Java bridge exists to let you call Objective-C code from Java (and vice versa). The bridge is so effective that you may not really notice it at all: You can write your Cocoa code, calling apparently Java classes and methods, without being aware of the bridge in most cases.

Bridge Performance Issues

There are two situations in which you do need to be aware of the bridge. In the first, you should realize that, yes, there is a slight effect on performance when using the Java bridge. This does not mean that Cocoa applications written in Java are slow: Most applications on personal computers spend most of their time waiting for user input. Even the fastest typist cannot keep up with today's processors. If you are writing an extraordinarily demanding application, you may need to consider this. For most people, that is not the case.

Finding Java Headers

The second occasion when you need to worry about the Java bridge is when you need to call a Cocoa framework method or use a Cocoa class and you do not have documentation for it in Java. Most of the Cocoa documentation is provided both in Java and Objective-C, but there are some lacunae.

In Project Builder, the Frameworks section of the project structure pane lets you examine the header files of your frameworks. These are in Objective-C (the file names end in .h). If you are writing Java, you can often guess at the Java syntax, but you need a definitive way to find out what the actual Java calling conventions and names are. JavaBrowser lets you do this.

Located in the Applications folder of the Developer folder (not in the standard Applications folder), JavaBrowser lets you browse the structure of any Java classes. To get to Cocoa, navigate through the browser hierarchy at the top as follows:

1. com

2. apple

3. cocoa

4. application or foundation (the AppKit framework is under application; the Foundation framework is under foundation)

The JavaBrowser window is shown in Figure 4-1. The three buttons at the bottom let you switch among views of class descriptions, source code (if available), and documentation.

Figure 4-1. JavaBrowser: Description View

The documentation view is shown in Figure 4-2. Next to the headers, buttons allow you to copy the text to the clipboard, from whence you can paste it into your application.

Figure 4-2. JavaBrowser: Documentation View

Most Objective-C classes are wrapped in this way, and you can access them using the syntax shown in JavaBrowser. Some—particularly basic classes in the Foundation framework—are morphed into standard Java classes (arrays, for example, are handled in this way). The functionality that you need is provided for you, but you use the underlying Java class, not the underlying Objective-C class.

There are a very few classes and methods that are not accessible from Java. Rarely do you need to use them in day-to-day Cocoa programming.

There is much more to the Java bridge, but this is probably all that you need to know for most purposes. The complete documentation for the Java bridge is available on Apple's Web site both as a PDF file and in HTML.[1]

Summary

This chapter summarized the high points of Java—particularly as they differ from C++ or Objective-C. The principles of Java are those of object-oriented programming: inheritance, polymorphism, and data hiding/encapsulation.

Java specializes in providing a particularly robust run-time environment and in providing a well-structured way of combining objects. Java's packages, interface/implementation structure, and ability to specify that methods, fields, or classes are not overridable (with the final keyword) provide a sturdy foundation.

Furthermore, Java's choice of not implementing multiple inheritance (although providing some of its features through interfaces) increases the manageability and maintainability of Java code. While multiple inheritance is one of the topics that can set off religious wars in the programming community, it is not one of the features that makes for easily maintained code.

Java is very close to Objective-C in its structure and in the degree to which it implements some important run-time features. By contrast, C++ is very sparse in making any assumptions about what happens at run time. Its power is focused on the compile-time language and its constructs.

---

1. http://www.devworld.apple.com/techpubs/macosx/Cocoa/ ProgrammingTopics/JavaBridge/JavaBridge.html).

Chapter 5
The Languages of
Mac OS X:
Objective-C

Cocoa is one of the principal programming tools for Mac OS X (the other is Carbon). It was developed in Objective-C; you can use Objective-C or Java to reference its application programming interface (API—the routines that do the work). Additionally, you can use C++ in your code to do application-specific processing using Objective C++. Integrating legacy C++ code with Cocoa is not a problem.

Just as with natural languages, choices of programming languages quickly spark passionate battles. In fact, while there are substantive differences among the three languages of Mac OS X, they have much more in common with one another than they have with traditional procedural languages. You would be quite justified in worrying what all the fuss is about, except for the likelihood that even express-

ing such a thought might subject you to suspicion on the part of the language purists.

This chapter starts with a brief summary of how the object-oriented programming languages developed and diverged. It continues with some highlights of Objective-C:

- *Dynamism*

- *Class and instance objects*

- *Protocols*

Note that these language chapters are highly interrelated, as they contrast the differences among the languages. For example, this chapter discusses Objective-C and C++ almost equally as it demonstrates the differences in the languages from the Objective-C side. The corresponding C++ chapter focuses at length on Objective-C and Java as it draws its own distinctions and comparisons.

Object-Oriented Programming Languages: Two Directions

The origins of object-oriented programming in the 1970s lie with Smalltalk and Lisp: development environments that were used for experimentation, development, and, later, production. The distinction between the language and the development environment was not clear (nor was it intended to be). In recent years, the Dylan language has rethought and extended these concepts; its popularity among developers (and lack of popularity among managers and end users) in many ways has repeated the experiences of Smalltalk and Lisp.

Objects and Messages

The initial model of object-oriented programming was of objects (often based on real-world models) sending messages to one another. Thus, documents sent draw messages to rectangles, employees sent timecard messages to payroll objects, etc.

When an object receives a message, it acts on it—typically by invoking a method or function of its own. C++ programmers usually emphasize the method or function; Smalltalk and Lisp programmers usually emphasize the message. Because the message commonly invokes a method of the same name, there is not a great deal of practical difference between talking about the draw message and the draw method. (There is a difference, but it is subtle.)

The Look of the Languages

The evolution of object-oriented programming has moved in two directions:

1. The objects of modern object-oriented programming are often not analogues of physical objects; they may be very esoteric and abstract objects.

2. The combined language/development environment of Smalltalk, Lisp, and Dylan has evolved into more or less separate worlds of languages (Objective-C, C++, and Java) and development/run-time environments (Cocoa, Java Virtual Machine, etc.).

The evolution of object-oriented languages has followed two main paths, both based on the C programming language. Objective-C added Smalltalk-like object and messaging syntax onto C; the result was intended to be as C-like as possible with the object-orientedness retaining its distinctive object/messaging roots. The other path—which led to C++ and then in a different way to Java—approached the problem as one of enhancing and improving C and incorporating object-orientedness into the language as if it had always been there.

As a result, Objective-C on the page looks very different from C and from C++. It is designed to emphasize and separate the distinctions. On the other hand, C++ looks very much like C because its object-orientedness has been deliberately designed to look C-ish.

There are advantages and disadvantages to each approach. As usual in the cases of both natural and computer languages, saying something so eminently reasonable and true will likely get your head handed to you on a platter.

Dynamism

Perhaps the most important feature of Objective-C as compared to C++ is its dynamism. Dynamic typing, binding, and loading/linking replace or expand features of a C++ compiler and are performed at run time.

Dynamic Typing

In C++, every object you refer to in your program is typed. You can use any of its methods—either methods declared in the object itself or methods in any of its ancestors. For example, the following syntax is legal in C++ and would allow you to ask a view object to return the shape at a given mouse location:

```
TShape* theShape = theView->
  GetShapeUnderMouse (mousePoint)
```

If the class of theView contains the following method

```
TShape* GetShapeUnderMouse (point mousePoint);
```

that code will work.

In MacApp, for many years most objects were descendants of TObject (they aren't now). Thus, the following method declaration would not allow you to write the line of code above:

```
TObject* GetShapeUnderMouse (point mousepoint);
```

GetShapeUnderMouse returns a TObject, and presumably TShape is a descendant of TObject; therefore, you cannot use a TObject as a TShape (although you can do the reverse). To avoid a compile-time error, you would need to rewrite the line of code as

```
TShape* theShape =
  (TShape*)(theView->
    GetShapeUnderMouse (mousePoint));
```

Even if `GetShapeUnderMouse` actually did return a TShape at run time, you would never get past the compiler. It has no way of knowing that the TObject return value of `GetShape-UnderMouse` could in fact be a TShape and that the code would therefore succeed.

This is not a matter of idle curiosity, because if you have dynamic typing, you can then have dynamic binding—which is the really big deal.

Dynamic Binding In the previous example, you could continue and write code such as the following to highlight the shape if it had previously been unhighlighted, or vice versa:

```
if (theShape)
  theShape->SetHighlight
    (!theShape->GetHighlight());
```

Presumably, `theShape->GetHighlight` returns a Boolean value indicating whether the shape is highlighted; the method `theShape->SetHighlight` sets the highlight value. This code snippet sets the shape highlight to the opposite of its current value.

This code will work for objects of type TShape or objects that are descendants of TShape (as TCircle, TRectangle, TTriangle, etc., might be). It will compile as long as TShape contains the methods

```
virtual boolean GetHighlight (void);
virtual void SetHighlight (boolean newHighlight);
```

If all of the objects in your application (or framework) are descended from a common ancestor such as TObject was for much of MacApp's life, you could not write the following:

```
TObject* theShape = theView->GetShapeUnderMouse
  (mousePoint)
if (theShape)
  theShape->SetHighlight(!theShape->GetHigh-
  light());
```

To avoid a compile error, theShape must be an instance of type TShape or one of its descendants. In the class hierarchy assumed here, GetHighlight and SetHighlight are methods of TShape, not of the ancestor TObject.

Dynamic binding moves the checking of whether GetHighlight and SetHighlight are methods of theShape from the compiler to the run-time environment. Thus, in Objective-C, the preceding code snippet (in which theShape is given no further definition than being of type TObject) would compile. It would generate a run-time (not compile-time) error if the actual object theShape as returned *at run time* from GetShapeUnderMouse did not support GetHighlight and SetHighlight.

Note that in Objective-C the common type for generic objects is **id**. Thus, the code snippet would read as follows:

```
id theShape = [theView
  GetShapeUnderMouse:mousePoint];
```

Dynamic typing has many design consequences for the development of frameworks and applications. In statically typed languages such as C++, there is a constant struggle to find the appropriate places for methods. Because a common ancestral class must contain the methods that all descendants need to use (such as SetHighlight), the temptation is either to load up an ancestral class with many methods—some of which will not apply to descendants—or to use multiple inheritance so as to provide several ancestors for each object, with each ancestor providing the set of methods appropriate.

In the latter case, you might have an ancestor object called HighlightableObject that you could mix into appropriate shape objects; other possible mix-in objects would be DraggableObject, EditableObject, etc. However you do it, though, at compile time your theShape object must have a `GetHighlight` method.

To see some of the intricacies involved here, look at the MacApp methods that read and write views. You will see the ping-ponging that goes on as views and subclasses of views are instantiated and generic TView methods interact with subview methods.

The C++ fragile base class problem just exacerbates this. The fragile base class problem is illustrated by the following scenario. If in the course of developing an application you discover the need to add a method to an ancestor of a class, all classes that descend from that class need to be recompiled. Thus, you can add `DrawResizeHandles` to a TCircle object with little difficulty; if your development process leads you to believe that you should really have a `DrawResizeHandles` method at the TShape level, TCircle and TRectangle (both of which may need it) will need to be recompiled—as well as TTriangle (which, for some reason, might not strictly need `DrawResizeHandles` but nevertheless will need to be recompiled due to the changes in TShape).

With dynamic binding, you can avoid bloated superclasses and minimize recompilation due to the fragile base class problem.

Dynamic Linking   The third aspect of dynamism is the ability to load and link code dynamically as needed. This capability is available to greater or lesser degrees even with languages such as C++; when combined with dynamic binding, however, the ability to assemble code on the fly presents many opportunities.

Class and Instance Objects

In languages such as Objective-C and SOM (the System Object Model), classes themselves can be run-time objects. As with the other issues discussed in this chapter, this can be a matter for esoteric speculation and argument; it also has practical implications.

Creating New Instances

In C++, you create a new instance with the `new` function:

```
Triangle* myTriangle = new Triangle;
```

The instance's constructor method is called automatically.

In Objective-C, if you have declared a Triangle object, you create a new instance by calling a method of the class object which creates a new instance.

```
Triangle* myTriangle [Triangle alloc];
```

By convention, the `alloc` method creates a new object. Note the difference: The C++ example uses a function (`new`) that is not an object-oriented construct; the Objective-C example uses an object-oriented construct in the form of the class object (Triangle).

Each declared class has a single class object that is referenced by the class name (Triangle here). You define methods for each class as being available either to the class object (such as `alloc`) or to the instance objects. The code

```
[myTriangle alloc]
```

would fail, because `alloc` is a class method (available only to Triangle and not to any specific instances such as myTriangle).

The distinction between class and instance methods is shown in their declarations. Class methods are preceded by +, and instance methods are preceded by –.

Here is a class declaration:

```
+ (Class)cellClass;
```

Here is an instance declaration:

```
- (BOOL)isLoaded;
```

Rather than relying on a constructor, you call an initialization routine (which by convention starts with `init`).

Thus, the code to allocate and initialize a triangle could be written as follows:

```
TTriangle * myTriangle = [[Triangle alloc] init];
```

As you can surmise, the result of the `alloc` method is an instance of Triangle on which the `init` method is called; the result is stored in myTriangle.

Class objects are of class Class; instances are objects of their given class.

Using Class Objects

Class objects can also be used for purposes other than simply as factories to create instances of themselves. If you have written C++ code, you may have experienced the joys of getting yourself wrapped up in Run-time Type Identification (RTTI), in which you need to find out whether an object that you happen to have is an instance (or descendant of) a certain class. This often happens when you are maneuvering around the limitations of static typing and binding—before coercing a descendant of TShape to a TCircle, for instance, it's a good idea to confirm that it is a TCircle.

A class object can return its class—not its class name (which you can derive from the class)—but a return value of type Class.

Protocols

C++ relies on class hierarchies to create objects—a class's methods are the ones it declares as well as those of its ancestors. With multiple inheritance, you can mix in a number of classes, each of which is targeted to specific functionality.

Objective-C does not support multiple inheritance, but it does support a multidimensional structure to create objects. As in C++, a class's methods include its own as well as those of its ancestors. In addition, you can declare protocols—which are collections of methods—that can mix into classes.

A protocol could consist of mouse management methods (you could have a protocol to implement the hypothetical DraggableObject mix-in class mentioned previously). Classes are said to adopt protocols; they conform to protocols if they either adopt them or are descendants of classes that adopt them.

Unlike mix-in classes in C++, protocols consist only of methods (not instance variables). Furthermore, protocols merely define the methods that the class adopting the protocol must implement. The protocol itself contains no implementations but is applicable only to the interface.

In declarations, a generic id can be qualified with a protocol. Thus id<NSCoder> refers to any object that adopts the NSCoder protocol.

Categories

A *category* is an extension to a class, somewhat similar to a subclass, but only to a certain extent. Categories are used to implement delegates and notifications in Cocoa.

In common use, a category (such as NSToolbarDelegate) extends another class—such as NSObject in this case:

```
@interface NSObject (NSToolbarDelegate)
- (NSToolbarItem *)toolbar:(NSToolbar *)toolbar
  itemForItemIdentifier:(NSString *)itemIdentifier
  willBeInsertedIntoToolbar:(BOOL)flag;

- (NSArray *)toolbarDefaultItemIdentifiers:
  (NSToolbar*)toolbar;

- (NSArray *)toolbarAllowedItemIdentifiers:
  (NSToolbar*)toolbar;
@end
```

Another category also extends NSObject—NSToolbarNotifications:

```
@interface NSObject (NSToolbarNotifications)
- (void)toolbarWillAddItem: (NSNotification *)no-
  tification;

- (void)toolbarDidRemoveItem: (NSNotification
  *)notification;
@end
```

Although they extend NSObject (that is, any object in Objective-C), these interfaces are found in the NSToolbar and NS-Notification interfaces (usually at the bottom of those files). You implement your code for them in your implementations of objects to which they will be attached as delegate or notification. In Java, you implement notifications and delegates at the bottom of the class files that will use them.

Keeping It Running

The strict compile-time type checking that C++ provides helps to make certain that you do not wind up calling a nonexistent method. In Objective-C, you have a choice: You can do that work yourself at run time or you can use static typing to have the compiler do the work for you.

As noted previously, an Objective-C object responds to a message that selects a method or function to invoke. Accordingly, the message may be called a *selector*—as it is in the following code snippet. All objects that descend from NSObject (and hence most of the objects you will be working with) have a `respondsToSelector` method to which you pass a selector that consists of the method you want to check:

```
if ( [anObject
  respondsToSelector:@selector (GetPoint::)] )
  ...
```

You can also use variables of type SEL to store references to selectors that you may use frequently:

```
SEL pointMethod;
pointMethod = @selector (GetPoint::);
```

Checking `respondsToSelector` is as natural to Objective-C programmers as checking for NULL objects is to C++ programmers.

Cocoa also provides a method of NSObject that you can override called `forwardInvocation`. This method is called (a forwardInvocation message is sent) in response to an unimplemented method being called in an object (that is, in response to an unidentified message). The unprocessed message is returned as a parameter to `forwardInvocation`; you can then use `respondsToSelector` on other objects to find an object to which to forward the message and to avoid a run-time error.

Syntax

In Objective-C, messages are sent to receivers, sometimes with parameters. For example, if you have a view object that responds to the `GetShapeUnderMouse` message with a point parameter that describes the mouse position, you can write it as

```
[aView GetShapeUnderMouse : thePoint]
```

All Objective-C messages are embedded in square brackets.

If there is more than one parameter, you may name the subsequent ones. For example, if `GetShapeUnderMouse` had a second parameter, you could rewrite the above code as:

```
[aView GetShapeUnderMouse : thePoint
  saveShape:YES]
```

The first parameter is never named.

Many Cocoa programmers prefer `YES` and `NO` to the constants `TRUE` and `FALSE`, respectively.

The result is returned and can be assigned to a variable. In this case, it is logical that an object be returned. All objects can be referred to as type id, so you could write

```
id theReturnedObject = [aView GetShapeUnderMouse :
  thePoint];
```

However, using static typing (that is, a specific type rather than the generic id) will cause the compiler to check that the call is legal. Many people would prefer the following line of code:

```
myShape * theReturnedObject =
  [aView GetShapeUnderMouse : thePoint];
```

Objective-C++

Objective-C++ is the set of Apple's extensions to the compiler in Mac OS X developer tools that lets you mix and match Objective-C and C++. No longer do you have to make a total commitment to one language or the other.

The most powerful use of Objective-C++ is in its ability to let you merge legacy code (often in C++) with new, Objective-C code. In such a case, you will find that your code generally stays on one side of the Objective-C/C++ fence or the other.

An example of the use of Objective-C and C++ together is found at the end of Chapter 6, which deals with C++.

Summary

This chapter summarized the high points of Objective-C for object-oriented programmers who are familiar with other languages. The rest of the syntax is quite comparable—interface and implementation files are used just as they are in other languages. Directives to the Objective-C compiler start with @, which is a change from other languages, but that shouldn't stump you.

What matters most about Objective-C is its dynamic nature, which makes much of the Cocoa frameworks possible. It also eliminates the need for some of the more complex C++ structures (in particular, multiple inheritance).

Protocols, for example, allow the creation of complex objects along two dimensions—one dimension of inheritance and another dimension of common functionality.

Objective-C is very much a product of the object-oriented world of the 1980s. It takes the then most popular programming language (C) and adds object-orientedness to it without touching the basic C syntax. It incorporates the very concrete notions of objects as message processors that were prevalent in Smalltalk, Lisp, and other early object-oriented systems.

Do not make the mistake of thinking that Objective-C is dated or old-fashioned. Its roots are different from those of Java and C++ but all of these languages evolved over time; the fact that they evolved in different environments accounts for some of their differences. If there were a clear developmental structure of A being supplanted by B, which in turn was supplanted by C, there would be no question that C is the preferred language. That is not the case, and there are reasons to use each of these languages today.

As people have used object-oriented programming techniques, their approach to architecture has changed. Objects have gotten smaller and smaller. In Java, the most recent object-oriented programming language, everything is an object—as you saw in Chapter 4.

Chapter 6
The Languages of
Mac OS X: C++

C++ is the other major language that you can use with Mac OS X. Perhaps the most widely used object-oriented programming language today, C++ has many partisans and experts; in addition, a great deal of existing code (tomorrow's legacy code) is written or is being written in C++.

You can use C++ with Mac OS X, and you are encouraged to do so. The mingling of C++ with dynamic object-oriented languages (Objective-C and Java) is no problem within the basic functional sections of your code. For the interface, you should use Interface Builder, which provides a consistent interface and a modern graphically oriented interface building environment. C++ has a limited role to play in that area.

This may worry you: What about all that existing code? What about your expertise? Have no fear—most of that code is reusable or easily modified, and your expertise is primarily at a higher level than language syntax. Your favorite C++ language tools are available with Mac OS X's dynamic languages. They may go by different names, and fierce partisans of one language or another may fight to the bitter end saying that the language structures aren't parallel, but from the practical point of view of the professional programmer, the differences are not great. What true differences there are all revolve around the issue of dynamism—dynamic binding, loading, and typing—as well as around multiple inheritance.

The tight integration of C++ code with Cocoa is accomplished with Objective-C++, a tool that is part of the second wave of Mac OS X development tools released in version 10.1. C++ on Mac OS X is used extensively in legacy applications and in the MacApp and PowerPlant frameworks that are used to build applications that run in the Carbon environment.

This chapter covers a few of the hot issues regarding C++ and Mac OS X.

The C++ Objective

"C with Classes" began its life at Bell Labs in 1979. It was designed from the beginning to be a production language—one that would be usable in real-world everyday projects. In this respect it differed from Smalltalk and Lisp, which were experimental languages. Smalltalk and Lisp (as well as Simula) convinced a number of computer scientists that there was indeed a practical benefit to the use of object-oriented programming. What was necessary was a way to bring it into the world where production programming was being done.

When C with Classes became C++ in 1983, the computing world had changed dramatically from what it had been only a few years earlier when C with Classes was born. The personal computer was well on its way to becoming the widespread phenomenon it is today. Programmers and users alike were turning from mainframes to personal computers because of the ability to do their computer work themselves without the mediation of large professional staffs.

In the early 1980s, personal computers were far from the powerful devices that exist today. The first Macintosh (1984) boasted 64K of memory. More than fifteen years later, a thousandfold increase in memory to 64MB is not uncommon; many computers ship with 256MB as standard—a 4000-fold increase.

In an earlier era, computer resources—memory, processor, and disk storage—were husbanded carefully. The first compilers on personal computers were designed to run in very small memory partitions at the expense of constant diskette swapping as memory structures were swapped to and from disk.

It is therefore not surprising that when a new language was developed it was designed to respond to the needs of the programming community. The single most significant design decision of C++ was the choice to move all possible decisions from run time into the compiler. It might take longer for the program to compile, but the finished code would run as quickly as possible.

This was a change from the designs of the predecessors of C++. Lisp and Smalltalk were dynamic languages—a lot happened at run time. They had reputations as being very slow (which they were), and object-oriented programming had a big hurdle to overcome because many people believed that it automatically meant at best sluggish performance of the final product.

The decision to make typing static (rather than dynamic) and not to support run-time binding was far from a mistake. In fact, you can argue quite convincingly that by making object-oriented programming feasible in the real world, C++ was largely responsible for moving it from computer labs to the workplace.

Today, processors are much faster, memory is plentiful, and disk space is cheap. Dynamic languages such as Objective-C and Java are not disadvantaged by their dynamism, although you can still hear legitimate concerns about the performance of Java (this is improving by the day—it is unlikely to remain a serious issue). If you go back and read some of the books about the evolution of C++, you will find emphasis on the need to keep the run-time performance of C++ programs as high as possible as well as on the need to make the code as portable as possible. The choices with regard to dynamism (specifically, the decision not to use it) are related to these concerns far more than to abstract designs.

C++ is not a dynamic language, and that's that. It was the right language at the right time, and every object-oriented programmer today owes a tremendous debt to the C++ designers who made the choices that made the language and the technology usable.

Consequences of Compile-Time Typing

By forcing the compiler to do as much work as possible, the run-time code is kept very efficient. The flip side is that in C++ design decisions and implementation choices must be made much earlier in the development process than is possible with dynamic languages.

Two consequences of compile-time typing are discussed in this section: the use of small, stack-based objects, and the fragile base class problem.

Small Objects Are Not Expensive

No matter how much the compiler and operating system try to minimize the impact, object-oriented programming and its attendant data structures do exert a cost at run time. Programmers have known this from the start; particularly in early days, the use of objects was quite limited. Because of the overhead involved in constructing and accessing objects, the objects tended to be fairly large structures.

Over time, it became feasible to use small objects—sometimes very small objects—in programs. Because much of the object management is done by the compiler, there is little run-time cost associated with these small objects. Furthermore, some frameworks have their own memory allocation routines that optimize the allocation and deallocation of these small structures; the OS memory allocation routines were often optimized for relatively large objects and data structures.

Small objects often have very brief lives. In MacApp, for example, you will find objects that wrap platform-specific structures such as points and rectangles. These objects are used precisely as the flat structures would have been used. That is, they are declared on the stack at the beginning of a function and are implicitly destroyed when control passes out of the function, as shown in this code snippet:

```
void TMyObject::DoSomething (void)
{
  int i = 0;
  CRect aRect;


  ...
}
```

On exit from the function, neither i nor aRect is available for use. The C++ compiler has taken care of preparing the stack to be cut back; it has also taken care to make certain that any constructors and destructors for aRect are automatically called.

In fact, many programmers use this feature to release memory structures automatically. If you create a small stack-based object that wraps a standard toolbox call, you can implement a single method—its destructor—and be guaranteed that it will be called automatically as necessary to deallocate auxiliary memory structures and other resources.

The referencing of methods within an object is done by the use of a virtual dispatch table for each class—a vtable—that is built at compile time by the compiler. These vtables make run-time dispatching extraordinarily efficient.

In Objective-C, there are no vtables. The dispatching is done at run time by highly optimized code that checks at that specific moment to find the method to call. With today's processors, the performance hit is rarely noticeable. However, because it is there and can be noticeable with a multitude of small objects, Cocoa rarely uses small objects such as the CRect object in the preceding code snippet. (NSRect in Cocoa is a struct, not a class.)

The Fragile Base Class Problem

The fragile base class problem is perhaps the most serious issue plaguing C++. Because all of the mapping of objects is done at compile time, every class's header structure must be known then. A change to any class's header requires recompilation of all of the classes that descend from it. This has caused severe problems as people have tried to reuse objects.

A number of attempts have been made to work around the fragile base class problem (including the System Object Model—SOM), but it remains a fundamental issue in dealing with C++.

Run-Time Type Identification and Exception Handling

Recent additions to C++ provide the ability for objects to query themselves and others about the classes to which they belong. This feature (Run-Time Type Identification—RTTI) is standard in Objective-C but was a long time coming to C++. The reasons it took so long were that not everyone was convinced it was a good idea and, more importantly, it required building and maintaining a run-time set of information about objects that C++ had never had to keep before.

Related to RTTI is native exception handling. The standard model for handling exceptions is shared by most contemporary programming languages—declare a try block in which you do the work, declare a failure block to which control is transferred if something fails, and finally declare a completion block that is executed if things work properly.

Multiple Inheritance

C++ supports multiple inheritance; Objective-C and Java do not. If you want to start a barroom brawl or language war, bring up this point. People have very strong feelings about it. In fact, to hear some people, multiple inheritance is the very essence of C++.

The History of Multiple Inheritance in C++

Multiple inheritance appeared in C++ in Release 2 (June 1989). It was not part of the initial design for C with Classes. So much for the "very essence of C++" argument!

Multiple inheritance is very useful and valuable; it is widely used in frameworks such as MacApp, and it clarifies the program structure. In its simplest form, multiple inheritance means that an object can have two superclasses. In his book on the development of C++,[1] Bjarne Stroustrup, the designer of C++, presents three cases in which multiple inheritance can be useful:

1. You can combine two completely separate objects into a third.

---

1. *The Design and Evolution of C++*, Bjarne Stroustrup. Addison-Wesley, 1994, p. 271.

2. You can combine related objects. For example, Strous-
    trup presents an abstract stream class, abstract input-
    and output-stream descendants, and finally a file
    stream class that merges the input- and output-stream
    interfaces.

3. You can combine an interface and implementation
    class to produce a fully configured object.

All of these are valid cases. The first can save recoding and re-
designing a new hybrid class; the second makes for more easily maintained code; the third may help you reuse utility
objects in a customized solution.

In practice, another aspect of multiple inheritance has become
obvious: Rarely do two objects of equal size and importance
become joined in the bonds of multiple inheritance (an exception is the structure of the symmetric input- and output-
stream objects in the second case cited). If you look at code
that uses multiple inheritance, there is usually a primary object that mixes in some additional classes of relatively small,
focused functionality; these classes are called mix-in classes.

It is not surprising that the mix-in class structure should be so
popular. It provides the advantages of multiple inheritance,
while avoiding the programming headache of managing an
object that truly has two equal parent objects. It is much easier
to live in the mix-in world with a primary object and the subsidiary, targeted mix-ins.

This usage of multiple inheritance is very important when
comparing C++ and its multiple inheritance to the single inheritance structures of Java and Objective-C. The functionality of the mix-in flavor of multiple inheritance is provided
through delegation and, to a lesser extent, through the use of
protocols. These are no substitute for the Grand Scheme of
Multiple Inheritance, but they are a very satisfactory substitute for the reality of the use of mix-in multiple inheritance.

C++ Delegation

In the nitty-gritty world of programming, multiple inheritance means that you can call three kinds of methods from a class that you create:

1. You can call methods that you declare and implement in that class.

2. You can call methods from the first superclass of your class.

3. You can call methods from the second (or nth) superclass of your class.

The implementation of multiple inheritance must make this possible. Object-oriented programming languages all provide for the ability to call methods from your class and from a superclass. It's calling a method from the second (or nth) superclass that makes for multiple inheritance—and the problems.

Language-Level Delegation in C++   An early attempt at implementing multiple inheritance used the concept of delegation. In your class's declaration, you could declare a delegate class. If you called a method that was not in your class and not in your superclass, the delegate class was given an opportunity to perform the command.

This language-level implementation of delegation caused problems. They were chiefly implementation problems for programmers—the relationship between delegate and primary class was close but not close enough. For example, in the multiple inheritance design as implemented today, you can override methods from any of your superclasses. In the delegation structure, you could override methods in your single superclass, but not methods from either the superclass or the delegate.

Another aspect of this problem was that while your class knew about the delegate, the delegate had no reference back to your class (unless you implemented one specifically). For these reasons, language-level delegation in C++ was dropped in favor of multiple inheritance.

Implementation-Level Delegation in Cocoa   You will find delegation used throughout Cocoa, and as implemented there these problems do not occur (at least not nearly to the extent they did in the early C++ experiments). Two types of delegation are used:

1.   You can declare a specific delegate variable for a class. Your class will send certain messages to that delegate for processing.

2.   You can use the forwarding mechanism that is based on overriding the NSObject `forwardInvocation` method. This method is called at the moment when neither the class nor its superclass can handle a method call (the moment when the second superclass in the C++ world would get a chance). Your `forwardInvocation` method receives all of the information about the method being called and can attempt to forward the message to any other object that can process it.

This structure provides much of the functionality of multiple inheritance in C++. It also makes several points even clearer than they are in C++:

•   There are clearly a primary object and subsidiary objects in the single superclass and possibly many delegates. This conforms to the way in which most programmers think.

•   You can control the calling of methods beyond your own class and your superclass. Whether you use delegation or forwarding, it is up to you to pass on the message.

•   You can control which other object gets the message. This control eliminates an area of ambiguity in C++ multiple inheritance, where there are many superclasses with possibly conflicting names. The way around this problem in C++ is to call a specific superclass's method, qualifying it with that superclass's name.

- Because you manually establish the link to other classes (either dynamically with `forwardInvocation` or by establishing a delegate), you can create whatever context-specific links forward and backward that you need.

Multiple inheritance is something people feel very strongly about. In practice, you can accomplish what you need to do either with C++ or with the Java and Objective-C structures. There are pros and cons of both approaches. As you may imagine, the Java and Objective-C architecture lends itself to dynamic processing much more so than the static structure of C++. (Of course as noted previously, dynamic processing may push error checking from the compile phase to the execute phase and from programmer to user.)

Cocoa and C++

Because the world of Cocoa is so bound up with dynamism, the static structure of C++ poses certain problems with integrating the dynamic objects of the Cocoa frameworks. Specifically, you can't subclass the framework classes in C++, nor can you (easily) call their methods.

Before you decide that this is a disaster, consider the implications. Most importantly, your C++ (or C) code can be used within Cocoa applications. Any existing code that performs application-specific functions can run quite happily in this world. The code that will have problems is existing C++ code that deals with the program interface.

If you are converting code to Mac OS X, that is far less of a problem than it might appear. Throwing out pages and pages of legacy C++ code in favor of using the standard interface is a benefit for everyone. You have less code to maintain and test, and you are guaranteed a consistent and conforming Mac OS X interface. *Throwing out legacy C++ interface code doesn't mean rewriting it—it just means that you don't need it anymore when you're using Cocoa.*

The existing code that performs the work of an application can remain as C++ code and can be called as needed in your application.

The only C++ code that needs rewriting is any interface-related code that does things that Interface Builder and Cocoa don't do for you. These types of tasks fall into two general categories:

1. Things that Interface Builder and Cocoa don't do and that you want to do because you're bringing a preconceived other interface along with you. In this case, forget it. Use the proper interface.

2. Things that Interface Builder and Cocoa don't do that are specific to your needs and that you must add. Although this code may live in your interface classes, it is truly application specific; you can call C++ code as needed. If it really is interface-related (involving drawing, for example), you may need to rewrite it to use the Quartz API, but you can access that from C. This is actually a very small amount of code for almost everyone. (For most people, it is no code at all.)

Should You Write in C++?   If you are converting an existing application to Mac OS X, you may choose to leave its functionality in C++ while using Interface Builder and Cocoa (together with Objective-C or Java). Depending on who has what skills (as well as the magnitude of the code base), it may be desirable to do a full-fledged port. This is an individual decision that must take into account deadlines, individual expertise, and other pertinent factors.

Using Objective-C and C++ Together

Objective-C++ is a front end to the Mac OS X version of the GCC compiler. It was introduced in Mac OS X 10.1. It allows you to use Objective-C and C++ together. As you have seen, the languages are very different, so their integration has been a delicate task. It is essential because there are large bodies of legacy code (usually C++) that people want to integrate into new applications. Also, although the goal is to eventually make all of the Mac OS X features available from both Carbon and Cocoa, many features of Mac OS 9 and earlier are available only in Carbon as of the initial Mac OS X releases. For either of these reasons, you may need to use Objective-C++.

The Objective-C++ integration is designed to function at this very high level; you cannot call Objective-C objects using C++ syntax, but you can call Objective-C objects using Objective-C syntax (or C++ objects using C++ syntax). You cannot create inheritance structures that cross language bounds: descendants of C++ objects cannot be Objective-C objects, and vice versa.

You can create objects with instance variables which are pointers to objects that are actually implemented in either C++ or Objective-C. You must use the appropriate language syntax in accessing these pointers to C++ or Objective-C objects: that is, you use C++ or Objective-C to make the calls. As a result, the individual lines of C++ or Objective-C code are mingled within your Objective-C++ file.

Keywords in the two languages often differ: `self` (Objective-C) and `this` (C++) are both ways of referring to an object itself. Because the syntax from both languages may occur in Objective-C++ files, the list of reserved words for Objective-

C++ consists of the union of the two languages' reserved words. You use the terms separately—self and this are still language-specific—but you may use both of them in appropriate contexts within the same file.

Project Builder invokes the Objective-C++ front end automatically for files with a suffix of .M or .mm.

Summary

Today, C++ is one of the most popular programming languages. Existing (and new) code written in C++ can be used within Mac OS X to implement application functionality as needed. The use of C++ in conjunction with Cocoa and Interface Builder is circumscribed; however, it is not so much a question of rewriting C++ interfaces as of jettisoning existing C++ code in favor of the frameworks and no (or little) custom interface code.

Chapter 7
The Frameworks of
Mac OS X: Cocoa

The primary framework for Mac OS X is Cocoa. It consists of two kits—Foundation and the Application Kit (AppKit). The AppKit classes provide the entire Aqua interface as well as most of the functionality that you deal with.

In this chapter, the fundamentals of Cocoa—both in AppKit and Foundation—are described. A lot of this discussion focuses on how it works: You do not often code or override the methods or objects described here, but this is how Cocoa does its jobs.

Many of the concepts pop up here and there in the work that you do have to do—for example, responders, events, and actions are critical to your work. You use them repeatedly as they are implemented in Cocoa (that is, without overriding them). Some people like to under-

*stand the architecture and concepts before looking at code; other peo-
ple want to examine code and then look at the concepts that lie
beneath it. If you are in the second group, you may want to read Part
III before continuing with the chapters in this part.*

Programming Design Terminology

Two general concerns apply to the Cocoa terminology in addition to the general principles of object-oriented programming:

1. Certain terms and conventions (services, connections,
   and outlets, for example) make it easier for you, your
   users, and consultants to use Mac OS X to construct
   customized applications and solutions.

2. Dynamism in the forms of dynamic typing and binding further expands the flexibility of Cocoa and makes
   much of Mac OS X's customizable interface possible.

As is often the case, nothing forces you to make your objects
usable in this way—you can decree what connections and interfaces exist and freeze them for all time. Likewise, you can
ignore dynamic binding and typing, keeping control over
your application and dictating how it is used.

When it comes to delivering value to users and customers, it
is far better to provide flexibility that allows them to do what
they want than to keep things "off limits" so that they don't
cause damage. Use the Cocoa error-handling routines and
run-time facilities to prevent, detect, and correct errors rather
than deluding yourself that preventing user access to your objects' functionality will yield a more stable system.

Objects

Everything is now an object, and sometimes their meanings
blur. At run time, an object is an instance of a class—a struc-

ture that has access to that class's methods and that has data values of its own. Other instantiated objects of that class have access to the same methods and have their own data values.

The class itself is the definition or template from which each object is instantiated. In Cocoa, the class is a run-time object of type Class; that object can instantiate an instance of its class. Thus, you might have a class defining an object of type Barn. At run time, an instance object of type Class exists for Barn. The Barn Class object can instantiate instances of barn such as `myBarn`, `yourBarn`, etc.

Unless otherwise noted, all references to objects are to run-time instantiations of classes—that is, to objects that exist in memory and can send and receive messages. "Class" is used to refer to the programming structures and in discussing code-writing or compile-time issues. This distinction is one of usage, not one of definition.

Events

If you have programmed for Mac OS, events and the event loop are familiar to you. Events may be generated by user actions (mouse clicks, mouse movements, etc.); they also can be generated by the system either directly or indirectly in response to user actions or for other reasons. For example, Cocoa supports the concept of *periodic events*—events that are sent at specific intervals to an application in response to a single request from it. Periodic events may be used by a window during mouse tracking.

If you have used MacApp, this may or may not be news to you. Deep inside MacApp is a standard event loop in which Mac OS events (data structures) are retrieved and immediately wrapped in MacApp event objects. You may have been dealing with Mac OS events as objects for years without realizing that at their core they are nonobject data structures.

Actions

Actions have more semantic meaning than events and often correspond to user commands. Cut, copy, paste, capitalize, in-dent, and page down are typical actions in Cocoa. Events are generated by the operating system in response to a user's interaction with the interface; actions are generated by objects such as windows, views, menus, and controls in response to lower-level events.

User actions (moving the mouse, clicking, etc.) often generate events—which may in turn generate actions in the Cocoa sense. Do not confuse user actions (a general interface concept) with the specifically Cocoa concept of actions that are certain types of messages.

Responders

In Cocoa, an object that can handle events and actions is a responder—usually a descendant of NSResponder. Applications, views, windows, and controls are all descendants of NSResponder and therefore can respond to events and actions.

The dispatching of actions differs somewhat from what you may be used to. In frameworks based on static languages such as C++ (MacApp and PowerPlant, for example), each object that can handle an event (applications, views, windows, and controls) is given a chance to handle every incoming event. Usually this is accomplished in a method such as `DoMenu-Command`, in which a gigantic switch statement has a case for each command that the object could handle. Commands that fall through the switch statement encounter a default block, which routes the command to the next object.

In Cocoa, the process is more direct. Given an action that needs a response, NSApplication finds a responder that implements that action by using the `respondsToSelector` method that all descendants of NSObject have. No longer does the object itself decide if and how it will respond to a command; instead, it doesn't receive the command unless it can respond to it—and it receives it not through a generalized command dispatching routine but rather as a direct call on its method that will process the command.

One of the most significant features of the Carbon libraries is their implementation of direct dispatching of events—by precisely this mechanism. As a result, MacApp and other Carbon-based applications can now provide the same efficiency of event handling that Cocoa does.

Responder Chain

Just as in other frameworks, events and actions are passed along from one element of the framework to another until one of them handles the request. This is done through a linked list of responder objects—each one points to its next responder or, if there is none, to null.

The framework takes care of following the responder chain through all of its elements. Typically, part of a window (a view or a control) is the *first responder*; if it cannot handle the event or action, it is passed on to its next responder—its superview (the view in which it is contained)—until its window is reached.

At that point, if the event or action has not been handled, the application moves on. There are normally three parts of the responder chain (each of which consists of its own linked list):

1. The Cocoa key window is the window to which all events and actions are directed.

2. The main window is the content window of data currently being worked on. The key window often is the content window; however, when a floating panel is interposed between the main window and the user, that panel becomes the key window. (This is one more step in the continuing saga of how to manage floating palettes.) The application sends unprocessed events and actions from the key window to the main window.

3. The application uses its own responder chain to attempt to process the event or action.

As in most other frameworks you may have used, this is a critical part of processing—and one that you can safely ignore most of the time.The framework will manage the responder chain in most cases.

Note, too, that actions can be dispatched directly to objects rather than going through the responder chain. When you connect an interface element to an object in Interface Builder, the method that you select is activated on demand. Thus, if you have a document (not an NSResponder), it can be directly connected to the Save menu command.

The choice of "responder chain" rather than "target chain" can be seen as more than merely semantic. In frameworks built on static languages, events and actions are sent *to* the elements of the chain. With its dynamic structure and the possibility of run-time introspection of objects, Cocoa can instead query the elements of the chain and send the event or action only to the object that *will* respond to it. The difference is subtle and general (there are cases where optimizations and structural concerns blur the architecture), but it is part of the flavor of Cocoa. Furthermore, this type of design is what makes the dynamic interface possible.

Delegates

As the penultimate step in each part of the responder chain (key window, main window, application), a delegate of the window or application is given a chance to handle the event or action. The delegate—which must be an NSObject—need not be a descendant of NSResponder. The window or application has a chance to forward the action or event to any object that it chooses (that presumably can respond to the event or action). If that, too, fails, then the ultimate step in each part of the responder chain is to pass on to the next part—from the key window to the main window to the application.

The use of a delegate is a very important part of the Cocoa architecture. For your application object (or a window or a view) to implement some functionality (responding to a message or a method call), it need only have a delegate that can do so. In other architectures, the application object (or window or view) would need to be subclassed to add the appropriate message or method call.

Outlets

An object often needs a reference to other objects with which it has to deal: A view may need to be able to communicate with its window, two views may need to mutually update data fields, etc. An outlet is just such a reference. Interface Builder can find such instance variables in your class definition and allow them to be manipulated by you or your users. It finds outlet instance variables by looking for the keyword IBOutlet in your header files (IBOutlet is defined to map to nothing, so it does not interfere with the compilation process).

Thus, the following declaration in a header file will be assumed by Interface Builder to be an outlet:

```
IBOutlet NSButton * myButton;
```

Early versions of Interface Builder require outlets to be typed as id rather than of specific types such as NSButton. If you are examining early Cocoa examples or legacy code, you may find many such outlets. Good programming practice is to type the outlets if your version of Interface Builder supports them. This allows Interface Builder to verify that connections are made properly—for example, that a button is not connected where a window should be.

With your outlets visible to Interface Builder, you can then connect them to graphical elements in your interface by using connections.

Connections

You connect outlets to interface objects. For example, a data entry field called "city" might be an outlet that is connected to a specific text field in your interface. Because Interface Builder can recognize your outlets, it can display the list of outlets for your object, allowing you to connect them to interface elements. Again, this differs from static language-based frameworks in which there is always a little snippet of code that you have to execute at run time to link the text field to the instance variable "city."

In this example, the outlet—a text field that is referred to by the outlet variable "city"—is in fact a data entry field. "Outlet" is a messaging concept and doesn't indicate the direction in which data flows in your application.

Actions

Connections are also made for actions—and here the direction of data flow is critical. Action connections are made from control objects (such as buttons) to the objects that you create. Actions not only have a source and destination, but also have a message that corresponds to a method of the receiving object. Thus, you can create an action connection from a button to an object you create and have it process the appropriate message of your object.

Interface Builder relies on methods of the form

```
- (IBAction) actionName: (id) sender
```

to find your object's actions. It generates a list of possible actions that your object can perform by compiling all of the action names into a list.

Like IBOutlet, IBAction maps to nothing, so it does not interfere with the compilation of your header file. Also, as with IBOutlet, IBAction was not present in the first versions of Interface Builder. Thus, you will find old-style action methods in some existing code:

```
- (void) actionName: (id) sender
```

AppKit

This section provides an overview of the structure of the AppKit classes. They are grouped into nine areas:

1. Interface

2. Fonts

3. Graphics

4. Color

5. Documents

6. Printing

7. Operating system support

8. International support

9. Interface Builder support

If the sheer size of Cocoa and its classes is daunting, consider that most of its classes just work—you don't have to worry about them. When you look at these areas, you can quickly see that many of them are probably not going to concern you. Fonts, for example, are set by the user in the Font panel and used by text objects—automatically. That's one area you probably do not have to worry about.

Likewise, color for text and other interface elements is set using the Color Picker, and you do not have to worry about it unless you need to implement a non-standard interface (which is probably not a good idea). The objects in question have their color choices set through the default behavior of interface elements. For many developers, international support is not an issue: Custom-written software developed for a school in France need not recognize the needs of a Mandarin speaker (but the capabilities are there if needs change).

Some of the more important Cocoa classes are described in brief in this section. They (and others) are discussed in more detail in Part III of this book.

Most of the objects described in this section are descendants of the fundamental Cocoa object, NSObject. NSObject is described later in "Foundation" starting on page 123.

Interface

By far the largest collection of classes is used to implement the Aqua interface. (In most frameworks that implement graphical user interfaces, the interface objects predominate.)

One problem with object-oriented frameworks has always been the fact that developers can override objects. True, this is one of the big advantages of such frameworks. When it comes to the interface, however, overriding standard elements has contributed to variations in functionality that confuse users and to difficulties in maintaining code.

Cocoa provides a number of ways to modify and extend interface elements without overriding them. In particular, delegation and protocols (such as MacApp behaviors) allow events to be passed off to custom-written objects that can provide functionality while leaving the underlying objects unscathed. If you are used to overriding objects (particularly interface objects), reconsider this choice before you do so with the Cocoa interface classes.

The interface classes are categorized into four major groups. Three of them are centered on objects that are descendants of NSObject itself. The fourth is a collection of objects that handle text.

NSEvent User-controlled applications are driven by events that normally are generated by the user. The most common of these are keystrokes, mouse movements, and clicking. Other events are generated by external events (network messages, for example) or by Cocoa or Mac OS X itself (periodic events in Cocoa fire on a regular basis once you have set them up).

An application needs to inspect each event that is sent to it; it can decline to do anything about the event, but it must examine each event that is sent to it.

NSResponder NSResponder objects can appear in the responder chain; they respond to events. Here you find the basic elements of a Cocoa application: windows, views, and the application itself. (In MacApp, the TEventHandler class is a common ancestor of views and the application object.)

NSCell Cells are relatively lightweight objects that can display text or images. They can also manage mouse tracking, selection, menus, actions, keyboard events, and the cursor. In this respect, they are like responders in general and views in particular.

However, cells are not responders or views—they descend directly from NSObject. Controls (descendants of NSControl such as NSButton) often have a cell associated with them to handle these generic activities. NSControl does descend from NSView and thus from NSResponder; it participates in the responder chain as appropriate and often passes off the processing of a specific message to an associated NSCell.

The problem of providing lightweight view-like objects to display text and images has evolved over time in all object-oriented frameworks. Clearly the text field that displays the label for a data entry field requires less functionality than the text field into which you can enter data.

Text The amount of code needed to properly handle text is enormous. Even without considering the demands of multiple languages and scripts, laying out text automatically (much less in response to user commands) is daunting. Users' expectations now are for the presentation of text on computer displays that matches or exceeds sophisticated typesetting on paper.

NSText and NSTextView are descendants of NSView (and thence of NSResponder). Both are designed to provide sophisticated text management so that you should not need to override them.

NSText is the more basic object: It displays text and implements actions allowing users to modify text styles. It manages wrapping of text across lines, and it can display graphics as part of RTF text. It implements clipboard support, including copying and pasting of fonts (as well as of text).

NSTextView provides further implementation of NSText (in fact, it is the object that you normally use in your applications). NSTextView provides additional support for rulers, services, and the storage of attachments (such as graphics).

Other Classes   Other interface classes handle menu items, status bars, toolbars, and the other Aqua interface elements.

Fonts

The font classes—NSFont and NSFontManager—are used by the Font panel, which users access to change their text font. The classes provide access to font information, but you rarely need to use them.

Graphics

The graphics area provides so much functionality that here, too, you may never need to get involved. Three of its classes are of particular interest.

NSImage   NSImage is the general image object. It reads image data and keeps track of multiple representations of it. The NSImage and NSImageRep structures are what makes it possible to create interface elements that display images without apparent regard to their type.

NSImageRep   An NSImage object contains an array of one or more NSImageRep objects. Standard objects are listed here:

- EPS images

- PICTs

- Bit-mapped graphics

- PDF images

- Images cached in memory (but with no instructions allowing them to be regenerated)

- Custom images that your application can create

When an NSImage needs to draw itself, it chooses from among its NSImageRep objects based on these criteria (in the following order):

- Color

- Resolution

- Depth (pixel depth or sample)

NSMovie   The NSMovie object can play QuickTime movies. Some of the QuickTime code exists here, but all of QuickTime is not available to this object.

Other Classes   Other graphics classes let you access cursors and the screen as well as OpenGL and the graphics environment.

Color

Like font objects, the color classes just work in most cases. NSColor and NSColorPicker are in this area; all interface elements work properly with them and you do not normally need to be concerned.

Documents

Documents are an area in which you do need to be very concerned if your application stores data. Note that the document architecture in Cocoa is much lighter weight than that of either MacApp or PowerPlant. In both of those frameworks, the document object is large and central. In Cocoa, the NSDocument object did not even exist until the late 1990s.

NSDocument The NSDocument object contains your document's data. It is a descendant of NSObject—not, as in frameworks such as MacApp, an event handler. However, documents can receive first-responder calls to save, revert, or print themselves.

The primary purpose of the NSDocument object is data management. If you use documents, you always override NSDocument.

NSDocumentController If you have more than one document or more than one document type, you use an NSDocumentController. This object intercepts File menu commands such as New or Open so as to carry them out.

In most cases, you do not need to override NSDocumentController; its default behavior works.

NSFileWrapper NSFileWrapper provides the in-memory versions of disk files. The default NSDocument and NSDocumentController methods normally handle file wrappers properly.

Printing

You rarely override the printing objects in Cocoa.

Operating System Support

A grabbag of objects provides support for help, copy-and-paste, spell checking, sound, and the desktop.

NSPasteBoard The pasteboard supports copy-and-paste on Cocoa. This object has had a difficult life when it comes to nomenclature. On the original Macintosh, it was referred to as the scrap or desk scrap; for users, it was the clipboard.

In Cocoa, the pasteboard structure is more complex than that found in other environments. At least five separate pasteboards exist to handle different types of shared objects:

1. Fonts

2. Rulers

3. Find text

4. Drag-and-drop data

5. Other objects

Most interface elements handle copy-and-paste properly, so you may never need to get involved with pasteboards.

NSWorkSpace The workspace object exists for each application. You use it to launch applications, copy files, and find the appropriate icons for files. It is somewhat like a programmer's Finder.

International Support

The input manager classes provide support for non-Roman alphabets.

Interface Builder Support

Three classes provide support for Interface Builder and its dynamic interface creation mechanism: NSNibConnector and its decendants, NSNibControlConnector, and NSNibOutletConnector.

Foundation

The Foundation framework provides the underpinnings for the AppKit framework. In the Carbon environment, the Core Foundation library lets Carbon developers get to the Foundation functionality. (See Chapter 9 for more details on the Core Foundation.)

Foundation's classes are grouped into 10 areas:

1. NSObject

2. Values

3. Strings

4. Collections

5. Operating system services

6. Notifications

7. Archiving

8. Objective-C language services

9. Scripting

10. Distributed objects

NSObject

NSObject and NSProxy are the basic objects from which all other objects descend—both those that are implemented in Cocoa itself and those that you create. This section describes NSObject in detail. In addition to the NSObject class, the NSObject protocol is also discussed here.

NSProxy, which supports objects that do not exist (such as objects that have not yet been instantiated) as well as distributed objects, is discussed in the final section of the Foundation framework.

Architectural Overview The issue of a common base object from which all other objects descend has been debated for a long time in the object-oriented community. The main disadvantage of a common ancestor is that a change to its structure requires recompilation of all objects that descend from it—the fragile base class problem. Of course, this argument loses most of its potency in a world where the fragile base class problem has been wrestled into submission (such as the dynamic world of Cocoa).

The argument in favor of a common base object is that all objects in the environment share certain characteristics and that you can rely on any object that you use to be able to perform certain tasks. Although static languages such as C++ let you inquire as to an object's class and dynamic languages let you inquire in more detail about not only the object's class but also the methods that it implements, it is still easier and more efficient to know that a certain set of tasks can be performed by any object with a certain ancestor.

This dogged problem is partly caused by the layering of object-oriented frameworks on top of operating systems. There is a critical barrier between the world of objects and the world of nonobject processing. In almost all cases, hardware does not deal with objects—in fact, it rarely deals with even such sophisticated concepts as data structures. It just moves bits and bytes around.

As you move from the hardware to the operating system, the bits and bytes are aggregated into data structures (strings, colors, files, etc.). Then, in what is traditionally called the application layer, a framework takes the data structures and encapsulates them into objects with which it works.

Special Objective-C Issues for NSObject   In Objective-C, each NSObject instance has a variable called isa. It points to the class object of that instance's class, and it is the route by which Cocoa is able to handle many of the introspective queries. In Java, this issue is handled by standard Java calls.

Special Java Issues for NSObject   Cocoa programmers working in Java rather than Objective-C need to note that a handful of Cocoa/Java classes do not descend from NSObject. These classes, such as NSDate and NSException, are implemented as descendants of the Java Object base class rather than as descendants of NSObject. In addition, some Objective-C structs (such as NSRect) are native Java classes.

Furthermore, NSObject in Java descends from the Java Object base class. As a result, some of the most primitive Objective-C methods (primarily those dealing with instance creation and initialization) are not present in the Java NSObject implementation; instead, the native Java Object methods that correspond to these are used.

NSObject Functionalities   NSObject—through its class and its protocol—provides basic functionalities shared by all objects in the Cocoa framework. These functionalities fall into the following categories:

- They provide means to initialize the class and then to create and destroy instances of it. (This process is referred to generically as *fabrication*.)

- Methods provide for *introspection* of the object—the class and superclass to which it belongs, to which what messages it responds, etc.

- *Identification* of a specific object—is this object the same as that one, for example—is supported. Identification differs from introspection in that introspection deals with the attributes and characteristics of the object, whereas identification deals with recognizing a specific object.

- *Message handling* is provided by NSObject, chiefly using the perform method.

- *Memory management* is implemented so that objects can be shared when needed but removed from memory when no longer in use.

- NSObjects can be archived and unarchived; this is done with their own methods and also by using the NSCoder protocol that NSObject adopts. The processes are grouped under *archiving and serialization*.

- *Error handling* is supported by NSObject.

Because of the significance of NSObject, each of these functionalities is described in more detail in the following sections. Most of the NSObject methods are described in this section.

Fabrication Allocation and initialization are used together when you manually create an object. You normally use a factory method that directly creates (allocates and initializes) an instance of the class required.

In Objective-C, you allocate an object using a Class method; you initialize it with an instance method.

```
+ (id) alloc;
- (id) init;
```

Conceptually, an invocation consists of:

```
myObjectClass * anObject = [myObjectClass alloc];
anObject = [anObject init];
```

anObject is an instance of the class myObjectClass; it is first allocated and then initialized. The second statement appears to replace anObject with itself: That is, its init method is called and the result is returned and overwrites anObject with the result of init. This coding is necessary because the init method can second-guess your initial object creation and return a substitute object (perhaps a more specific subclass of myObject than the general one you created).

In reality, most allocation and initialization are done with a single line of code that calls both the Class and instance methods:

```
myObject* anObject =
  [[myObjectClass alloc] init];
```

This line of code appears over and over in Objective-C Cocoa programs.

Objects that are located farther down the inheritance tree from NSObject may have more complex `init` methods that take parameters or that have different names. For example, NS-View has an initialization method that takes the view's framerect into account:

```
- (id)initWithFrame:(NSRect)frameRect;
```

Within the implementation of such initialization methods, a call to

```
[super init]
```

must be made (or to a comparable initialization method). These inherited calls must be made so that initialization proceeds all the way up to the basic NSObject `init` method. (The absence of these inherited calls is a frequently encountered bug. It is particularly insidious because the object is allocated and appears non-nil in a debugger, but when you attempt to use it—thousands of lines of code later—it is corrupted.)

Having allocated an object, you must deallocate it when you are done with it:

```
- (void) dealloc;
```

You override this method if you have data structures to release or if you have subsidiary objects to release. It is called from `release` and `autorelease` (methods of the NSObject protocol, discussed later in this chapter).

Thus, in Objective-C, you call `alloc` and `init` to create an object. You override `dealloc`; it will be called when needed.

In Java, you use standard method creation and construction calls to create instances of classes.

The new function creates an instance of a class, as in

```
myObjectClass anObject = new myObjectClass;
```

You do not explicitly call an `init` method; rather, a constructor is automatically invoked based on the name of the class and the parameters passed in the `new` call. Thus, Java would expect to find a method such as the following for it to call when you execute the previous line of code:

```
public myObjectClass() {
  super();
}
```

Just as in Objective-C, the call to the inherited constructor is essential. The call to `new` and the constructor can take matching parameters, such as the following pair:

```
myObjectClass anObject = new myObjectClass
  (file, size);

public myObjectClass (String theFile,
  NSRect theSize)
   super (theFile);
   _size = theSize;
}
```

Parameters to the constructor can be passed along to the superclass's constructor, used to set instance variables, or both—as is the case here.

Java handles garbage collection, so you do not have to call a `dealloc` method. A related concept—the `finalize` method of Object—exists, and you can override it if necessary. It is called during garbage collection just as an object is about to be destroyed. Java will automatically reclaim all of the object's memory, so you do not need to do anything about that. If you have memory structures or other data of an object that Java will not recognize, however, you may need to provide an override of `finalize`.

One frequent Cocoa use of `finalize` is to remove an object as an observer of notifications (since the object will no longer exist). Here is such a `finalize` method (they are scattered throughout Cocoa Java programs).

```
protected void finalize() {
  NSNotificationCenter.defaultCenter().
    removeObserver(this);
}
```

Introspection Particularly in the dynamic environment of Mac OS X, it is important that objects be able to examine themselves. Some of the compiler-time error checking you may be used to in less dynamic languages does not occur, and rather than allow a program to crash or misfunction, you need to do that checking at runtime.

In Java, this is done by using the Class class (that is, the class named "Class"), and the term "reflection" is used rather than "introspection." The relevant methods include `getSuper-class`, `isInstance`, `getFields`, and `getMethods`.

For example, consider the code to discover whether a method exists in a given class. First, you obtain the class; one way to do this is from an instance of the class.

```
Class theClass = anObject.getClass();
```

Because `getClass` is a method of Object, all Java objects respond to it appropriately. Next, if you want to see if that class responds to a given method, you can use the following code:

```
java.lang.reflect.Method aMethod = null;
aMethod = theClass.getMethod("someMethod", null);
```

Objective-C has methods that are comparable to the Class and java.lang.reflect methods in Java. Here is one that is similar to the Java example just shown and that is the one that you use most often: the test to see whether an object responds to a given message or selector (that is, whether it contains a specific method).

```
- respondsToSelector: (SEL)aSelector;
```

The selector is the complete description of the method you are looking for including its name and any optional parameters. The following are all selectors:

```
(SEL)comparator;
(SEL)aSelector name:(NSString *)aName
  object:(NSString *)anObject;
(SEL)operation error:(NSCalculationError)error
  leftOperand:(NSDecimalNumber *)leftOperand
  rightOperand:(NSDecimalNumber *)rightOperand;
```

Identification Identification routines let you compare and identify objects based on their content. Here, too, there are some differences between Objective-C and Java. Perhaps the most obvious one is the way in which you refer to an object itself: use self in Objective-C and this in Java. These two lines of code are comparable:

```
[self doIt]; //Objective-C
this.doIt(); /Java
```

The tests for two identical objects are also different in Objective-C and Java:

```
- (BOOL)isEqual: (id) object; //Objective-C
public boolean equals(Object anObject); //Java
```

Note that these tests are methods of NSObject in both Objective-C and Java, but they have different names (equals is a method of Object in Java, and is overridden by NSObject so as not to drive Java programmers mad).

What is important to note is that in your descendants of NSObject in either language, you can override equals or isEqual. This means that you can determine what equality is for specific objects.

Message Handling While all object-oriented languages and frameworks can handle messages (whether they are called messages or function calls), one of the very significant advantages of Cocoa and its dynamic nature is that it can reroute messages on the fly. The previously noted methods `re-spondsToSelector` and the comparable Java code discussed previously let you find out if an object can handle a message. If it does, you can then cause the method to be invoked (or the message to be sent, depending on your semantic preference).

If, in Java, you have found a method using the code shown previously,

```
java.lang.reflect.Method aMethod = null;
aMethod = theClass.getMethod("someMethod", null);
```

you can invoke that method by using the Object `invoke` method:

```
if (aMethod != null) {
  theResult = (resultType)aMethod.invoke(null);
```

To actually do this, you should catch the possible exceptions:

```
java.lang.reflect.Method aMethod = null;

try {
  aMethod = theClass.getMethod
    ("someMethod", null);
  } catch (NoSuchMethodException e) {
}

if (aMethod != null) {
try {
  theResult = (resultType)aMethod.invoke(null);
  } catch (IllegalAccessException e) {
    theResult = null;
  } catch
   (java.lang.reflect.InvocationTargetException e)
  {
    theResult = null;
  }
}
```

In Objective-C, you can do a comparable feat. You rely on the `performSelector` method of Objective-C and NSObject; it takes a single parameter—a (SEL) that is usually exactly what you have just tested in `respondsToSelector`:

```
if (anObject respondsToSelector: (SEL)theMethod) {
  [anObject performSelector: (SEL)theMethod;
];
```

However, the framework will normally do much of this work for you. If an object receives a message to which it cannot reply (that is, it is asked to perform a method or function that it does not have), it is then sent a new message—`forwardInvocation`. The original message is wrapped in an NSInvocation* object. You can extract the message to use in a call to `respondsToSelector` for another object. If you find an object that can respond, you can redirect the message.

Memory Management   Memory management is an important parts of modern frameworks and languages. Too much time has been spent tracking down memory leaks and mysterious crashes from data structures that were not allocated when necessary—or were pulled out from underneath code that assumed they were there.

In Foundation, the process is made as simple as possible. When you want to make certain an object is around at a later time, you send the `retain` message; you balance each `retain` message with a `release` message. In a great many cases, this is done automatically for you. For example, the NSArray object allows you to put objects into an array that can then be manipulated with its searching and sorting methods. NSArray calls `retain` for each object it adds to its array; it calls `release` when it removes objects from the array. In this way, an object in an NSArray can never accidentally be deallocated while it is in the array.

Autorelease pools provide an even easier way to manage objects. Here, you send the `autorelease` message to an object instead of a `retain` message; it is automatically added to the current autorelease pool—which is merely a collection of objects that can be released at a given time. When the pool itself is released, each object in the pool is sent a `release` message—you don't have to balance `retain` and `release` calls.

A single autorelease pool exists for the life of your application, although you can create others (and usually do for each thread in a multithreaded application). As balancing `retain` and `release` calls is a potentially time-consuming programming chore, using `autorelease` is a valuable tool. The disadvantage of `autorelease` is that the `release` messages are not sent until the entire pool is deallocated. Thus, if you have an object that you want to retain and could release almost immediately, using `autorelease` will keep it around until the current autorelease pool is deallocated.

The actual mechanism that is used is a reference count in each object that is incremented by one for each `retain` call and decremented by one for each `release` call. When the count falls to zero, the object is deallocated.

Archiving and Serialization   In Java, the java.io.Serializable interface lets you write out objects without further ado. Its subinterface, java.io.Externalizable, lets you customize the reading and writing.

In Objective-C, NSObject provides basic support for archiving and distribution. Archiving refers to placing representations of objects on disk; distribution refers to copying objects to other address spaces.

Archiving relies on NSCoder objects that are discussed in "Archiving, Serialization, and Distribution" on page 474. Table 7-1 shows the archiving methods of NSObject in Objective-C. In practice, you frequently use NSCoder (which is available both in Objective-C and in Java) to create serialized data that you then store in dictionaries (see "NSDictionary" on page 137).

Table 7-1. NSObject Archiving Methods

`classForArchiver` `classForCoder`	Return a Class object to be used during archiving or coding. The default is the object's own Class.
`replacementObjectFor` `Archiver`	Returns an id of an alternative object to archive by `anArchiver` (NSArchiver*). This allows you to read and write less complex objects than your run-time objects.
`awakeAfterUsingCoder`	The counterpart of the replacement Object methods. Its single argument `aCoder` (NSCoder*) has just created the object; you can substitute another.
`replacementObjectForCoder`	Returns an id of an alternative object to encode by `encoder` (NSCoder*). This allows you to read and write less complex objects than your run-time objects.
`setVersion` `version`	You can provide a version for objects that are archived. This helps you manage change in your software. Set: `anInt` (int). Get: returns an int.

Error Handling In Objective-C, NSObject itself has only one method to directly handle errors—`doesNotRecognizeSelector`. It is called by the run-time environment when a message sent to the object cannot be processed.

Normally, `doesNotRecognizeSelector` is called as the only statement in the default `forwardInvocation` method and an error is generated. You override `forwardInvoca-`

`tion` to attempt to process the message before `doesNotRec-ognizeSelector` is called.

NSInvocation This small object wraps a message that cannot be processed in Objective-C. Note that messages being forwarded must have a fixed number of arguments; some methods (such as NSArray's `initWithObjects`) that use variable numbers of arguments are not allowed.

Values

These objects include dates, numbers, and the like. Here is where you are most likely to find differences between the Objective-C and Java versions of Cocoa.

The Java implementation, for example, contains an NSRange object—a descendant of the primal Java Object class. In Objective-C, NSRange is a type. NSRange consists of two integers, and the overhead of creating such a small object as an object (rather than a type) in Objective-C is not worth the effort. NSRect, NSPoint, and NSSize are treated similarly: They are objects in Java, and they are types in Objective-C.

NSData NSData is an undifferentiated collection of bytes. It is frequently used as a return value from a method. Another method casts the NSData object to a more specific type.

NSValue NSValue is an Objective-C class that wraps a simple value (an integer, for example). It exists so that such values can be used in places where objects are required, such as within an NSArray object. It is not needed in Java, since integers and everything else are objects in that language.

Strings

The Objective-C NSString class and the native Java string class are both used to manage strings. Two Cocoa classes are of particular interest: NSFormatter and NSAttributedString.

NSFormatter NSFormatter objects—available in both languages—edit, display, and validate string entries in cell objects. (Cells contain controls such as text fields.) Two standard formatters—NSGregorianDateFormatter and NSNumberFormatter—are provided. You can override NSFormatter yourself to provide additional functionality.

Note that NSFormatter objects take localization rules into account. Thus, you probably do not need to create your own NSFormatter object to implement those features.

NSAttributedString An NSAttributedString adds styling attributes to the characters of a basic string (NSString in Objective-C or string object in Java). It contains such a string as part of its data structure.

NSAttributedString uses "attributed" in the sense of a string with styling attributes rather than in the sense of ascribing. Thus, the stress in pronouncing its name is on "at," rather than "trib."

Collections

Collection objects manage multiple data values.

NSArray In traditional programming, arrays and iterators were widely used. With the advent of object-oriented programming, various collection objects have been devised that incorporate the iterators. Many of them also include sophisticated searching mechanisms.

NSDictionary The NSDictionary object is a very powerful construct of Cocoa. It is just a set of key/value pairs, but it can be quickly accessed and can be stored to and retrieved from disk (see "Dictionaries" on page 377 for an example of its use). NSDictionary objects are used extensively in Cocoa. Perhaps because of their name, many people think they are appropriate for large amounts of data. In fact, they are useful for storing any amount of data that can be named. (Because NSDictionary keys must be unique, naming is important.)

NSSet Unordered sets of data are supported by the NSSet class.

Operating System Services	Foundation operating system services include locks, tasks, and threads. For most purposes, you can let the frameworks take care of these for you.
Notifications	Notifications are part of the Cocoa messaging system: One object can register its interest in another object and certain events. An object posts a notification when it does something; Cocoa takes care that the appropriate other objects are notified.
	Notifications are used for such events as window movement or resizing, application launching or activating, and the like. What is important about notifications is that the posting of the notification and the receipt of the notification are separate; an application does not notify individual objects that a window has moved. See "Notification" on page 404 for more information.
Archiving	The NSCoder class and its descendants, NSArchiver and NSUnarchiver, are used to move objects from memory to files or to flattened data structures suitable for writing or transmitting to other computers. They provide recursive processing, so that an entire collection of objects (or graph of related objects) can be reconstituted at a later time or at another location.
Objective-C Language Services	NSUndoManager, NSException, NSAutoreleasePool, NSAssertionHandler, and several other utility classes provide support for constructs of Objective-C itself.
Scripting	Support for AppleScript is located in the Foundation framework (not the AppKit). Scripting is described in Chapter 28.
Distributed Objects	Finally the Foundation framework lays the basis for managing objects across a network. The key to this is the NSProxy object.

NSProxy, like NSObject, is a base object or root class. It adopts the NSObject protocol, so it provides all of the functions of introspection (`isKindOfClass`, `isMemberOfClass`, etc.), messaging (`performSelector`, `respondsToSelector`, etc.), and memory management (`retain`, `release`, `autorelease`, etc.) that are included in that protocol.

On its own, NSProxy has seven methods. In addition to the standard allocation and deallocation methods, it has the `forwardInvocation` and `methodSignatureForSelector` methods of NSObject. These allow NSProxy to do its work. When an NSInvocation is received to which it cannot respond (and that is any invocation), it passes it on to the object for which it is standing in. At that moment, it may be necessary for that object to be instantiated, or for a link to an object somewhere else to be established. The methods of NSProxy are shown in Table 7-2.

Table 7-2. NSProxy Methods

`alloc`	The basic method to allocate the object.
`dealloc`	Called from a `release` method. You override this method if you have data structures to release or if you have subsidiary objects to release.
`class`	Returns the Class object.
forwardInvocation	You pass an `Invocation` (NSInvocation*) on to the object that the NSProxy is representing— possibly instantiating that object at the time.

Table 7-2. NSProxy Methods (Continued)

`methodSignatureForSelector`	You override this method to return the NSMethodSignature* for `aSelector` (SEL). Normally, you call the `methodSignatureForSelector` method of the object that the NSProxy is representing—possibly instantiating that object at the time.
`description`	Returns an NSString*; the default implementation returns the class name in the string. You can override it to provide additional information to debuggers.

Because NSProxy is a base class and not a descendant of NSObject, it has only the NSObject protocol methods available.

Summary

If you have used other frameworks, you will be struck with how similar Cocoa is to them. After all, graphical user interfaces rely on menus and windows, and there's only so much you can do with them!

Cocoa differs from other frameworks in its dynamism, and in the fact that its class structure is much less deep than it is in some heavily overridden frameworks (particularly MacApp). Furthermore, its utility objects such as dictionaries allow for data hiding (encapsulation) as well as very fast development since the single data-handling structure can be accessed as needed.

Chapter 8
The Frameworks of
Mac OS X: Carbon

Carbon is a set of libraries that constitute a framework (in the Mac OS X sense of the word). It is most notable for the ways in which it differs from Cocoa:

- *You can program Carbon applications in C++.*

- *You can modify existing applications to run in Carbon, taking advantage of many of the Mac OS X features.*

- *Carbon applications can run on both Mac OS X and on legacy systems—Mac OS 8.1 and later and earlier.*

This chapter shows you how Carbon fits into Mac OS X. It next shows you the structure of the Carbon frameworks, and it then explores the Carbon event model and how it differs from older programming styles on the Macintosh.

Where Carbon Fits In

Apple's first attempt at moving to the UNIX-based world that is now Mac OS X met with heavy resistance from developers. Apple provided an environment that would run then-existing software (it is now called Classic, then it was Blue Box), but the new features of the operating system were to be available only to freshly written applications using the Rhapsody framework (which is now Cocoa).

The gap between Blue Box and Rhapsody was just too large for people to swallow. After listening to customers and developers, Apple added Carbon to the picture.

Classic

Perhaps what is most important about Carbon is that it is not the Classic environment. In the Classic environment on Mac OS X, applications run as if they were running on Mac OS 9 (they are, in fact). They have that interface, and they have none of the modern features of the Mac OS X operating system such as protected memory. While a feature such as protected memory is a behind-the-scenes issue, the look and feel of the applications makes it clear to most users that they are running in the Classic environment.

There are some user interface differences between Aqua and Classic that can be annoying if you have to switch back and forth between them (it is the switching that causes the problem). When coupled with the lesser stability of the Classic environment when compared to Mac OS X, it is clear that Classic is a remarkable achievement, but it still is a second-class environment in which to run programs.

Carbon allows applications to access the features of Mac OS X, but Carbon applications do not run in the Classic environment. That is the most significant difference from a user's point of view since it is the most noticeable.

Carbon—and Cocoa—have been works-in-progress along with Mac OS X during the period of developer preview releases and the public beta testing of Mac OS X. All three products have evolved, and they continue to evolve. It is Apple's stated goal that both Carbon and Cocoa will have access to all features of Mac OS X. Thus, while a technology such as Services was not available from Carbon at the time of the first public release of Mac OS X, that represented only the then-current state of the Carbon libraries and not a design decision.

Mach-O and CFM

On Mac OS 9 and earlier, executable code is stored in code fragments; it is unpacked as needed by the Code Fragment Manager (CFM). The format of these files is referred to as PEF (Preferred Executable Format), but CFM is also sometimes used to refer to them.

Before the PowerPC chip powered Macintosh computers, a separate format was used. Code segments were stored in the resource fork of two-forked files, and they were loaded as needed.

On Mac OS X, the preferred format is Mach-O, but PEF files can also run. Mach-O files cannot be executed on Mac OS 9 and earlier.

In addition to the question of which executable file format can run where, the question of which development environment can generate which format matters:

- CodeWarrior can generate Mach-O or PEF files.
- Project Builder can generate only Mach-O files.
- MPW can generate only PEF files.

Depending on the project you are working on, your choice of development environment may already be made for you.

Carbon as a Mac OS X Preview

Because Carbon applications run directly in Mac OS X, they can take advantage of a number of the new features of the operating system including

• Protected memory

• Preemptive multitasking

• Virtual memory

• Aqua

From a user's point of view, of course, the biggest advantage is Aqua.

Carbon as a Classic Porting Tool

You can use Carbon not only to take advantage of new Mac OS X features, but also to help port older applications to Mac OS X. Some APIs are not available in Carbon; porting an application to Carbon will force you to get rid of extraneous or old-fashioned code.

Printing   Printing has been redesigned on Mac OS X, and there are new calls for printing. If you are using a framework such as MacApp or PowerPlant, you may not even notice this change. That's because you do not call the methods that have changed.

68K Calls   There is still legacy code around that calls nonexistent functions from the long-gone Motorola 68K architecture. No longer is this harmless; it will not compile with the Carbon libraries.

Hardware Access   Direct access to hardware is gone for the most part on Mac OS X. All such access needs to go through Darwin. Code that accesses hardware directly will not compile (usually in disk drivers or in games that draw directly to the screen buffer).

Trap Table Trap patching is gone. This was a very elegant architectural touch in the original Motorola chip. If you had to call a low-level subroutine, you jumped to a specific address—and the processor then jumped again to a memory location that was the value of the address. This intermediate address was called a trap. You could patch the trap. When you or anyone else called that trap, the patched code was executed.

Over a period of years, people stopped having much idea what would happen when they called a trap. It might be patched or not, and if patched, who knew what that code did?

Control Panels and Extensions Like trap patching, control panels and extensions were good ideas that got out of hand. They, too, allowed the operating system to be extended in one way or another. Unfortunately, sometimes these extensions conflicted with one another (and with trap patches). The combination of trap patches, control panels, and extensions meant that users really had very little idea what was going on in their operating system—and technical support people were just as much in the dark.

The Mac OS X structure is quite different. Just about everything is an application. The Darwin core is as small as possible, and the pieces of the operating system (the Finder, Classic environment, Dock, communications, and the like) run as individual processes. (You can see them with Process Viewer.)

Because of this fundamental architectural change, programs that were control panels or extensions or that relied on them must be rewritten to run under Carbon.

Carbon for Good Code

Code that has been converted to Carbon is generally of better quality than the pre-Carbon version. First, rewritten code often benefits from past mistakes and from improved programmers' skills. Second, Carbon does not allow you to do some of the things that are not part of good contemporary programming practices.

Perhaps the most important change to your code is the use of opaque data structures and accessors in Carbon. The data structures of the original Macintosh toolbox were available to anyone. Now, you must access them through accessors, and you have Apple's commitment that even though the underlying data structures most likely will change, the accessors will continue to work .

One such change is in process now. Much of the human interface code is not reentrant which means that it cannot be called from two different threads at the same time. This code—and there is a great deal of it—is gradually being changed to make it thread-safe. When this mammoth project is completed, the human interface methods will run much faster, particularly on multiprocessor computers. If you use accessors, you will take advantage of these changes whenever they occur.

Carbon for Maintenance

If you have existing code to port to Mac OS X, you can move gradually from Classic to Carbon as you have the time. You can adopt minimal Carbonization, then add new Carbon features, and finally move to Cocoa. It is not unreasonable to plan for this to occur over a period of many years.

The investment people have in legacy code is enormous. It cannot just be thrown out and rewritten (and redocumented and retested). As perhaps the biggest single developer of Macintosh code, Apple is well aware of this.

If you are considering converting code, first take an inventory of what you have. Here are some points to consider:

- Do you have the source code?

- Do you have all of the source code (critical files have a tendency to get lost)?

- Can you compile with the current best interfaces from Apple? The Universal Interfaces from Apple are available on http://developer.apple.com. Get the latest version and check that you can compile.

- Can you compile with the current development environments? Many legacy programs require legacy compilers.

Recompile your code with the latest Universal Headers and the latest version of your preferred development environment. Then test it. It cannot be stressed enough that you must make certain that the entire compile-build-run process works successfully before you start making modifications.

Once you have a successful build, download the latest Carbon libraries from http://developer.apple.com/macosx/carbon/index.html and start to work.

As always, if you are using a framework such as MacApp or PowerPlant, you may be able to skip many of these steps. However, you cannot skip the step of making certain that you can compile and run in the latest development environment. In the case of a framework, you need to add the current version of it to your checklist of dependencies.

Carbon Frameworks

This section provides a roadmap to the Carbon frameworks. While CarbonLib runs as a shared library on Mac OS 8.1 and later, it runs as a framework on Mac OS X, and that distinction is not noted further in this section.

Apple has approached Carbon from two directions. In the first, the company has looked at all of the toolbox calls for Mac OS 9 and decided which to convert to Carbon and which not to convert. The vast majority of toolbox calls have been converted. Where they have not, Apple's documentation generally cites a reason. For example, Apple events—even on Mac OS 9—provide a higher-level and more sophisticated way of communicating between programs than the PPC (program-to-program communications) toolbox. Added to the fact that the PPC toolbox was closely tied to the Mac OS 9 (and earlier) architecture, this meant that Apple saw little reason to convert the PPC toolbox. In as many cases as possible, Apple provides this sort of information: Toolbox calls are not just marked "unsupported" but a reason and a replacement are provided. (Note that in the case of libraries or sets of calls, the workarounds and replacements may be provided at the top of a file rather than repeated for each individual call.)

The second approach to Carbon has been to look at the features provided in Mac OS X and not in Mac OS 9 and provide as much access to as many of them as possible through Carbon. The combination of these two efforts is producing a sophisticated set of frameworks on which developers can build applications for some time. The no longer supported toolbox calls for the most part were replaced many years ago, but they were left in place. Now, it is time to clean up legacy code.

Apple continues to update the Carbon libraries (for Mac OS 8.1 and later) and the Carbon frameworks (for Mac OS X). The latest information is available at http://developer.apple.com/techpubs/macosx/Carbon/CarbonSpecification/CarbonSpecTOC.html.

While Carbon on Mac OS X consists of frameworks, it is not the sort of application development framework that Cocoa, MacApp, or PowerPlant is. In the latter frameworks, you focus on fairly high-level programming, leaving human interface and basic functionality to the framework. With the lower-level Carbon frameworks, you are responsible for more of the programming.

In Cocoa, for example, it is easy to create a descendant of NS-Document; if you set the appropriate parameters, Cocoa will take care of saving the document (according to the format you specify), reading it (again, using your format), and displaying "Do you want to save" sheets and other interface elements.

On Carbon, you display the sheets, take care of the reading and writing, and otherwise do programming that is more procedural than object-oriented. This may be more comfortable for you; it also may fit in with code that you have already been working on. Eventually all aspects of Mac OS X will be equally available from Carbon and Cocoa, so you can choose whichever environment is more convenient.

In Cocoa, there are 19 major sets of objects; they are grouped into 9 AppKit and 10 Foundation sets. In Cocoa, there are 29 frameworks grouped into three sets:

1. Carbon frameworks. These frameworks provide most of the mid-level Carbon support: CarbonSound, CommonPanels, HIToolbox, HTMLRendering, Print, Help, NavigationServices, SpeechRecognition, OpenScripting, IBCarbonRuntime, ImageCapture, NSL, Security-HI, and URLAccess.

2. Application services. These provide high-level support, including user interaction: Apple events, ATS, ColorSync, CoreGraphics, FindByContent, LangAnalysis, LaunchServices, PrintCore, QuickDraw, and SpeechSynthesis.

3. Core services. These are the lowest-level routines for Carbon: CarbonCore, NSLCore, OSServices, OT, and SecurityCore.

This section provides a brief description of each framework. It should provide you with an overall roadmap so that if you want to program a specific part of Mac OS X—ColorSync, for example—you should be able to find the name of the framework in which that support code is listed. Given the framework name, you can search for it in Apple's online documentation (on the Web or installed from the Developer CD).

Note that Apple documentation presents groups of managers; the structure presented in this chapter corresponds to the set of frameworks that Project Builder provides you in a default Carbon application. For more information on any specific framework, search for its name on http://www.apple.com/developer.

Carbon Frameworks

CarbonSound   Most Sound Manager calls from version 3.3 are supported. Earlier calls are not, but QuickTime frequently can replace their functionality.

CommonPanels   ColorSync and the Color Picker are located here, along with their support routines.

HIToolbox   This framework contains the basic human interface elements: dialogs, windows, lists, and the like. Most of the interface is located here. The old Standard File manager is not supported; it is replaced by NavigationServices. (Apple has been requesting developers to make this transition for years.) Also gone is support for editions—an approach to dynamic documents that was elegant and sophisticated but was rarely touched by users and not very frequently implemented by developers.

HTMLRendering   This framework lets you draw in a window based on HTML descriptions of what is to be drawn. It includes the data loading functions to retrieve data.

Help   Here is the support for Apple Help, which is described later in this book in Chapter 14.

IBCarbonRuntime   These are the calls to create windows and menus from Interface Builder nibs. (See Chapter 12 for more about Interface Builder and nibs.)

ImageCapture   These are the routines used to identify still cameras and devices and to download images from them.

NSL   The Network Services Location manager provides support for locating network services available for a computer. Its primary method is `NSLStandardGetURL`, which brings up the dialog you see in the Finder's Connect to Server command in the Go menu. This may be the only NSL method you need to call, as it handles all intermediate processing. When it returns, the value of the last parameter (`userSelectedURL`) is the URL of the selected service—or a null string if nothing was selected.

NavigationServices   NavigationServices handles the standard open and save dialogs that allow users to navigate through the directory structure (on their own computer or on a network) and through recent and favorite folders. It replaced the Standard File Package some time ago; Standard File is no longer supported on Carbon in Mac OS X.

OpenScripting   Open Scripting Architecture (OSA) is the Apple event mechanism that supports AppleScript and other scripting languages. It contains the routines necessary to parse object descriptions, to identify properties, to handle recording, and to process events.

Print   The Carbon Printing Manager replaces the Classic printing mechanism, and if you are converting an application, you may have some work to do. Fortunately, it is not burdensome in most cases. The Printing.h header file from Classic is no longer available (nor are its routines). In its place, you use the headers in the Print frameworks—PMApplication.h, PM-PrinterBrowsers.h, and Print.h. Each of the Classic printing calls generally has a corresponding call in the new Print framework.

A chart of old and new names is available at http://developer.apple.com/techpubs/macosx/Carbon/graphics/CarbonPrintingManager/Carbon_Printing_Manager/index.html.

If you are using MacApp, you probably never called Classic print manager routines anyway, so these changes do not affect you—they have already been done in the conversion of MacApp.

SecurityHI This framework provides access to the Keychain Manager. You can use it to let users update their keychains with passwords from within your application. In addition, you can use it to retrieve passwords from a keychain so that users do not have to reenter them in your application.

SpeechRecognition The built-in speech recognition API is supported in this framework.

URLAccess The URL Access Manager lets you send and receive data to and from a URL using FTP, HTTP, or HTTPS. Local files (file:///) are supported, as are proxy servers, compression, and extraction from Stuffit archives.

Application Services

AE This library supports Apple event scripting. It is the higher level set of APIs than the Open Scripting Architecture framework in the Carbon frameworks.

ATS Apple Type Services provides support for Unicode and other text.

ColorSync These are the support routines for color matching.

CoreGraphics These are the routines that let you access Quartz for low-level drawing.

FindByContent   This is the support for Sherlock searching; you can implement it in your own applications for high-speed data retrieval.

LangAnalysis   This provides morphological analysis, and it is currently available only for Japanese.

LaunchServices   Launch Services are used to find the application to open an application and otherwise find out that type of information about files and URLs.

PrintCore   These are the higher-level routines to support the Print framework in the Carbon frameworks section.

QuickDraw   These are the two-dimensional drawing routines that support QuickDraw on Carbon (that is, they implement QuickDraw calls by using Quartz).

SpeechSynthesis   These routines generate speech from your application.

Core Services

These frameworks provide the low-level support for Carbon.

CarbonCore   The bulk of the Carbon implementation is here. You will find everything from date and time utilities to the Alias manager in this framework. If you need a utility and don't find it in another framework, here is the place to look.

NSLCore   This is the low-level support for network services location (the Connect To dialog).

OSServices   Operating system services include power and disk partitioning.

OT   Open Transport provides communications architecture support at the transport level of the OSI architecture. If you are writing application programs, you usually do not need this.

SecurityCore   These are the low-level routines that interact with the human interface security routines (including the Keychain Manager) from the Carbon frameworks.

Carbon Events

You do not need to adopt Carbon events when you Carbonize your application. However, doing so makes your application run a little faster—and it makes other applications on the same computer run much faster. The Carbon event model (which is similar to the Cocoa event model) allows for direct dispatching of events to the object in an application that needs the event.

Old-Style Events
(WaitNextEvent)

Before Carbon events, each application ran its own event loop. Somewhere within the outer block of an application (either an application object or a plain, C- or Pascal-based application), a loop like the snippets given in this section can be found.

A `while` loop is at the core of the responsiveness of all user-driven applications. The faster it executes, the faster a user's keystroke or mouse event will be picked up by the program. The utmost responsiveness is guaranteed by keeping all extraneous processing out of the event loop.

Unfortunately, extraneous processing means everything other than what this program is doing. If you are transferring files in the background, sending email, or doing anything else on your computer, those tasks compete with a processor that is heavily loaded with this `while` loop—which is itself waiting for a user event.

This problem becomes increasingly acute as more and more processes run on a computer, and as more and more events need to be attended to. This simple model—grab the processor and keep it waiting until the user deigns to press a key or move the mouse—is very inefficient in a shared environment.

SimpleText Event Loop Processing In Apple's SimpleText from 1996 (version 1.4d16), here is part of `DoEventLoop`:

```
do {
  pWindow = LMGetFirstWindow();
    // walk all of our windows, even invisible ones

  DoAdjustCursor(pWindow);
  gotEvent = WaitNextEvent(everyEvent, &gEvent,
    DetermineWaitTime(pWindow), gCursorRgn);
  trueGotEvent = gotEvent;
 ...
} while (!gAllDone);
```

This loop runs over and over, checking for events of interest. Dispatching of events is done later within this same method. For mouse clicks, the process consists of stepping through where the mouse is clicked and what interface element is beneath it:

```
PointtheMouse, tipLocation;
shortnewBalloon = iNoBalloon;
RecttempRect;

// find out where the mouse is
SetPort((GrafPtr) GetWindowPort(pWindow));
GetMouse(&theMouse);

// and only do something if we are within the window
  itself
if (PtInRect(theMouse, &GetWindowPort(pWindow)-
  >portRect))
{
  // is it in the vertical scroll bar?
  if (pData->vScroll)
  {
    tempRect = (**(pData->vScroll)).contrlRect;
    if (PtInRect(theMouse, &tempRect))
    {
```

As you can see, the process involves `if` statements within `if` statements. This code—often exactly this code—appears in many non-object-oriented Macintosh programs.

MacApp Event Loop Processing In MacApp, here is some framework code that runs the main event loop. The `while` loop calls a MacApp method, `PollEvent`, which does similar work to that shown in SimpleText.

```
void TDispatcher::MainEventLoop()
{
  fIdlePhase = idleBegin;
  while (!fDone)
    PollEvent(kAllowApplicationToSleep);
}
```

If you follow the code of the `TDispatcher::PollEvent` method through, you will find the code that actually handles events. This code is common to all event loop-driven applications. In SimpleText (not built to an application framework), all of the testing was done in-line. In MacApp, the same testing done in SimpleText occurs in MacApp framework methods—but while the code is simpler, the same process is carried out (Where is the mouse? What lies beneath it?).

```
void TDispatcher::DoToolboxEvent(TToolboxEvent*
  event)
{
  // For Toolbox events, fIdentifier == fEven-
  tRecord.what
  if (event)
  {
  switch (event->GetIdentifier())
  {
    case mouseUp:
    HandleMouseUp(event);
    break;

    case mouseDown:
    HandleMouseDown(event);
```

```
break;

case activateEvt:
HandleActivateEvent(event);
break;

case updateEvt:
HandleUpdateEvent(event);
break;

case keyDown:
case autoKey:
HandleKeyDownEvent(event);
break;
```

While a certain degree of grouping of types of events can be done (`HandleMouseUp` and `HandleMouseDown`, and `HandleActivateEvent`), nevertheless each possible event that the program handles needs to be placed into a gigantic `switch` statement. In practice, you will find multiple sections of code like this one to handle different types of events.

When you finally get to a specific type of event, you call a method in your application to handle it. For example, `HandleKeyDownEvent` in TDispatcher is called to handle all of the keystrokes. (That method call is underlined.)

Direct Dispatching with Carbon Events

Direct dispatching moves all of this processing out of the application and into the operating system. It involves a different structure, but all the pieces of the preceding code architecture are still present.

If you are used to handling events either in the old style or in other event-driven architectures, you will recognize the concepts and much of the terminology in this section. If this is your first experience with event handling, you will find this an overview, but you may need to examine more code than is provided in this chapter to become comfortable. Fortunately, this code is as routine as it can be—the dispatching of mouse events is the same as dispatching keyboard events.

One way to think of the difference between the old `Wait-NextEvent` architecture and direct dispatching is that all of the testing and sorting that you used to do after you got an event is now done before it, so that the operating system can dispatch the event correctly.

When you work with events, you need to be able to describe them in the abstract and in the concrete: you must be able to identify a mouse click abstractly, and you need to be able to get information about a specific mouse click that has happened. (This is true also of the older event-handling architecture, but direct dispatching with Carbon events uses different terminology.)

Identifying Events Identifying events relies on a pair of values: an *event class* and, within that, *event kinds*. (This is very similar to the structure of Apple events—in that case, there are events, and there are kinds within them. Apple events are not Carbon events, but there can be similarities.)

There are nine classes of events. For each of those classes, some of the kinds of events in those classes are shown in the following list along with the defines for the classes:

1. Application events (launching and quitting, bringing to the foreground or background, another application starting or terminating) `kEventClassApplication`

2. Commands (menu items chosen, enabled, or disabled) `kEventClassCommand`

3. Control (checkboxes, buttons, pop-up menus—clicked, created, or destroyed) `kEventClassControl`

4. Keyboard (key down/up, modifier key pressed) `kEventClassKeyboard`

5. Menu (mouse down in menu, menu hidden/displayed, menu item enabled/disabled) `kEvent-ClassMenu`

6. Mouse (mouse down/up, mouse move, mouse move with button down) `kEventClassMouse`

7. Tablet (touch, pen enters/leaves) `kEventClassTablet`

8. Text input (character typed, selected text, update text) `kEventClassTextInput`

9. Window (created/destroyed, activated/deactivated, made visible/invisible, content region: cursor moved in or mouse click in, moved, resized, minimized, to be moved, to be resized, to be minimized) `kEventClassWindow`

You normally use the defines for classes and kinds. To uniquely identify an event, you need both, and the `EventTypeSpec` struct declared in CarbonEvents.h combines both of them.

Using Specific Event Information In the older architecture, you could examine data within events that your application obtained from `WaitNextEvent`. In Carbon, you cannot examine the data structures within events; instead, you use accessor methods to get the data you are interested in. (This is better programming practice, and in general this sort of coding style makes issues such as reentrancy and thread safety much less troubling than is the case when people access internal data structures.)

Following are the accessors for Carbon events. The first four take a single parameter—and EventRef, which is a reference to an event (it is what you receive when Carbon dispatches an event to you).

1. `GetEventClass` (returns the event class identifier).

2. `GetEventKind` (returns the event kind identifier).

3. `GetEventTime` (the time as a floating point number—EventTime—when the event occured).

4. `GetEventRetainCount` (the reference count of the event; you rarely need to use it).

5. `GetEventParameter`.

Everything else about an event is accessed through `GetEventParameter`. While this may look daunting, in practice, it is very simple to use.

```
OSStatus
GetEventParameter(
  EventRef          inEvent,
  EventParamName    inName,
  EventParamType    inDesiredType,
  EventParamType *  outActualType, /* can be NULL */
  UInt32            inBufferSize,
  UInt32 *          outActualSize, /* can be NULL */
  void *            outData);
```

You will find constants in CarbonEvents.h that identify event parameters for each event. Comments are all in the same format:

```
Parameters for command events:
  kEventCommandProcess
    --> kEventParamDirectObject
          typeHICommand
    --> kEventParamKeyModifiers
          typeUInt32 (optional)
```

From this, you should understand that the `kEventCommand-Process` kind of the command event class has two parameters:

1. `kEventParamDirectObject` is of type `HICommand`, and it is always present.

2. `kEventParamKeyModifiers` is of type `UInt32`, and it may or may not be present.

To extract the command from a command process kind of command class event, declare an HICommand and then call `GetEventParameter` as follows:

```
HICommandcmd;

GetEventParameter(inEvent,
    kEventParamDirectObject,
  typeHICommand, NULL, sizeof(HICommand), NULL,
  &cmd);
```

You will then be able to access the fields in `cmd`. (You will see code to do this later in this chapter in "Programming the Event Handler" on page 165.)

To reference an optional field such as `kEventParamKeyModifiers`, you need to check the OSStatus return value as follows:

```
HICommandcmd;

if (GetEventParameter(inEvent,
    kEventParamDirectObject,
  typeHICommand, NULL, sizeof(HICommand), NULL,
  &cmd) = noErr)
  …
```

The reason for this is that the parameter is optional, and `GetEventParameter` might not return anything.

`GetEventParameter` is perhaps the most frequently used method in handling Carbon events. Although it has seven parameters, you normally care only about two: the event you pass in (which you receive from Carbon), and the value you want out (the last parameter). In between, you use the constant and type from CarbonEvents.h, and you specify the size of the item to be returned.

Setting Up Direct Dispatching Here are the steps involved in setting up direct dispatching:

1. *Identify* the event targets. (This is a design and planning step; you don't write code as part of it.)

2. *Define* the events that you will handle. (These are the conditions of the `switch` or `if` statements that you used to test the incoming event in the old architecture.)

3. Program the code to *handle* those events. (This is the code that was executed in the body of the `switch` or `if` statements.)

4. *Install* the event handler (step 2) in your application.

5. *Run* the application event loop to let the operating system receive events and dispatch them to the handler you wrote in step 2.

The example code in this section is based on the Carbon SimplerText example that is in the CarbonLib package. Note that SimpleText in CarbonLib uses Carbon but with the older-style `WaitNextEvent` architecture. The definitive guide to events and event dispatching is the Event.h interface located in the HIToolbox framework inside the Carbon frameworks. Because of the importance of the methods in this file, they are heavily documented there.

Identifying Event Targets Direct dispatching of events involves the concept of an event *target*. (You may prefer to think of a target as the *context* of an event—that is a less common terminology, but it may help you to understand the concept.). In either case, the issue is simple: An event (such as a mouse click) is paired with a particular action performed by the event handler (such as closing a window) in the context of a particular object, or when that object is the target.

Put another way, a mouse click in a window's close box has a different meaning than a mouse click on an OK button in a Save dialog, and that in turn has a different meaning than a mouse click on an OK button in a warning dialog.

In old-style event processing (such as the code snippets given earlier in this chapter), all events were received by the main event loop in the application, and they were dispatched by that code to the appropriate routines to handle the events. This dispatching of incoming events involves the nested `if` statements or `switch` statements that you saw in the previous code snippets.

Event targets in Carbon can be the application itself, windows, menus, or controls (such as buttons, checkboxes, and the like). If you identify a very specific target, you can avoid much of the testing to see how an event should be handled. In some cases, no testing is required because a given target handles a given event in only one way. For example, an OK button is a control, and it can be a target. If you identify it as such, then an incoming mouse click event can be dispatched without further ado to a routine that does whatever a click on the OK button should do. You do not have to test further.

In practice, windows are often the best targets for events in the user interface. Making each control a target carries things to extremes.

A target must be able to distinguish between the events that it receives. If it receives mouse clicks, for example, it needs a mechanism to know which mouse click occurred in an OK button and which occurred in a Cancel button.

One common case is distinguishing among control elements such as buttons. When you create such controls in Interface Builder, you can assign a four-character code to each one.

Events that are received by a window have access to these codes, and you can easily construct a `switch` statement that lets you route events appropriately. You do not have to test where the mouse was clicked to find out what interface element was clicked on; you will receive that information directly from the event parameters.

The way you do that is to check the `commandID` value of the command that is in the event. The code shown previously gets that command:

```
ICommandcmd;
GetEventParameter(inEvent,
  kEventParamDirectObject,
  typeHICommand,
  NULL,
  sizeof(HICommand), NULL, &cmd);
```

Access the command `ID` of the control that sent the event by using `cmd.commandID` (`commandID` is part of the HICommand struct). You can then use that to dispatch various routines:

```
switch (command.commandID) {
  case kMyFirstCommand:
}
```

You are responsible for defining `kMyFirstCommand`, and you must assign the same value to the control in Interface Builder.

When you are deciding what to use as event targets, look for a middle road between no differentiation (that is, sending all events to the application) and no consolidation at all (sending events to specific buttons). As noted previously, the window will be the most likely target.

Then, as a reality check, make certain that you will be able to distinguish among the events your target receives. Look in CarbonEvents.h to see what parameters will be available—you will use them (along with the event class and kind) to differentiate events. If you cannot differentiate between events based on this information, you must split them into two or more targets, in each of which the events are unambiguous, or you must provide additional information in your application for the disambiguation. (For example, if you are handling mouse clicks in objects that move—as in a game or drawing program—you will need to make certain that you are storing the current locations of those objects so that you can use them with the mouse location information that is part of the events you receive.)

Defining the Events   When you have decided on a target, you need to define the events that it will receive. You do that by creating an `EventTypeSpec` or an array of `EventTypeSpec` elements. Each element contains a class and kind constant, as the following code snippet illustrates:

```
static const EventTypeSpec sAppEvents[] =
{
  {kEventClassCommand,kEventCommandProcess},
  {kEventClassCommand,kEventCommandUpdateStatus},
  {kEventClassMenu,  kEventMenuEnableItems}

};
```

This information will be used when you install an event handler. If you will be installing two event handlers, you will need two arrays: one for each of the sets of events that each handler will be responsible for. Whether you use one or more event handlers depends on how you program them. The next section shows you how to do that.

Programming the Event Handler   An event handler receives the events you have set up for it and then processes those events. These event handlers have very similar structures; the window event handler from SimplerText is partially shown in this section.

As a general rule, a `switch` statement separates the incoming event based on its class; within those separations, different event kinds are handled. (Note that the event kind is located in the call to `GetEventKind` before `GetEventClass` only to simplify the code.)

In the case of `kEventClassWindow` and `kEventWindow-DrawContent`, the application's `TXNDraw` method is called (it is underlined). Later on, in response to `kEventClassCommand` and `kEventProcessCommand`, the application's `ProcessCommand` method is called. While your methods may vary, you will probably have an event handler that looks very much like this.

Now you can see the significance of having one or more arrays of event definitions. You either separate the incoming events as shown here—in `switch` and `case` statements—or you separate them in advance by installing separate event handlers. If you installed all `kEventClassWindow` events into one handler, and all `kEventClassCommand` events into another, you would not need the outer `switch` statement in this code. Do what makes sense and what makes the code cleaner.

The event handler must have three parameters and return an OSStatus. The prototype is as follows:

```
pascal OSStatus HandlerName (
  EventHandlerCallRef nextHandler,
  EventRef theEvent, void* userData);
```

You can install a two-stage event handler in which the prototype is little more than a shell that calls a more customized handler such as the one that follows (not that `userData` is missing). This two-stage process is described in the following section.

```
OSStatus TTextWindow::HandleEvent(
  EventHandlerCallRef handler, EventRef inEvent)
  {
    OSStatusresult = eventNotHandledErr;
    UInt32kind = GetEventKind(inEvent);
```

```
switch (GetEventClass(inEvent))
{
  case kEventClassWindow:
    if (kind == kEventWindowDrawContent)
    {
    TXNDraw(fObject, NULL);
    }
  else if (kind == kEventWindowSizeChanged)
    {
    Rectbounds;

    GetWindowBounds(GetPlatformWindow(),
      kWindowContentRgn, &bounds);
    TXNResizeFrame(fObject,
      bounds.right - bounds.left,
      bounds.bottom - bounds.top, fFrameID);
    }
    result = noErr;
    break;

  case kEventClassCommand:
    if (kind == kEventProcessCommand)
    {
    HICommandcmd;


    GetEventParameter(
      inEvent,
      kEventParamDirectObject,
      typeHICommand,
      NULL,
      sizeof(HICommand),
      NULL,
      &cmd);
    result = ProcessCommand(cmd);
    HiliteMenu(0);
    }
    break;
```

The existence of the ProcessCommand is a matter of judgment and style (just as is the choice of how many handlers to install). In SimplerText, `ProcessCommand` is merely a large `switch` statement. It could just as easily be programmed in-line in the handler, but that would make the code less readable. Here is the beginning of `ProcessCommand`:

```
switch (command.commandID)
{
  case kHICommandUndo:
  TXNUndo(fObject);
  result = noErr;
  break;

  case kHICommandRedo:
  TXNRedo(fObject);
  result = noErr;
  break;
```

You can see how the event handler and `ProcessCommand` use `GetEventParameter` as described previously in this chapter to get the command identifier of the object that sent the command.

Installing the Event Handler Having defined the events to which the target responds and having written the event handler, you next need to install that event handler for those events.

This is a multistep process, and it may take some getting used to. Fortunately, there are many examples and tutorials on the Developer CD. Also, if you use MacApp 15 or later, much of this work is done for you. Furthermore, this process is pretty much the same for most event handlers in most applications. You can use this code with very little modification (save for your specific handler routines).

The basic installation process involves calling `Install-EventHandler`. It takes six parameters:

1. First, you pass in the target as an `EventTargetRef`. It is a window, the application, and so forth.

2. The handler itself is passed in as a universal procedure pointer (UPP) created with the `NewEventHandler-UPP` function. It needs to be packaged as a UPP so that a reference to it can be stored until the callback is needed. If that callback needs to cross the boundary between Mach-O and CFM (for example, when a Carbon application is a CFM app), this step is essential.

3. You then specify the number of events that this handler will respond to.

4. Next, you pass in an array of those events.

5. You can pass in a pointer to any data that you want; that pointer will be returned to the event handler whenever it is called.

6. You can also specify an `EventHandlerRef` pointer. If you provide it, it will be created and returned to you when InstallEventHandler completes. You can use this pointer to dynamically add and remove events from the handler as the program executes.

Macros are defined to install event handlers for windows, the application, menus, or controls. These simplify or eliminate parameters in the basic procedure call. For example, `InstallWindowEventHandler` takes as its first parameter a `WindowRef` pointer, and it calls `GetWindowEventTarget` on that `WindowRef`. These two sets of code are identical:

```
InstallWindowEventHandler (theWindow, theHandler,
  numTypes, typeList, userData, &handlerRef);

InstallEventHandler (GetWindowTarget(theWindow),
  theHandler, numTypes, typeList, userData, &han-
  dlerRef);
```

The Carbon examples on the Developer CD show you how to create and install simple event handlers. Here is a slightly more complex case that you can expand to cover many of the real-life situations you may encounter. (It is from Simpler-Text.) It demonstrates the interaction of the userData pointer and the handlerRef during event-handling callbacks.

1. Write the handler. This step is the same for all event handlers and the code always looks something like this:

```
OSStatus TWindow::HandleEvent(
  EventHandlerCallRef inRef,
  EventRef inEvent)
  {
  OSStatusresult = eventNotHandledErr;

  switch (GetEventClass(inEvent))
  {
    case kEventClassWindow:
      switch (GetEventKind(inEvent))
      {
      case kEventWindowClose:
      this->Close();
      result = noErr;
      break;
      }
  };

  return result;
  }
```

2. The actual handler that you install needs to conform to the prototype with the three arguments mentioned earlier. Thus, here is the shell prototype that you will install. Note that all it does is to rearrange the incoming parameters (specifically, casting userData to a TWindow*) and then call the customized handler from step 1.

```
pascal OSStatus TWindow::EventHandlerProc(
  EventHandlerCallRef handler,
  EventRef event, void* userData)
  {
    return ((TWindow*)userData)->
```

```
      HandleEvent(handler, event);
}
```

3. To install the event handler from step 2, you need to package it as a UPP:

```
EventHandlerUPP
TWindow::GetEventHandlerProc()
   {
   static EventHandlerUPP handlerProc = NULL;

   if (handlerProc == NULL)
     handlerProc = NewEventHandlerUPP(
       EventHandlerProc);

   return handlerProc;
   }
```

4. You need to define the events to be handled:

```
const EventTypeSpec events[] =
{
  {kEventClassWindow,kEventWindowActivated},
  {kEventClassWindow,kEventWindowDeactivated},
  {kEventClassWindow,kEventWindowClickContentRgn},
  {kEventClassWindow,kEventWindowSizeChanged},
  {kEventClassWindow,kEventWindowDrawContent},
  {kEventClassCommand,kEventCommandProcess},
  {kEventClassCommand,kEventCommandUpdateStatus},
  {kEventClassMenu,kEventMenuEnableItems}
};
```

5. Now, you actually install the event handler (which will call the secondary event handler) for the specified events. The userData parameter is passed in as this—the object in which this line of code is placed. It is coerced into a TWindow* object when the handler is called, and the HandleEvent method of the object is called.

```
InstallWindowEventHandler(fWindow,
  GetEventHandlerProc(), 1, &closeEvent, this,
```

```
&fHandler);
```

6. The fHandler variable passed into `InstallWindow-EventHandler` is returned with a reference to the handler that has been installed. You can use that to modify the events that are attached to the handler:

```
AddEventTypesToHandler(fHandler, numEvents, list);
```

Running the Event Loop Having identified your targets, defined your events, programmed your event handlers, and then installed them, you need to start the Carbon event loop running. Usually you do so in your `main` function. Here is the code:

```
RunApplicationEventLoop();
```

In the Carbon event model, there is much more setup than in the older architecture using `WaitNextEvent`. However, as you have seen, much of the same code is used—it is just used in different places. There is less code, though, because the looping and dispatching are moved into the operating system.

You could argue that until an operating system has control of the scheduling of events, it cannot begin to handle multiple users and applications. The architecture of Mac OS X relies on multiple applications and threads instead of a big amalgam of control panels, extensions, traps, and the like. Centralized dispatching is essential to making it work. The more applications that use the Carbon event model, the more responsive a computer will be.

Summary

Carbon is a framework on Mac OS X (a set of shared libraries on Mac OS 9 and earlier). You can move existing C++ code relatively easily to Carbon; you also can program new applications in Carbon, taking advantage of your experience in the world of C and C++.

Carbon applications take advantage of many of the Mac OS X features automatically; they can take advantage of others if you do further programming. In particular, the direct dispatching Carbon event model allows your application to run efficiently (and other applications to run efficiently) in the shared environment of Mac OS X.

While Carbon at first was thought of as a transitional technology, it is here for the long haul—the Finder itself is written in Carbon, and everything that it can do, both functionally and in terms of interface, can be done in Carbon.

With two major application development frameworks, Cocoa and Carbon, Mac OS X provides a variety of choices in terms of design and programming languages for developers. Completing the suite of development tools are Core Foundation and the Apple Class Suites, the topics of the next chapter.

Chapter 9
The Frameworks of
Mac OS X: Core
Foundation and Apple
Class Suites

There is an enormous amount of C++ code in the world. Much of it was written for the Macintosh, and still more was written for other platforms. If you have C++ code, or if you feel most comfortable writing C++ code, you can do so on Mac OS X. Cocoa is accessible primarily to Java and Objective-C programmers; Java applications can also be written for Mac OS X (as Java applications in addition to Cocoa applications). But C++ remains a workhorse and Apple has not forgotten C++ programmers. This chapter provides an overview of three major C and C++ technologies on Mac OS X: Core Foundation, MacApp, and Apple Class Suites.

Core Foundation is a Carbon framework (on Mac OS X—on Mac OS 9 it is a library) that provides access to the Cocoa Foundation framework. It can be used to share data among all of the Mac OS X frameworks and development tools.

About to enter its third decade, MacApp has tracked the development of object-oriented frameworks, the Macintosh, and graphical user interfaces. This section provides a very brief overview of MacApp, and it shows you how to find out more about it in the most definitive way possible: by exploring the code in a browser.

Apple Class Suites (ACS) represents a relatively recent project to pull some of MacApp's functionality out of the framework and make it available to people using other frameworks and even people not using a framework at all.

Core Foundation

Core Foundation provides fairly low-level functionality that is otherwise provided either by basic language constructs (such as character arrays—strings), common libraries, and other tools. They are packaged into reusable programming entities that incorporate error checking, sensitivity to location (for strings, dates, and so forth), and the other features that make the difference between starting from scratch each time you write a program and building on the powerful accomplishments of others (and yourself).

Core Foundation Syntax

In object-oriented frameworks, some objects—particularly small ones—have frequently been declared as `struct` syntax elements rather than as true objects. (In Cocoa, this is true of NSRect, for example. Before the advent of stack-based objects in MacApp, it was equally common there.) From the programmer's point of view, there is no difference between using such object-like `struct` elements and using true objects.

However, the use of `struct` elements is not satisfactory in all cases. Core Foundation uses a syntax that lets you work as if you were in an object-oriented world while not necessarily being there.

Given an object (myObject), you can invoke one of its methods (aMethod) in various ways in the object-oriented languages:

```
myObject.aMethod(); //Java or C++
[myObject amethod]  //Objective-C
```

In the Core Foundation syntax, you would write such a statement as

```
aMethod (myObject);
```

If parameters were used for aMethod, they would appear in this way:

```
aMethod (myObject, param1, param2, param3);
```

This structure is not object-oriented (although its implementation may or may not be). However, because it is at least object-oriented-like, you can refer to Core Framework elements as objects.

Note that some methods—particularly creation methods—depart from this convention. Creation is described later in this section.

Opaque Types

Within the Core Foundation code, macros, and defines, this is all sorted out so that the right thing happens. Part of the way in which this is done is by hiding everything within the Core Foundation elements from view. You can get to the contents only by using accessors such as in the following.

A CFNumberRef object (value) is declared (and created elsewhere). You can use an accessor for such an object to retrieve its value as an integer type (kCFNumberIntType) and place it into the int, currentValue.

```
int currentValue;
CFNumberRef value;
...
CFNumberGetValue(value, kCFNumberIntType,
  &currentValue)
```

This is what Core Foundation code looks like: lots of constants and accessors.

Creating and Copying Core Foundation Objects

As you can infer from the type names, Core Foundation objects are references to underlying data structures. As always when you deal with references, you need to be aware of just how you are manipulating memory.

First, creating Core Foundation objects is always done with methods that include "create." These methods take as their first parameter an allocator that creates the appropriate underlying object and reference to it. Default allocators exist for all Core Foundation objects, and you use them by passing NULL as the first parameter. The following code snippet demonstrates the use of a string creation routine. A CFNumber object is created with the default allocator (NULL), from a kCFNumberIntType type that is located in currentValue.

```
value = CFNumberCreate(NULL, kCFNumberIntType,
  &currentValue);
```

Next, copying an object needs to use an explicit copy routine; replacing a reference to one object with another handles only the references, not the underlying objects. Whenever copying makes sense, use routines such as the one that retrieves a user preference for a given application (appName) and given preference key (sortDirection):

```
direction = CFPreferencesCopyAppValue(
  sortDirection, appName);
```

The allocator that has been used to create a Core Foundation object is hidden away inside its opaque data structure; when it needs to be copied, that same allocator is used. In this way, you can (carefully!) change the actual data elements that are allocated and used by a Core Foundation object. More to the point, this is the mechanism by which Cocoa objects—such as NSString and NSDictionary—wind up inside Core Foundation objects such as CFString and CFDictionary. (Apple calls this "toll-free bridging.")

Memory Management and Thread Safety

Core Foundation objects use reference counts, which enables them to be shared among various threads and by several routines within a single thread. For the most part, if you are writing a single-user, single-thread application, you can ignore the reference counts because the default behavior typically is correct.

Memory management is implemented with reference counts: Each time a section of code starts to use an object, it increments the reference count. When you are finished with an object, you decrement the reference count. Incrementing the reference count is done explicitly with CFRetain; it is done within the processing of all CFCopy... and CFCreate... routines. You must balance these calls with calls to CFRelease when you are finished with an object.

CFRelease decrements the reference count; when it hits zero, the framework will delete it. You never explicitly free or delete an object.

Core Foundation objects are often distinguished between mutable versions and immutable versions. This is part of preparation for thread safety. An immutable object is read-only once it has been created. In other words, an array cannot be added to or deleted from, and a dictionary cannot be updated.

Mutable versions of objects need to be locked to make them thread-safe.

Core
Foundation
Services

Core Foundation routines are organized into 10 clusters of services. Each of them is described briefly here. (These are not Mac OS X services that allow data- and functionality-sharing; rather, they are services in the common sense of the word.)

Base Services   These services consist of basic definitions (true and false) as well as allocator support and two important utility functions, CFEqual and CFHash. They operate on the underlying data structures within the Core Foundation references. Always use CFEqual to compare two Core Foundation objects. Whereas the equality operator (==) checks to see if two Core Foundation object pointer references are the same, CFEqual checks whether they have the same value or are otherwise equal but not necessarily the same memory structure.

Bundle Services   These routines provide support for loading bundles containing resources such as images, sounds, and localized strings.

Collection Services   Arrays, dictionaries, and sets are located in Collection Services. They are among the highest-powered Core Foundation constructs. In particular, dictionaries (NS-Dictionary underneath it all) are used to store preferences and other unformatted data for an application.

Plug-In Services   The code-loading facilities here allow you to implement plug-in support. If you do not use these routines, you probably will use Bundle Services to load customized code modules.

Preference Services   One of the most useful services is Preferences Services. Using dictionaries, it implements preferences for keys that you specify in your application. It manages multiple users so that the preferences you store and retrieve are appropriate to the logged-in user. (An example of the use of Preferences Services is found later in "Preferences and Defaults" on page 386.)

Property List Services These routines convert property lists to and from XML. Note that property lists require CFNumber objects; if you happen to have a number you can use Utility Services to convert it.

String Services One of the largest sets of services supports strings. String Services handles Unicode and respects the localization choices for the user and computer. Much of the nasty little character manipulation code you may have written in the past is written for you in String Services.

URL Services These routines let you parse URLs and use them to load the resources to which they point (`CFURLCreate-DataAndPropertiesFromResource`). A significant amount of Internet interface exists in this set of services.

Utility Services This is the catch-all location for date and time manipulation, routines to swap byte orders, and the like.

XML Services XML Services converts XML data to data structures such as trees.

Apple Class Suites

When MacApp became an enormous framework, it was very difficult to extract small pieces from it for use on small projects. Apple has started to pull out some of the building blocks into the Apple Class Suites (ACS).

ACS consists of small, stack-based entities (objects or object-like objects). You use them as you would any other C type, and you do not have to worry about creating them with `new` or disposing of them when you are finished (although you can allocate them on the heap if you want).

The elements of the Apple Class Suites provide error checking, and they throw C++ exceptions as you would expect if problems occur. They mimic and/or wrap Core Foundation framework objects; using them can help you make the transition to Cocoa.

They are classified into the following categories:

Appearance Interface elements

Containers Arrays, lists, iterators, and maps (These are being phased out in favor of equivalent C++ standard library containers.)

Core Memory management, pointers and handles, and exception handling

Files Files, streams, resources, and file type handling

Help Support for help and assistance

Imaging Graphics objects such as points, rects, patterns, regions, grafports, and basic text handling

Memory Memory management

Patterns Events, properties, and tasks

QuickTime Media management

Stream Reading and writing data

Text Parser

Threads Thread management

TidyHeap Debugging

Toolbox Windows, date and time utilities, resources, menus, Apple events, and clipboard support

MacApp

MacApp is widely used both for commercial products and for in-house projects. (The first version of Photoshop is one of the MacApp applications along with many other Apple products, including Apple System Profiler.) It has provided developers with the ability to present the Macintosh look and feel to users with a minimum of customized programming. Today, MacApp is Carbonized, which means that the Aqua interfaces (and the Carbon event model) are part of your application with almost no effort on your part.

Moving forward into the future, Cocoa plays a similar role for projects that are beginning now. Maintenance of existing code and continuation of ongoing projects frequently require the use of MacApp.

MacApp Design Considerations

Three important design considerations influence MacApp: the Macintosh interface, C++, and multiple inheritance.

Macintosh Interface   In almost all cases, MacApp implements the standard Macintosh interface. You can create ugly windows and put OK buttons in counter-intuitive locations, but the default behavior of the interface elements is normally what a Macintosh user would expect.

While this is not big news to users of frameworks, it is a big deal to others. When you are working outside a framework, you may have to implement the functionality of interface elements and controls; nonstandard behavior can easily creep in.

C++   Although it was originally written in Pascal, MacApp has been based on C++ for a decade. It uses advanced features of C++, such as templates and exceptions, as well as many components from the C++ standard library, such as strings, vectors, and maps. The use of these features influences the structure of MacApp.

Multiple Inheritance   One of the most important C++ features that is implemented in MacApp is multiple inheritance. Whether you approve of multiple inheritance or not (some people abhor it), a framework design that integrates it as thoroughly as does MacApp requires a basic understanding of the technology.

Classes that are designed to be used in multiple inheritance are prefixed with "M." The primary MacApp objects descend from these, but only from two or three of them. For example, TEventHandler, the superclass of views, windows, documents, and commands, descends from MDependable_AC and MStreamable_AC. These are lightweight classes that manage objects on which others depend and that can be streamed to or from disk.

Farther down the inheritance tree, TDocument descends both from TEventHandler and from MScriptableObject (which is where its AppleScript capabilities come from).

Nomenclature   In general, the multiple inheritance classes can be recognized easily by their "M" and their functionality can normally be surmised from their names. The bulk of the framework consists of MacApp classes that begin with "T," a legacy from the Object Pascal days in which objects were declared as types.

Other classes begin with "C." These are the lightweight Apple Class Suites objects that are described later in this chapter (see "Summary" on page 188).

Browsing MacApp in CodeWarrior

Finding your way through the MacApp class hierarchy is easy when you have a class browser like that in CodeWarrior. You need to set a project preference to create a browser. You do so by choosing YourProjectName Settings from the Edit menu; in Build Extras, click Activate Browser.

You then open a browser from the Window menu. Figure 9-1 shows a browser for part of MacApp.

If you are trying to track down a class, you can type in the beginning of its name; the browser will scroll to the class. With a class selected, you can move to its superclass with the left arrow on the keyboard. To the right of a class name, you may find an arrow; clicking on it will expand/contract the subclasses of that class (if they exist).

Figure 9-1. MacApp Browser

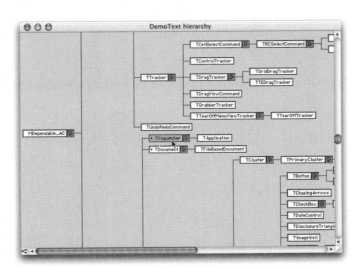

To navigate the multiple inheritance hierarchy, use the small arrow to the left of the class name as shown in Figure 9-2. If there is no small arrow, the object does not have multiple ancestors. When you select the class you want to examine, the browser will automatically be repositioned to it.

If you double-click a class, you will open it in its own class window as shown in Figure 9-3. In brief, this window provides you with a list of the class's methods (upper left), its fields (upper right), and the code for the selected method in the lower pane. Other controls let you explore the source code file, add or eliminate elements from the ancestors, and so forth.

The easiest way to work through the MacApp framework is just to trace the code (as was done in the previous chapter). The CodeWarrior class browser is a very efficient and easy way to do this.

One of the attractions of MacApp is that the entire source code is available to you. This means you can modify it—if you want to. Remember that modifying MacApp source code may well leave you out on a limb when future versions appear. (There is a reason that only the first version of Photoshop was written with MacApp; development of both products diverged at that point.)

Figure 9-2. Multiple Inheritance in the Class Browser

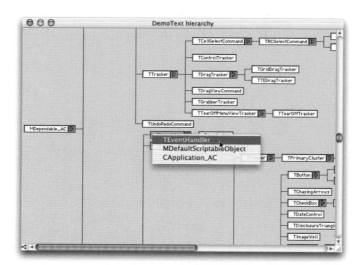

Differences Between MacApp and Cocoa

The major classes of MacApp parallel those of Cocoa—not surprising, given that they both do much the same thing. There are some significant differences, however. It is remarkably easy to start a battle among programmers about which architecture is better. In fact, that is among the most trivial of issues. Your job is to understand the frameworks you work with and to use them to their best advantage. If studying another framework helps you understand its benefits and avoid its mistakes, that is less trial-and-error work for you.

Menu Manipulation   Although the target chain (MacApp) and responder chain (Cocoa) are conceptually very similar, Cocoa takes care of enabling menu commands for you in most basic cases; in MacApp, you need to do so yourself.

Figure 9-3. Class Window

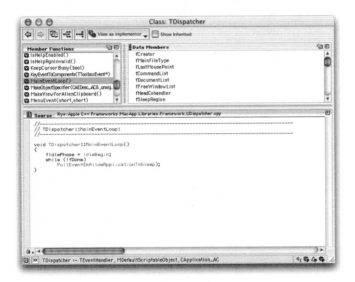

TDocument/NSDocument   TDocument is a heavyweight object that is a descendant of TEventHandler (itself comparable to NSResponder). NSDocument is a much lighter-weight object, and it does not descend from NSResponder. NSDocument is primarily concerned with data storage; TDocument also handles many user events, and it finds itself in the target chain much of the time. Because a member of the target chain can set up menu commands, TDocument normally does a lot more menu manipulation than does NSDocument.

TWindow/NSWindow   In MacApp, TWindow is a special case of TView, and thus it can do anything a view can do (and more). In Cocoa, NSWindow is a separate object, and it is not a descendant of TView; it can do less of what TView does.

Adorners and Behaviors/Delegates   Cocoa implements delegates that can receive events originally sent to their owning objects. MacApp has two features that show some similarity. Adorners are small objects that normally do rendering for images. They can be attached to views, and you can designate them to be called before or after the drawing of the view. In this way, you can change the rendering behavior of a view object without overriding it.

Behaviors are event-handling objects that can be attached to any event handler (document, view, and the like). They are called before the main event handler's code is called. In this way, they extend event handling without overriding the primary object.

Delegates provide a somewhat similar mechanism for adding functionality to objects. They are more general than adorners and behaviors, but they do address a similar design issue.

Summary

Core Foundation provides wrappers for the basic Cocoa Foundation framework classes for C and C++ programmers working with Carbon. The wrappers not only allow these classes to be used, but also allow them to be wrapped with error checking and other useful benefits.

In a similar way, Apple Class Suites wraps basic language elements of C++ and basic MacApp functionality so that they can be used independently of one another. Both of these tools help you be as productive as possible in as short a time as possible.

Furthermore, MacApp, the original Macintosh application development framework, allows you to write complex applications that automatically use the standard user interface. You may write new applications in MacApp, but more likely you will modify existing ones to use Carbon (automatically, with the latest version of MacApp) or Cocoa.

With each of these tools, not only are you able to be more productive, but you also can produce more sophisticated applications that employ advanced error handling and the latest human interface advances for Mac OS X.

Part II
Designing for Mac OS X

This part of the book focuses on designing for Mac OS X, using its development tools, and managing your project. In it, you will find chapters about the complete product life cycle, from planning the project, to managing the source code during development, to packaging the resultant application for distribution.

The primary development tools from Apple are Project Builder and Interface Builder; each gets its own chapter here. There are also chapters on Apple Help as well as on prototyping and testing.

Chapter 10
Planning Your Project

Given the abundance of programming tools and development frameworks that are a part of Mac OS X, the temptation to jump in and get started can be great. However, planning a project in advance will help to assure its success. This chapter provides a brief overview of some of the most important issues to consider—both in general terms and in the specific context of Mac OS X.

You can use Interface Builder and the Cocoa framework to develop sophisticated proof-of-concept demonstrations that will help you, your users, your managers and funders to understand what it is that you want to do. Some of those techniques are described in this chapter; references to other parts of the book are also provided to help you take advantage of these tools.

In particular, Chapter 13, Prototyping and Testing, provides additional information on some of these techniques. As a very broad rule of thumb, consider proof-of-concept demonstrations as described in this chapter to be among the exploratory tools you use to start a project and to get its initial approval and funding. Prototyping is what you do during the project as you experiment with different ways of doing what has already been approved and funded. (Note that you can use Cocoa and Interface Builder for prototyping anything; you need not use them in your final project.)

Thus, this chapter focuses on what you have to do at the beginning of a project:

- *Set your objectives.*

- *Know your user.*

- *Build on the past.*

- *Choose your resources.*

- *Use Mac OS X features.*

You have probably heard all of these instructions before (and will hear them again), but if your project is to succeed—even if it is a one-person project that you do on your own time—they are essential. Fortunately, Mac OS X makes it easy to carry out these steps.

There is one overriding theme to this chapter: Know what is already there. Even if your project exists only for you to become familiar with development on Mac OS X, start from existing software products and see what they do and how they do it.

Set Your Objectives

Scores of books and articles have been written about projects (software and otherwise) that devour years of effort and enormous amounts of money, only to go up in flames. Post-mortems often reveal that either there was no agreement on what the project was supposed to have done or, if there was, the scope or scale of the project was unclear.

Many projects have multiple objectives: You may want to learn something about developing on Mac OS X, learn object-oriented frameworks, or produce a program to calculate various statistics for your work. Make certain that you know what all of the objectives are and how they relate to one another.

Write down the objectives. A small piece of paper should be sufficient (if it is not, the objectives are not clear enough). Keeping the objectives in your head is not a good idea—you need the concrete words on the back of an envelope or on a folded piece of paper in your wallet. Be specific.

Justify the Project

Next, justify writing your project. Remember that a wide range of tools exists on Mac OS X. Before you start out, consider using them—either for the project or for prototypes. In particular, look at the following:

- **Productivity tools**. Can AppleWorks with its spreadsheet and database documents do what you want? What about FileMaker or products in the Microsoft Office suite?

- **AppleScript**. Can you add your functionality to a scriptable application? Doing so will let you write only your mission-specific code while letting you use the user interface of the underlying applications.

- **Existing software**. Use the various resources on the software section of Apple's Web site to search for products that might do some or all of what you need to do (the URL is http://www.apple.com/software).

Traditionally, the barriers between from-scratch programming (the kind "real" programmers do) and scripting of application software has been large. With Mac OS X, Apple is providing a range of development tools to everyone: Apple-

Script comes in every installation, just as all the developer tools and compilers do.

If you need to justify your project to management (or to yourself), having done this research will help you make your arguments. You will be able to hone in on the features that are necessary to the project that cannot be provided by other resources; in more than one case, a decision has been made that the cost of special development is not justified for such features. In many other cases, though, it is.

Develop Proofs of Concept

Even if productivity tools, AppleScript, and existing software do not do what you need to have done, they may be useful in developing working prototypes and proofs of concept. Use them to put together something that (sort of) looks like and acts like the program you intend to write.

Many developers are leery of proofs of concept and prototypes. They have learned from experience that many users see the prototypes and then wonder why additional months (or years!) of effort are needed to finish an apparently finished program.

The objective is to prove that something is feasible. You and the user should both understand that. Feasibility means many things in a project. It may mean refining a formula or calculation that is key to the program. It also may mean proving that your Mac OS X application can communicate with a corporate database (that particular proof may require work on both the Mac OS X side and the database side). Yet another typical proof of concept is a demonstration so that someone can understand the process that you are proposing to implement in your program.

If there is anything tricky about any part of your proposed project, pull it out and prove it as early as possible. Most of the biggest fiascoes involve interfaces among disparate systems and other types of predictable difficulties that could have been dealt with at the start of a project when time was available.

Proofs of concept often are bits and pieces of programs. You may have one little program that proves out your corporate database connection; another program may prove that your users can understand the process you are dealing with.

Proofs of concept may fail—but it is better for them to fail than for an entire project to fail.

Some programmers actually prefer to work on proofs of concept than on products that will ship. If you have a team of programmers, look for those people who never finish things and leave loose ends around. A proof of concept just needs to work—no one cares what it looks like or if all the error handling is in. By the same token, if you have perfectionists who always finish every last aspect of their work, they may be unhappy doing proofs of concept.

Know Your User

Programs written for casual users should differ from those written for people who sit at a computer all day long. You can use Interface Builder and Cocoa to quickly come up with drafts of a user interface that you can use for experimentation. Avoid deciding how users think and behave in the absence of research (formal or informal). Customer service representatives who enter data while talking on the phone to clients have a very different point of view from management and programmers, for example. Your experiments need not involve your project at all: Ask your potential users which products they like and which ones they do not. Ask them what annoys them and what makes their lives easier.

Use Appropriate Language

Particularly if you are a consultant working on a project for a client, learn the language. Will your software deal with "clients," "users," "patrons," "prospects," or "customers"? Not only the interface but the software itself should reflect the domain in which it functions. This is all the more critical if ongoing maintenance will be provided by other people.

If you do invent language, make certain that it is clear and consistent, and that users understand it. Then use that terminology. For new terminology, create a document of definitions, including screen shots and diagrams. You can learn from Mac OS X itself. A wide variety of newly named interface features are part of its interface—the Dock, toolbars, and drawers, among them. There is little confusion because their names are used consistently.

For interface elements and guidelines, use *Aqua Human Interface Guidelines*, Appendix B, and *Apple Publications Style Guide*. Both are available in PDF format from Apple's Web site. Their locations move periodically, so search on their titles.

Build a Usable Interface

Test the interface with real users. There is more on this later in this chapter, but for now recognize that usability testing is a critical part of every project, and you need to plan for it. Also, the results of good usability testing frequently require reprogramming and redesign, so you need to plan for that, too.

Consider the Non-interactive User

More and more, people are coming to understand that these expensive machines on their desks can do productive work when their users are off gallivanting around. Make your application scriptable (and recordable and attachable) with AppleScript. Also, consider making it available as a command line tool. By using the standard CGI interface, you can also make it available through an HTTP (Web) server. By all means, do not rule out any of these possibilities; if possible, include them.

One tip for preparing for non-interactive use is to thoroughly factor your interface from the functionality. There is more on this in Part III of this book.

Building on the Past

Look at what you have. Most organizations (and individuals) have a vast amount of preexisting code. Some of it is reusable; other parts of this code store should be rewritten…someday. Learn from Apple's example: The Finder in Mac OS X was not written from scratch. One of the reasons that it is written in Carbon rather than Cocoa is so that some parts of the Mac OS 9 Finder code could be included in the first releases of Mac OS X. (Another, far more important, reason was Apple's desire to demonstrate the long-term viability of Carbon to developers.)

It is always nice to have brand new code with the latest and greatest features. Unfortunately, brand new code may come with bugs; it certainly comes with the need to document and test it thoroughly.

Choose Your Resources

Once you know what you are doing (your objective), who you are doing it for (your user), and what building blocks you can reuse, it is time to assemble the resources for your project.

The most crucial resource is the people on the project. After that, you have choices to make with regard to development environments, frameworks, and languages. Those choices are intertwined, but they are presented here separately.

People

For now, Mac OS X is a new experience. Some developers welcome these new adventures, while others do not. Given a choice, it seems obvious (but bears repeating) to select the people who will enjoy working on a new project. The fact that you cannot wait to use Mac OS X (or any new development process) does not mean that everyone shares your view.

Development Environment

Shrink-wrapped versions of Mac OS X ship with Project Builder and Interface Builder from Apple. They are also available for downloading from http://www.apple.com/developer. (You can register at a number of developer levels, including online and student developers, which incur no charge.) They both run under Mac OS X and produce Mac OS X code. For new projects that need to run on Mac OS X, they are an excellent choice.

For projects that need to be developed to run on Mac OS 9 and earlier as well as on Mac OS X, you need to be able to generate code that runs on Mac OS 9. CodeWarrior is an excellent environment for this.

In the world of Java, both Project Builder and CodeWarrior provide development environments. In addition, JBuilder from Borland (http://www.borland.com/jbuilder/) is an excellent development tool for Mac OS X.

Framework

If you are building on to an existing application that uses MacApp or PowerPlant, in most cases it is worthwhile continuing with those frameworks. Both allow you to modify your code (if necessary) so as to compile Carbon versions.

For new projects, consider Cocoa as a development framework if the code does not need to run on legacy systems. If it does, MacApp may be the best choice.

Language

You can choose any of the three major languages of Mac OS X: Objective-C, Java, or C++. The religious wars between Java and Objective-C partisans are unlikely to abate; however, for the vast majority of applications, it really does not matter what language you use. What matters is that the code that is written is correct and maintainable.

The language choices are related to frameworks and run-time environments:

- Objective-C almost always means Cocoa is the framework. Although you can write non-Cocoa Objective-C code, that is an unusual case.

- C++ suggests Carbon along with PowerPlant or MacApp.

- Java may mean Cocoa with the Java bridge. You also can use Java to write applications that do not use Cocoa at all. If you are writing cross-platform Java applications, this is your best choice.

Use Mac OS X Features

You can write a Cocoa-based application that looks and feels like a 20-year-old Cobol application. (It's not easy, but it certainly can be done.) By the same token you can (with a very great deal of effort) write an application that sort of looks like the most sophisticated Mac OS X application using Fortran.

The point is that the tools, frameworks, and languages do not guarantee what a program looks like or how it runs. They help you accomplish your goals, and they make it easier to work within the Mac OS X architecture, but by themselves they are not enough.

In some ways Mac OS X features are so pervasive that they may affect everything in your planning process. In other words, you may get here, think for a few moments, and go back to the beginning of the chapter. Never fear: Good planning and development is always an iterative process.

Many Mac OS X features come automatically with the modern tools: preemptive multitasking, protected memory, and the like. In two areas, however, you have issues to consider. These are the user experience and the application structure.

User Experience

User experience covers the look and feel of the application. For many people, it *is* your application. The following items are the points to consider adopting.

Apple groups them into Good, Better, and Best categories. That is more or less the order in which they are presented here.

That order is not arbitrary. The first two items ("Good") are those items that affect your application when it is not running (its icons) and, while it is running, other applications. In other words, the first two items influence the look and feel of the entire computer running Mac OS X—including the operating system and other applications. Your adoption of Mac OS X features is critical to being a good citizen.

Cocoa, Carbon, and Java Using these frameworks and tools, you will automatically take advantage of the Aqua interface and the internal features of Mac OS X. It is important to note that while the Classic environment is a critical part of Mac OS X, it is designed for the transition process so that users' applications will not break and so that developers will not be forced to modify their software on Apple's schedule, rather than on their own.

However, the Classic environment is obviously not the best way to run an application. All applications within the Classic environment are linked so that one of them can bring down the environment and all other Classic applications. It is important to get out of Classic and into Cocoa, Carbon, or Java as quickly as possible. [Good]

Early adopters of Mac OS X started by running Classic applications almost all of the time—that is all there was. However, with the programs that ship with Mac OS X (Mail and Internet Explorer among them), and with Carbonized products such as FileMaker and AppleWorks, these early adopters gradually moved out of the Classic world. Now, it is sometimes a surprise to notice Classic starting up when a laggard application is launched.

Quality Icons   Your application's icon is visible even when it is not running. Each application on the computer needs to implement quality icons to make the desktop, Dock, and Finder look their best. [Good]

System Appearance   The Aqua interface comes with Cocoa and with a Carbonized framework such as MacApp. [Better]

Layout Guidelines   Space the controls in your windows in accordance with the Aqua interface guidelines. As you will see, this is very simple in Interface Builder. You can use the guidelines that appear automatically when objects are correctly sized and placed. (See "Designing with Interface Builder" on page 269.) [Better]

Apple Help   Implement HTML-based Apple Help. Having a standard help system across all of the applications on the computer makes the user experience substantially better. (See Chapter 14, Developing Help and Assistance.) [Better]

Window Layering   On Mac OS 9 and earlier, all of an application's windows moved forward at the same time in response to activation or a mouse click. On Mac OS X, you can layer windows. This makes it easier for users who are working in two windows that happen to be in two different applications. (Cocoa takes care of this for you.) [Best]

Help Tags   Help tags provide additional assistance to users by identifying elements in the interface. Fortunately, Interface Builder makes adding help tags a very simple matter. [Better]

Sheets and Drawers Sheets and drawers—as well as tool-bars—are important new interface elements of Mac OS X. Incorporate them, but use them properly. Sheets immobilize a window (rather than an entire application) until they are dismissed. Drawers are the perfect place to store information or controls that are occasionally needed. Toolbars provide customizable controls that can appear at the user's command. All are useful, and all clearly say "Mac OS X." [Best]

Data Browser Replacing the List Manager in Mac OS 9 and earlier, the Data Browser (Carbon) and its Cocoa counterparts (NSOutlineView, NSTableView, and NSBrowser) provide sortable, movable, and resizable columns. Known informally as "That ListView Thing," the Data Browser is documented in Tech. Note 2009—http://developer.apple.com/technotes/tn/tn2009.html—you can see it in the Finder's Save and Open dialogs. [Best]

Application Structure

The appearance of your application reflects its underlying structure to a certain extent. However, there are aspects of its structure that are apparent to users only as they work with your application.

Scriptability Make your application accessible to Apple-Script. This means making it scriptable, recordable, and connectable. Users can then access its functionality in batch mode or as part of a complex work flow.

Command Line Entry Similarly, consider making some or all of your application's functionality available from the command line. When someone is sitting at a computer, the most expensive part of that picture is the individual: Requiring someone to press the keys or click the mouse is frequently a waste of time. The command line interface to Project Builder is a good example of this. (See "Building from the Command Line" on page 238.)

Services   Finally, consider making all or part of your application a service—or using services provided by others. Users (and developers) complain of "feature bloat"—applications that become swamped with more and more features that need to be programmed, tested, and documented, and which users have no idea exist.

Write what you need to write, do what you do best, and rely on the operating system and others to provide the rest.

Summary

The basics of planning a project apply to Mac OS X projects as they do to all others. However, the use of Interface Builder and Cocoa as rapid prototype development environments can take a lot of guesswork out of your development.

Having planned your project, it is time to get started. The next chapter focuses on Project Builder (with some additional comments about the use of CodeWarrior at the end). Then it is on to Interface Builder and the other steps of actually creating a Mac OS X project.

Chapter 11
The Tools of
Mac OS X:
Project Builder

Project Builder is Apple's integrated development environment (IDE) that is part of the Developer Tools suite accompanying Mac OS X. You can use other tools to develop software for Mac OS X. CodeWarrior from Metrowerks has been a critically important Macintosh development tool for many years, and it remains so in the world of Mac OS X. It is covered briefly at the end of this chapter. For Java, JBuilder (as well as CodeWarrior) provides a sophisticated IDE for development.

Project Builder occupies a special place in the world of Mac OS X development tools. First, it runs only on Mac OS X (JBuilder and CodeWarrior run on other platforms, including Mac OS 9 and earlier). In addition, Project Builder is the tool that is used internally at Apple to build its software—including Mac OS X itself. This matters because you can rest assured that anything that is done anywhere in Mac OS X or in the scores of applications that are distributed with it can be compiled using Project Builder.

This chapter provides an overview of Project Builder:

- ***Getting Started with Project Builder*** *introduces you to the concept of an integrated development environment and shows you where its components come from.*

- ***Using Project Builder*** *is your roadmap to using Project Builder. The three areas of the IDE (project structure, tools, and editor) are described.*

- ***Building Projects*** *explores targets, build styles, and build phases. You may never give these a second thought, but if you are building a large application or working on a project that involves a number of people, these features can save you time and confusion.*

- ***Building from the Command Line*** *shows you how to use Project Builder with Terminal and how to construct batch processes with it.*

- ***Working with CodeWarrior*** *provides a very brief look at the Metrowerks IDE that has played a pivotal role in Macintosh development.*

Other chapters provide additional development information:

- *Chapter 12, "The Tools of Mac OS X: Interface Builder" starting on page 245 for help with menus, windows, and other interface elements.*

- *Chapter 15, "Packaging Your Application" starting on page 311 includes information on packages, nibs, bundles, and the critical info.plist features.*

- *Chapter 16, "Managing Your Code" starting on page 325*

includes source code management (SCM) tips for using the Concurrent Versions System (CVS) built into Project Builder.

Note that this chapter is based on Project Builder 1.0.1 (v.63).

Getting Started with Project Builder

Project Builder is installed in the Developer folder at the root of your computer. You should see it in the Applications folder there. If you do not, use Sherlock to search your disk. If that fails, check your installation disc and Apple's developer Web site (http://developer.apple.com).

Using an Integrated Development Environment

An integrated development environment brings together the tools you need to edit, compile, link, and debug applications. Even today, some people prefer to use one tool for editing, another for compiling, and so forth.

IDEs are among the most complex applications in existence, and their users (developers) are among the most demanding. As a result, they pose significant user interface challenges to their designers. Furthermore, many IDE users use the tool for hours and days on end as they develop applications. As a result, if you are new to the world of IDEs you may find the interface to any of them daunting; if you are familiar with an IDE other than Project Builder you may find that it looks different from the one you are used to (every one looks different).

This chapter walks you through Project Builder and helps you to get started using it. If you are not a full-time developer, you will find many features that you may not need to get started. In time, you may want to return to this chapter or to the online assistance to explore some of those features. In any case, do not take one look and throw up your hands: All IDEs are complex, but they save you time and make you more productive than you would otherwise be.

Where Project Builder Comes From

Like much of Mac OS X, Project Builder relies on industry-standard and open-source software. Among its components are the GNU compiler, the GDB debugger, and CVS. Apple has integrated these tools with its own editor and other development tools; all of them are wrapped in the Project Builder graphical user interface (as well as in the command line version of Project Builder).

Project Builder itself is an excellent example of how you can leverage existing code (including cross-platform C code) with the Aqua interface to create sophisticated Mac OS X applications.

GNU Compiler   An Apple modification of version 2.7.2 of the GNU C compiler from the Free Software Foundation[1] is at the core of Project Builder. It is used to compile C, C++, Objective-C, and Objective-C++ code.

If you have Objective-C code, it is most likely compiled with this compiler. However, if you have C or C++ code that has been used in the past, it may have been compiled with another compiler. As always when you switch compilers, take a moment to review warning (and even error) messages. The GNU compiler is more stringent than some other compilers in some cases.

GDB   Also from the Free Software Foundation, GDB is a debugger. It allows you to run your program in a controlled manner, stop it at breakpoints, examine variables, and change values of variables while the program has stopped.

---

1. Free Software Foundation, 59 Temple Place - Suite 330, Boston, MA 02111-1307 USA, http://www.gnu.org/.

CVS A third major component of Project Builder is CVS— the Concurrent Versions System is an open-source, network-transparent, version control system that is used for projects such as Mozilla (Netscape), KDE and GNOME (graphical interfaces to UNIX and Linux), and the Darwin core of Mac OS X. For more information, see "Managing Your Code" starting on page 325.

When to Use Project Builder

Project Builder runs on Mac OS X and creates code for Mac OS X. In that simple sentence you find the answer to the question of when to use Project Builder.

- If you need to create code that will run on Mac OS 9 and earlier without recompilation, you will need another tool to do that. Project Builder handles C, C++, Objective-C, and Java, but the code that it generates is in the Mach-O format and therefore can only run on Mac OS X. (Of course, you can create, edit, and debut your code in Project Builder and later compile it in another environment to run on Mac OS 9 or earlier.)

- If you need to run your IDE on Mac OS 9 or earlier, you must use another tool.

Using the Command Line

Finally, note that the `pbxbuild` command in Terminal can be used to run Project Builder's core. You can set up scripts to run overnight to recompile your projects (this is what Apple does internally). The command line interface is described later in this chapter ("Building from the Command Line" on page 238).

Using Project Builder

Like most IDEs, version 1.0.1 of Project Builder provides a single window with access to all of its tools. The window is resizable, and its component panes can be resized, too. The basic Project Builder window is complex, but if you take a moment to look at its components, you will see that it actually consists of only four basic areas:

1. A customizable toolbar at the top

2. A project structure pane at the left

3. A tool pane at the right

4. An editor pane at the lower right

These are identified on Figure 11-1.

Note that the actual image of the window has been slightly exploded or torn apart so that the three separate panes are more clearly visible; also, they are outlined in the figure. The black rectangles surrounding the three panes do not appear in the actual window.

The panes are all resizable. You can expand the project structure pane horizontally. You can also resize the tool pane vertically; doing so automatically resizes the editor pane so that together the tool and editor panes take up the entire right side of the Project Builder window. The window itself can also be resized.

The project structure and tool panes have tabs along their edges; these tabs change the contents of their views. The editor pane contains controls along its top. All of these are described in the sections that follow.

Changes to the appearance but not the functionality of Project Builder will appear in subsequent versions.

Figure 11-1. Project Builder

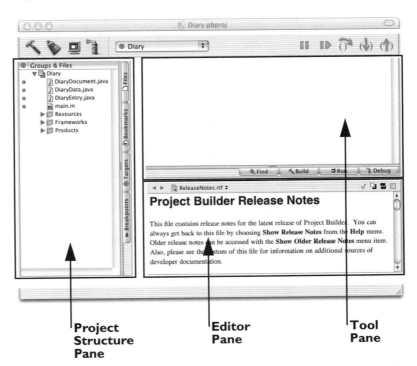

Project
Structure
Pane   Editor
Pane   Tool
Pane

**Project
Structure Pane**

At the left, the project structure pane shows you the elements of the project. Four tabs let you examine these elements:

1. **Files** lets you see the project's files in a logical grouping that is independent of those files' locations on disk.

2. **Bookmarks** lets you bookmark lines of code in your project files so that you can quickly return to them.

3. **Targets** lets you specify what will be built; Project Builder allows you to declare multiple targets so that you can build your files in many different ways.

4. **Breakpoints** are used in debugging; they are the locations in your code where execution will stop and allow you to examine or set variables.

Files The Files tab lets you examine the files and groups of your projects as shown in Figure 11-2. This is a logical structure of your project's files; they may exist on disk in this structure, but they also may exist in a wildly different structure.

Rearrange files by dragging them up and down in the file list. Create new groups by selecting several files (use command-click if they are not contiguous in the list) and then choosing Group from the Project menu. Alternatively, create a new group from that menu, name it, and drag files into it.

Figure 11-2. Files and Groups

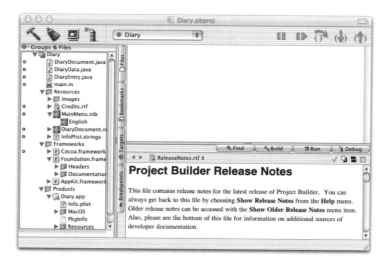

You can drag files or folders into the files view of the project status pane from a Finder window. You can also use the Add Files or Add Frameworks command in the Project menu to add them. When you add a file, the sheet shown in Figure 11-3 will ask you to specify how its inclusion should be handled.

Because files in your project can exist anywhere on your disk, Project Builder needs to know whether inclusion in the project should entail copying the file to the project directory. In addition, the reference style pop-up lets you specify whether the file's path should be treated absolutely or relative to the project. For imported folders, you can choose to have them handled as a group or not. Finally, you can select in which—if any—of the project's targets the file should be included. If this is daunting, rest assured that for most cases, simply leaving the defaults and clicking Add will do the trick. You may get in trouble if you subsequently move or rename files, but if you do not, you should be okay.

Figure 11-3. Adding a File to a Project

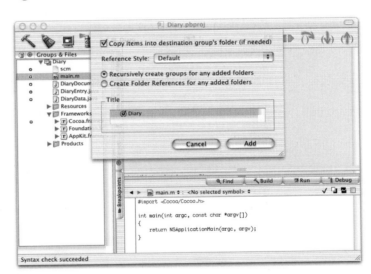

You can use the disclosure triangles to view files within groups. If you click a file, it is editable in the editor pane as shown in Figure 11-4. If you double-click the file, it will be opened in its own editing window inside Project Builder; CONTROL-double-click will open the file in its preferred application rather than in Project Builder. (RTF files, for example, will be opened in TextEditor.)

The column with a target icon at the top (just to the left of the Groups & Files title) indicates which files are part of the current target. To add a file to the current target, click next to its name; to remove it, click the small circle again.

If you are running source code management using CVS, a column at the left of the Groups & Files view will show CVS status. You can see such a column at the far left of Figure 11-3; it is not present in 11-4.

Sometimes you will see a file name in red, which indicates that it cannot be found on disk. This may be an error; however, in the case of the files in the Products folder, it is not. Products contains all of the output of your Project Builder project (your application, for example). At the beginning, it is listed in red inside the Products folder; after a successful build, it is in black—and it is located on disk.

Figure 11-4. Editing a File in the Editor Pane

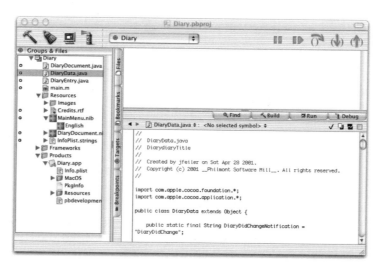

Bookmarks The second tab from the top of the project structure pane lets you bookmark sections of your code for quick reference. You simply select the text you want to bookmark and then choose Add to Bookmarks (COMMAND-OPTION-DOWN ARROW) from the Navigation menu. Click a bookmark to go to it in the editor pane; double click it to open it in its own window as shown in Figure 11-5. Remove bookmarks by selecting them, then choosing Delete from the Edit menu.

Figure 11-5. Bookmarks

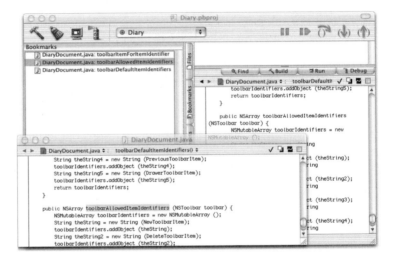

Targets Use the third tab to organize your project's targets. A target is what you are building. It can be an application, or it can be a collection of precompiled headers that need to be compiled and then built into a project. By organizing your files and targets properly, you can set up complex dependencies. See the Project Builder examples and documentation for more information on how to create such dependencies. Targets themselves are discussed later in this chapter (see "Using Targets" on page 237).

Breakpoints   The fourth tab on the project structure pane lets you manage the breakpoints that you use in debugging.

Although the views within the project structure pane handle different aspects of your project, all four of them are structural. Files (and groups of files), bookmarks, targets, and breakpoints all are part of the structure and organization of your project.

Editor Pane

The editor pane contains the code for the currently selected file in the Files tab of the project structure pane. A variety of tools at the top of the editor pane help you maneuver through the project. Three of those tools involve pop-up menus; they are shown in Figure 11-6.

The first pop-up lets you quickly select from the editable files in the project. Note that this pop-up presents the files alphabetically; the Groups & Files view in the Files tab of the project structure pane provides a structured view of the files.

Next, a pop-up lets you see the functions or methods within the current file. Selecting any one of the items will immediately bring you to the code in question. (The project must be indexed to do this.)

Finally, a pop-up at the right (identified as the counterpart icon) provides quick access to header files referenced within the file you are editing—either explicitly or implicitly by your use of items declared in the header files.

Figure 11-6. Project Builder Editor Pop-up Menus

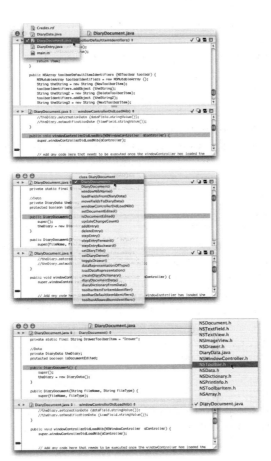

The combination of these pop-up menus lets you quickly maneuver through your project as you are tracking down code. But there are even more controls in the editor pane; they are shown clearly in Figure 11-7.

Figure 11-7. Editor Controls

At the left, the pair of horizontal arrows function just like a Web browser's back/forward buttons: They take you to the previous (or next) file that you were viewing in that window. They are very useful in conjunction with the pop-up menus that take you to other files.

At the right, the check mark icon lets you compile the one file in the window to check its syntax. The next icon lets you switch between header (.h) and implementation (.m) files. The two rightmost icons split the window into two panes (as shown in Figure 11-6) or combine panes (as shown in Figure 11-7).

COMMAND-double-click a class name to see its definition.

Tool Pane

The tool pane is at the upper right of the Project Builder window. It contains four tabs to let you manage four of the basic tools:

1. Find

2. Build

3. Run

4. Debug

Find   Two forms of Find are available in Project Builder. The Find menu provides both. The simplest form is the single file find (COMMAND-F). Use it to find and/or replace text within the open file. The Find tab on the tool pane provides access to the Batch Find feature. It is shown in Figure 11-8.

Figure 11-8. Batch Find

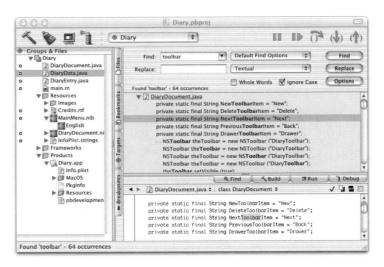

In the tool pane you first specify the string for which you are searching; click Find to carry out the search. The results are shown in the tool pane. You can scroll through them and click any line to view it in context in the editor pane.

You also use the Find tab to do a batch replace across a number of files. This is a two-step process. First, do a find. Second, enter the text you want to replace and click the Replace button.

The Options button opens the Find Options dialog shown in Figure 11-9. You can customize Batch Find (and save your customizations).

Figure 11-9. Find Options

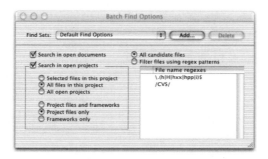

Build Organizing a project's files and editing them are well and good, but the primary goal of Project Builder is to actually help you build projects. Click the hammer icon at the left of the toolbar to build your project. The tool pane will display the Build view; alternatively, you can click the Build tab in the tool pane to open the view shown in Figure 11-10. Error messages appear in the tool pane along with warnings and informational messages. Because Project Builder integrates all of its tools, you can click error messages in the tool pane and go to the corresponding line of code in the editor pane.

Figure 11-10. Building a Project

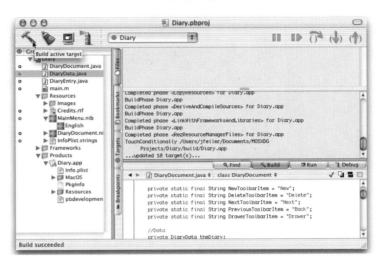

If you need to remove all compiled files from your project, the Clean icon (the broom to the right of the hammer icon) will do so.

Run The Run tab shows you run time console messages from the application as shown in Figure 11-11. You actually start to run the project by using the Run icon, which is the third icon on the left of the toolbar in the default configuration. While your program is running, the icon changes to a Stop sign as shown in Figure 11-11. Clicking it stops the program.

Note that sometimes when you launch your application from Project Builder, you may not see its interface. Unless it has immediately crashed (see the Run tab of the tool pane for that cheery news), you can find it in the Dock; click its icon to bring it forward.

Figure 11-11. Running a Project

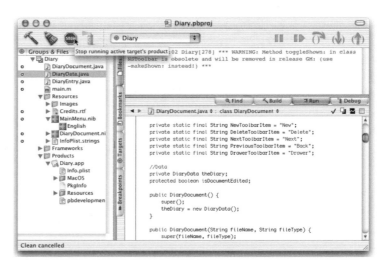

Debug The final tab in the tool pane lets you work with the debugger that is part of Project Builder. You launch the debugger with the Debug icon in the toolbar (the bug spray).[2]

When you launch the debugger, the icon changes to a Stop sign, and the tool pane switches to the Debug view shown in Figure 11-12. You can stop the debugger at any time by clicking the Stop sign.

The debugging view is complex (as are all debugging views). At the top, the Console display contains messages that your program may write out. Two panes within the main part of the debugging window provide a stack crawl (at the left) and a list of variables (at the right). In the case of complex structures, you can click the disclosure triangles to see the constit-

---

2. Close examination of the Debug icon shows that it uses organic bug control products and its aerosol components do not affect global warming or the ozone layer.

uent parts. At the right, the current value of each variable is shown.

If variable names or variable data are not clearly visible, resize the Project Builder window or resize the columns in this view.

Figure 11-12. Debugging

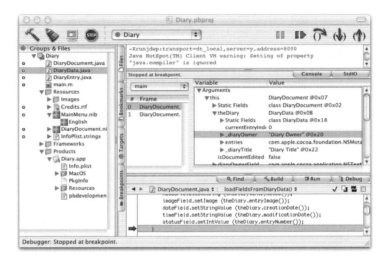

You can control where the application stops by setting breakpoints. You do this by clicking in the breakpoint well (the column at the left of the editor pane). In Figure 11-12, one breakpoint is set—at the bottom line.

When the debugger reaches a breakpoint, it stops, and the variables are displayed as they exist at that moment. It is very common to set a breakpoint at the end of a method or function (or just before a `return` statement). By doing so, you can check the values that have been calculated within that function. An enormous number of bugs are caused by variables that have not been set properly—and this technique catches that.

You can add breakpoints to your project while the debugger is stopped—just click next to the lines on which you want to break. You can also temporarily disable breakpoints by clicking them.

The Breakpoints tab in the project structure pane lets you manage breakpoints as shown in Figure 11-13. It shows you which breakpoints are enabled. You can click a breakpoint and go to the code; you also can select a breakpoint and delete it from the project (using the DELETE key). (You can also remove breakpoints by dragging them into the main part of the editor pane, where they will just disappear.)

Figure 11-13. Breakpoints

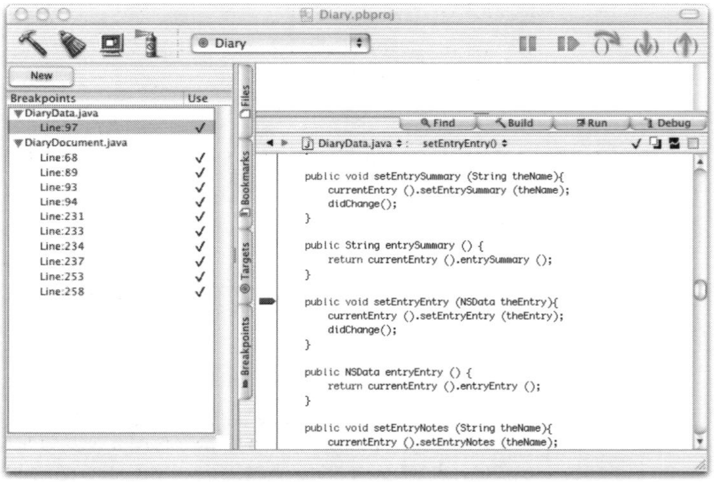

You start the debugger running with the spray can icon; execution stops at the first breakpoint. Thereafter, you control execution with the five icons at the right of the toolbar:

1. The first one pauses execution.

2. The next one continues the program, which runs until the next breakpoint.

3. The third icon (step over) continues to the next line of code, but it does not stop in a called function. In other words, if the next line of code invokes a method or function, you will stop after completion of that method or function.

4. The fourth icon (step into) steps into the next line of code within a function or method. This is helpful in tracing problems down through function calls.

5. The fifth icon (step out) runs the application until the end of a function or method is reached. This is useful.

Using the last three icons can help you avoid setting multiple breakpoints. Set one where you start to have trouble, then use these icons to maneuver through the code.

Configuring the Toolbar

The Project Builder toolbar is configurable. You can move the debugging icons out of it (or place them somewhere else in the toolbar). You configure it just as you would any toolbar: You can use the Customize Toolbar command in the Window menu, or you can use the contextual menu as shown in Figure 11-14 (CONTROL-click in the toolbar to bring up this menu).

When you get new releases of Project Builder (or of any Cocoa application), look in the Customize Toolbar sheet to see if there are new features to add. Sometimes the default toolbar is left unchanged to provide continuity for existing users, but new features may be ready for you to use them. In Project Builder 1.0.1 the Build Styles pop-up menu is not in the default toolbar, but you can add it. (See "Build Styles" on page 236.)

Figure 11-14. Configuring the Toolbar

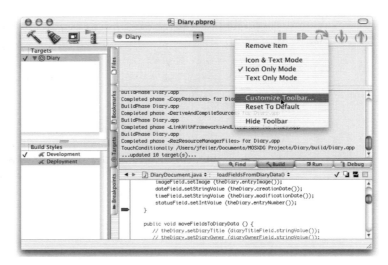

Creating a New Project

This is all well and good, but how do you get to a new project? Project Builder comes with a number of templates from which you can choose in the New Project command of the File menu as shown in Figure 11-15.

As you can see, a variety of options are available. You can create IOKit drivers, frameworks, and other special-purpose projects. In most cases, you will choose either a Cocoa, Carbon, or Java application.

Cocoa Applications In the case of Cocoa, you need to choose which language you want to use—Objective-C or Java. The choices that do not identify a language use Objective-C.

The other choice to make is whether you want a document-based application. Regardless of whether it is based on Objective-C or Java, a document-based application comes with an NSDocument object created for you. It will be opened automatically when the application is launched, and it is linked to its own window. If your application does not store data on disk, there is no need to use a document-based application.

Carbon Applications   Carbon applications come in two varieties: plain and nib-based. Nib-based applications let you use Interface Builder to create the interface; others use templates to create and load their windows, menus, and other resources.

It is worth noting that another type of Carbon application is widely used: one based on MacApp. If you want to create a MacApp-based Carbon application, start from the MacApp framework and create a new project (or modify one of the examples). You can then edit it in Project Builder.

Figure 11-15. Creating a New Project

Java Applications   The third choice you may make is to create a Java application. This is a pure Java application. If you want to create a Cocoa application that you write in Java, choose one of the Cocoa templates.

Other Choices   You can experiment with the other templates to see what they produce. In each case, it is worthwhile creating a new project, building it, and attempting to run it just to see what Project Builder does automatically for you—and what that type of project is.

After you have selected your project template, you will be prompted to name it and to select its location.

Creating a New File

Project Builder also has templates for files, as shown in Figure 11-16. You open this window by choosing New (not New Project) from the File menu.

Figure 11-16. Creating a New File

Building Projects

When you start from a template, the targets are set up for you automatically. As you proceed, you may wish to add targets and to otherwise modify the project. Use the examples that ship with Project Builder to examine how targets are set up.

There are two sections of the Targets view. At the top, you can list all the targets for a project. At the bottom, you can list and select from build styles (which are described later in this section).

Note that the vast majority of projects have only a single target; it may have multiple styles (such as debugging and deployment). This section provides an overview of features that you can explore in depth if you need them for large projects.

Files and Build Phases

With a target selected, yu can use the Files & Build Phases tab in the editor pane as shown in Figure 11-17.

Figure 11-17. Targets: Files & Build Phases

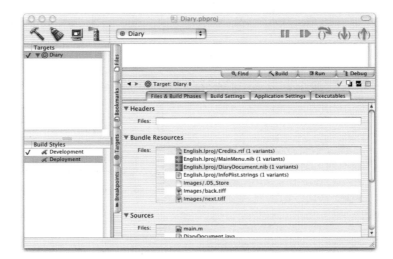

This lets you select headers, source files, and the like for your target. If you have used a template and added files only through Project Builder, you may not have to touch this. The the Add File sheet shown in Figure 11-3 lets you select which targets a file should be added to—and it completes this information for you automatically.

Build Settings

The second tab lets you control build settings as shown in Figure 11-18. Build settings let you specify what you are building and what to do with it (whether to install it, for example).

Figure 11-18. Targets: Build Settings

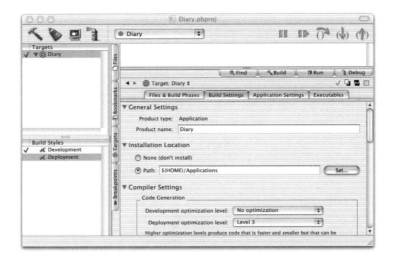

Here is where you can specify the compiler, linker, and debugger that you want to use (if they are not the default ones). You also can specify search paths for headers, frameworks, libraries, and classes.

Application Settings

The third tab lets you set attributes of the product that you are building—an application, framework, or whatever. (The tab is appropriately renamed; it is not available for projects in which it does not make sense.) The first part of application settings is shown in Figure 11-19.

Figure 11-19. Targets: Application Settings

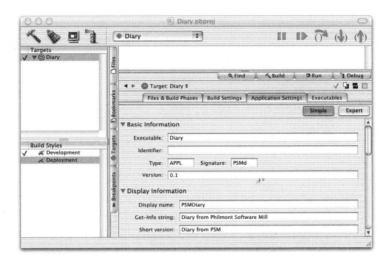

Here is where you specify the application's name and type. (Many of the application settings options are involved with handling application and document types.) You also specify information such as the version in this part of the Targets tab.

As you can see in Figure 11-19, some of the information that you provide here consists of strings that will be visible to users in the Finder; when you localize an application, you need to modify these. These strings and some of the other settings here can be set manually in the info.plist file for the project.

Figure 11-20 shows more of the application settings. For Cocoa applications, you need to set the principal class and main nib file so that the application can be properly launched. If you are using a subclass of NSApplication (the default templates do use NSApplication), you must modify this entry. Also, if you change the name of the default nib file, you must also make a change here.

Figure 11-20. Targets: Application Settings (Cocoa-Specific and Document Types)

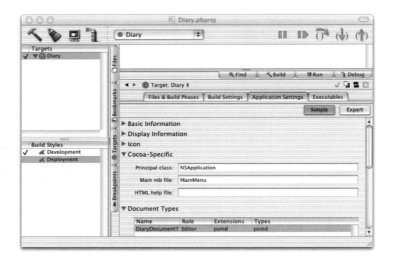

Figure 11-21 shows further type information for the Finder.

Note that you can click the Expert button at the right (just below the tabs) to use another interface. This lets you enter data in the property list directly as shown in Figure 11-22.

Figure 11-21. Targets: Application Settings (Type Information)

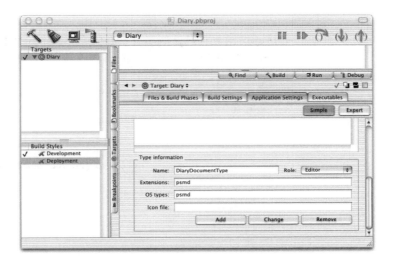

Figure 11-22. Targets: Expert Application Settings

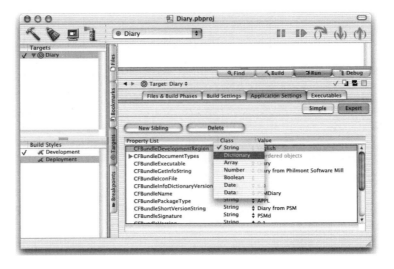

Executables

The Executables tab shown in Figure 11-23 lets you specify information for Project Builder to use when it executes your application—either in its debugger or when you click the Run icon. (For Java applications, here is where you can choose which debugger to use.)

As with most of the target settings, you can usually work with the default values; you need fuss with them only for advanced cases or when you are trying to integrate other compilers or complex projects into your environment.

Figure 11-23. Targets: Executables

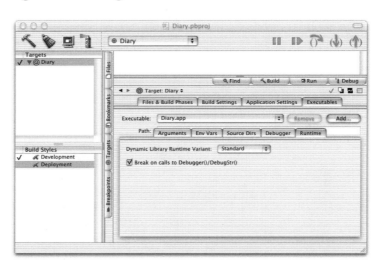

Build Styles

Build styles (shown in Figure 11-24) let you use the same target for debugging, development, or production.

You can select the style you want in the lower part of the targets view. You also can add a pop-up menu to the toolbar as shown in Figure 11-24 so that you can quickly switch between build styles.

Figure 11-24. Build Styles

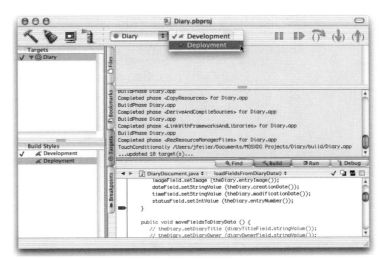

Using Targets

The point of build styles, targets, and all of the other choices described in this section is to enable you to write your code and then quickly switch among various ways of compiling and executing it. If you find yourself modifying the code to include or exclude debugging features, get yourself up to the Project menu and add a new target, build style, or build phase.

You create dependencies among targets simply by dragging one target (the dependent one) onto another target. Project Builder automatically builds all dependent targets for you.

Two special types of targets are worth noting:

1. Aggregate targets are nothing more than wrappers of other targets. You can use them for overnight or other periodic mass builds. Just pile all of your various targets into an aggregate target, and when you build it, they will all be rebuilt.

2. Legacy targets are built using the standard `make` tool. As you will see in "Creating a Disk Image" starting on page 317, you can have a very small shell script dependent on a rather large build. If the shell script is responsible for creating an installation disk image, that legacy target (and its dependent target) will automatically produce the installation package.

This section has provided a walk-through of some of the features in the Targets tab of the project structure pane. Many more options are available. Remember that Project Builder is built on standard tools; if you want to set flags or options for the compiler, you can do so here—and they will be the same flags or options that you are used to.

Building from the Command Line

You invoke Project Builder from the command line in Terminal by using the `pbxbuild` command. Its syntax is very similar to that of `build` as the following examples show. By default, this command builds a project in the default directory. Thus, if you set your directory to that of a Project Builder project and type `pbxbuild`, the project file will be located and built.

By default, the output will be placed in the tmp directory; you can change that by setting DTSROOT (for example, to the root, as in the following):

```
pbxbuild install DTSROOT=/
```

Options to install or clean along with the build can also be set:

```
pbxbuild -install
pbxbuild -clean
```

You also can select a build style, as in the following:

```
pbxbuild install -buildstyle "debugging"
```

If you are doing an overnight rebuild of everything, you might build and rebuild debug, deployment, and other development style versions of your project.

Working with CodeWarrior

CodeWarrior from Metrowerks was the first major graphical IDE for the Macintosh PowerPC. Before CodeWarrior, most development on the Macintosh was done using Macintosh Programmer's Workshop (MPW), which combined compilers, linkers, resource editors, and the like in a command line environment or graphical IDEs from Symantec/Lightspeed. (Even earlier, the Lisa Workshop, which ran on the Lisa, was used to develop the original Macintosh software and applications.)

CodeWarrior's compilers outperformed those in MPW from the start. The reason for this was that the MPW compilers (as was the case with all of MPW) were designed to work in the smallest possible memory configurations. As a result, they were heavily disk-bound, reading and writing intermediate results throughout the compilation process. CodeWarrior, coming along in a later environment with faster processors and much larger memory configurations, sucked up large chunks of code and worked on them in memory, spitting out compiled or linked code in an efficient manner. (The reason that this is worth noting is that it demonstrates once again how important it is for memory management to be handled by the operating system, as it is in Mac OS X, rather than being implemented in individual applications.)

Today, CodeWarrior runs on Macintosh and Windows computers as well as Linux, Solaris, Java, and other platforms; it generates code for Mac OS 9 and earlier, Mac OS X, Windows, and Java. It ships with a sophisticated application development framework, PowerPlant, which many people have used to develop Macintosh applications. From the start, it has been a critical tool for MacApp development.

CodeWarrior provides many of the same types of features that Project Builder and all other IDEs provide. CodeWarrior's approach involves windows that are less complex than those of Project Builder. In addition, CodeWarrior defines targets somewhat differently than does Project Builder.

Using CodeWarrior with MacApp

One way to get started with CodeWarrior is to download the complete current MacApp, including the Apple Class Suites, from http://developer.apple.com/tools/macapp. Drag the downloaded folder to wherever you want it on your disk. Within the ACS folder, you will find a CodeWarrior support folder (it may be called CWP7—CodeWarrior Pro 7—or it may have some other name). Within the CodeWarrior support folder, you will find a MacApp folder, and within that, an Examples folder. From CodeWarrior, you can open any of the example projects, or you can open one of the Standard Examples projects that contains all projects. Figure 11-25 shows the Files tab of one example, Nothing (the smallest MacApp program).

Before building any of the examples, you may need to build the MacApp libraries. They are located in MALibraries, next to the Examples folder in the MacApp folder. Note, too, that in addition to the CodeWarrior support folder, you will find a Project Builder support folder (PB Support). It contains comparable files. Do not move folders around: Both PB and CW support folders rely on the locations of the common source code that they reference.

You can add files to a project by dragging them into the window; likewise, you can move them around. (All of this is like Project Builder.)

Figure 11-25. CodeWarrior: Files Tab

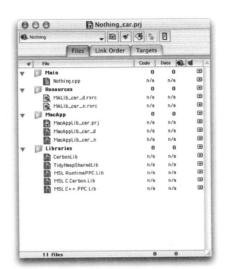

Targets in CodeWarrior are shown in Figure 11-26. As in Project Builder, targets can contain subtargets, and the IDE manages the dependencies. However, unlike in Project Builder, targets in CodeWarrior can differ from one another in that some are for debugging purposes and others are not. (In Project Builder, this is handled with build styles.)

CodeWarrior provides a host of settings for projects; these settings include whether the code that is output will be for Mac OS 9 and earlier or for Mac OS X.

Figure 11-26. Code Warrior: Targets Tab

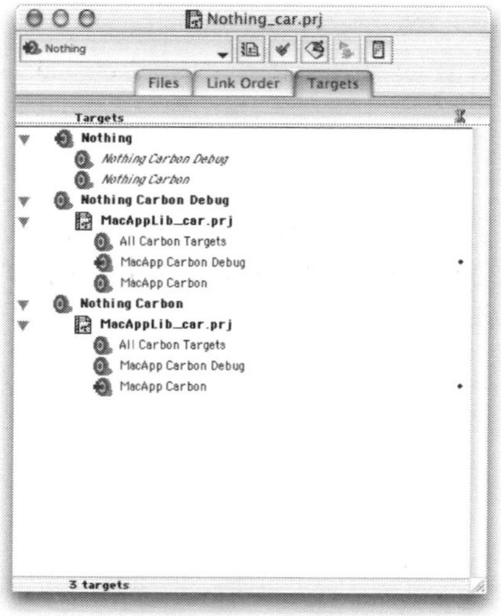

Exporting Projects from CodeWarrior

If you have a project in CodeWarrior, you can export it and import it into Project Builder. Use the Export Project command in the File menu to create an XML representation of the project.

Summary

This chapter has provided a basic overview of Project Builder. Examples abound both on the Developer CD-ROM and on Apple's developer Web site; there is additional documentation on both of those locations.

The easiest way to get to know any IDE such as Project Builder or CodeWarrior is to use it. One important tip will help you get the most out of your experimentation: Do not start from scratch. Take a MacApp example or a Cocoa example and open it in Project Builder. Build it, and then run it. Explore what you have done and what the settings are. It is a rare programmer who really starts from scratch on a project. In most cases, people take an example that is close to what they want and work from it; they add features, remove others, and gradually morph the example into their finished product. Apple's example code contains copyright notices that encourage this sort of use.

With Project Builder helping you manage your code, you can turn to Interface Builder to work on your interface. That is the topic of the next chapter.

Chapter 12
The Tools of
Mac OS X:
Interface Builder

Interface Builder is the graphical tool that you can use to design your Cocoa-based interface. It is much more than just a graphical design tool, however. It helps you create the shells of interface classes that you will implement in Project Builder; it also reads Project Builder header files and imports the relevant parts into its own environment. The Aqua human interface guidelines are implemented in Interface Builder, too. Guidelines appear dynamically as you move objects around so that you can position them appropriately.

After a brief overview, the chapter focuses on three major areas of Interface Builder as it is used with Cocoa:

- ***Using Interface Elements***. *This section shows you how to* *add menus, windows, and views to your interface, and how to make them work with your application's code.*

- *__Designing with Interface Builder.__ The Aqua guidelines and dynamic measurement tools are presented here, helping you to make your interface look as good as possible (and be as useful as possible).*

- *__Programming for Interface Builder.__ Actions, outlets, responders, and other programmatic issues are described here. The concepts are really not that hard to understand, and you do not have to do much with them, but you do need to know what they are.*

Following these sections, you will find a discussion of using Interface Builder with Carbon.

Apple provides extensive documentation on Interface Builder, including step-by-step tutorials. This chapter does not attempt to duplicate that documentation, so you may wish to go through one or more of the tutorials. You can do so before, during, or after the time you read the chapter. The tutorials tell you what to do, while this chapter is a bit more oriented toward "why."

Interface Builder is opened automatically when you double-click a nib file in the Groups & Files view of the project structure pane in Project Builder. You also can start from Interface Builder to create the interface for a project that does not yet exist. For most people, it is easiest to start in Project Builder and create a new project using one of its templates and then to move into Interface Builder.

Note that this chapter is based on Interface Builder 2.0.1 (v194).

Interface Builder Overview

Interface Builder edits nib files—the files that contain information about each interface element (menus, windows, and views, for example). This information consists at a minimum of the size and location of objects ensuring that they can be created on the user's display as needed.

Technically, nibs are *wrapped files*: They contain design-time files, run-time files, and resources such as images, and each of these is a separate file. In Project Builder, you can click on the nib file to open it in Interface Builder, but you can also use the disclosure triangle next to its name to see its component files for various languages; those component files are also visible on disk within a xxx.lproj folder, where xxx is a language name. The nib file appears within the lproj folder, and you can view its contents by clicking on the nib file in the Finder while holding down the CONTROL key.

The display of objects from a nib file's information is done by the application program. When it is a Cocoa program, Cocoa itself handles most of the nib operations automatically. Cocoa objects in nib files contain far more information than their size and location. Objects that you declare as descendants of Cocoa objects (custom views, for example) have their ancestor's information stored in a nib file, but when you actually load the nib file your own code is invoked to display the object and set data values.

It is important to note this point, because it means that custom views will need programmatic attention in most cases when they are being placed in a window if they contain data other than standard view information.

Cocoa and Carbon Nibs	Cocoa's views and menus are always stored in nibs; in Carbon, they may or may not be. Older Carbon applications do not use nibs (they were not available). Today, they are available, and if you are writing a Carbon application from scratch, you can use Interface Builder to design its interface and to cre-

ate nibs. This makes it easier for you to work in both Carbon and Cocoa environments because your work will be similar. Carbon treats nibs differently from the way in which Cocoa does, but your work is much the same.

Main Nib File

Each Cocoa application normally has a main nib file. It is created for you automatically from each of the standard templates. If you change the name of the main nib file, you need to set the new name in the application settings for the target (look for the section titled Cocoa-Specific in that pane). It is much easier not to change the name of the main nib file from that provided by the Project Builder template.

Your main nib file and its contents are automatically loaded when the application starts up. This is essential because this file contains your application's menus, and they must be there as soon as the file appears on your display.

In addition to the menus, this nib file normally contains any controllers you may have (as in model-view-controller), at least the application's main window and its views, formatters, and contextual menus for that main window.

Additional Nib Files

In some ways, nib files are like resource forks in Mac OS 9 and earlier. Additional nibs can be loaded on demand. This means that you can load the minimal resources for your application (menus and main window) and then load the resources that are relevant to commands that the user issues.

It is common to pair a nib file with a document in your application. The document's windows and views are thus intimately connected to it. (Actually, you pair a nib file with a document class; the document class and the nib file's objects are instantiated for each document that is created. If you run the TextEdit example and create several documents you will see this in action.)

The main nib file for your application is specified in the application pane of the target as mentioned previously. If you instantiate an object that has its own nib file, you need to identify that nib file. In your descendant of the NSDocument class, for example, override `windowNibName` as shown here (assuming that your nib file's name is DiaryDocument):

Java:

```
public String windowNibName() {
   return "DiaryDocument";
}
```

Objective-C:

```
- (NSString *)windowNibName {
    return @"DiaryDocument";
}
```

Hooks for Nib File Creation

A nib file is opened automatically when your application is launched; in the NSDocument class, it is opened when a document is created. The actual loading of the nib file is done by a window controller. Documents with one window each have a default window controller. If your document has multiple windows, you need to override the window controller so that it can handle the windows. (An example of this is provided with Project Builder.)

For NSDocument descendants, the method `windowControllerDidLoadNib` is called after the nib has been loaded. At that point, everything has been instantiated and is about to be displayed. This is the moment for you to intervene if you need to dynamically set data in some of the views in the window or otherwise programmatically adjust the nib's contents before they are displayed.

You do this with an override of `windowControllerDidLoadNib`. You must start by calling the inherited method;

thereafter, you can do anything that you want. Some code from Diary is shown here. (The code in italics is the sort of code that you add—everything else should be included as is in your application.)

The underlined code calls a method that stores document data into the text and image fields in the view. It then creates a toolbar for the window. Toolbars must be created dynamically—you do not create them in Interface Builder. There is more on them in "Implementing Toolbars" starting on page 440; this is part of that recipe.

Java:

```
public void windowControllerDidLoadNib(
  NSWindowController  aController) {
    super.windowControllerDidLoadNib(aController);

    this.loadFieldsFromDiaryData ();

    NSToolbar theToolbar = new NSToolbar
      ("DiaryToolbar");
    theToolbar.setVisible (true);
    theToolbar.setDelegate (this);
    theToolbar.setDisplayMode (1);
    theToolbar.insertItemWithItemIdentifierAtIndex
      ("New", 0);
    theToolbar.insertItemWithItemIdentifierAtIndex
      ("Delete", 1);
    theToolbar.insertItemWithItemIdentifierAtIndex
      ("Previous", 2);
    theToolbar.insertItemWithItemIdentifierAtIndex
      ("Next", 3);

    theToolbar.allowsUserCustomization ();
    (aController.window()).setToolbar (theToolbar);
}
```

Objective-C:

```
- (void)windowControllerDidLoadNib:
    (NSWindowController *)windowController {
```

```
[self loadFieldsFromDiaryData];

toolbar = [[NSToolbar alloc] initWithIdentifier:
  @"Diary Toolbar"];
[toolbar setVisible:true];
[toolbar setDelegate:self];
[toolbar insertItemWithItemIdentifier:
  NSToolbarNewItemIdentifier atIndex:0];
[toolbar insertItemWithItemIdentifier:
  NSToolbarDeleteItemIdentifier atIndex:1];
[toolbar insertItemWithItemIdentifier:
  NSToolbarPreviousItemIdentifier atIndex:2];
[toolbar insertItemWithItemIdentifier:
  NSToolbarNextItemIdentifier atIndex:3];
[[windowController window]setToolbar:toolbar];
}
```

Another hook involved in nib file creation is awakeFromNib; it is called for each object that has been created from the nib. For document-based applications, overriding windowControllerDidLoadNib is usually best: Everything is created and is just about to be displayed. Even custom classes require very little fiddling other than setting their initial values. Before starting to program adjustments to your nib objects, look at the examples to see how they are done.

Nib Windows in Interface Builder

When you open a nib in Interface Builder, you normally see a window with tabs at the top. The main nib for a Cocoa application appears at the top of Figure 12-1. An application with multiple nibs (such as a document-based application) has two nibs that you can open as shown at the right of Figure 12-1. (In Carbon applications, only two tabs appear in nib files: the Instances tabs as shown here and the Images tab.)

Three objects appear by default in your nib file:

1. **File's Owner**. This icon represents the object owning the nib. For a main nib, it is your application object (usually an instantiation of NSApplication itself). In

the DiaryDocument nib, File's Owner represents the owning object—the customized DiaryDocument class that overrides NSDocument. In either case, File's Owner is normally set up for you by the Project Builder template.

2. **First Responder**. This is used to dispatch events to objects throughout your application; it is described later in this chapter (see "First Responder" starting on page 277).

3. **Font Manager** and other objects needed by your application may be automatically inserted into the main nib.

Figure 12-1. Interface Builder Document Windows

A main nib also has a MainMenu object that contains your application's menus. If you double-click it, you open the Menu editor shown in Figure 12-2.

You can rename menus by double-clicking their names and typing new names. As you will see in the next section, you can also add menu commands and new menus.

Figure 12-2. Menu Editor

Using Interface Elements

You manipulate most of the interface elements in Interface Builder. You need not do so—you can create your interface elements programmatically, but it is easier to use Interface Builder.

This section shows you how to create interface elements; "Programming for Interface Builder" starting on page 271 shows you how to make them active. You deal with three main interface elements:

- Menus
- Windows
- Views

Menus

There are two types of menus in Cocoa applications: menus that appear in the menu bar at the top of the display, and contextual menus that appear when you CONTROL-click on an interface element.

A palette of interface elements is available to you; if it is not visible, choose Palettes from the Palettes submenu of the Tools menu. The palettes in Cocoa and Carbon applications are different; furthermore, you can customize palettes in Cocoa. As a result, your palette may not look like the ones shown here, but it should be similar. At the top, buttons let you choose the pane containing the type of interface elements you want to work with. Click the menu button as shown in Figure 12-3.

From here, you can drag prepared menus into the menu bar. Existing menus will move aside for your new menu. Be certain not to be creative with your placement of menus. The area with which you can play is between the Edit menu and the Window menu. The Apple, application, File, and Edit menus must be the first four menus; the Window and Help menus must be the last two.

Figure 12-3. Menus Palette

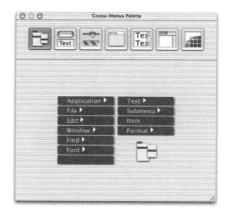

You can select any item in the menu and examine its attributes with the Info window from the Tools menu's Show Info command, shown in Figure 12-4.

The Info window is used to examine and set values for many Interface Builder objects. Its pop-up menu at the top lets you switch among a variety of displays, of which Attributes is only one. The others will be shown throughout this chapter. The attributes vary for different types of objects. For menu commands, as you can see here, you can set key equivalents, initial settings, and a Tag ID.

The Tag ID is available for all palette items; it is passed to you in events and you can use it to dispatch them in the Carbon event model.

Figure 12-4. Menu Attributes

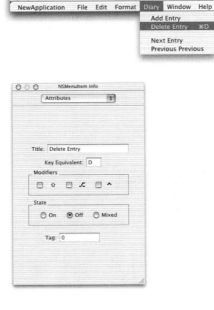

Connecting
Interface
Elements for
Actions

Now comes the most powerful part of the Interface Builder mechanism—connecting interface elements to commands and to one another. Holding down the CONTROL key, you drag from a menu command to the object that you want to respond to that command. When you release the mouse button, the Info window will open to the Connections pane of the object from which you drew the connection.

Figure 12-5 shows a connection drawn from the Delete Entry menu command to the First Responder object in the Main-Menu nib file. In the Info window that is open, you can see that the Connections pane shown is for an NSMenuItem (this is in the Info window's title bar).

Figure 12-5. Menu Connections

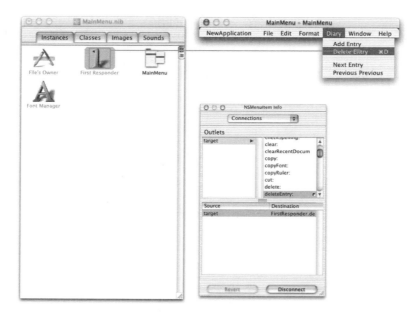

Sometimes multiple outlets appear in the left side of the upper part of the window; at least one will. If there are multiple outlets, you select the one to which the action will be sent. Here, there is only one (target), so you move to the right-side list and select the action (or "method" or "message") of the target that you want to occur.

To complete the connection, you click the Connect button at the bottom right. Once the connection has been made (as it has been in Figure 12-5), the button changes to a Disconnect button so that you can undo your handiwork.

This process is repeated frequently as you build an interface. To have an interface element cause an action to occur in another element (for example, to have a menu command cause a document object to delete an entry), do this:

1. *Establish the connection.* From the element that will start the event (the menu command, the button, etc.), CON-TROL-drag to the object that contains the object that will receive it (the document, the application, etc.). First Responder is a special type of object, which is frequently used; it is described later in this chapter.

2. *Select the object that will receive the event.* In the Info window, select the object in the receiving object that will get the event. Sometimes only one possibility ("target") exists; in other cases, there are multiple choices. A drawer, for example, will contain a `parentWindow` and a `contentView`; it also contains a `delegate`. Even without knowing much about what is going on, it is usually not hard to guess at what you are dealing with. Beyond that, the examples and Apple documentation provide full information. Remember that interfaces are usually simple; they are complex only in the variations that users can ring from the basic themes. An interface that itself is fundamentally complex is usually unsuccessful.

3. *Select the action.* From the scrolling list at the right, select the action that is to occur.

4. *Complete the process.* Click connect.

Sometimes there is no immediate action to perform, but you need to connect one interface element to another one. This is the case in the next section, where you will see a drawer connected to its content view as well as to its parent window. The process in that case is three steps: Make the connection, select an object, then click Connect.

If you are not comfortable with the process yet, have no fear: It is repeated throughout this chapter. In addition, you can work through the step-by-step Interface Builder examples and gradually you will find that the process installs itself automatically in your fingers; you will not have to think about it.

The process of connecting objects described here works for menu commands as well as for windows, views, and controls, as you will see in the following section.

Windows

The windows palette is shown in Figure 12-6. Drag a window, a window with a drawer, a panel, or a drawer itself into the nib window to create that object in the nib.

Figure 12-6. Windows Palette

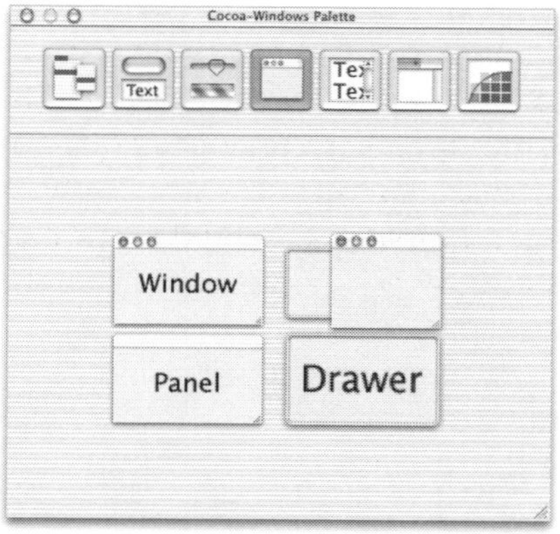

Whenever you create an object from a palette, you set the relevant attributes as shown in Figure 12-7.

Figure 12-7. Window Attributes

Figure 12-8 shows an example of the second type of connection referred to previously: It establishes a link, but no action is specified. This is a very common type of connection in Interface Builder.

Connecting Interface Elements for Outlets

The connection is drawn from the window's title bar to the File's Owner object in the nib. This means that any event sent to the window will be passed on through this connection if it is not handled by the window. The delegate outlet in the File's Owner object is the connection to which the window is linked. (These connections are called *outlets*, but that term sometimes confuses people because it implies a directionality that may not always be obvious.)

Figure 12-8. Window Connections

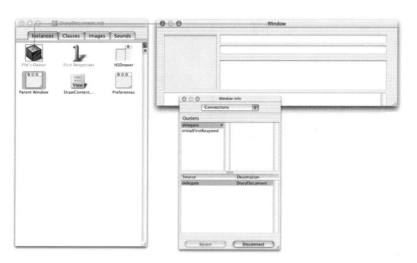

As you can see in the lower part of the Info window's Connections pane, the delegate has been set to the DiaryDocument object. Thus, an event sent to the window (a generic window, after all) will ultimately be passed on to the DiaryDocument custom object. In many cases, you have choices among a number of outlets (as, in fact, you do here).

You can quickly set up relationships among interface elements. For example, if you have an NSDrawer object in your nib, you can connect it to a parent window as shown in Figure 12-9.

From the NSDrawer object, CONTROL-drag to the window's menu bar. In the line shown in Figure 12-9 and other figures in this chapter, the small rectangle shows the start of the connection.

From the Connections pane in the Info window, set that connection to be to the parentWindow outlet. This really is not very difficult; in fact, it is quite obvious as soon as you start doing it. And in this particular case, you can drag a window and its drawer from the palette into your nib file, and the window, drawer, and content view are all created and connected for you automatically.

Figure 12-9. Connecting a Drawer to a Window

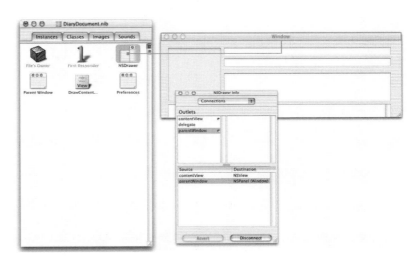

A drawer has no visible information; it contains a content view into which you place your interface elements. To link a view to a drawer, forge another connection as shown in Figure 12-10. From the drawer, CONTROL-drag to the view and set it as the contentView as shown here.

You will note in the Connections pane of Figure 12-10 that two of the outlets—contentView and parentWindow—have dots to their right. That indicates that they are connected. You can click on either one and see the details of that connection in the bottom of the window. You can also select any connection and disconnect it with the button at the bottom right of the window.

Figure 12-10. Connecting a Drawer to its Contents

Views

Views are used within windows to display information and to provide objects for user actions (*controls*). The two views palettes are shown in Figures 12-11 and 12-12.

You drag the type of view you want to use into a window and place it where you want it. As you can see, buttons, sliders, image wells, and a host of other interface elements are available. If you are tempted to create your own, consider whether you really need to do so (the answer is usually no).

Note that you can drag any of these views directly into the nib file. You place them in a window when you are preparing that window for display. However, if you want to create a set of views that will be programmatically placed into a window, you can do so. Remember to set the Tag ID so that you can retrieve the view hierarchy from the nib and add it to the window when you are ready to do so.

Figure 12-11. Views Palette

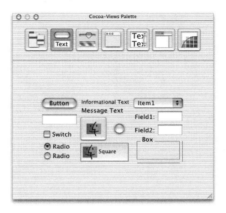

Figure 12-12. More Views Palette

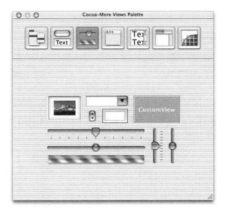

All of the views allow you to set their size in the Info window as shown in Figure 12-13.

Figure 12-13. View Size

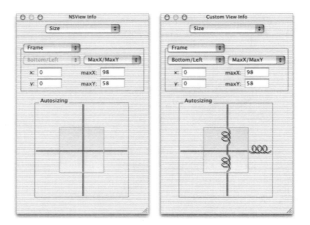

You can experiment with these settings very easily in Interface Builder. Set the size for a view within a window (either here or by sizing it directly) and then test the interface—Test Interface (COMMAND-R) from the File menu. This works for most of the Interface Builder changes that you make.

In the view Size pane, you can not only set location sizes, but also use the spring and struts to indicate if a view should be placed at a fixed location from its superview (or window) edges or should spring to relative positions. As you will see as you click on the springs and struts—the lines from the view to the border—they alternate between coiled spring-like objects that indicate flexibility and struts that indicate fixed dimensions.

If you have a set of views that need to be placed together within a resizable window, group them or place them within some containing view so that their relative sizes and locations among themselves remain constant.

As always when you drag an object from a palette into your nib file, you set its attributes using the Info window. Figure 12-14 shows the attributes for a variety of views. Each view functions the same way but has different attributes. You can experiment with each one to see how it works.

The following three views are commonly used for displaying images and text. Note that they come complete with their own menu commands; the appropriate items in the Edit and other menus are enabled for each view as necessary.

Image Views   You can place an image in an image view—or a user can do so if it is marked as Editable in the attributes. As you can see from Figure 12-14, you can control the image's placement and sizing within the image view.

Text Fields   These are used for brief (usually one line) entries of text. Use them for a name or address field, for example.

Text Views   These views can contain large amounts of text. Memory is the only constraint on their size. You can set attributes to allow Rich text and even the inclusion of graphics. A text view brings with it all of the standard text editing commands, including Find/Replace and Spelling.

Figure 12-14. Image, Text Field, and Text View Attributes

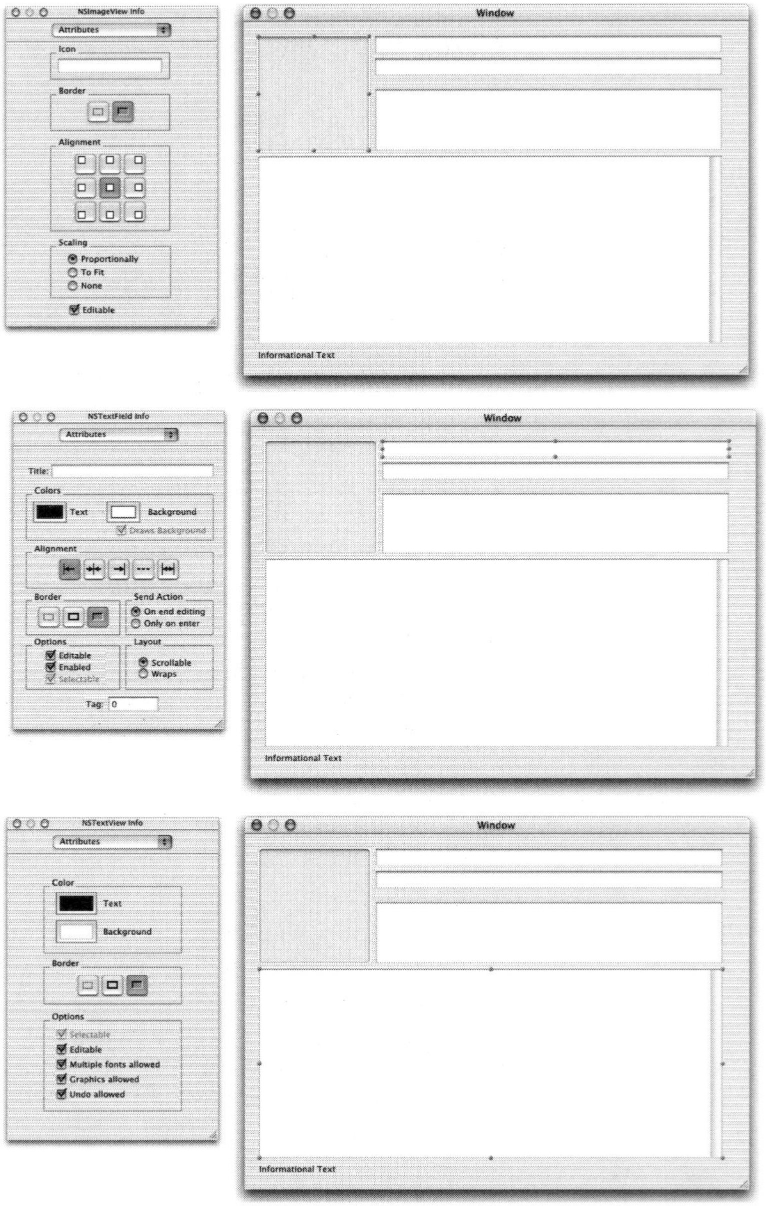

Figure 12-15 shows tabulation views from the palette. These views allow you to group data together.

Figure 12-15. Tabulation Views

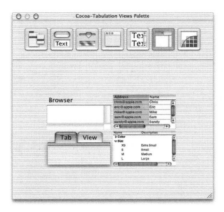

One of the most frequently used of these views is the tab view, shown in Figure 12-16.

Figure 12-16. Tab Views

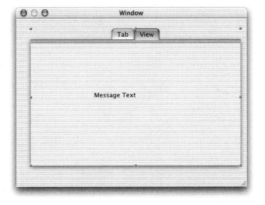

You can drag other views and controls into a tab view as shown in Figure 12-17. To do so, you must select one of the tabs and double-click so that the edit focus is visible.

Figure 12-17. Editing a Tab View

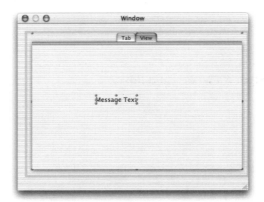
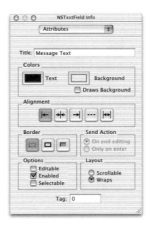

In Figure 12-16, the tab view itself is selected; changes that you make to it affect the entire assemblage of views. In Figure 12-17, the focus ring surrounds the selected tab, and you can add subviews to the selected tab. (If you do not see the difference, look at the area around the tab view and just inside the window frame.)

Designing with Interface Builder

As you move interface elements around in Interface Builder, guidelines appear as shown in Figure 12-18. These guidelines suggest where you should place objects and how you should size them so that they appear as suggested in the Aqua human interface guidelines. (If the guidelines are not visible, you can turn them on from the Guides submenu of the Layout menu.)

Figure 12-18. Guidelines

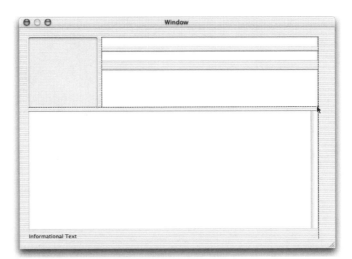

There are two sets of guides: Aqua guides, which help implement the interface, and user guides, which you can create to organize your window's design. Taken together, these guides contribute enormously to making your interface look consistent not only with itself but also with the Aqua guidelines. It is worth playing with the guidelines a bit. Move and resize your interface elements so you can see how the guidelines appear. Some of their measurements (distances between objects, for example) are absolute. Others are calculated to make similar objects (text fields, for example) of similar sizes. This second category of guidelines is ultimately under your control.

In addition to using the guidelines, you can have Interface Builder measure distances for you. Select an element in a window; then, holding down the OPTION key, move the mouse around. Measurements will appear from the selected object to the object under the mouse as shown in Figure 12-19.

Figure 12-19. Measurements

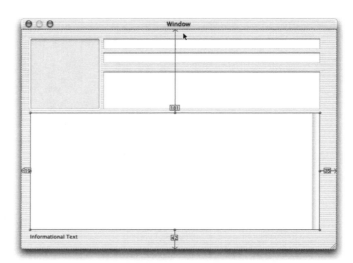

Finally, you can use the Show Layout Rects command from the Layout menu to see the display shown in Figure 12-20. This is particularly useful when you are trying to align shadowed objects and objects that contain text. It is usually more pleasing to align baselines of text objects even though the outside boundaries of those objects may not be aligned. Layout rects can help you decide what should go where. (Note that the guidelines handle this case well; layout rects help you do additional troubleshooting.)

Figure 12-20. Layout Rects

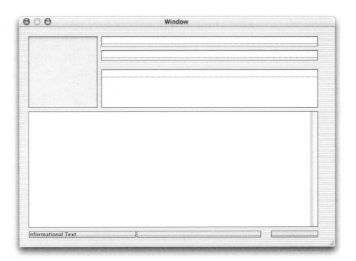

Programming for Interface Builder

Everything that you have seen so far in this chapter has involved Interface Builder and the methods of its default objects
(with one exception). Most of your interface will involve these
default objects and their methods. However, the mission-crit-
ical parts of the interface will normally involve custom objects
and the methods that you write in Project Builder.

Use the Classes tab to examine the classes of the objects in
your nib file. That tab is shown in Figure 12-21.

In the two columns at the right, you will see outlets and actions, with a number next to each one indicating how many
there are. Outlets are the connections to objects that have been
described in this chapter (a `parentWindow` outlet in the NS-
Drawer object, for example). Actions are the methods that are

called when user actions occur (the `deleteEntry` method was referred to previously).

Figure 12-21. Interface Builder Document WIndow: Classes Tab

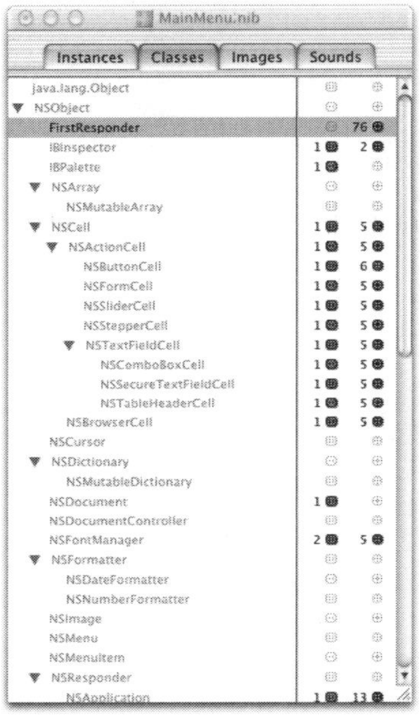

Objects built for Interface Builder have a variety of outlets and actions that are visible in the Classes tab of the nib file. With a class selected, you can add an outlet or action from the Classes menu. You can name it, and then it will show up in the appropriate Connections pane. You can then use the Create File command in the Classes menu to create a header file in your Project Builder project.

You can also work the other way. That is, you can create files in Project Builder and use the Import Classes command to bring them with their outlets and actions into Interface Builder.

The step-by-step tutorials walk you through this process. However, you will soon see that in real life once the initial skeletal interface is built, you normally need to synchronize the files manually. This is done so that the code you add to Project Builder files is not overwritten by Interface Builder.

Actions

Actions are listed under the appropriate classes in the Classes tab; they are implemented in your project files. All action methods have the same format. Here is a sample action that was referred to earlier in this chapter:

Java:

```
public void deleteEntry (Object Sender) {
  theDiary.deleteEntry();
  this.loadFieldsFromDiaryData ();
}
```

Objective-C:

```
//interface - .h file
- (IBAction)deleteEntry:(id)sender;

//definition - .m file
- (IBAction)deleteEntry:(id)sender
{
  [theDiary deleteEntry];
  [self loadFieldFromDiaryData]
}
```

All actions take one parameter. In Objective-C, it is sender (lowercase) and of type id. In Java, it is Sender and of type Object.

The Java action returns void. The type of the Objective-C action is null, but the defined constant IBAction is used for clarity and to help Interface Builder in scanning header files.

As you can see from the code, the action methods can do anything you want. They have full access to all of the objects and variables of the files in which they are located. Sometimes an action is one line of code; other times it is many lines.

In designing your actions, remember that they will be linked to interface elements. As a result, they should be simple. In some cases, a complex action in your code may call several simpler actions. This allows various interface elements to call the components of the complex action.

Outlets

Outlets are the connections that you make from one object to another—this button in the user interface is connected to the myButton variable in the code, for example. They do not involve a single action (as is the case with a menu command), but they are linked for the course of the program's execution.

Typically, your outlets include interface elements that you need to deal with programmatically. For example, here are the outlets for DiaryDocument (in part):

Java:

```
private NSTextField diaryTitleField;
private NSTextField diaryOwnerField;
private NSTextField titleField;
private NSTextField subtitleField;
```

Objective-C:

```
IBOutlet NSTextField *diaryTitleField;
IBOutlet NSTextField *diaryOwnerField;
IBOutlet NSTextField *titleField;
IBOutlet NSTextField *subtitleField;
```

As you can see, in Objective-C, you identify outlets with IBOutlet. In Java, they are simply private to the object.

It is not necessary to create such outlets. However, if you need to load or unload data from interface elements, your code needs to be able to get to the fields of your interface. Thus, you declare them as outlets. You need to link them up in the interface. You have actually seen how to do this already; here it is again with further explanation.

Connecting Outlets

CONTROL-drag from an interface element to the object that contains the outlet you want to connect. In the case of a document-based application, the File's Owner object of the document nib file is set to the document class (MyDocument, by default), and the outlets you add to MyDocument are shown in the Connections pane as you see in Figure 12-22.

Figure 12-22. File's Owner Connections

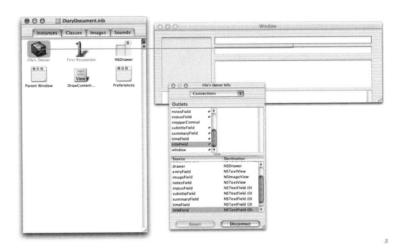

The `titleField` outlet was declared in code like that shown in the previous section. It is connected to the text field in the window in this manner. What is typed into the text field when the program is running can be accessed by your application by using the `titleField` variable it contains. Likewise, the application can initialize that field to a given value by setting the `titleField` contents programmatically.

In the case of documents, the override of `windowDidLoad-NibFile` is where you do this loading.

The other piece of legerdemain that lies behind this window is how the outlets get into the File's Owner object. The document template sets File's Owner to MyDocument (which it creates automatically). You may choose to rename that class (and you should).

You can see that in Figure 12-23. Select File's Owner and look at the Attributes pane in the Info window. You can change the File's Owner class to another class if you want to.

Figure 12-23. File's Owner

The list of classes in the Info window comes from the classes listed in the Classes tab of your nib window. You can add a class by using Subclass from the Classes menu. You also can automatically add a class by choosing Read File from that same menu (if you have declared the class in the imported file).

If you add a class with Subclass, whatever class is selected in the Classes list will be subclassed. If none is selected, the command is not available.

The outlets (and the actions) for your classes appear in the same ways: either by reading from a file in which they are declared or by choosing the Add Outlet or Add Action command for a selected class. The step-by-step tutorials walk you through this, and you will get used to it very quickly.

First Responder

Finally, the issue of the First Responder needs to be dealt with. First Responder is the head of the target chain (in MacApp terms). It is the object that gets the mouse click or keystroke first. It changes as the program executes, and you rarely set it. (Your objects may resign from that role or refuse to ever become a First Responder, but you rarely aggressively grab First Responder status.)

The First Responder is listed in the Classes list, but it is not an object in the sense that the others are. Instead, it is whichever of those objects happens to be the First Responder at a given moment. You need the First Responder when you need to send an event to an object that you cannot identify in the nib window.

An example is the `deleteEntry` action, which was connected to the menu bar earlier in this chapter. The menu bar is in the main nib. The `deleteEntry` action is an action of the DiaryDocument class; DiaryDocument shows up as File's Owner in the secondary nib file. You cannot make a connection across nib files, so you cannot connect the menu command to the File's Owner object in the secondary file. (If you could, you could connect it to the `deleteEntry` action and be done with it.)

What you do is add the `deleteEntry` action to the First Responder "object" in the main nib file. You can make a connection from the menu command to the First Responder, and you can choose that action. When this actually occurs, Cocoa will search the responder chain for the first responder that responds to `deleteEntry` (i.e., that can process it). It will find that object in the DiaryDocument object that is in the responder chain. (If you have several documents open, there may be several objects lying around, but only one will be in the responder chain—the one associated with the active window.)

In this way, the command is sent appropriately. You need to add actions to First Responder in the main nib for any menu commands that act on objects in other nib files; you may need to add other such actions as well.

Instantiating Controllers and Other Objects

In this chapter, all of the objects in the nib files have been dragged from palettes. This is correct for most interface elements. However, if you have invisible objects (such as controllers of views or data structures), you instantiate them by selecting the appropriate class in the Classes pane and then choosing Instantiate from the Classes menu. An instantiation of the class appears in the Instances tab.

Using Interface Builder with Carbon

Project Builder supplies two Carbon templates: one for nib-based applications and one for non-nib-based applications. Using nib-based applications means that you can use Interface Builder to design your interface.

Working with Interface Builder and Carbon

The main difference you will see in using Interface Builder with Carbon applications is that the outlets and actions are gone. You design your menus and windows, but there are no connections to set. You must programmatically handle the events. But Interface Builder provides significant help in setting all this up, as you can see in Figure 12-24.

Figure 12-24. Using Interface Builder with Carbon Applications

Perhaps the most important factor is the command identifier—`easr` in this case. That is the command ID that you will be able to isolate in your event-handling routine. In a variation of the code presented in "Programming the Event Handler" on page 165, you can write this section of code in your event handler:

```
case kEventClassCommand:
  if (kind == kEventProcessCommand)
  {
    HICommandcmd;
    GetEventParameter(inEvent,
      kEventParamDirectObject,
      typeHICommand,
      NULL,
      sizeof(HICommand),
      NULL,
      &cmd);
    switch (command.commandID)
      {
      case "easr":
        ...
        result = noErr;
        break;
```

You simply place the appropriate case element into your handler, and you carry out the actions for the button you created in Interface Builder. (You can follow the Interface Builder and Project Builder Carbon examples for step-by-step guidance through this process if you want.)

Programming for Carbon Nibs

If you create a nib-based Carbon application from the Project Builder template, the basic code will be created for you. First, the nib (called main, by default), is created:

```
err = CreateNibReference(CFSTR("main"),
  &nibRef);
require_noerr( err, CantGetNibRef );
```

Then, the main menu is extracted from that nib:

```
err = SetMenuBarFromNib(nibRef,
  CFSTR("MainMenu"));
require_noerr( err, CantSetMenuBar );
```

The window is also extracted:

```
err = CreateWindowFromNib(nibRef,
  CFSTR("MainWindow"),
  &window);
require_noerr( err, CantCreateWindow );
```

The nib is disposed of (its contents having been extracted):

```
DisposeNibReference(nibRef);
```

The window is shown, and the event loop is started:

```
ShowWindow( window );
RunApplicationEventLoop();
```

Summary

Interface Builder lets you design interfaces for both Cocoa and Carbon applications. With Cocoa, you can also use it to make connections between interface elements and the outlets and actions in your Cocoa code.

Interface Builder can be used not only to help implement your application, but also to assist in prototyping, as the next chapter shows.

Chapter 13
Prototyping and
Testing

With Project Builder and Interface Builder, you have incredibly powerful tools that let you build an application in record time. The temptation is to think that you can use them to build an application quickly. You can do that, but you can also use them to build prototypes of your application. It may sound boring or seem a waste of time, but if you plan to build your application from scratch two or even more times, it will be more robust and more successful.

Far too many projects are done simply by writing code, compiling it, and then moving on. If you are a professional developer or if you are a serious student or hobbyist, and if you value your efforts and want to write good (or even excellent) code, you need to recognize that just getting something to compile and run is not good enough.

This chapter examines the roles of prototypes, ways to shape the interface, and ways to create the testing environments you need to bring your project to fruition. You can use design tools such as Macromedia Director for prototyping, but you can also use the quick development tools in Project Builder and Interface Builder to do so.

The Roles of Prototypes

Prototypes are mock-ups of your application (or parts of it) that to a greater or lesser extent resemble what you think the final product will look like. In the planning phase of your project, proofs of concept are used to make sure that what you want to do can be done. Once you have started to actually develop your project, you use prototypes to explore alternative design strategies—both internally and externally.

Many people do not understand how to use prototypes effectively. They can be used as general practice for the main project, but they also can be used very effectively to explore specific areas. Focusing your prototypes (there can be many) will mean that your final project can proceed more smoothly.

Prototyping Development Tools

Sometimes a prototype is used to address a specific question that arises in development. For example, if you are new to Mac OS X programming but have a background in C++ programming on another platform, you might want to try coding part of your application in MacApp and Carbon using the C++ language with which you are familiar. You might want to also try coding that same part of your application in Cocoa, using either Java or Objective-C.

If you keep an open mind, you will probably discover that there are pros and cons to each option. What many people realize is that the bulk of the work is involved in designing your application and its objects, and that the high-level design is remarkably transportable.

Because it is so easy to develop with modern tools such as Project Builder/Interface Builder, and because object-oriented frameworks like PowerPlant, MacApp, and Cocoa are so efficient, it is often much faster to actually conduct such an experiment rather than argue about which environment is best. The biggest development cost is likely to be programmer resources (whether you have a staff of 100 or are trying to fit some extra hours into your weekend to get your pet project done). Make the choice based on the people, not abstract arguments about technology.

Fortunately, the developer tools included with Mac OS X allow you to perform such an experiment without purchasing additional compilers or development environments.

Visualization of Concepts

A very common use of prototyping is to explore alternative interfaces. Most of the time, computer programs involve visualization of concepts—sometimes they are simple concepts, such as words on a piece of paper, but at other times the concepts are quite abstract, such as conformance to accounting standards.

Part of the task of creating an application program is successfully identifying these concepts and providing visualizations that make sense to the users. The first attempt is likely not to be the best one, and the users need an opportunity to experiment with interfaces. Prototyping lets them do so. (There is more on this later in the chapter in "Shaping the Interface" on page 287.)

Process Definition

In addition to providing a visualization of the concepts, you may need to define the processing your program carries out. Increasingly, corporate policies and procedures exist only inside their application programs: The days of separate policies hammered out carefully in meetings are gone in many cases.

Part of the definition process is looking for loopholes and exceptions. The programmer needs to provide code that handles all of the possible situations that may occur; corporate planners may not have done this.

You can describe these exceptional events all you want, but when you put a prototype in front of a user and say, "What should happen next?" it sometimes has a way of focusing attention on the issue.

Advance Versions

Sometimes you need an early version of the product to show to people—documentation writers, investors, managers, marketers, or even your friends. During the course of development, the full application from time to time will not be usable. You can keep a minimally featured prototype around to be used for demonstrations. It is much better to have a robust and reliable (but incomplete) prototype for these purposes than to have a non-running (or crashing) real application.

The danger of these prototypes is that people can draw erroneous conclusions from them. You need to remind people that they are not complete, and that the final product will look different.

Training

If you are using new technologies, use a prototype to familiarize yourself with the tools you will be using. The first Cocoa application you write will probably not be terrific (and that also applies to your first Java application, your first Pascal program, and so forth).

Practicing with tutorials can be very useful, but taking the time to write something that actually might be used in your application is even more useful. Treating it as a throw-away training experience is the most useful of all.

Skunkworks

Finally, the skunkworks aspect of prototypes cannot be ignored. More than one project has seen the light of day as a result of a prototyping experiment that took off and was carried out without (or even despite) management's supervision.

All of these uses of prototyping rely on the ability to quickly develop those pieces of an application that are the subject of inquiry. Project Builder and Interface Builder are unmatched as prototyping tools.

Shaping the Interface

While you are prototyping and developing your design, the interface gets the lion's share of attention. The world of application interface design is still evolving, and although standards are taking shape, there is still not a consensus as to what skills are required to design successful interfaces and to critique them. Everyone has an opinion (and not too many people have logical arguments to back up their opinions). Unless you are designing a work of art on the computer, your major focus is usability and clarity: People should be able to use the interface, and they should be able to understand the information that it conveys.

Using Interface Builder for Prototypes

Use Interface Builder for prototyping all phases of your application. Not only can you easily create windows (and alternative versions of windows), but you can also create output displays through Interface Builder.

Whereas in the application itself users will click a button named Compute or Go and cause the program to generate results, you can link the Compute or Go button to a new window that contains results you have typed in yourself. In this case, you are not worrying about the calculation, you are concerned about the best way of presenting the results to users.

Typically, time with users is scarce, so make the most of it. If you have two or three output displays, present all of them together. Some users are so impressed with any display (and so pleased to be asked their opinion) that they will agree to almost anything. Showing them several alternatives (not too many) indicates that there is a real choice to be made and that you do want them to pay attention.

One important point to remember is that the results you format should be correct. You may know that it does not really matter what the values of numbers are in the formatted display, but to a user who understands the data, it is hard to see past a display that has absurd data in it.

Using Interface Labs

In designing interfaces, try to observe real users working with the interface. This can be done in a formal lab where you sit behind a two-way mirror, but you can also do it informally at a user's desk.

Your job at this point is to watch and listen. Do not show users how to use the interface, and certainly keep your hands off the mouse and the keyboard. Watch the mistakes they make (at this stage of the game, those mistakes are likely to be your interface design mistakes).

Preserving Innocents

Because the design process is iterative, you need to preserve innocent users—people who have not been part of the design process. Remember that the users of your software may well approach it without the background of your testers, so you need to test the final interface on people who have not been through the testing mill.

Testing

Once the prototypes have served their purposes and your full project is under way, you need to be prepared to test the code that is developed. Setting up test schedules and test environments has to be done very early in the project.

If the project is big enough, you may be able to have a separate testing staff. It is very hard for the people who have actually developed a project to successfully test it and find errors in it. This applies to projects of all sorts. This book, for example, has benefited from editing and comments from close to a dozen people at the publisher (Morgan Kaufmann in San Francisco), the production staff at Academic Press (in Boston), individuals at Apple, and a variety of other people. In reviewing early drafts of this book, each of those people has found typographical and other errors that none of the others found.

Unit Testing

Unit testing is also sometimes called programmer testing. It is the testing that an individual developer does on a component that is created. It should include all of the relevant aspects of testing—functionality, failures, and interface.

System Testing

System testing involves testing the product as a whole. When a testing staff is involved, the staff usually picks up at this stage after the individual (programmer or unit) testing is completed.

Primary Functionality

The first test of a product is that it does what it is supposed to do. Unfortunately, for many products, the testing stops here.

Testing Failures

You have to test that the program fails properly. Error messages should be provided, and they should be correctly spelled and should not themselves cause further problems. It is very common that error-handling routines themselves fail; this is because the code is rarely executed and even less frequently tested.

Testing Interface Errors

You also need to test interface errors—errors that come in from the outside world. They can be user errors, but they also can be errors involving other applications.

Too many occurrences of the same interface error may suggest a problem with the interface design. In other cases, you merely need to make certain that the error is caught and handled properly.

Test Suites and Regression Testing

You cannot just play around with a program to test it. You need a test suite that provides a controlled way of exercising as much of the product as possible.

Regression testing is a highly controlled form of testing changes to applications. When a change is made, it is tested—and the entire test suite is rerun. In environments where software reliability is critical (financial services, for example), such testing is essential.

Changes during the testing process need to be controlled formally. Normally, such changes are bundled together so that test suites and regression testing can be done as few times as possible.

Test suites can simulate functionality of a product, but they cannot always duplicate real-life conditions. For example, timing issues (and the problems that arise in multithreaded applications) are very hard to duplicate in a testing lab. For this reason, public or beta testing in real-life conditions is often added to the mix.

Public/Beta Testing

When you are satisfied that you have done as much as possible, you can let people actually use the product. This type of testing is not done in a lab, but happens wherever people use the product. It is relatively informal and uncontrolled, and as a result, you normally need quite a few beta testers to get good feedback. After all, not everyone will use the product extensively; those who do, may not encounter problems. Even those who encounter problems may not report them.

Did you participate in the public beta testing of Mac OS X? Did you find errors or have comments? Did you send them to Apple? It is just like voting: If you do not make your voice known, you have no legitimate right to beef.

Beta testing is sometimes used for other purposes, including getting feedback on general product issues, marketablity, and the like. It also is used for major software products to generate publicity and to draw attention to the forthcoming product.

User Testing

Users should test their software—particularly if they rely on it for critical processing. During the period of concern over Y2K problems, one startling discovery was that many individuals and corporations had no idea whether their software worked properly.

In the case of shrink-wrapped, mass-market products, flaws are often known. However, in the case of vertical market software or custom-written software, bugs are not always discovered.

It is common for users to install upgrades to their software without understanding what those upgrades will do. You should encourage users to create a test environment so that they can find these things out before problems occur.

It is not always easy to go to users (who may in fact be your employers) and tell them that you think there are flaws in your code. But in the long run, including users in the test scenarios will make for better products and better relations.

Summary

Using the quick development features of Project Builder and Interface Builder, you, your users, and your developers can play with a remarkably lifelike version of your application. The sooner this happens, the better, because changes made to prototypes and pseudocode are always cheaper than changes made during the actual implementation process.

Chapter 14
Developing Help and
Assistance

*Somehow or other people have gotten it into their heads that help—
at least in the world of technology—is bad. For developers, it seems
to be an admission that their elegant interfaces are not perfect (people have trouble understanding them). For users, the mere existence
of help and assistance seems to threaten their independence and su-
periority over an inanimate chunk of silicon and plastic.*

*Maybe it is a sign of the times: Help (and helplessness) seem to con-
jure up a long-distant world of strapping damsels in distress and co-
quettish knights in shining armor. Today, everyone just knows how
to do everything—and if you don't, you wing it. Or so it seems.*

*Perhaps this strange antipathy to help and assistance can be over-
come by recognizing that help is not some weird afterthought in a*

software project but instead is part of the entire suite of documentation and information that makes the product usable and makes people understand what they can do with it.

This chapter helps you understand how to develop help and assistance on Mac OS X. The technology (Apple Help and the Help Viewer) goes back to Mac OS 8.6, so it is nothing new to old hands at the Macintosh—both users and developers.

Providing Help

Your application is just a bunch of code that requires a user's actions to place it in motion. How a user works with your code and what is done with it depends on your code, on the user, and what the user understands about the code.

This range of information about the code is provided by a host of different mechanisms and media, one of which is help. Following is a summary of the most common communication tools for software.

Documentation
Documentation is printed or PDF online documentation that users can refer to. It may include step-by-step tutorials as well as discursive examples, endorsements, questions-and-answers, and so forth.

Increasingly, PDF versions of documentation are placed on vendors' Web sites (and on internal sites for internal custom-written software). This has two very important impacts on the way in which people use documentation:

1. Because the documentation can be located, read, and printed on demand, most people know where it is and how to get it. Missing manuals are not a major problem.

2. Because documentation is available online, you can no longer assume that readers of your documentation have your product. Many people read or scan documentation before buying a product.

Advertising

Advertising and promotional materials also provide general information. Together with documentation, they help people understand what they can do with a product. (In many cases, the vast majority of users do not know most of the features of the products that they use every day. This is particularly true of office productivity tools.)

Onscreen Information

Onscreen information is the material that is presented at all times to a user. It consists of the names of interface elements, snippets of text ("include your area code with your phone number"), and the like. It is chiefly characterized by being there whether the users wants to see it or not.

Note that much information on screens—particularly crowded ones—is ignored.

Aspects of Help

The user may seek out documentation (and even advertising); more often those media require little, if any, action on a user's part. Help, on the other hand, is provided only when the user asks for it. It is a very different type of communication. You should recognize several important principles of help.

Impasse and Frustration People ask for help when they cannot do something. In very special cases (chiefly flirtation or extreme cases of obnoxiousness), people do ask for assistance in tasks that they can do, but these situations are rare in the world of software.

Your user is frustrated. Everything that your assistance does should be focused on getting the user back on track. This leads to the second principle.

Task-Oriented Focus Help should always be task-oriented. "This is the toolbar" is not help. It is part of a tour or travelogue through the interface. It does not matter to the user what you can do with the toolbar—the user wants to print or send an email message. If the toolbar can do that, fine; if not, who cares?

If the user is trying to do something that is illogical or impossible, your help must point that out, but it should be pointed out in the context of helping the user do what can be done. Sometimes this is impossible: There is just no way that you can create a movie using an email program, in most cases. In addition, if the user is truly off base, your prepared help is likely not to be of any help (you really were not expecting people to search for the Create Movie menu item in your email program). Leave some opening for users—a technical support number or email address, a Web site, or the like.

Avoid Naming Interface Elements You need to name interface elements when you refer to them in documentation and advertising. This is because you cannot insert an image of the object in question whenever you refer to it.

In your documentation and advertising, it is critical to name interface elements consistently so that people can understand the imaginary interface world you are creating. In online help, however, you can refer to objects on the screen much more simply. Tool tips, for example, appear next to objects. You do not have to say "Drag and drop images to the Image Well" or even "Drag and drop images here"; instead, you can say "Drag and drop images" because the location is identified by the mouse position and the tool tip that appears.

If you name objects in your online help, people will go looking for them. Users are remarkably resourceful, and will provide rather lovely explanations for why they assume that the Image Well is not the object to which the mouse is pointing and to which the tool tip is attached.

Recognize Experience   Once a user has made it into your program, you must assume a knowledge of menus, windows, buttons, and other basic controls. True, some users are amazed to learn after years of using a Macintosh computer that they can resize a window, but such users are the exception rather than the rule.

In the particular domain that your application focuses on, recognize experience as well. If you are providing a program to help keep track of sheep- and goat-breeding, the phrase "small ruminant" requires no explanation.

In general, users like a software application to match their level of expertise closely. They will endow it with all sorts of imaginary attributes in order to do so. Do not spoil the illusion by breaking this bond either with over simplification or with sudden confusing jargon.

Don't Be Cute   Finally, remember the first principle: Your help-needing user is frustrated and at an impasse. This is the wrong time for cuteness.

Help Buttons

Help buttons (usually indicated with a question mark) launch application help. Since such buttons are usually located on specific windows, the program can launch fairly appropriate help information for each one.

Help Viewer is the foundation of Apple Help; it is used to display information for the user. Some applications use other help delivery mechanisms (this is particularly true of cross-platform applications that need to provide consistency within their applications).

Tool Tips and Help Tags

Tool tips and help tags are brief messages that appear if a user holds the mouse over an interface element for a few seconds. The easiest way to create a tool tip is in Interface Builder: Select the interface element, choose Help from the pop-up at the top of the Info window, and type in your tool tip as shown in Figure 14-1.

(The two terms—tool tips and help tags—are similar in meaning, but *tool tip* is used in Cocoa and *help tag* is used in Carbon.)

Figure 14-1. Entering a Tool Tip in Interface Builder

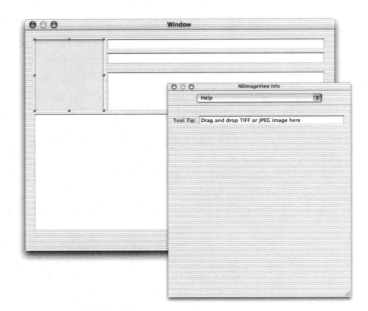

The field in which you enter the tool tip in the Info window is not large; in fact, it is probably a bit larger than the best tool tips are. In writing tool tips, you should consider these issues:

- Add information; if you have nothing to add, omit the tool tip. Not every interface element needs a tool tip.

- Make the tip active, not descriptive. In the example shown here, the user finds out what to do ("drag and drop") as well as additional information not obvious from the interface ("TIFF and JPEG images").

- Limit the tip to one item. Do not write a tip that refers to multiple interface elements. The one exception to this is in the case of closely spaced objects such as radio buttons. You can attach a tool tip to the view that groups those button so that it—the combination of buttons—receives the tip.

- As you can see from Figure 14-1, you cannot provide alternative tips for alternative states of the object. What you write must apply to selected/unselected items, active/inactive controls, and so forth.

Contextual Menus

Contextual menus appear when the user holds down the CONTROL key while holding the mouse button over an interface element to which a contextual menu is attached. You create contextual menus in Interface Builder: Simply drag a menu from the palette into your nib file and add the commands that are relevant. Attach those commands as you normally would attach any menu commands to interface elements and actions.

Next, attach the contextual menu to the interface element. Holding down the CONTROL key, drag from the element to the NSMenu as shown in Figure 14-2.

In the Connections pane of the Info window, select the menu outlet. All views have a menu outlet, so you can attach a contextual menu to any type of view in Interface Builder.

You can create a single contextual menu and attach it to a variety of interface elements if they all have the same contextual menus and actions. If some of the menu commands have different meanings (such as Clear, which might clear a particular field), you cannot do so.

Remember that many standard interface elements (such as text fields and text views) come with their own contextual menus. If your window has a background view, you can connect it to a contextual menu (you cannot connect a window to a contextual menu).

Contextual menus can address the task-oriented aspects of help that have been described earlier. They also can serve the purpose of answering, "What can I do now?" in addition to or instead of "How do I...?"

Figure 14-2. Connecting a Contextual Menu to an Interface Element

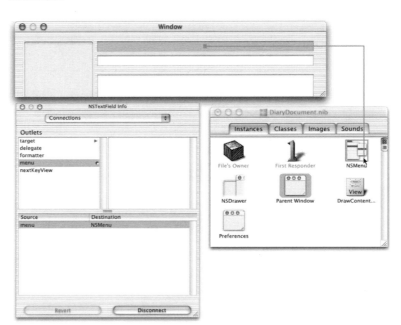

Contextual menus also can be used to extend the interface. This is sometimes a risky avenue to take, but it works in some circumstances. One example is the case in which you may want to open an application package in the Finder to see its constituent files. Using the Info window, you can open its resources, but the various files are normally not shown in the Finder. The contextual menu that appears when you CONTROL-click on a Finder icon includes a Show Package Contents command that you can use to open it up in its own Finder window. This is a typical power user feature; however, because it is included with a common feature (contextual menus), there is no guarantee that only expert users will use it.

Even so, this approach can be a useful way of providing two sets of commands to users of your application. Just realize that there may be unforeseen side effects from people exploring commands that you thought were hidden.

Help Menu

Finally, the Help menu at the right of the menu bar provides users' entrance to Apple Help and the Help Viewer. Help menus have undergone changes over the years as interface designers have come to understand the most productive way of organizing assistance.

At one point, all help was collected in the Help menu, resulting in a plethora of help commands. What this meant was that the frustrated user not only had to confront the inability to complete a task but also had to deal with the mystery of where the key to the problem might be located.

With Apple Help, a single entry (YourApp Help) is provided for entrance to Help Viewer. From there, the user can navigate to other help resources. This seems to work most effectively.

Help Viewer

Help Viewer displays help in windows like that shown in Figure 14-3. The window layout is standard across all applications. The body of the help material is written by you using HTML 3.2. This means that plug-ins, forms, and Java are out. Basic formatting, headers, images, and anchors are in.

Full documentation for Apple Help is available at http://developer.apple.com/ue/resources.html. Apple Help is available on Mac OS 8.6, OS 9, and OS X; on OS X you can access it from Classic, Carbon, or Cocoa. The links on the user experience page cited here will help you find the documentation; much of it is located under Carbon, but you can use it from Cocoa, too.

Figure 14-3. Help Viewer

In the Help Viewer window shown in Figure 14-3, you can see an image tag, a header (H1) tag—Taking pictures of the screen—and several paragraphs of text.

At the bottom left, an anchor lets users open the Grab application (for which this help is provided).

At the top of the window, users can search your help; they can also use the button at the lower left to go to the main help window.

Searching and Indexing Help

If a user decides to search, the current set of help—known as a *help book*—is searched as you can see in Figure 14-4. Searching is based on text as well as on keywords that you specify in a special tag at the top of a help page. It is an HTML meta tag, and it looks like this:

```
<META NAME="KEYWORDS" CONTENT="QuickTime QuickTime
  video QuikTime">
```

You do not need to repeat keywords that are in the body of the page; however, concepts that are not referenced by name are useful to add to keywords. In addition, misspelling or alternative spellings that users may indulge in should be provided as shown in the previous example ("QuikTime").

Figure 14-4. Searching within a Help Book

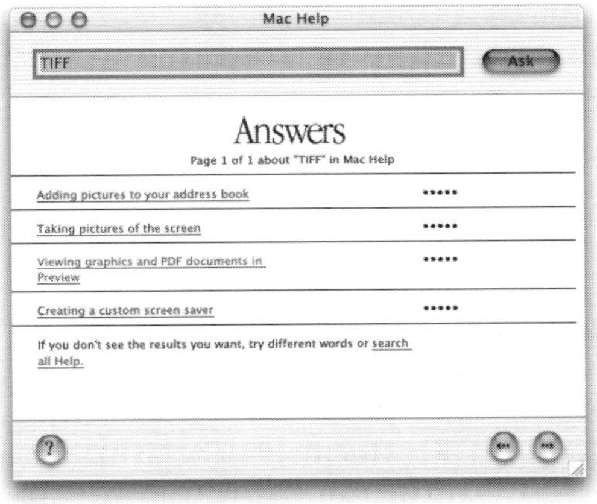

You can split a single page up into segments; each one can then appear separately in the search results.

The results of the search are summarized based on yet another meta tag. In the first result shown here, the following tag would appear at the top of the HTML file:

```
<META NAME="DESCRIPTION" CONTENT="Adding pictures
  to your address book">
```

The user can select any of the results to view. If they are not satisfactory, the Help Viewer instructions invite users to search all of help—that is, all installed help books. The results, as you can see in Figure 14-5, come from a variety of applications.

Figure 14-5. Systemwide Help

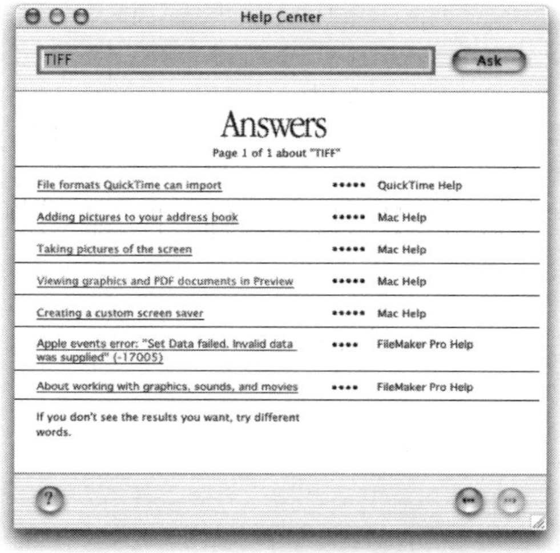

A meta tag that is used frequently on Web pages lets you control indexing with more detail:

```
<META NAME="ROBOTS" CONTENT="...">
```

The possible values for the content of the ROBOTS tag are as follows:

- INDEX (the default)
- NOINDEX (skip the entire page—use for tables of contents)
- KEYWORDS (use only keywords, not the text)
- SEGMENTS (indexes only the segments on a page)
- ANCHORS (indexes only the anchors on a page)

If a user chooses the button at the lower left, the systemwide Help Center containing all currently installed help books is shown as in Figure 14-6.

To prepare an index, you drag the folder containing all of your help files onto the Apple Help Indexing Tool; all relevant indexes will be created. This tool is available as part of the Carbon SDK; further information on using it and on preparing help is in that SDK as well as on Apple's Web site. You also will find documentation there on more advanced topics such as integrated Web-based HTML pages with your help files.

Figure 14-6. Help Center Shows All Help Books

Anchors and URLs

You can place anchor tags in your help files; from the HREF attribute you can reference several Help Viewer-specific schemas.

Help Center To load the Help Center page (shown in Figure 14-6), use the following syntax:

```
href='help:goto_helpcenter=user'
```

The Developer Help Center is loaded with

```
href='help:goto_helpcenter=developer'
```

Automated Searching   Launch a canned search (such as for the word "keyboard") in a specific help book this way:

```
href='help:search=keyboard book=Diary%20Help'
```

This example also demonstrates that you must use HTML-compliant names. That is, special characters—such as a space—must be encoded; %20 is the code for a space.

A canned search in all system help books looks like this:

```
href='help:search=keyboard'
```

The first example produces a result such as that shown previous in Figure 14-4; the second produces the results in Figure 14-5.

AppleScript   To start an AppleScript, use this syntax:

```
href='help:runscript="OpenPalette"'
```

A single string is passed to the AppleScript. You specify it as follows:

```
href='help:runscript="OpenPalette"string="tools"'
```

It is your responsibility to make certain that the AppleScript can accept and properly process such a string.

Launch an Application   You can launch an application if you know its location by using the following syntax:

```
href="~/Applications/Diary"
```

Additional commands are described in Apple's documentation. Note that most of Apple Help is also available through a public API; you can carry out these commands and open the Help Viewer programmatically.

Help Viewer Contents

All of the general comments about help that were provided at the beginning of this chapter apply to Help Viewer content. In addition, two important points should be kept in mind.

Use AppleScript Users appreciate the "do it for me" feature of AppleScript. There has been some concern that providing too many AppleScript choices would create a group of users with no understanding of what they are doing, but research by Apple has shown nothing but contented users. Remember, it may take you a day or two to develop an AppleScript, but you will be saving many users many hours and days of work—each.

Avoid Interface Images Users click on buttons; they move scroll bars; they have been trained to interact with the interface. You can add images to your help content, but avoid directly placing interface elements (screen shots or parts of screen shots) into the help content. Users will click the image.

If you feel that you must put an image of all or part of the interface into your help content, make it clear that it is an image. You can provide it with a jagged border that looks as if it is a scrap of paper; you can also "break the frame" of the image—provide an arrow pointing into the middle of the image—so that it is clear that it is not a set of live controls.

The best choice is to keep the interface where it is—on the desktop and in application windows—and to keep the very special Help Viewer and its functionality separate.

One thing does not work: Do not place text in the help window saying "This is only an image, do not try to click the button." It is like waving a red flag at a bull.

Installing Help

From Cocoa or Carbon, it is very easy to install Help Viewer content through Project Builder. Here is the recipe.

Create the Files Prepare your help files using the meta tags described here and in the Apple documentation. Place them all in one folder.

Add Suffixes Make certain that all help files have a suffix of .html or .htm.

Index the Files Drag the folder to the Apple Help Indexing Tool (in the Carbon SDK) to index all of the files.

Set Application Values Click the Target tab on the project structure pane. Inside the Application Settings tab, set the following:

1. Set `Identifier` (under Basic Information). This must be a unique name for your application. The Apple examples use the Java naming convention to provide unique names; you can follow that. It is the reverse of your domain name followed by a name that is unique within it. Thus, the identifier for sketch is com.apple.CocoaExamples.Sketch. The item in the property list that this sets is `CFBundleIdentifier`; it must be set and must be unique for help to work.

2. Use the Expert button to set `CFBundleHelpBook-Folder` to the name of the folder within your project that contains the help files (this is the folder that you indexed). Normally, this folder is inside the English.lprog (or French.lprog) folder on disk. The name is the name of the folder within your project; it is not a fully qualified path name.

3. Also with the Expert button, set `CFBundleHelp-BookName` to the title of your help book as defined in your title page using a meta tag like the following. Replace "Diary Help" with your own help title; the name AppleTitle is used for all help files.

```
<META NAME="AppleTitle" CONTENT="Diary Help">
```

Summary

Whether your application is a shrink-wrapped consumer product or an in-house application for a single department (or single user—even yourself), it is not complete without an appropriate level of assistance and help.

Apple Help is available in both the Cocoa and Carbon frameworks, and it provides an HTML-based help system that can integrate Web updates dynamically.

When you have finished with your help system, you are ready to package your product for distribution. The next chapter shows you how to do that.

Chapter 15
Packaging Your Application

On the original Macintosh, applications were more or less based on a single file. Over time, that single file, with its data and resource forks, was joined by various support files. In addition, user preferences (not to mention user data) cluttered the application; these files showed up in a variety of folders (Preferences inside the System Folder, for example). As a result, installation became tricky. Furthermore, moving an application from one computer to another was not always easy—there were many pieces to remember.

On Mac OS X, applications come in self-contained packages that group their various files together. User preferences show up in each user's Library folder, and documents are normally placed in the Documents, Pictures, and Movies folders for each user.

To provide easy-to-install (and easy-to-move) applications to users, it is best to provide them with a single thing that they can work with for installation and reinstallation. Three basic mechanisms are available on Mac OS X:

- *You can use the output of Project Builder to create an installable application.*

- *You can prepare a disk image that, as a single file, can be sent over the Internet and then opened as a disk image on the receiving computer.*

- *You can use Package Maker to create a package that will be installed by the installer.*

This chapter shows you how to do all three. It ends with some tips on testing and troubleshooting installation problems.

Packages, Bundles, and Installation Locations

A bundle contains all of an application's resources, including its code. The entire bundle appears as one file to users; they can move it around as they see fit. If they use the Info window to look at an application, they can see its localized resources from the Application Files pane. To open an application's bundle to see its contents, users need to use a contextual menu.

CONTROL-click on an application to bring up the contextual menu, and then choose Show Package Contents to open a Finder window that shows the application's contents. Note that this is a special Finder window; you can navigate down into the folders of the application, but you cannot navigate up and out of it—that is, you cannot move into the application's containing folder from such a window. (This process is shown later in this chapter in "Creating a Disk Image" on page 317.)

Application bundles are folders whose names end with the .app extension. The Finder hides the extension and presents the folder as an application icon so that to the user it appears to be a single file.

In addition to applications, other types of bundles are frameworks, debug or profile versions of applications, and plug-ins that are loaded on demand by applications (including Interface Builder, which relies heavily on palettes).

Installation Locations

Normally, applications are installed either in the systemwide Applications folder (/Applications) or in an individual user's Applications folder (~/Applications). They also may be located on the local area network.

The Finder looks in these locations for applications; Cocoa looks there for services. Applications located in other places will probably function properly, but they may not appear properly in the Finder and their services may not be exposed.

Note that ~/Applications may not be created in default installations of the operating system. If you create it, you should alert the user.

Drag-and-Drop Installation

Because an application bundle appears as one file, dragging and dropping it is the easiest way to install and remove it. An installation program (such as Installer) can be used to handle more complex installations.

Installation Packages

When you use the Apple Installer, you combine the application bundle and a variety of other files into an installation *package* (a file with a .pkg suffix). The Installer reads the package file, manipulates it (decompressing its contents, perhaps), and then installs its package in the appropriate locations.

Creating an Application Bundle with Project Builder

The simplest way to create an application bundle is to use the Project Builder Deployment build phase as shown in Figure 15-1.

Figure 15-1. Deployment Build Phase (Files & Build Phases)

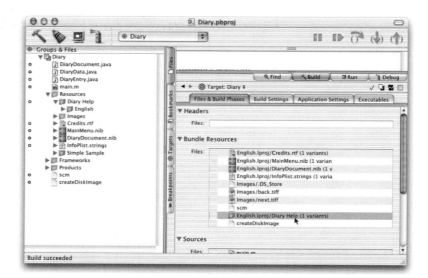

You normally do not need to do anything here: The figure is presented to show what Project Builder does for you. Note that in the Groups & Files view of the project structure pane at the left, all of the project files have been organized—as you normally do. In particular, note the Diary Help folder that is located within the Resources folder.

At the right, the highlighted line shows that Project Builder has automatically included the Diary Help folder in the bundle resources. It has noted that one variant (English) exists. The rearranging of file names (involving lprog.English) is automatic.

When you build a deployment version in Project Builder, you do have to make a few adjustments in the Build Settings pane. In particular, you need to set a location for the compiled application to be placed in. This is shown in Figure 15-2.

The variable $HOME specifies the user's home directory. Thus, this application will be installed in a user's Applications folder, not in the systemwide Applications folder.

Figure 15-2. Deployment Build Phase (Build Settings)

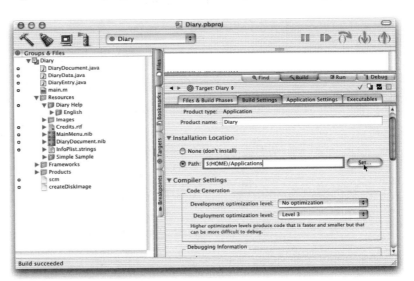

On successful completion of the build, the application—viewed as a single icon in the Finder—is placed on disk. You can open it using a contextual menu as shown in Figure 15-3. Choose Show Package Contents to see the contents of the wrapper folder that is the application bundle.

Figure 15-3. Opening an Application Bundle with a Contextual Menu

The contents of the application bundle are shown in Figure 15-4. Note in particular the Diary Help folder; it is located inside English.lprog.

Figure 15-4. Contents of an Application Bundle

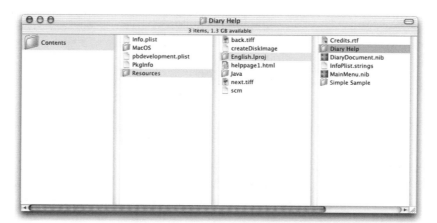

Next to the Diary Help folder are the two nibs that the application uses. The application executable code is located in the MacOS folder (along with any Classic executable code that may be present). This collection of files and folders is similar to the contents of the project folder, but there is no source code here.

Note, too, that you cannot scroll the browser in Figure 15-4 to the left: The Contents folder inside an application folder is not part of the Finder's file hierarchy, and you cannot look at the folder in which it is located. You can access all files and directories within the application bundle from the command line (but the Finder access described here is usually sufficient).

Creating a Disk Image

A somewhat more complex method of creating a single file for users to install your application is to create a disk image. This is suitable for sending via email or transferring using FTP. Transferring an application bundle over a network may cause problems because it will appear as a folder or directory; its special application qualities appear only on Mac OS X, and mostly only when the Finder is involved.

Engineers from Apple demonstrated the following technique at the 2001 World Wide Developers Conference. It subsequently was posted to the Project Builder mailing list (http://www.lists.apple.com/mailman/listinfo/projectbuilder-users). This type of information is a good reason for joining both the Apple Developer program and the mailing list.

Project Builder's multiple target structure allows one target to depend on another. When you combine the dependencies with the ability to have a target that consists only of a shell script, you can create the following elegant process. Simply put, it makes your project's compile-and-build target a dependent target of a legacy target that runs a shell script, which itself packages the newly built application in a disk image.

Figure 15-5 shows how you set up such a process. Create a legacy target (such as Disk Image Creator). In the Custom Build Command pane of the selected target, make three entries:

1. Set the tool to /bin/sh.

2. Set the arguments as shown. Specify the size of the disk image (8000 is used in this example), and set the name of the image to be created (replace outimg with your own image file name).

3. Locate the directory in which the files exist (your project directory).

Figure 15-5. Legacy Target

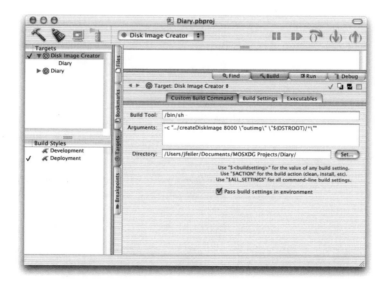

When you build a deployment version of this target (set the deployment build phase in the lower left, as shown), the script will be run to create the disk image. If your build is lengthy, you can launch the whole process from the command line. Use cd to change the directory to your project's directory, and then type

```
pbxbuild install -target "Disk Image Creator"
```

(You can also drag and drop your project's directory into Terminal: type cd and a space, then drag the folder onto the command line.)

Here is the script you need to use. It should be added to your project but not attached to a target.

Note that files created by the build are placed in a temporary destination root (DSTROOT) folder; from there, they are moved to the disk image.

```
#! /bin/sh
#
# createDiskImage

# Requires three or more args
if [ $# -lt 3 ] ; then
echo "usage: $0 <ImageSizeInMegabytes>
  <NameOfImageWithNoExtension>
  <FolderToCopyToImage> ..."
exit 1
fi

# Grab the size and image name arguments.  Leave
  the rest of them in $*
imageSize=$1
shift
imageName=$1
shift

# Create the image and format it
echo
```

```
echo "Creating ${imageSize} MB disk image named
  ${imageName}..."

rm -f ${imageName}.dmg
hdiutil create ${imageName}.dmg -megabytes
  ${imageSize} -layout NONE

hdidOutput=`hdid -nomount ${imageName}.dmg | grep
  '/dev/disk[0-9]*'`

sudo /sbin/newfs_hfs -w -v ${imageName} -b 4096
  ${hdidOutput}

hdiutil eject ${hdidOutput}

# Mount the image and copy stuff
hdidOutput=`hdid ${imageName}.dmg | grep '/dev/
  disk[0-9]*'`
sleep 4 # This sleep is needed and there seems to
  be no way to know when the image is mounted...

echo "Copying contents to ${imageName}..."
while [ $# -gt 0 ] ; do
  echo "...copying ${1}"
  /Developer/Tools/CpMac -r ${1}/Volumes/${image-
  Name}
  shift
done

hdiutil eject ${hdidOutput}

# Compress the image
echo "Compressing ${imageName} disk image..."

mv ${imageName}.dmg ${imageName}.orig.dmg
hdiutil convert ${imageName}.orig.dmg -format UDCO
  -o ${imageName}
rm ${imageName}.orig.dmg

echo "Done."
echo
```

Creating an Installer Package

The Apple Installer is used to install Mac OS X itself and many other software products on your computer. Its initial screen is shown in Figure 15-6.

Using the installer rather than drag-and-drop is a good idea when the installation is complex and when subsidiary files (licenses, Read Mes, and the like) need to be managed.

An installation package contains one or more application bundles; these may be archived automatically and dearchived during the installation process. In addition, other files and scripts can be included in the package.

Figure 15-6. Apple Installer

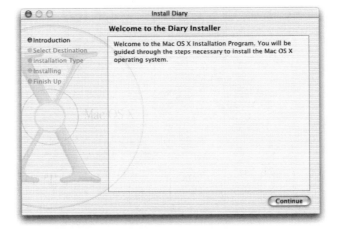

Setting Up Your Files

Package Maker is included with the developer tools, and it allows you to easily create installer packages. To begin with, create a distribution root folder (DSTROOT) and assemble the files that you need to include in the package. Normally, this will be the Project Builder output from a deployment build, but you may include other files.

When you first launch it, the control window shown in Figure 15-7 appears. The first two entries are for the DSTROOT directory in which you placed the Project Builder output; the resources directory is where you should place the additional files that are needed during the installation.

Using a Read Me File

If you include a ReadMe file with a suffix of .txt, .rtf. or .html in the resources folder, it will be displayed in the Important Information pane of the installer.

Using a License

If there is a file named License.txt, License.html, or License.rtf in the resources folder, it is displayed in a sheet at the appropriate point in the installation process.

Figure 15-7. Package Maker

The other fields and options on the Package Maker form are self-explanatory. Additional information is available from the online help included with Package Maker.

Testing Installations

Be sure to test installations of your software. Users typically do not do many installations, and they may install your software only once. Your installation should work the first time. If it does not, you may have lost your chance to have people use your software ever again.

The basic test of an installation should be done on a computer that has never had your software installed on it. This is because if your installation accidentally does not include something that happens to be on your test computer, you will not find the mistake.

One common way of handling this testing situation is to keep your hard disk partitioned into two sections. Keep one or two gigabytes for a cleanly installed operating system; use the rest for your work. When you need to test an installation, reformat the small partition, install a fresh copy of Mac OS X, restart with that partition as the startup disk, and see if the installation works. If it does not, the most basic user installations will fail.

You should do additional testing in other environments (particularly if there are certain configurations that you know will be used). In addition to the installation, test that everything works properly. Pay particular attention to first-time bugs that cannot be easily reproduced. At one time, for example, MacApp applications crashed if you attempted to print a document on a computer on which no document had ever been printed since the operating system was installed (in other words, on Mac OS 7—where this occurred—the Chooser had never been used to select a printer). The typical response of users (and testers) was to test if there was a problem with printing. They printed something—and selected a printer in the Chooser to do so. They then ran the MacApp application again, and all was well. Their troubleshooting actually solved the problem, and it was some time before the true bug was discovered.

Summary

Wherever possible, use a simple drag-and-drop installation for your applications. On a single computer or on a local area network, you can use the application bundle created by Project Builder to do this.

If you need to send the application bundle across the Internet, consider packaging it in a single file such as a disk image. That single file will be handled properly by other operating systems it may encounter on its travels.

Finally, consider using Package Maker and the Apple Installer for more complex installations.

Chapter 16
Managing Your Code

In part because all of your source code is stored electronically, it is important to keep track of it and the various versions of it. Whereas early programmers could always go back to their punched cards, programmers now cannot go back to yesterday's version (or the version from 10 minutes ago) unless some kind of management structure is in place.

Project Builder incorporates the Concurrent Versions System (CVS) that is widely used for open-source projects. You can access most of the commands that you need through its SCM (source code management) menu.

How Source Code Management Works

The basic idea behind source code management is that a central location—called a *repository* in CVS—contains all versions of all files associated with a project. Each version of each file is identified by date and with an informational note that is placed there by a programmer.

You check out files to work on them; you check them in (with notes) when you are done with them. This means that you do not have to save entire copies of a project folder as you experiment.

Source code management tools function in one of two ways:

1. When a programmer starts to work on a file, it is checked out. No other programmer can check out a modifiable version of the file. (Programmers can also check out read-only versions of files without affecting other people, but they cannot modify them.)

2. Anyone can check out a file at any time. When it comes time to check it in, the programmer must merge it with the then-current version of the file (which may have been modified in the meantime).

CVS uses the second mechanism. It is particularly well suited to large projects on which many people may have checked out many files but which may never be checked back in (the checkouts are used for experimentation, for example). This describes many open-source projects.

Because the check-in process requires the person checking in the code to compare it to the current version, a source code management system normally includes file merge and compare software (as does CVS).

Source code management is essential on large projects; it is at least as critical on small, one-person projects. It is used so that versions of code can be identified—whenever you reach a stopping point, you can set a version to which you can return. That may be automatically at the end of a day, but it may be at the end of fixing a particular bug or solving a particular problem. Programmers expect to be able to quickly revert to any previous version of their software. This avoids the practice of storing copies of your code in folders with names like "Friday Good" or "Tuesday Before Restructuring."

If you are used to working on your own, SCM may be a change. Actually, it turns out to be very simple and convenient. You set up your repository and put all your code in it, and then you check it out as you need it. This means that if you want to take your code with you on an iBook or Power-Book, you just connect to your repository and check everything out; you do not have to worry about copying files. When you need to synchronize files, you can easily do it through Project Builder.

Source code management manages all kinds of files for you. Anything that involves multiple files and multiple versions—including large word processing projects—can benefit from the organization of source code management. You can use the CVS command-line syntax in Terminal to check files other than Project Builder files in and out. For more information on CVS, see http://www.cvshome.org.

Setting Up CVS

Project Builder provides access to the check-in and check-out features of CVS. However, you need to set it up first. If you already have a CVS code repository on a network, you can skip this step. Your network or project coordinator will provide the information that you need.

You need to use the command line in Terminal for this setup. However, once it is done, you can just use Project Builder. The steps outlined here are very simple. Even if Terminal scares you, go ahead and try them.

Create the project as you normally would in Project Builder; if you already have a project, you can start with it. Although the whole point of using CVS is to keep a safe copy of your project, start by copying the entire project folder just in case something goes wrong.

Create Your CVS Repository Directory

Start by creating the repository for all of your CVS files. This directory can be anywhere on your computer or local area network, but it must be accessible to everyone who will need to check files in and out. In many places, this directory lives on a file server that is protected with an uninterruptible power supply (UPS) and that is automatically backed up to tape or some other medium on a regular (at least daily) basis. Note, too, that this central repository can be of tremendous value to outsiders. It should not be located on a public Web server unless you intend to make your code open source.

Once you have created the directory for your CVS files, use Terminal to let CVS know where it is. You can set the environmental variable CVSROOT for this purpose:

```
setenv CVSROOT /Users/jfeiler/Documents/codeCon-
    trol
```

Use Terminal's drag-and-drop to drag the directory (folder) from the Finder into this command line following CVSROOT. Replace `/Users/jfeiler/Documents/codeControl` in this line of code with your actual repository directory name.

All of your CVS projects will be placed in this directory. You can change this directory from time to time by using the `-d` option with CVS commands on the command line. That specifies a specific directory for one CVS command. You need to do this if you are switching between a local code repository and a networked one (such as Apple's Darwin repository).

If you are using a repository to synchronize your files between a portable and desktop computer, create one repository and check out files from it to either computer. If you create two repositories, you will be asking for trouble, as you will then be in the multiuser world all by yourself. One repository—even (especially!) for multiuser projects—is essential to manage code properly.

Import Your Project

Next, import your project into the repository directory you have just created.

Go to the directory in which your project is located. Use the `cd` command to change the Terminal directory to that directory (type `cd`, then drag and drop the folder onto the command line—remember to leave a space after `cd` and before you drag and drop the folder).

Next, use the `cvs import` command to import the contents of your default directory. The `-m` (message) option lets you specify the check-in message; if you do not enter it, you will be prompted for it. After that, you specify three required variables:

1. The name of the project repository directory to be created within the main repository directory. In the example shown here, it will be `Diary/rdir` (`rdir`—repository directory—is often used in contrast to `wdir`—working directory).

2. A vendor name. For most purposes, you can simply name the project. `Diary` is used for the vendor name here. (This matters when you are working with third-party code that will need to be merged later on into other CVS systems. For merging within your own repository, you can set this to any value you want in most cases.)

3. A release name. This, too, matters when you are working with other parties. Here, Start is used.

```
cvs import -m "Converting Diary" Diary/rdir
  Diary start
```

CVS will report if there are any conflicts: When you are setting up a project, there should be none. You are using a new directory for a new project.

Check Out Your Project

You have moved all of your files into the CVS repository; now you need to get them back again. The round trip will have equipped them with the CVS information that lets you check them in and out.

Go to a directory in which you want to work. To prevent any possible confusion at this point, you might consider creating a new directory in your Documents folder—calling it work may keep it separate from other folders you already have.

Back in Terminal, change your directory to this new one: use the cd command (type a space after it), and then drag and drop the folder you want to use.

Check out the entire directory of files using this command:

```
cvs checkout Diary
```

where Diary is whatever vendor name you used in the import command described previously.

The entire directory of files that you checked in should be placed in your new directory. You can now quit Terminal and move into Project Builder.

Open your project file in this new directory from Project Builder.

Using Source Code Management in Project Builder

After this, when you open your project, Project Builder will automatically add a column to the left of Groups & Files view in the project structure pane as shown in Figure 16-1. If it does not do so, see "CVS Preferences" on page 338.

Figure 16-1. CVS Column

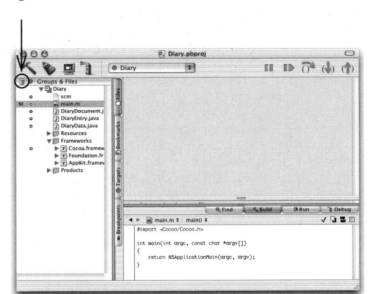

Note that source code management in Project Builder is implemented using CVS. In the future, alternative source code mechanisms could be used. As a result, the more general term—SCM—is used from here on.

File Status

Each file in the SCM repository will be identified with a symbol letting you know its status:

- Blank (space). Repository and local versions of the file are the same. (Note this is based on the check-in information; SCM does not scan the files to confirm that they are the same. It is possible to fool CVS—but it is not easy, and it is not a good idea.)

- ? The file is not a SCM file.

- U. The file on your disk needs to be updated with a more recent version from SCM.

- A. You have added a file locally but not to the repository.

- R. You have removed a file locally but not from the repository.

- M. You have modified a file locally, but not moved it to the repository.

- C. A conflict occurred during a merge or update.

- -. The folder is not known to SCM.

If you are working alone on a project and using SCM to keep track of your work, the only symbols you will care about are blank (no problem), M (modified), A (added), and R (removed).

If you are working on a multiperson project, you also may see U or C.

You can add, remove, or check in files to the repository through Project Builder. Creating new projects or adding folders (not files) to a project needs to be done through Terminal.

Note that the initial importing of a project will import all of the folders; this is sufficient for many projects, and the subsequent files that you add to the project can be managed with Project Builder alone.

Version Info

You can select any file in the Groups & Files list and see its SCM status by using the Show Info command from the Project menu as shown in Figure 16-2.

Figure 16-2. Info Pane

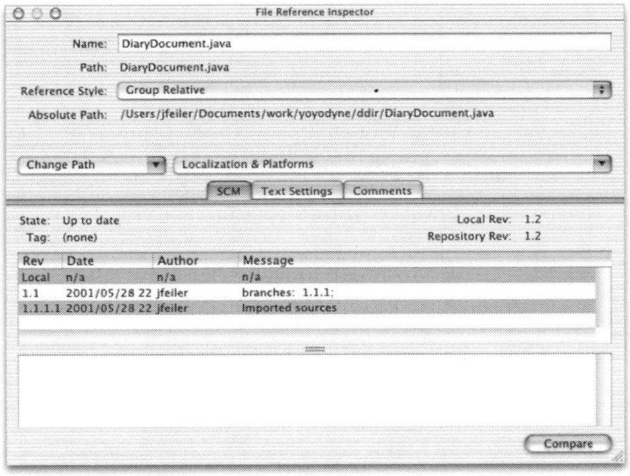

This pane is available for files that are not under source code management, but the version information is available only for SCM files. Note the message column: When you have versions that go back several months (or years!), those messages become increasingly important.

Comparing Files

You can select any two versions of a file (COMMAND-click) in this window and compare them by using the button at the lower right. Comparing files is one of the most important tools in source code management. As Figure 16-2 indicates, you can compare versions that are not consecutive. This is particularly useful when a fix to one problem has introduced another error and you need to go back to the last clean version.

The FileMerge window is shown in Figure 16-3. Each file is shown in is own pane, and you can clearly see additions, deletions, and changes.

Figure 16-3. FileMerge

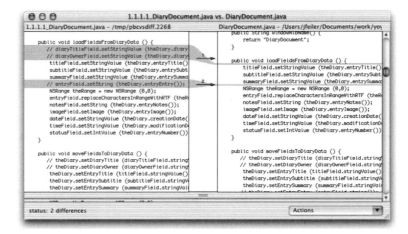

FileMerge is a separate application with its own preferences, as shown in Figure 16-4.

Figure 16-4. FileMerge Preferences (1)

On multiuser projects, each user can have separate preferences. This helps in navigating through files that others have modified. Additional preferences are shown in Figure 16-5.

Figure 16-5. FileMerge Preferences (2)

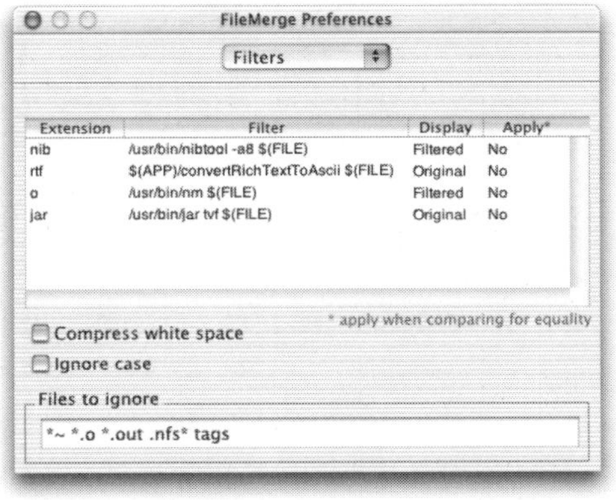

Checking Files In (Commit)

When you have modified a file locally, it is marked with an M as shown in Figure 16-6. When you are satisfied that you are at a point where the code should be checked in, select the file and choose Commit Changes from the SCM menu.

Remember that checking a file in is a way of protecting it from accidental deletion or modification (unless the entire repository is destroyed). On a multiuser project, you should not check in code that does not work unless there are extenuating circumstances. (For example, multiple changes from a variety of programmers may be required to implement a single feature; until all are checked in, none may work properly.) On a single-person project, you can use the repository for daily backups, and there is no reason to worry about checking in buggy code.

Figure 16-6. Modified File

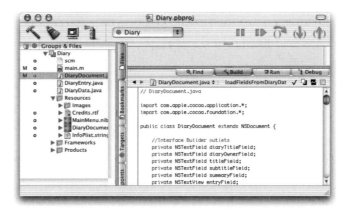

You will be prompted to enter a message as shown in Figure 16-7. This message will appear in the Info window (see "Version Info" on page 333).

Figure 16-7. Enter a Message

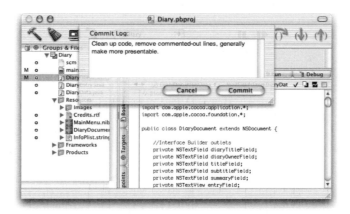

Once the file has been checked in, it is no longer marked with an M. Note that you must check in each file individually; in

Figure 16-8, you can see that one modified file is no longer marked with M (it has been checked in), but the other one still needs to be checked in.

Figure 16-8. After Commit

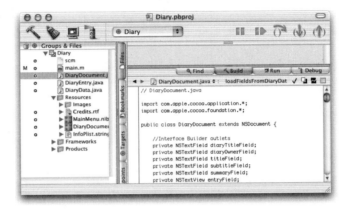

Reverting

One particularly helpful tool of code management is the ability to quickly revert to a previous version of a file as shown in Figure 16-9.

Figure 16-9. Reverting

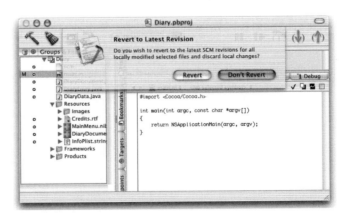

To do this, you select a file in the Groups & Files view and then choose Revert to Latest Revision from the SCM menu. This lets you throw out your changes if you have been wandering off on an unproductive track.

Before reverting, consider saving a copy of your locally modified file in case you were on the right track after all.

CVS Preferences

The Project Builder preferences include a CVS Access pane as shown in Figure 16-10.

Figure 16-10. CVS Preference

If you are having problems, make certain that CVS is enabled here. Also, it is a good idea to save files before SCM operations. The radio buttons controlling when SCM status is obtained are most important in multiuser projects where file status may change while you are working on files.

Logging In to a Remote CVS Server

CVS servers manage many large projects (Mac OS X, for example). They also manage open-source projects. If you want to access Apple's open-source code for Darwin, for example, you use CVS.

First, go to the Apple public source page (http://public-source.apple.com/) and register. You will need to select a user name and password.

Then, you need to set your CVSROOT to the remote directory. You can modify the CVSROOT environmental variable or use the -d option in cvs commands. Here is the Terminal code to modify the environmental variable for Darwin open source:

```
setenv CVSROOT :pserver:YOURUSERNAMEHERE@
  anoncvs.opensource.apple.com:/cvs/Darwin
```

Then log in with

```
cvs login
```

You should receive the following response:

```
(Logging in to @anoncvs.opensource.apple.com)
CVS password:
```

Type your password, and you should be connected to the code repository. You can then proceed to check out the source code using the same check-out procedures outlined previously in this chapter.

Summary

The likelihood of any software development project moving from start to finish without any interruptions, backtracking, or revisions is minimal. When more than one person is involved, the challenges of coordination are magnified.

Managing source code is a normal part of everyday, professional software development—even for students and hobbyists. Because Project Builder provides you with integrated source code management, there is no reason not to use it—and many reasons to do so.

This part of the book has led you from the initial planning of a software development project through its prototyping, implementation, and packaging. The next part of the book looks at the details of writing for Mac OS X.

Part III
Writing for Mac OS X

This part of the book shows you how to create Mac OS X applications. Each chapter focuses on a different aspect of functionality—documents, windows, and the like. Many of these chapters refer to a simple Diary application that is described in the first chapter of this part. Sections of its source code appear with annotations in the appropriate chapters. You can download the application (and the source code) from the author's Web site—http://www.philmont-mill.com. Select the Mac OS X area and then follow the link to Mac OS X Developer's Guide.

For a complete reference to all of the classes in the Mac OS X frameworks, refer to the documentation on the developer CD-ROM and on Apple's Web site. The focus of this part of the book is on showing you the sorts of things you can do and then pointing you in the direction of additional information. You should have read Part I, and you should be familiar with the programming concepts described there. If you need additional assistance, consult the Apple documentation.

Chapter 17
Applications

This chapter begins with a walk-through of the Diary application. It continues with the code that you need to use to create that application. As you will see, the application object in the Cocoa framework is critical—but its default behavior is almost always satisfactory. The boilerplate code that Project Builder creates for you is generally usable without modification.

In the final part of this chapter, a brief summary of the Carbon application object in MacApp is provided. You will also find a guide to deciphering Classic and Carbon applications that have been written without the benefit of frameworks (in case you need to modify or convert such applications to Cocoa).

A Walk-Through of Diary

It is easier to understand programming concepts when portions of code are at hand. The problem is always to have examples that are complex enough to shed light on real-world problems but not so complicated as to require more explanation of the example than of the concept.

One application program is used for many of the examples in this part of the book. It is of moderate complexity, and it touches on many of the issues that most Mac OS X developers need to know about. Inside Diary, you will find the following functionality:

- Windows and views, including text fields and text views, buttons, scrollers, and images

- A drawer

- A customizable toolbar

- Documents that can be saved and reopened

- Automatic dirtying of documents after changes

- An undo feature

You will find wonderful examples from Apple on the developer CD-ROM. Among them, you will find TextEdit and Sketch—very sophisticated authoring tools for text and graphics. However, as many developers have found, the opportunities to write from-scratch editing applications are few and far between. More often, the need to read and write structured data and to perform calculations on it is what needs to be done. That is what Diary does.

What Diary Does

Diary is a program that is designed to help people keep diaries. People who keep diaries on paper often start either with blank notebooks or with preprinted books that have space on each page for a date or other identifying information.

Diary presents a more structured but still flexible approach to the wide variety of diary-keeping. As is always the case when you start to work on an application program, it is important to define its scope and to know exactly how you and the user expect it to work. (Even if you are both developer and user, you need to come to this mutual agreement.) You have to understand the data you are working with before you can adequately represent it in windows and views or store it on disk.

Here is the scope and purpose of Diary. It starts from the seven types of diaries that Thomas Mallon describes in his excellent book, *A Book of One's Own*[1]:

1. Chroniclers: These people keep a day-by-day (or irregular) record of goings-on.

2. Travelers: Many people who do not otherwise keep diaries or journals do so when they travel. Sometimes these diaries are kept for their own sake; other times they are kept to help identify photographs or video clips as well as to keep track of purchases for customs.

3. Pilgrims: After embarking on a personal or spiritual search, many people keep track of their progress (or lack of it) in attaining inner goals.

4. Creators: Artists, writers, scientists—and even computer developers—keep track of their experiments and the development of their ideas and projects.

5. Apologists: These people need to explain or promote themselves or their causes. As Mallon writes, they include not only politicians such as Nigel Nicholson and Richard Nixon, but also "unappreciated artists; nebbishes turned killers; those denied their dreams because they were the wrong age, or the wrong sex, or

---

1. *A Book of One's Own: People and Their Diaries*, Thomas Mallon. Ticknor & Fields, 1984.

just in the wrong place"; and "lovers, spurned and scornful, hurt and bewildered, proud and defiant."

6. Confessors: Sometimes only a diary can be trusted with thoughts and questions about life. According to Mallon, confessional diaries are most often the province of adolescents.

7. Prisoners: With nothing to do all day and all night, prisoners often use diaries to pass the time.

Mallon's book is used as an informal user specification in the Diary application. You may think it odd, but in practice, user specifications take many forms. The book describes the process quite thoroughly, and it analyzes the data involved. Figuring out what types of data storage will be needed is up to the developer.

Diary Entries

Taking these types of diaries as the basic need for the Diary program to fulfill, its basic entry window is shown in Figure 17-1.

Title and Subtitle At the top of the window are two text fields: the title and subtitle of the entry. Each diary entry for each of the types of diaries can use these fields. For the chronicler, they can be year, month, and date; for the traveller, they can be location and date (or time).

If you wanted to make this program more specific, you could force these fields to be dates. However, if you look back at the types of diaries, you will see that this choice does not fit with some of the requirements.

Alternatively, you might consider making these fields prepared items in a pop-up menu; they might also carry edits with them so that they are unique. Again, the overall scope of this project argues for totally customizable titles and subtitles. (However, these are all good projects for you to pursue to learn more about programming for Mac OS X by modifying Diary in these ways.)

Figure 17-1. Basic Diary Entry

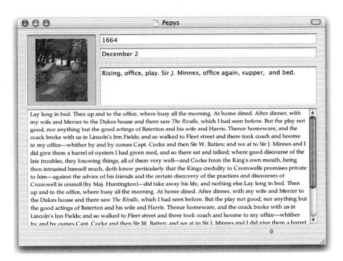

Summary Below those fields, another text field allows a summary of the entry to be displayed. For creators, such a summary might be the problem to be solved or the experiment to be conducted. For others, it can be a literal summary, a quote or phrase overheard, or anything brief and textual that applies to the entry.

The summary field is longer than the title and subtitle in the view shown in Figure 17-1. The larger field suggests that you can enter more data. The fact that the field is not placed within a scroller suggests to the user that only the visible amount of data should be entered. (In fact, much more can be typed, but it will be hard to see.) Gradually, you will learn how to use the Aqua interface elements not just to show people what they can do, but also to suggest to people what they should not do—enter long summaries.

Image To the left of these three fields, an image field is available for graphics to be pasted or dragged into it.

The choice of a single image field suggests to a user that this is primarily a text-based diary. Picture diaries are usually called scrapbooks, and if you were designing one it would look quite different. The image is subsidiary to the text, and this program does not allow for editing. You can edit images in any of a variety of programs.

If you want to modify Diary, you can add image editing features to it.

Text The large scrolling text view in the center of the window allows Rich text to be entered (with formatting and styles). This is the body of the entry, and it is essentially unlimited.

Drawers for Notes

Diary uses many features of the Aqua interface. For example, there is a drawer that you can open as shown in Figure 17-2.

Figure 17-2. Drawer Lets You Enter Notes

A drawer is a good interface element to use to let people have easy access to information or controls that they sometimes need. If you read Mallon's book, you will see that people frequently annotate their diaries; they also often make contemporaneous notes that they later expand into full entries. Both purposes ideally fit a drawer: an object that can be there if needed and closed up if not needed.

Toolbars

Toolbars are another important new feature of the Aqua interface. They are appropriate for icon-driven commands that you may need close at hand (or not, if you close the toolbar). Because a toolbar may not always be open (and because users may not know how to do so), it is important that all toolbar commands also appear in the menu bar. However, while the commands in the menu bar may be scattered among a variety of menus, in the toolbar, they are all equally available. The Diary toolbar is shown in Figure 17-3.

Figure 17-3. Toolbar Lets You Control the Window

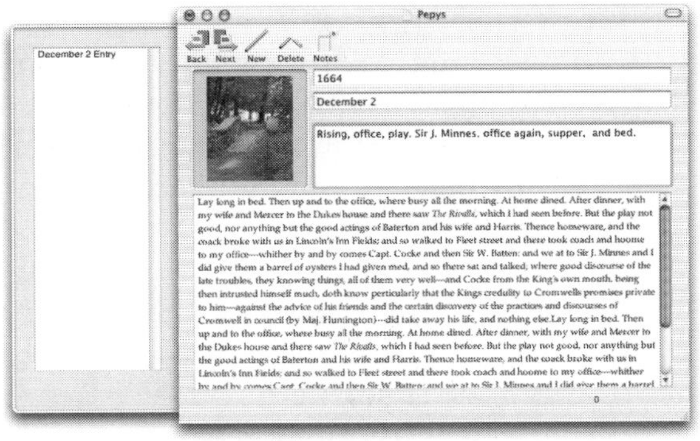

Diary Data Structure

The windows in the previous figures have shown a single Diary entry. Obviously, a diary contains many entries. The data structure used in Diary is not uncommon. In fact, it is very similar to (indeed, borrowed from) the data structure in Sketch, a Cocoa example.

A Diary document contains two types of data:

1. Diary Data. This data consists of the Diary name and the name of its owner. There is one set of Diary data per Diary document (i.e., one owner and title).

2. Diary Entries. Within the Diary, a variety of entries—each in the format of the windows shown in these figures—are stored. At run time, these entries are placed in an array in the Diary Data. Any number of entries can exist, but there is only one entries array.

If you create a document-based Cocoa application in Project Builder, a document object—MyDocument—is automatically created for you. In the Diary program, you will see that two other classes are created: DiaryData and DiaryEntry. They correspond to the two types of data described here.

Where to Put the Data

In developing a document-based application, you always have to consider where the data will live. In the TextEdit example, it lives within the document itself; in Sketch and Diary, it lives primarily outside the document object in custom objects.

The Model-View-Controller paradigm comes into play here. As noted previously, the classic MVC architecture omits documents and data storage. (NeXTSTEP and the original Open-Step similarly omitted documents. The NSDocument class became part of OpenStep only after Apple purchased NeXT. The document-based computing paradigm was added in 1997.)

You can view your document as a controller, a model, or both. There is an attraction in leaving the data (your model) "pure"—that is, untouched by any platform or framework considerations. Such code can easily be ported from one environment to another, with the visualization (view) and manipulation (controller) code rewritten for whatever particular environment it is in. In such a case, your document must be a controller for the data. It must store and restore it. (Storing and restoring is almost always platform- and/or framework-specific.)

On the other hand, you can take the stance that the data in the model can manipulate itself as asked by the controller—and that manipulation can include storing and retrieving it. Such a choice means that the model data must know how to use the framework's storage mechanisms; as a result, it is no longer platform- or framework-agnostic.

The choice made in Sketch (and in Diary) is to make the document more of a controller than a model. In both cases, it asks the data to store itself, and the data uses Cocoa calls to do so. In TextEdit, the document itself contains the data; there is no choice to be made, as model and controller are one object.

Yet a third architecture can be used: You can make the document a controller and yet keep the model pure by having the data objects call routines in the controller, which then interact with the platform or framework. This is a more complex structure, but it does keep the input/output routines out of the data model.

Each of these architectures is justified, and each has been used both in demonstrations and in production software. Some of the choices are a matter of flipping a coin; others are influenced by whether you are writing for multiple frameworks or classes. The architecture used in Diary and Sketch seems to strike a happy medium: It is highly structured, yet it is not so complicated that it cannot be modified and maintained. It also avoids a problem that the all-in-one approach of TextEdit sometimes has: By mixing model and controller functionality, you can lose sight of which is which and it can be more difficult to modify the software. (As an exercise, try to find where the data in TextEdit is stored.)

Thus, in Diary, you will find that the document object has a reference to a single DiaryData object; in turn, that object has an array of DiaryEntry objects. As you will see in Chapter 18, this structure requires that the entire data structure be initialized when a new empty document is opened: A DiaryData object with an array of one DiaryEntry is created.

A Walk-Through of the Diary Classes

In both Java and Objective-C, there are three primary classes in Diary. They are described throughout this part of the book, but this walk-through shows you what they are and what their primary methods are.

The classes are:

1. DiaryDocument—the document

2. DiaryData—the contents of the diary as a whole, including a list of entries

3. DiaryEntry—each of the entries within DiaryData

Here are the major sets of methods in these classes. Methods within them are described throughout this part of the book. (Not all methods are listed here.)

DiaryDocument

DiaryDocument is the main document; it is the File's Owner object in Interface Builder, and it is the object for which actions and outlets are exposed in Interface Builder.

Constructors and Initializers for the Class These are the standard Objective-C and Java routines you would expect.

Support for Document and Window Creation As the Interface Builder document window is loaded at run time, `windowNibName` and `windowControllerDidLoadNib` are called. The latter method is called at the end of window creation, which is where most interface elements are initialized and fields are set.

Interface Support Actions   The basic action methods include `addEntry`, `deleteEntry`, `stepEntryForward`, `stepEntryBackward` and `toggleDrawer`. They are connected to menus in Interface Builder and they are dynamically connected to toolbar items at run time.

Accessors and Changers   As the highest-level object in the application, this object is connected to interface fields. Accessors retrieve data for the interface; changers change data and dirty the document.

Updates, Changes, and Dirtinesss   A critical role of documents is to manage changes, updates, and dirtiness so that documents are saved when needed and the display is redrawn when appropriate. Methods such as `isDocumentEdited`, `updateChangeCount`, and `diaryDataDidChange` do this.

Persistence (Storage)   The objects in the document and its subsidiary objects need to be flattened into a form that can be written to disk: `moveFieldsToDiaryData` moves data from the interface elements into data objects, and then `createDiaryDictionary` and `diaryDocumentData` provide a data object to be written out by `dataRepresentationOfType`.

Persistance (Retrieval)   In the other direction, `loadDataRepresentation` reads data and passes it on to `diaryDictionaryFromData`, from whence `loadFieldsFromDiaryData` moves it into the interface.

Toolbar   Three toolbar delegate methods are implemented to support the toolbar: `toolbarAllowedItemIdentifiers`, `toolbarDefaultItemIdentifiers`, and `toolbarItemForItemIdentifier`.

DiaryData

Following are the sets of methods for the main data model class, DiaryData.

Constructors and Initializers for the Class As in DiaryDocument (and most other objects), these are the methods you would expect.

Accessors These methods set and get data from the object's variables. Note that this application structure places changers and managers of document dirtiness at the highest level; some Apple document architectures place changers at the lowest (model) level.

Action Support These methods are called by the actions from the document. They are not Interface Builder actions themselves (which are in DiaryDocument), but rather methods such as `addEntry`, `deleteEntry`, `stepEntryForward`, and `stepEntryBackward`.

Changes One method—`didChange`—is called to generate a notification that is propagated up to the DiaryDocument class (and anyone else who may be interested in it).

Persistence (Storage) The `loadDiaryToDictionary` method is called from the DiaryDocument `createDiaryDictionary` method.

Persistence (Retrieval) The `unloadFromDictionary` method is called from the DiaryDocument `diaryDictionaryFromData` method.

DiaryEntry

Within the DiaryData object, a set of individual DiaryEntry objects is created. Following are the primary methods for that class.

Constructors and Initializers for the Class These, too, are the methods you would expect.

Accessors   These methods get and set instance variables. The note in the previous section about changers applies here, too.

Persistence (Storage)   The `propertyListRepresentation` method creates a new dictionary object and populates it with this entry's data. Each DataEntry object generates its own dictionary; all of these dictionaries are consolidated into a Diary-wide dictionary.

Persistence (Retrieval)   From the DiaryData `unloadFrom-Dictionary` method, the static (Java) or class (Objective-C) method `entryFromPropertyListRepresentation` is called to create a new entry; it, in turn, calls `loadProperty-ListRepresentation` to load the instance variables for that entry.

Using NSApplication

The application object in Cocoa runs everything. You rarely override the default application class. Whether you are writing in Java or Objective-C, main.m is the same:

```
int main(int argc, const char *argv[])
{
    return NSApplicationMain(argc, argv);

}
```

NSApp—The Application Object

A global NSApplication object (called NSApp) is created and run. In addition, the main nib file is loaded. As you saw in Part II, this allows an application to be launched and to execute if it uses nothing but the standard Cocoa objects (and you can do quite a lot with just them). However, if you need to perform computations or calculations, or if you need to store and retrieve data, you will need to implement your own custom classes. If a nib file encounters a customized object—such as a view or an override of NSDocument—the appropriate objects are instantiated using the code that you have written, and action methods are called as needed based on the interface activity.

What this means is that if you want any code that you have written to execute after the launch, it must be sparked by a custom object's activity (and that activity can be no more than its display in a window that was opened from the main nib file).

Unlike in some other frameworks (such as MacApp), you do not override the basic application object. You have your code invoked by attaching it to an object that is displayed in the first window that opens. This is not nearly so complicated as it may sound—it is rather obvious. It is a very rare case in which you want to execute code in the context of a graphical user interface without some visible manifestation of that code. If someone opens a document from within your application (or drags a document onto the application icon), the user expects a window to appear. Sure enough, Cocoa creates a document, opens a window, and links the two if you are using the basic template from Project Builder. Doing something automatically behind the user's back and without a window to report on the activity violates most user interface guidelines.

Application Delegation

Some programmers do feel the need to manipulate the application object. In Cocoa, the way to do that is to attach a delegate to the NSApp object. Like behaviors in MacApp, delegates get a chance to respond to events or messages that are sent to the primary object; any of the delegated methods can be called from your custom object. Unlike with some Cocoa delegates, you can implement as many or as few of the NSApplication delegate interface methods as you want. Construct a descendant of NSObject (that is, any Cocoa object), and implement whatever you want. Then attach that object to NSApp in Interface Builder. Alternatively, you can use the following code.

In Java:

```
NSApp.setDelegate (yourObject);
```

In Objective-C:

```
[NSApp setDelegate:yourObject];
```

The NSApplication delegation methods are shown in Table 17-1. As you can see, they focus on being able to instruct the application (through its delegate) to automatically open or print files, to indicate if it should open files in response to a user request, and to terminate. There is not much else that the application object can do that you should want to influence. Of course, you can call methods of NSApp at any time if you want to do so. Normally, you do not do so except to get references to a key window or other global entity. Even in those cases, you normally work with more general methods, as you will see later in this book.

Table 17-1. NSApplication Delegate Methods

Java	Objective-C
`public abstract boolean applicationOpenFile (NSApplication theApplication, String fileName)`	`- (BOOL)application: (NSApplication *)sender openFile: (NSString *)filename`
`public abstract boolean applicationOpenFile- WithoutUI (Object sender, String fileName)`	`- (BOOL)application: (id)sender openFileWithoutUI: (NSString *)filename`
`public abstract boolean applicationOpenTempFile (NSApplication theApplication, String fileName)`	`- (BOOL)application: (NSApplication *)sender openTempFile: (NSString *)filename`

Table 17-1. NSApplication Delegate Methods (Continued)

Java	Objective-C
| ```
public abstract boolean
  applicationOpenUntitled-
  File
    (NSApplication
    theApplication)
``` | ```
- (BOOL)applicationOpenUn-
  titledFile:
    (NSApplication *)sender
``` |
| ```
public abstract boolean
applicationPrintFile
    (NSApplication
    theApplication,
    String fileName)
``` | ```
- (BOOL)application:
(NSApplication *)sender
    printFile:
    (NSString *)filename
``` |
| ```
public abstract boolean
applicationShouldHandle-
  Reopen
    (NSApplication
    theApplication,
    boolean flag)
``` | ```
- (BOOL)applicationShoul-
  dHandleReopen:
    (NSApplication *)sender
  hasVisibleWindows:
    (BOOL)flag
``` |
| ```
public abstract boolean
applicationShouldOpen-
  UntitledFile
    (NSApplication
    theApplication)
``` | ```
- (BOOL)applicationShoul-
  dOpenUntitledFile:
    (NSApplication *)sender
``` |
| ```
public abstract int
applicationShouldTerminate

Return values are 0 (ter-
  minate immediately), 1
  (cancel a termination
  request), and 2 (wait
  for a call to replyToAp-
  plicationShouldTermi-
  nate before proceeding)
``` | ```
- (NSApplicationTermina-
  teReply)
  applicationShouldTermi-
  nate:
    (NSApplication *)sender

NSApplicationTerminateRe-
  ply values are:
NSTerminateNow, NSTermi-
  nateCancel, and NSTermi-
  nateLater
``` |
| ```
public abstract boolean
applicationShouldTerm-
  nateAfterLastWindow-
  Closed
    (NSApplication
    theApplication)
``` | ```
- (BOOL)applicationShould-
  TerminateAfterLastWin-
  dowClosed:
    (NSApplication *)sender
``` |

**Application
Notifications**

Delegates get a chance to respond to messages sent to the application object (or, if you prefer the terminology, they can respond to calls on the application object's methods). The Cocoa notification system fills in the other side of the process: It allows the application object to communicate outwards to objects that have registered as wanting to be notified about events. (The notification system is described more fully in "Notification" starting on page 404.)

Delegation and notification remove most of the legitimate reasons for overriding NSApplication; the messages and methods that cannot be accessed through those structures should very rarely be overridden. NSApplication methods can be accessed directly by using the global NSApp object. They are not overridden, and the most frequently used methods are those that return shared objects. However, remember that you are likely to be able to get access to those objects (windows, for example), through objects such as window controllers that automatically are attached to your document.

The NSApplication notifications are shown in Table 17-2. Their names are generally self-explanatory; more details are available in the Cocoa electronic documentation both online and on the CD-ROM. As you can see, these notifications are sent primarily when the application is being hidden or unhidden, launched, or terminated. There also is a notification that is sent when the screen parameters change. In general, these notifications are needed for you to be able to update windows that need to be changed to reflect environmental changes rather than user actions. (One attractive feature of the notification system is that if you do need to know when one of these events has taken place, you no longer need to search in the framework code to see which application method is called at that time and how to override it. Even if future releases of the framework move processing from one method to another, the notifications will still be generated.)

Table 17-2. NSApplication Notifications

```
applicationDidBecomeActive

applicationDidHide

applicationDidFinishLaunching

applicationDidResignActive

applicationDidUnhide

applicationDidUpdate

applicationWillBecomeActive

applicationWillHide

applicationWillFinishLaunching

applicationWillResignActive

applicationWillUnhide

applicationWillUpdate

applicationWillTerminate

applicationDidChangeScreenParameters
```

Applications in Carbon and Classic

You may need to modify legacy MacApp applications or adapt them to Cocoa or Carbon. MacApp handles application objects differently from Cocoa. Also, you may be called upon to handle non-framework applications from legacy applications. There, too, the application structure is different.

MacApp and TApplication

In the Nothing example, the smallest subclass of TApplication is created: a constructor, a destructor, and an override of `Do-MakeDocument` that creates the document (and thence the window).

In `main`, a small section of code creates the customized TNothingApplication object and then runs it (`InitUMacApp` initializes MacApp itself).

```
InitUMacApp(3);// Initialize MacApp; 3 calls to
  MoreMasters

TNothingApplication aNothingApplication;
aNothingApplication.Run();
```

The C++ constructor is called when the object is created:

```
TNothingApplication::TNothingApplication() :
  TApplication(kFileType, kSignature)
{
// So we can create the view object by name and
// So my view will be substituted when MacApp® cre-
  ates the "default view"
REGISTER_SIGNATURE_AC(TDefaultView, kStdDefault-
  View);
}
```

This constructor relies on templates to create the view for the Nothing example. In practice, you can either do that or programmatically create a view by overriding `TDocument.Do-MakeViews` when you override TDocument for your own document. In some cases, both practices are followed.

The destructor is empty, but the `DoMakeDocument` override is not:

```
TDocument* TNothingApplication::
  DoMakeDocument(CommandNumber, TFile* itsFile)
{
#pragma unused (itsFile)
return TH_new TDocument;
}
```

You must override `DoMakeDocument` to create a document for your application. In this case, a standard TDocument is created; in almost all other cases, you create your own document—something like a TMyDocument. (Remember that this example focuses on the smallest possible MacApp program, not the most useful one!)

Compared to Cocoa, these differences emerge:

1. Always subclass the application object (TApplication) in MacApp; rarely, if ever, do so in Cocoa.

2. Standard objects such as windows and views are created automatically from your nib file in Cocoa (the nib file is almost always built in Interface Builder). In MacApp, they are created programmatically (in overrides of `TDocument.DoMakeViews`) or from templates.

3. As you have subclassed TApplication, it is easy to override any of its methods to gain access to the application at critical points; with Cocoa, do so with delegation and notification.

Applications without Frameworks

Applications built without frameworks have yet another structure—in fact, two of them. The typical `main` function does some initialization; it then contains the main event loop or it calls a function that runs the event loop. In the older architecture, this is based on `WaitNextEvent`. In the Carbon direct-dispatch structure it is done differently. The Carbon direct-dispatch structure was described in "Direct Dispatching with Carbon Events" starting on page 157.

It is unlikely that you will be writing a new application from scratch that uses the old style of event dispatching (`WaitNextEvent`). But it is quite possible that you will have to read or modify legacy applications, and for that reason you need to know how events were handled in them. Here is `main` from the NetSprocketsTest example that you can download from the Apple Developer site:

```
void main(void)
{
OSErrerr;
short m = 5;

SIOUXSettings.autocloseonquit = true;
SIOUXSettings.asktosaveonclose = true;
SIOUXSettings.initializeTB = false;
SIOUXSettings.setupmenus = false;
SIOUXSettings.standalone = false;

MaxApplZone();

for (;m == 0;m--) // alloc the master pointers
  {
  MoreMasters();
  }

  err = Initialize();

  EventLoop();

  ShutdownNetworking();

  AERemove();
  ExitToShell();

}
```

The `EventLoop` function (underlined) is called and remains in an infinite loop until the user quits as you can see here:

```
void EventLoop(void)
{
EventRecordevent;

gDone = false;
while (! gDone)
  {
  WaitNextEvent(everyEvent, &event, 60, nil);

  // go ahead and handle the event just
```

```
// in case we have and idle
DoEvent(&event);


    }
}
```

The underlined function does the actual dispatching; its beginning is shown here:

```
void DoEvent(EventRecord *event)
{
  OSErrerr;
  shortkind;
  longmenuChoice;
  PointthePoint;
  Booleanactive;
  WindowRefwindow;

  window = FrontWindow();

  SIOUXHandleOneEvent(event);

  switch(event->what)
  {
    case nullEvent:
    HandleNetwork();
    break;

    case mouseDown:
    HandleMouseDown(event);
    break;

    case mouseUp:
    break;

    ...
```

This example was written in 1996. Note how the amount of application-handling code you need to write has decreased from that time—first with the MacApp framework and then with Cocoa (where you do not have to write any such code).

The structure of the application that is shown here is fairly standard for older non-framework Macintosh applications. Thus, if you need to modify or convert such a program, go immediately to `main`, find the event loop (or the call of the event loop function), and track down the event-dispatching code. Much of it will be handled by the framework (MacApp or Cocoa), because most of it is involved with moving windows, manipulating menus, and the like. Search out the application-specific code, and you will see what you need to modify or convert to Cocoa.

With the advent of Carbon, direct dispatching of events is now the preferred method of handling them.

Summary

This chapter has provided an architectural overview of applications—both in Cocoa and in Carbon (for MacApp and for non-framework applications). It also has shown you the structure of the Diary application and of its data—this example will be used extensively throughout this part of the book.

This overview sets the stage for the remaining chapters in this part of the book. You need to know what the application object can do for you, but now you need to see what tools are available for it to use. Then, you can come back and implement the application properly.

From the overview of the application, the next chapter focuses on the smallest units: the building blocks and data elements that you use.

Chapter 18
Building Blocks and Types

From the large architectural and application overview of the previous chapter, this chapter moves to the lowest level: the building blocks and basic types of Cocoa and Carbon. It starts by outlining the steps you can take to create a data strategy and ways that you can use this strategy to help you build a prototype and then progressively more complete versions of your application.

Next, you will find an introduction to the basic types of Mac OS X, along with information about how to create them programmatically. (There are significant differences between Cocoa and Carbon as well as between Java and Objective-C.)

Among the most useful building blocks of Mac OS X are collections—arrays, dictionaries, and sets. These can be immutable (that is, they are of fixed size and contents), or they can be mutable. All are described here.

Property lists provide a convenient way of storing information; they work together with XML to manage information without your needing to worry about formats and field widths. They are implemented using the dictionaries described in this chapter.

Preferences (Carbon) and defaults (Cocoa) pull together even more of these technologies to help you provide customization for specific applications, specific users, and specific computer environments.

A section showing you how to create objects in Objective-C and Java concludes the chapter.

Creating a Data Strategy

Data modeling, data strategy, and normalization are all terms that refer to the same basic concept: creating a coherent view of the data in your project. As noted Chapter 17, the first and most crucial step is understanding the data you must deal with.

Experienced developers do not just take a user's word as to what the data is: They look at samples of the data. Look for patterns, and look for anomalies. If something seems wrong, it may be a legacy of an old system—or it may be that you or the user does not fully understand the data.

The following slight paraphrase of an actual conversation is presented without comment. Experienced developers may smile ruefully—or top it with their own experiences. "Ninety-nine doesn't mean 99: we use it to indicate 'No Answer.' It's OK, because we use 65 to mean 80 or greater, so a real value of 99 would be coded as 80, unless it was missing, in which case it would be 99."

Once you feel comfortable with the data, you need to develop and implement your data strategy. Three steps are key to this process:

1. Factoring data and interface elements

2. Fishing data through the objects

3. Implementing the strategy

Factoring Data and Interface Elements

Whether or not you use the model-view-controller paradigm as your guide, it is important to separate interface elements from data elements. The consequence of this is that your code can be transported from one platform or framework to another; it also means that you can incorporate external code (in C or another language) easily. Keep a solid wall between the customizations of your environment and the substantial reality of the data.

When you use Interface Builder, it is easy to create a simple application as well as interfaces to even complex ones. As you saw in "Outlets" on page 115, it is easy to connect interface elements to fields in your customized code. You can then write that code to use the data accordingly.

However, remember that Interface Builder lets you connect to the interface elements. Although you can use them to store data (and, in fact, they must store data at least temporarily to display it), for most applications, you need to move the data from the interface elements into local variables (fields of your objects).

Here, for example, is code that does the following:

1. Declares a text field in an object

2. Declares a data field in that object

3. Sets the text field to the data field's value

4. Retrieves its value—which may have been changed by the user

This code is based on the Diary code. It is simplified, and intervening lines have been removed.

Here is the Java code:

```
private NSTextView notesField; //1
private String _notes; //2
notesField.setString (_notes); //3
_notes = (notesField.string()); //4
```

Here is the same code in Objective-C:

```
IBOutlet NSTextView *notesField; //1
NSString * _notes; //2
[notesField setString:[ _notes]]; //3
[_notes:[notesField string]]; //4
```

At this degree of simplicity, there is no substantive difference between having a separate variable (_notes) and using the text field (notesField) to store the data: After all, you can always use the string message/function to retrieve that data. But remember that if you want to separate the interface elements from the substantive elements, you want to keep objects such as the text view out of the model.

A simple (and very common) example of why this is useful occurs when you change the type of the interface element. You can place a string in a text field or a text view (the text view scrolls and is suitable for longer text). If you write your code using a string variable such as _notes, it is a trivial matter to change the interface element; however, if you carry the text field or the text view into your calculations, you will need to make adjustments. In particular, although text fields respond to the stringValue message/function, text views do not: You must use string instead.

Even more important is the case in which your interface elements must represent different data at different times. In the

Diary example, for instance, the window contains the data for whatever diary entry is current. Users can click the Next and Previous buttons to move back and forth in the diary. As they do, the data for the then-current entry is placed into the interface elements. If the data itself is stored in the interface elements, you could have only one set of data displayed. (You could, of course, have multiple copies of the interface elements and move them into and out of the display window, but this would be awkward, inefficient, and slow. You will find some programs that do this, but it is a poor choice.)

Fishing Data Through the Objects

The name of the actual data field starts with an underscore. Any such convention is good (this one is particularly common). It reminds programmers that this is private, internal data that should normally be accessed through an accessor—as the next section shows you.

Implementing Accessors Accessors let objects set or retrieve data without the programmer having to worry about how it is stored. Here, the third and fourth lines in the previous example are rewritten using accessors.

Java:

```
this.setEntryNotes (notesField.string()); //3
notesField.setString (this.entryNotes()); //4
```

Objective-C:

```
[self setEntryNotes:[notesField string]]; //3
[notesField setString:[self entryNotes]]; //4
```

The entryNotes and setEntryNotes methods are simple accessors that hide the variable _notes from view. Here is their code:

Java:

```
public String entryNotes () {
  return _notes;
}
```

```
public void setEntryNotes (String theNotes){
  _notes = theNotes;
}
```

Objective-C:

```
- (NSString*)entryNotes
{
  return _notes;
}

- (void)setEntryNotes: (NSString *)theNotes;
{
  _notes = theNotes;
}
```

One issue that arises with the use of accessors is that of dirtying the underlying document—that is, requiring it to be saved when it is closed. If accessors dirty a document, they cannot be used for setting values that do not dirty the document, such as when an existing document is reread from disk and its values need to be set to the stored—undirtied—data.

A good way around this issue is to use accessors only to access data and changers (or whatever you want to call them) to dirty the document and call the accessor.

Combining Accessors with Factored Objects When you combine these accessors with the DiaryData and DiaryEntry objects described in Chapter 17, you get the actual code that is used in Diary, as you can see in the following code snippets. The accessors just shown become methods of a subsidiary object (theDiary—an instance of DataDiary in this step), and the data element itself (_notes) is declared there:

Java:

```
theDiary.setEntryNotes
  (notesField.string()); //3
```

```
notesField.setString
  (theDiary.entryNotes()); //4
```

Objective-C:

```
[theDiary setEntryNotes:[notesField string]]; //3
[notesField setString:[theDiary entryNotes]]; //4
```

This may seem like a lot of effort, but in practice it is simple. You will quickly get used to accessors if you are not used to them now. Your code will be more stable and maintainable, and it will be easy for you to develop prototypes quickly.

The process of using accessors in this way is like that of fishing a cable through a wall or behind furniture: Its course may be serpentine, but the end result is well crafted.

Implementing the Strategy

In fact, the sequence of steps in the previous section provide a roadmap to quick and accurate software development. If you know that you will be structuring your data in this way, you can start by declaring the data elements in your most basic class (your MyDocument object in most cases). This is the wrong place for them, but you know that you will move them.

Create accessors in that class that access the data element by name—as in `_notes = theNotes`. Except for the references within these accessors, never use the variables directly. Instead, use your accessors. This will allow you to prototype the interface using Interface Builder. You may finish the interface, but more likely you and your users will take some time to work with it, tweak it, and experiment with using it.

Meanwhile, implement the next portion of your data strategy. In Diary, that involved creating both the DiaryData and the DiaryEntry objects. Create a DiaryData object when your document is initialized, and then place the declarations of these variables in that object (remembering to remove them from the document object). In addition to the declarations, create accessors in the subsidiary object. Then, change the code in your document to use the accessors rather than the variables directly. That means changing

```
_notes = theNotes;
```

to

```
theDiary.setNotes (theNotes);
```

Once you have done that, your document object is free of the knowledge of the variables that you temporarily inserted in it (and your prototype should still work).

Of course, the DiaryDocument object contains a DiaryEntry object, which is where the actual _notes field should live. Follow the same process again. Create a DiaryEntry object when you initialize the DiaryData object. Declare _notes there, and write accessors for it. Then, in DiaryData, remove the direct references to _notes and replace them with calls to the DiaryEntry object's accessors.

In DiaryDocument, you will have this code:

```
theDiary.setNotes (theNotes); //Java
[theDiary setNotes: theNotes]; //Objective-C
```

In DiaryData, you will have the following:

```
theDiaryEntry.setNotes (theNotes); //Java
[theDiaryEntry setNotes; theNotes]; //Objective-C
```

You are not done yet—the DiaryData object still contains a number of DiaryEntry objects. Use the same process to convert a local variable (theDiaryEntry) to use an accessor. The accessor you will create in DiaryData returns one DiaryEntry object—the current one. (How that is determined will be described elsewhere.)

You can thus rewrite the two lines of code as follows:

```
(currentEntry()).setNotes (theNotes); //Java
```

```
[[self currentEntry]setNotes: theNotes];
 //Objective-C
```

You gradually move the actual variable declarations deeper and deeper into your data structure. As you do so, the accessors change in the same way at each level:

1. They start out in the document class accessing the variable (_notes) directly; that variable is also declared there.

2. You move the variable down one level, and you change the accessor to call an accessor at the lower level.

You continue this process until the data elements are located where they belong.

The use of accessors is normally presented as a way of making your code "pure" and implementing architectures such as model-view-controller. In practice, you can use accessors as shown here to help get an early version of your code up and running quickly.

Some people point out that all of these accessors use processor time to execute; they can make an application program sluggish. While theoretically true, in practice accessors add very little overhead to a program. There is one exception to this. If the accessors run across a network so that those calls involve telecommunications, they can be unacceptable. For non-networked applications (or for those in which the data and accessors are on a single computer), the delays are not significant.

Basic Types and Objects

Armed with a data strategy and your accessor-based design, you are ready to actually declare and use variables. Mac OS X provides a number of basic types in both the Cocoa and Carbon environments.

You may be used to writing code and using the types of Java and the C languages directly. You will find that the types declared in the Foundation framework (Cocoa) and in the Core Foundation (Carbon) are more powerful than the raw types. Specifically, you will find that these objects provide you with the ability to read and write them, compare them, and transform them without writing much of the code once had to write.

The very simplest types—integers and booleans—are not wrapped in these foundation classes. All other basic types are.

In Cocoa, these are all classes. In the Apple C++ frameworks and Core Foundation when running on Mac OS X, they generally wrap the Cocoa classes in C++. You use them as if they were objects, but they may not be. Thus, in this section, the terms type and object are used interchangeably.

Collections

In addition to the simple data types described in the previous section, Mac OS X provides a number of more sophisticated tools. These range from the collections, property lists, and preferences described in the remaining sections of this chapter to data types and objects that are designed for specific purposes (such as visualization). The latter types and objects are described later in this part of the book.

Collections let you handle groups of objects as a single entity. Traditional programming structures let you handle a basic collection—arrays. *Dictionaries* provide a powerful feature of Cocoa and of Carbon: You can place entries into them and identify each entry with a key. Unlike the ordered, numeric keys of arrays, keys of dictionaries are strings and are not ordered. Finally, *sets* let you place entries into an unordered, unkeyed set—just like a mathematical or logical set (in fact, exactly like such a set).

Arrays

Arrays are based on the NSArray class; they function just as arrays do in standard programming languages. However, they provide a number of additional features:

- The `containsObject` method returns true if an object is in the array—you do not have to iterate through and test each element until you find a match.

- Given an object, `indexOfObject` returns its index in the array (a RangeException is thrown if the object is not in the array). Again, this saves you writing iteration code.

- If you do need to iterate through an array, you can use the `objectEnumerator` (or `reverseObjectEnumerator`) method to return an enumerator (in Java or Objective-C).

- As you might expect, a `count` method returns the number of elements in the array.

One of the differences between these arrays and traditional arrays is that they need not be typed—they contain objects. If it makes sense to you, you can create an array that contains decimal numbers, instantiations of custom classes, and images.

Dictionaries

Arrays provide ordered and numbered access to collections of objects; dictionaries use keys. Each key is a value that can be hashed (usually a string), and it is paired with any object that you want. Like arrays, dictionaries can contain dissimilar objects, provided that they all descend from a basic object (such as NSObject in Objective-C or Object in Java).

Dictionaries provide some functionality similar to that of arrays in these commonly used methods:

- The `count` method returns the number of key/value pairs in the dictionary.

- Given a string containing a key, `objectForKey` returns the appropriate object (if it exists).

- Two methods—`keyEnumerator` and `objectEnumerator`—return enumerators that iterate through keys and objects, respectively.

Dictionaries are useful for storing large and small amounts of data. As Sketch (and Diary) demonstrate, they are particularly useful for storing a handful of data values for objects in an application. Rather than worry about formatting or tagging data to identify it, you can simply store an object's data in a dictionary. The entire dictionary can be converted to a property list (see "Property Lists" on page 384) and the property list, in turn, can easily be stored on and retrieved from disk. Each of the objects in your application has its own dictionary.

Here is how Diary unloads data from a dictionary (it is modeled on Sketch). There are three steps involved:

1. Create constants for the dictionary keys (that is, constants to identify the data you will store).

2. Declare your local variables.

3. Unload the dictionary.

Because dictionaries have unique keys, this architecture works very well if each object that you are storing has the same set of unduplicated data. It is even more efficient when the objects you are storing have some of the same data elements (in other words, some might have a background color, others might not). It does not work if the objects might have multiple entries for a key. If you can create multiple keys (rather than multiple entries), it will work. Thus, instead of a "phone" key, you might have "home," "work," and so forth.

Create Constants for Keys You can hard-code the keys for your dictionary entries in your program. In fact, it is a good idea to do so. In Java, place them at the top of your Java class file like this:

```
private static final String entryIDKey =
  "entryID";
private static final String entryTitleKey =
  "entryTitle";
```

In Objective-C, you can define these constants at the top of your .m file (not the .h header file): that is because they are totally private and no other part of the application should know about them.

```
NSString *entryIDKey = @"entryID";
NSString *entryTitleKey = @"entryTitle";
```

Other key constants are declared in Diary in the same way as these.

Declare Local Variables Although they are not part of dictionary maintenance, you will need local variables into which to unload the dictionary. Following are the declarations from Diary.

Java:

```
private String _ID;
private String _title;
private String _subtitle;
private String _summary;
private NSData _entry;
private String _notes;
private NSImage _image;
private String _creationDate;
private String _modificationDate;
```

Objective-C:

```
@private
  NSString * _ID;
  NSString * _title;
  NSString * _subtitle;
  NSString * _summary;
  NSData * _entry;
  NSString * _notes;
  NSImage * _image;
  NSString * _creationDate;
  NSString * _modificationDate;
```

Set Local Variables from the Dictionary   When you have read the dictionary in from storage, you can unload it into your local variables. The following code snippets show you how you can do that. There are two issues that you should note in particular:

1.   This code does not use accessors; it refers directly to the local variables. Some people prefer not to use accessors for this low-level initialization of variables; others use accessors in all cases—both for low-level initialization as well as for data entry and ongoing changes during run time.

2.   The variables that represent simple data types such as strings are set directly. This dictionary (like that of Sketch) contains an image. For such objects, you need to declare a local variable such as obj, test to see that it exists, and then set it. If you do not do so, you may wind up passing a null object to the NSUnarchiver method that does the unarchiving. (For more on archiving, see "Archiving" starting on page 475.)

Java:

```
Object obj;

_ID = (String)dict.objectForKey(entryIDKey);
_title = (String)dict.objectForKey(entryTitleKey);
```

```
_subtitle = (String)dict.objectForKey
  (entrySubtitleKey);

_summary = (String)dict.objectForKey
  (entrySummaryKey);
_entry = (NSData)dict.objectForKey(entryEntryKey);
_notes = (String)dict.objectForKey(entryNotesKey);
_creationDate = (String)dict.
  objectForKey(creationDateKey);
_modificationDate = (String)dict.
  objectForKey(modificationDateKey);
obj = dict.objectForKey(entryImageKey);
if (obj != null) {
  _image = (NSImage) NSUnarchiver.
    unarchiveObjectWithData((NSData)obj);
}
```

Objective-C:

```
id obj;

_ID = (NSString *)[dict objectForKey:entryIDKey];
_title = (NSString *)
  [dict objectForKey:entryTitleKey];
_subtitle = (NSString *)
  [dict objectForKey:entrySubtitleKey];
_summary = (NSString *)
  [dict objectForKey:entrySummaryKey];
_entry = (NSString *)
  [dict objectForKey:entryEntryKey];
_notes = (NSString *)
  [dict objectForKey:entryNotesKey];
_creationDate = (NSString *)
  [dict objectForKey:creationDateKey];
_modificationDate = (NSString *)
  [dict objectForKey:modificationDateKey];
obj = [dict objectForKey:entryImageKey];
if (obj) {
  _image = (NSImage *)
    [NSUnarchiver unarchiveObjectWithData:obj];
}
```

Note that the Dictionary Manager is used to manage the natural language dictionaries for spell-checking. Dictionaries are implemented with the Cocoa NSDictionary object and with CFDictionary routines in Carbon.

Sets

In addition to arrays and dictionaries, sets provide unordered, unidentified collections of objects. They, too, have the common methods you would expect:

- You can count the number of elements in a set with `count`.

- To manipulate the elements of a set, you may want to use `allObjects`, which returns the set as an array.

- One of the most basic set operations is determining whether an object is a member of a set; `containsObject` does this.

Mutable Collections

Each of the objects described here is immutable in its basic form. That is, you can initialize it from a file, array, or other data structure, but you can then neither add to it nor remove items from it. In both Cocoa and Carbon, companions to NSArray, NSDictionary, and NSSet let you modify them; they are named NSMutableArray, NSMutableDictionary, and NSMutableSet.

When you are reading data from a file, you may build a mutable collection. However, once you are finished reading, you can pass it along as an immutable object for other purposes. In addition, if you are repeatedly storing data into a collection, you obviously need to make it mutable.

Here is the other side of the dictionary unloading process just described: the code in Diary that loads a dictionary prior to writing it out. First, a new mutable dictionary is created; then the various data fields are stored with the declared keys. Note the special treatment of the `_image` object.

Java:

```
NSMutableDictionary dict =
  new NSMutableDictionary();

dict.setObjectForKey(_ID,entryIDKey);
dict.setObjectForKey(_title,entryTitleKey);
dict.setObjectForKey(_subtitle,entrySubtitleKey);
dict.setObjectForKey(_summary,entrySummaryKey);
dict.setObjectForKey(_entry,entryEntryKey);
dict.setObjectForKey(_notes,entryNotesKey);
dict.setObjectForKey(_creationDate,creation-
  DateKey);
dict.setObjectForKey(_modificationDate,
  modificationDateKey);
if (_image != null) {
  dict.setObjectForKey(NSArchiver.
    archivedDataWithRootObject(_image),
    entryImageKey);
}
return dict;
```

Objective-C:

```
NSMutableDictionary *dict = [NSMutableDictionary
  dictionary];

[dict setObject:_ID forKey:entryIDKey];
[dict setObject:_title forKey:entryTitleKey];
[dict setObject:_subtitle
  forKey:entrySubtitleKey];
[dict setObject:_summary forKey:entrySummaryKey];
[dict setObject:_entry forKey:entryEntryKey];
[dict setObject:_notes forKey:entryNotesKey];
[dict setObject:_creationDate
  forKey:creationDateKey];
[dict setObject:_modificationDate
  forKey:modificationDateKey];
[dict setObject:
  [NSArchiver archivedDataWithRootObject:_image
  forKey:entryImageKey]];
return dict;
```

Property Lists

Property lists use XML to store pairs of property names and values. They are used pervasively in Mac OS X. Property lists with their property name/value pairs are similar to dictionaries. In fact, it is simple to convert a property list to a dictionary, and vice versa. On disk, a property list is often an editable XML text file; when you access it from a program, it is a standard NSDictionary.

You can use property lists to store dates, numbers, booleans, and strings. In addition, NSData or CFData types can be stored in them. Most importantly, arrays and dictionaries that contain those types can also be stored in property lists.

The diaryDocumentData method in the DiaryDocument class stores a dictionary into a property list which is then written out to disk (this is based on Sketch). Objective-C and Java differ in their handling of this process. In each case, the underlined code does the actual conversion from a dictionary to a string containing a property list.

In Objective-C, you can convert a dictionary into a property list by simply calling its description method:

```
- (NSData *)diaryDocumentData {
  NSDictionary *dict =
    [self createDiaryDictionary];
  NSString *string = [dict description];
  return [string
    dataUsingEncoding:NSASCIIStringEncoding];
}
```

The process is a little more complex in Java. The first line calls a method that contains code like that seen previously in this chapter: It creates a dictionary and stores objects into it using the data in local variables and the predefined keys. Next, a string property list is created from that dictionary. The remaining code (starting with NSMutableStringReference) is used to optimize Java bridge performance.

```
public NSData diaryDocumentData() {
  NSDictionary dict = createDiaryDictionary();
  String plistStr = NSPropertyListSerialization.
    stringFromPropertyList(dict);

  NSMutableStringReference mutStrRef =
    new NSMutableStringReference();
  NSData data;
  mutStrRef.setString(plistStr);
  data = mutStrRef.dataUsingEncoding
    (NSStringReference.ASCIIStringEncoding, false);
  return data;
}
```

On the opposite side, you can convert a string containing a property list into a dictionary. In Diary, the diaryDictionary-FromData method does this. It takes a data value as a parameter, converts it to a string, and then loads it into a dictionary. The underlined code does the actual conversion from the string containing the property list to the dictionary.

Java:

```
public NSDictionary diaryDictionaryFromData
  (NSData data) {
  NSStringReference strRef =
    new NSStringReference
      (data,
       NSStringReference.ASCIIStringEncoding);
  NSDictionary dict =
    (NSDictionary)NSPropertyListSerialization.
      propertyListFromString(strRef.string());
  return dict;
}
```

Objective-C:

```
- (NSDictionary *)diaryDictionaryFromData:
  (NSData *)data {
  NSString *string = [[NSString alloc]
    initWithData:data
    encoding:NSASCIIStringEncoding];
  NSDictionary *dict = [string propertyList];
  [string release];
  return dict;
}
```

Preferences and Defaults

Mac OS X uses property lists to store preferences and defaults for applications as well as to store information about them. The Core Foundation framework implements preferences and defaults; they are available both for Carbon and Cocoa applications.

Systemwide preferences and defaults are one of the most important aspects of the Mac OS X user experience. They help to make multiple users' experiences correct on a given computer. Also, they make a single user's experience correct when running in a networked environment. You may have implemented preferences and defaults on other platforms or on Mac OS 9 or earlier, but you should look at the Mac OS X structure because it will make your life (and your users' experiences) easier.

Default Domains

Five domains are used for defaults. When an application is searching for a default value, each of these domains is searched in turn.

Argument This domain contains values that can be entered on the command line in Terminal. They apply to the single execution of an application that is being invoked at that time.

Application An application can store its own default values and preferences. This domain is specific not only to an individual user. This information is stored in ~/Library/Preferences in each user's home directory.

GlobalDomain This domain contains global settings for each user. Such settings can include units of measurement as well as preferred languages (and their order of preference).

Languages In the languages domain, preferences for each language are stored. A user may specify (in the global domain) what language should be used at the moment; any number of languages may contain preferences that come into play if the user changes the language preference in the global domain.

Registration Preferences are set at the registration domain. This is created when an application is installed, and it is specific to the computer (not the user).

Preference Names

A variety of preference key names are predefined for your used. They include names such as CurrencySymbol (to specify $, £, or ¥, among other choices. Note that CurrencySymbol is independent of language settings. English speakers may well refer to yen (¥), just as Spanish speakers may refer to pounds (£).

A variety of date and time constants are available. Keys such as ThisDayDesignations (which let you specify the string to be used as the current day—"today," by default) let your application take advantage of a user's preferences.

Setting Preferences

You can set preferences at any time that you want. Normally, you do so either when the user clicks OK in a preferences dialog or when some information that you know should be saved is modified. (Sometimes the two interact, as when the preference is to save passwords, window locations, and so forth.)

Saving General Preferences Following is the code to save a preference that consists of a number or object. These snippets assume the following:

- `key` is a string constant that names the preference
- `val` is an object that contains the preference
- `longKey` is a string that names a second value which contains...
- `longVal`, a long value (not an object) that contains a second preference

In Carbon, you must pass your application's name (in the constant `kCFPreferencesCurrentApplication`) in to the functions; in Cocoa, the `standardUserDefaults` object is already set up properly.

Cocoa/Java:

```
NSUserDefaults defaults
  NSUserDefaults.standardUserDefaults();

//to remove a default value
defaults.removeObjectForKey (key);

//to add/change a default value
defaults.setObjectForKey (val, key);
defaults.setLongForKey (longVal, longKey);
```

Cocoa/Objective-C:

```
NSUserDefaults *defaults =
  [NSUserDefaults standardUserDefaults];

//to remove a default value
[defaults removeObjectForKey:key];

//to add/change a default value
[defaults setObject:val forKey:key];
[defaults setLong:longVal forKey:longKey];
```

Carbon:

```
CFPreferencesSetAppValue (key, val,
  kCFPreferencesCurrentApplication);
CFPreferencesSetAppValue (longKey, longVal,
  kCFPreferencesCurrentApplication);
CFPreferencesAppSynchronize (
  kCFPreferencesCurrentApplication);
```

As you might surmise, other similarly named methods let you save integers, floats, and the like.

The actual saving of preferences occurs when the Synchronize method is called. In Cocoa, it is called for you automatically in most cases. In Carbon, you need to call it explicitly as shown in this code.

Saving Window Positions   It is very common to want to save window positions. A method of NSWindow lets you do so automatically. It makes its own calls to the preferences manager automatically whenever a window is moved.

Java:

```
myWindow.setFrameAutoSaveName ("Data Entry");
```

Objective-C:

```
[myWindow setFrameAutoSaveName:@"Data Entry"];
```

Pass the name of the window into the method, and Cocoa will take care of everything for you. The window name must be unique; otherwise there is no way of keeping preferences straight.

Using Preferences

Having saved preferences, you need to retrieve them. Following is the code to do so in both Java and Objective-C. If you are saving default data, one useful place to insert this code is in your NSDocument override of windowDidLoadNib; it is called after the nib is loaded and before it is displayed, so that is the right time to set text fields and the like.

Cocoa/Java:

```
NSUserDefaults defaults =
  NSUserDefaults.standardUserDefaults();
NSString val = defaults.stringForKey (myKey);
```

Cocoa/Objective-C:

```
NSUserDefaults *defaults = [
  NSUserDefaults standardUserDefaults];
NSString *val = [defaults stringForKey:myKey];
```

Carbon:

```
CFStringRef val = CFPreferencesCopyAppValue
  (myKey, kCFPreferencesCurrentApplication
```

Creating Objects

There are some important differences between Java and Objective-C relating to the way in which objects are created. The code snippets in this section demonstrate some of them.

The snippets also demonstrate a programming style that you may or may not want to emulate. Some programming languages (such as Java and Objective-C) initialize variables to appropriate defaults—usually 0 or null/nil. Other programming variables leave uninitialized variables just like that—with no value. This is one of those topics that can raise a fierce argument among programmers. On one side is the position that it is wrong—morally wrong—for a compiler or operating system to interfere in any way with a programmer's code (and that includes setting default values). On the other side is the argument that the compiler or operating system should try to catch errors or clean up code (such as mistakes that arise from uninitialized variables).

Regardless of which side of the argument you take (if any), you may want to initialize your variables as shown here. As you can see, in most cases, they are initialized to neutral but nonzero values (such as "entry title"). This means that when you are debugging your code, you can use the debugger to check the values of variables and watch as they change from 0 (which the compiler and operating system set) to your default value (such as the values here) and then to a real value.

In practice, as soon as this method is called to initialize a diary entry object, the default values are overridden with actual data.

Constructors and `Init` Methods A constructor in Java must start with a call to `super`—the constructor of its ancestor (this is marked as 1 in the Java snippet). In Objective-C, the `init` method must start with a call to `[super init]` which does the same sort of thing. Note that `[super init]` returns an object which is stored in `self`; the Java constructor does not return a value.

Creating Objects Simple variables are set with replacement statements as is the case for `_ID`, `_title`, and so forth. Variables that are references to objects need to have objects created for them. `_entry`, which is an NSData object, falls into this category (underlined in both snippets). In Java, you create a new object by calling its constructor; the constructor may have parameters or—as is the case here—may not.

In Objective-C, there is a somewhat more complex mechanism for creating objects as shown in this line of code:

```
[[NSData alloc] init];
```

Remember to read from the innermost brackets outwards. This code does the following:

1. It calls a Class object (NSData) to allocate an instance of itself.

2. It then calls the instance's `init` method.

In practice, you reuse this line of code over and over: All that you change is the name of the class that you are instantiating (NSData in this case). Note that in some cases, you call object-specific `init` methods such as the `initWithFrame` method of NSView.

Setting Objects to Nil You create objects—such as the `_entry` objects—when you know you will need to refer to them. In other cases, objects are created on demand. In Diary entries, for example, images can be supplied by the user. Thus, the `_image` object is left as null until the user places an image into the entry.

It is possible for the user not to enter any data into the `_entry` object; in that case, the expense of creating that object and storing it goes for naught. In practice, though, that is a rare occurrence. This is an example that illustrates how knowing your application and its data (and how people deal with them) can help you to write more efficient code.

Java:

```java
public DiaryEntry () {

    super (); //1

    _ID = "0";
    _title = "entry title";
    _subtitle = "entry subtitle";
    _summary = "entry summary";

    _entry = new NSData(); //2

    _notes = "entry notes";

    //image is null //3

    _creationDate = (String)new NSDate().toString();
    _modificationDate = _creationDate;
}
```

Objective-C:

```objc
- (id)init {

    self = [super init]; //1

    if (self) {
        _ID = @"0";
        _title   = @"";
        _subtitle  = @"";
        _summary  = @"";

        _entry  = [[NSData alloc] init]; //2

        _notes  = @"";

        _image = nil; //3

        _creationDate  = [[NSDate date]description];
        _modificationDate  = _creationDate;
    }
    return self;
}
```

Summary

For most applications, the structure of the data elements and their basic manipulation lie at the core of the design. This chapter has shown you the basics of modeling data, using basic objects, and using the powerful collection classes available in both Cocoa and Carbon such as dictionaries. Property lists and preferences are implemented using these tools, and they, too, are your basic building blocks for applications.

With them, you can move on to implementing your application. The next chapter focuses on the events and actions that drive its processing.

Chapter 19
Making It Happen:
Events, Responders,
Delegates, and
Notification

Having dealt with the big picture (applications) and the smallest building blocks, it is time to turn to how they work together. This chapter examines how the application and its objects animate those building blocks and the more complex objects that you create in your applications.

The most basic concept in this chapter is that of events—*they cause the application to take some action. Sometimes they are initiated by users (mouse clicks, for example), and other times they are generated by the application itself. (They also can arrive from the operating system or from other applications.)*

Objects in your application respond to events. Called responders, *they include views, buttons, and other interface elements.*

Delegates *provide a way for an application and its objects to pass events along to other interested objects.*

The notification *system in Cocoa does just what its name implies: It allows one object to automatically notify others (which it may not even know about) when something has happened.*

Note that a number of the concepts in this chapter are required to implement toolbars. The complete code for implementing toolbars is given in Chapter 20; see "Implementing Toolbars" on page 440.

Events

In all graphical user interface frameworks, events provide a mechanism for managing the event loop and for letting the application and its objects know when something needs to be done. Events always are a request for an application to do something if it deems it appropriate. The application may decide not to process an event, but it is always a request for action in the sense that if the application does in fact respond to an event, that is not incorrect. Events are not informational: They may trigger actions.

Types of Events

There are two types of events:

1. Basic, system-level events include mouse clicks, activation of an application, menu selection, and keyboard events. Implementations of events normally call the inherited method.

2. Action events are defined within your application. They include higher-level concepts such as saving a document, resizing an image, and finding or replacing text. Implementations of actions may or may not (often not) call the inherited method.

Basic Events These are known and defined both in Carbon and in Cocoa. Basic framework objects such as windows contain code to handle these events where appropriate. Thus, you can rest assured that when you create a window in Interface Builder, it will be activated when you click it, and its resize box (if you enable it) will work properly. (In Classic applications written without a framework such as MacApp or PowerPlant, you had to actually write the resizing code!)

If you create a new interface element and subclass a standard class (such as a window), all of these events will be handled for you automatically. The one issue that you need to address is that of overriding a basic method (such as `mouseUp` or `keyDown`). If you do so, you must call the inherited method so that if you do not handle the event it is properly passed on. The purpose of the responder chain is to allow each object in turn to have a chance to handle an event until one of them does so. If you do not pass the event on, you break the chain and the application becomes unresponsive.

Action Events These are your application-specific events (actions in Interface Builder). When they arrive at one of your objects, you must handle them there; you may pass them on to other objects, but you do not pass them on to the default objects in Cocoa since they will not know about your own events.

Event Formats

In Cocoa, events are objects—descendants of NSEvent. In Carbon, as in the Classic environment, events are packaged as data structures. Unlike events in the first Macintosh versions, events in Carbon are now pointers to opaque structures; that means that you cannot access fields within the pointer. An event is passed around the system in a pointer of type EventRef, and you use routines such as `GetEventParameter` to get a parameter out of the pointer. (This is an accessor to a data structure; it is functionally identical to an accessor to an object's data in the object-oriented world.)

You use accessors to get information out of the event objects and data structures. For all practical purposes, you program using the two types of events in much the same way when it comes to getting data from the event.

The data in the event consists of general information such as the time at which the event occurred as well as information identifying the specific type of event (a mouse down, for example) and data that applies only to that specific event (such as a location).

Timers

Timers are a special type of event: They fire repeatedly according to the parameters that you set. Each time an NSTimer fires, an event of the type that you specify is sent.

Timers are part of the design that moves the event loop processing from individual applications into the operating system. In the old days, periodic events were handled by individual applications. Each one kept track of when it needed to perform tasks, and in the constantly repeating event loops, such tasks were initiated as needed.

Using timers is much more efficient for the computer's total environment. It also removes code from your application, making it easier to maintain.

Responders

Most objects that respond to events are descendants of the NSResponder abstract class. The abstract class has stubs for many common actions that responder objects implement, but because it is an abstract class, they are not full implementations. (See "Selectors" on page 401 for information on how to deal with this situation.)

The abstract class implements the mechanism for building the responder chain and for manipulating it. Thus, almost all objects that are in the responder chain are descendants of NSResponder.

NSDocument demonstrates why there is a little ambiguity in the previous paragraph. It is a direct descendant of NSObject, but is not an NSResponder. However, it can respond to certain events. Its Save action, for example, is connected to the Save menu command. Because it is not a responder, it never appears in the responder chain, and therefore its other actions are not processed through the chain. Many of its actions are invoked indirectly by objects that are responders and do appear in the responder chain—window controllers, for example, as well as views, windows, and the application itself.

Windows are critical players in the responder chain. Mouse clicks and keystrokes go to the active window (the key window) and to its responders; then, they go to an application's main window (if it is different from the key window). From there, they are sent to the application itself.

At each stage of the process, an NSResponder can pass the event off to a delegate (see "Delegates" on page 403). Once an object handles an event, it is not propagated farther up the responder chain.

However, when an object handles an event, it may pass that event on to its superclass (or even to an entirely different object). There are two chains of linked objects in play at that time:

1. The responder chain is the linked list of objects that will respond to any event that comes in.

2. An individual object's inheritance tree or other ad hoc linked list of objects is the chain that will process a specific event.

Working with
the First
Responder

In reality, you do not care at all about the responder chain, with the exception of the first responder (the head of the chain). Cocoa just manages everything for you. The first responder, though, may require your intervention.

Setting the First Responder You usually set the first responder using Interface Builder when you design your windows. However, there also are two general methods that you can use to set the first responder. Both are methods of NSWindow.

The first, makeFirstResponder, is used dynamically to make an object (usually a view in the window) become the first responder at that moment. The second, setInitial-FirstResponder, is used to set the first responder for the window in general.

Java:

```
public native boolean makeFirstResponder
  (com.apple.cocoa.application.NSResponder);

public native void setInitialFirstResponder (
  com.apple.cocoa.application.NSView);
```

Objective-C:

```
- (BOOL)makeFirstResponder:
    (NSResponder *)aResponder;
- (void)setInitialFirstResponder:(NSView *)view;
```

You rarely need to use these methods, as the default behavior is intuitively correct in most cases. Furthermore, not only is it correct, but changing it may also make the user confused. (One case in which you may need to set the first responder is when you have a text entry view within a scroller.)

Accepting First Responder Status Far more common than setting the first responder is specifying whether an object will allow itself to become a first responder. By default, views return false when their `acceptsFirstResponder` function is called. This means that unless you actively allow a view to become a first responder (whenever it is called upon to do so), it will not.

With Interface Builder, you can set this using the Enabled option on a control's Attributes pane in Show Info.

Selectors

Periodically, it is necessary to refer to a method of an object or to a procedure so that it can be manipulated as data. Objects in the responder chain need to be able to provide information as to whether or not they implement a given action that has been requested (this is needed not only to carry it out but also to preflight actions so that menu commands can be properly enabled or disabled).

In other cases, a specific action needs to be attached to a toolbar item, to a notification, or to an undo stack.

In Carbon, Universal Procedure Pointers (UPPs) identify procedures in much the way that is needed. In Cocoa, two similar mechanisms are used: one for Objective-C and the other for Java.

Objective-C Selectors   A type, SEL, exists in Objective-C. A method of NSObject lets you query whether the particular descendant of NSObject you are interested in handles the message.

```
- (BOOL)respondsToSelector:(SEL)aSelector;
```

In usage, you can check whether `anyObject` responds to the `drawMe` message:

```
if ([anyObject respondsToSelector:@selec-
  tor(drawMe:)])
```

You need to use selectors when you are attaching actions to dynamic objects. For example, if you are creating a toolbar item, you set its action as follows:

```
[item setAction: @selector(stepEntry:)];
```

Java Selectors   Java does not have a SEL type. Instead, an NS-Selector class is used to identify a method, and `java.lang. reflect.Method` is used to determine if a class has a given method. This is somewhat different from the `responds-ToSelector` method of NSObject in Objective-C, since in Java the query reflects a given method in a given class; in Objective-C, `respondsToSelector` reflects only a given method in any class. Practically, this enormous conceptual difference does not matter in most of the work that you do.

You construct an NSSelector using the method name and an array of parameters for the given class. You can obtain these by calling the class method of the class; the array of parameter types for NSNotification is {NSNotification.class}, that of NS-View is {NSView.class} and so forth. Here is the code to create a selector on the fly:

```
new NSSelector ("stepEntry",
  new Class[]{DiaryDocument.class})
```

This creates a selector identifying the `stepEntry` method of the DiaryDocument class.

You can use this to set an action for a toolbar item in the following way:

```
item.setAction (new NSSelector ("stepEntry",
  new Class[] {DiaryDocument.class}));
```

Sometimes you need to set a number of actions and need the class parameter types repeatedly. You can store them in an array and use that variable as follows:

```
Class arrClass [] = {DiaryDocument.class};
item.setAction (new NSSelector
  ("stepEntry", new Class[] arrClass);
item2.setAction (new NSSelector
  ("reverseStepEntry", new Class [] arrClass);
```

Sending Actions   Two methods let you send a specific selector to particular objects. Cocoa uses these methods internally, and you do not have to worry about them in most cases.

The first is a method of NSApplication. You specify both the target and sender; if the target is nil, the responder chain is traversed.

```
public native boolean sendActionToTargetFromSender
  (
  com.apple.cocoa.foundation.NSSelector,
  java.lang.Object,
  java.lang.Object)
```

```
- (BOOL)sendAction:(SEL)theAction to:(id)theTarget
  from:(id)sender;
```

You can ask any NSResponder to attempt to perform an action; you pass into it the object that is the parameter of the action method using its id.

```
public boolean tryToPerform(
  NSSelector anAction,
  Object anObject);
```

```
- (BOOL)tryToPerform:(SEL)anAction with:(id)anOb-
  ject;
```

Delegates

Many objects allow you to set a delegate for them; the delegate implements certain methods that augment the primary object's functionality. In many cases, this means that instead of overriding the primary object you can attach a delegate to it.

The easiest way to attach a delegate to an object is in Interface Builder. Draw a connection (CONTROL-drag) from an object to another one; attach the connection to the delegate outlet in the Info window.

You may need to attach a delegate to an object programmatically—again, toolbars require this. The toolbar object itself implements only the most basic functionality. It requires a delegate to tell it what the default items are, to identify the allowable items, and to provide it with an NSToolbarItem for a given identifier. In the Diary example shown in Chapter 20, the document object (an override of NSDocument) is the delegate and implements these methods.

Sometimes, a delegate is required to implement some or all of a set of methods. Other times, the delegate can pick and choose. The documentation of an object's setDelegate method will list the required methods for the delegate. If you attempt to attach an inappropriate delegate to an object, an error message appears in the console window.

In Objective-C, when you set a delegate using setDelegate, the delegate object is not retained. You should call retain on it (and later release it when the primary object is deallocated).

Notification

As objects within a single application (or several applications) interact, their ability to notify one another of specific events happening to specific objects makes for efficiencies both in coding and in running applications. For example, many interface elements reflect the states of the system and other applications (a font menu that contains the currently installed fonts is one such case). Without a notification structure, whenever you update your interface (redisplay your menus, redraw a panel, etc.), you need to go out and find what the current state is: have fonts been installed or uninstalled, has another application started or stopped, etc.

Using notifications, you can check the state of the system and other applications when you first present your user interface and register an interest in changes to those states. Then, instead of checking the states each time you re-present your interface, you can happily continue to display your initial states until notified otherwise.

Of course, notifications can be used for many other purposes than keeping your interface up to date; the example given here just happens to be a common case.

Performance and Development Issues Objects can communicate with one another in various ways:

- An object can obtain a reference to another object and send messages to it, invoking its methods. This requires that the first object have a reference to the second and know what methods it has.

- A less tightly coupled structure lets the first object send messages to the second via an intermediary. The intermediary object (often a delegate of the first object) needs to know what messages the first object might send and what messages to pass on to the second object. The intermediary can function as a translator, converting one API to another.

- The least tightly coupled structure has no links between the objects. The first object posts notifications about possibly interesting events that it has processed; the second object responds to those notifications for those objects in which it is interested.

This last structure is the most sophisticated; it allows the greatest degree of independence among objects and therefore the maximum amount of object reuse and encapsulation (both of data and of functionality). Theoretically, you can construct a system in which objects know nothing about one another but simply post and respond to the appropriate notifications.

Be aware that this structure—which may allow significant savings in development time—may exert a toll at run time. In practice, the objects must know something about one another; if they don't, you are likely to wind up with a glut of notifications (most of which are not acted on). Even worse, objects that expect to receive notifications may not act on them because the notifications are not what they expected to receive.

A further difficulty with implementing notification-based architectures lies in the fact that many programmers remain uncomfortable with the idea. They simply don't trust the system to do the right thing; they are much more comfortable with using the 50-year-old paradigm of procedure calls. However, to move into a robust, sophisticated, multiuser model (even the limited version of it that consists of multiple applications running simultaneously on a single computer), it is necessary to trust the framework that you use.

Furthermore, overuse of notifications can make debugging excruciatingly difficult, because you do not know why pieces of code are suddenly executing (or not). But this fact is not an argument against using notifications—it is an argument for keeping them clear and simple so that they can be debugged.

The notification design, when properly used, can extend the economies of object-oriented programming as individual programmers become more and more expert in their own objects' functionalities and need to know less and less about other objects. Emotionally it may feel better to control all of your application's objects and their methods; unfortunately, that is a dead end, leading to closed systems, unmaintainable code, and compromises with object-oriented design that will produce code that is just as spaghetti-like as the worst legacy Cobol code (it just will take longer to reach that point because the object-oriented technologies will sustain you longer than Cobol did).

NSNotification An NSNotification object is at the heart of the notification system. Although you can subclass NSNotification, doing so is likely to defeat the elegant simplicity of the design. A notification object has three fields:

1. The notification's name is an NSString that you select. Senders and receivers of notifications should agree on this string; it is usually much easier for development teams to agree on a string name for a notification than for a data structure or other shared information.

2. A notification contains a reference to an object. This is usually the object that posts the notification (that is, the object that causes the action that the notification reflects). This object may be nil; it also may be another object, but that design starts to muddy the clear design of the notification system.

3. The notification may also contain a dictionary that contains any additional information that the notification might need. For example, if several fields of a view are involved in a notification, the dictionary may contain keys such as "Field 1 view" and "Field 2 view" that are linked to specific objects. The dictionary is optional.

The flexibility of the notification lies in its simplicity. The dictionary lets you pass specific information in a common format along with the notification. If you are familiar with Apple events, you will notice that this structure is quite reminiscent of the Apple event structure in which the common syntax allows an Apple event to contain very specific descriptors of meaning to its senders and recipients but which are transparent—but transmittable—to others.

You can subclass NSNotification, but doing so immediately makes your events less general. If you need to pass additional information, pass it in the dictionary included with the notification. Don't subclass NSNotification.

Once you have decided that you have something to notify other objects about, you post the notification to the default notification center for your task. The notification center contains utilities for creating NSNotification objects.

NSNotificationCenter The notification center for each task serves as the clearinghouse for all notifications within that task. Notifications can be created by any object in the task and posted to the notification center. Independently, any object can register itself as an observer of notifications. As noted in the previous section, a notification has a name and optionally has an object (usually the originator of the notification) and user information in a dictionary.

Observers can register to receive notifications based on name or originating object—or both, or neither. If the registration omits both the name and object, all notifications within the task are forwarded to it; if either or both are provided, only those notifications from the chosen object or with the given name are forwarded. When registering, an observer passes in a selector, which is a reference to one of its methods that will be invoked by the notification center. If a notification needs to be forwarded to an observer, that observer's method will be called and the NSNotification object passed as the single argument to it. You may name this method anything you want (but something like ProcessNotification wouldn't be such a bad idea). The NSNotification center makes very few demands on either notifiers or observers; the architecture is simple and robust.

A notification center uses an NSNotificationQueue to manage the notifications. The notification queue normally functions as a first in–first out queue, but the default NSNotificationQueue also provides the ability to merge similar notifications ("coalescing") and to remove events matching some criteria (name, object, etc.). Changing the way in which notifications are enqueued or dequeued can lead to problems later, so unless you are absolutely certain that you know what you are doing, stay out of the NSNotificationQueue. You are likely to optimize the performance of your application in a single-user, single-processor, non-networked environment... and lay the grounds for a disaster later on. Assume that the notification center uses a first in–first out queue and furthermore assume that it may function asynchronously (even though it does not in the simplest case).

Using Delegates and Notifications

Here are some code snippets from the Diary example that show how you can use delegates and notifications.

Receiving a Notification

The `loadFieldsFromDiaryData` method in Diary Document gets the current Diary entry via an accessor in DiaryData, and then it moves the object's data into the interface fields. When the data is changed anywhere in the application, a notification is posted, and the interface is refreshed with the new data.

Java:

```
public void loadFieldsFromDiaryData
  (NSNotification notification) {
    titleField.setStringValue
      (theDiary.entryTitle());
    subtitleField.setStringValue
      (theDiary.entrySubtitle());
    summaryField.setStringValue
      (theDiary.entrySummary());
```

Objective-C:

```
- (void)loadFieldsFromDiaryData:
  (NSNotification *)notification {
    [titleField setStringValue:
      [theDiary entryTitle]];
    [subtitleField setStringValue:
      [theDiary entrySubtitle]];
```

```
[summaryField setStringValue:
    [theDiary entrySummary]];
```

Note that you implement these methods, but you may never call them. The point of notifications is that the dispatching is done by Cocoa. In fact, in Diary, you sometimes call these methods directly without a notification—in `windowCon-trollerDidLoadNib` they are called to move data from the current entry object that exists after opening a window into the interface:

Java:

```
this.loadFieldsFromDiaryData (null);
```

Objective-C:

```
[self loadFieldsFromDiaryData:nil];
```

Notification receivers have a single argument, an NSNotification, which can be null as in this case. If it is not, you can use data from the NSNotification object which was put there during the registration process described next.

Registering for Notifications

Registering for notifications is done before you could possibly need one. In Diary, `windowControllerDidLoadNib` in DiaryDocument is used to register for notifications.

The `addObserver` method registers your code for a notification. In most cases, you register with your task's default notification center, which you can obtain dynamically from the NSNotificationCenter object.

There are four arguments to the `addObserver` method:

1. The first is the object to be notified.

2. The second is the method in that object to be called.

3. The third is a string that, if it is part of a posted notifi-

cation, triggers this action. (Such strings are part of many header files—windows, views, NSApplication, and so forth; they can also be your own.)

4. The fourth is an object that, if it is part of a posted notification, triggers this action.

Note that either 3 or 4 will trigger the action.

Java:

Java uses NSSelector objects to register for a notification. You typically create them dynamically as in the underlined line of code in the following snippet. You specify the method to be called when the notification is received, and you pass in the parameters for the class specification. This is boilerplate code starting from the arrClass declaration; all you normally change is the name of the method to be called and the name of the notification. In the first notification, for example, when the `DiaryEntryDidChangeNotification` is received, `loadFieldsFromDiaryData` is called.

```
NSNotificationCenter center =
  (NSNotificationCenter)
    NSNotificationCenter.defaultCenter();

Class arrClass [] = {NSNotification.class};

center.addObserver
  (this,
    new NSSelector ("loadFieldsFromDiaryData",
      new Class[] {getClass()}),
    DiaryEntryDidChangeNotification,
    null);

center.addObserver
  (this,
    new NSSelector ("diaryDataDidChange",
      new Class[] {getClass()}),
```

```
        DiaryEntryDidChangeNotification,
          null);

    center.addObserver
      (this,
        new NSSelector ("moveFieldsToDiaryData",
          new Class[] {getClass()}),
        DiaryDisplayWillChangeNotification, null);

    center.addObserver
      (this,
        new NSSelector ("loadFieldsFromDiaryData",
          new Class[] {getClass()}),
        DiaryDisplayDidChangeNotification,
          null);
```

The notification strings are defined here:

```
public static final String
  DiaryDisplayWillChangeNotification
    = "DiaryWillChange";
public static final String
  DiaryDidChangeNotification
    = "DiaryDidChange";
public static final String
  DiaryDisplayDidChangeNotification
    = "DiaryEntryNeedsDisplay";
public static final String
  DiaryEntryDidChangeNotification
    = "DiaryEntryDidChange";
```

Objective-C:

Objective-C uses a selector data type for the second parameter as shown here:

```
NSNotificationCenter* center;

center =
  [NSNotificationCenter defaultCenter];
```

```
[center
  addObserver:self
  selector:@selector(loadFieldsFromDiaryData:)
  name:DiaryEntryDidChangeNotification
  object:nil];

[center
  addObserver:self
  selector:@selector(diaryDataDidChange:)
  name:DiaryData.DiaryEntryDidChangeNotification
  object:nil];

[center
  addObserver:self
  selector:@selector(moveFieldsToDiaryData:)
  name:DiaryDisplayWillChangeNotification
  object:nil];

[center
  addObserver:self
  selector:@selector(loadFieldsFromDiaryData:)
  name:DiaryDisplayDidChangeNotification
  object:nil];
```

The string declaration in another header is shown here:

```
NSString *DiaryDisplayWillChangeNotification
  = @"DiaryWillChange";
NSString *DiaryDidChangeNotification
  = @"DiaryDidChange";
NSString *DiaryDisplayDidChangeNotification
  = @"DiaryEntryNeedsDisplay";
NSString *DiaryEntryDidChangeNotification
  = @"DiaryEntryDidChange";
```

Posting a Notification

Posting a notification does not require registration. You frequently receive more notifications than you send, as you can use the declared notifications of documents, views, windows, the application object itself, and other Cocoa objects. These are sent at appropriate times; you need merely register to receive the notifications.

For your internal processing, however, you frequently post notifications to yourself to provide consistency among interface elements. In Diary, for example, calling the addEntry method in DiaryDocument causes a notification to be posted:

Java:

```
public void addEntry (Object Sender) {
  theDiary.addEntry();
  NSNotificationCenter.defaultCenter().
    postNotification
    (DiaryEntryDidChangeNotification, this);
}
```

Objective-C:

```
- (IBAction)addEntry:(id)sender
{
  [theDiary addEntry];
  [[NSNotificationCenter defaultCenter]
    postNotificationName:
    DiaryEntryDidChangeNotification object: self];
}
```

This is the first notification registered in the code in the previous section; it causes loadFieldsFromDiaryData to be called. Thus, the following processing occurs:

1. The DiaryData addEntry method is called: It creates a new DiaryEntry object and makes it the current entry.

2. As a result of the posting of the notification, the Diary-Document's loadFieldsFromDiaryData method is called. It uses an accessor to retrieve the current entry from DiaryData—the new entry—and it loads its data into the interface fields.

Delegates versus Notifications

The `windowShouldClose` method is a delegate of NSWindow. It is implemented in the TextEdit example document class. It runs when the NSWindow's `windowShouldClose` message is sent/method is called and is passed on to its delegate—the document, in this case.

Java:

```java
public boolean windowShouldClose(Object sender) {
  return canCloseDocument();
}
```

Objective-C:

```objc
- (BOOL)windowShouldClose:(id)sender {
  return [self canCloseDocument];
}
```

Delegates are specified in the header of the class to which the delegate will be attached (in other words, NSToolbar specifies the delegate methods you implement in the document or window that will be the delegate). They are called as needed, and their structure is variable. In many cases, including those shown here, a delegate returns a boolean indicating whether a proposed action can take place. Thus a delegate is prospective in nature.

The notification methods are called automatically through the notification center. In general, notifications are retrospective: They are called after something has happened. Furthermore, their structure is not open as is that of delegate methods. Notifications pass an NSNotification object from which you need to extract the relevant information for your processing.

Summary

With its events and responders, Cocoa is similar to a number of other application development frameworks. However, it adds the powerful delegate and notification systems to more traditional event handling.

You can combine event handling and the basic building blocks of the previous chapter to implement sophisticated applications in Mac OS X, but one more thing is needed: the visualization in windows. That is the topic of the next chapter.

Chapter 20
Visualization: Views and Windows

The heart of a graphical user interface is its graphics—its views, windows, images, and the other visual elements that appear on your computer's display. This chapter examines how to handle those elements in Mac OS X.

The sections of this chapter focus on:

- *Views—the basic graphical elements of the interface*

- *Windows—the containers of views, images, text, and other graphical elements*

- *Images—JPEG, TIFF, or other images that are displayed in the interface (but are not part of its interactivity)*

- *Toolbars—one of the most attractive features of the Aqua interface*

- *Drawers—an "ooh" feature of Aqua that demonstrates that windows need not be rectangular*

Note that controls—buttons, sliders, pop-up menus, and the like— are dealt with in Chapter 21.

Looking at Views

In the C++ frameworks of MacApp and PowerPlant, views are a generalized class that descends from an event handler class. Windows are a specialized type of view.

In Cocoa, views and windows are descendants of a similar type of object—NSResponder. However, windows and views are equal descendants of NSResponder: Windows are not descendants of views.

It should scarcely be surprising that an enormous amount of work has gone into handling the windows in graphical user interfaces. After all, they are the interface for most users. A number of different strategies have been used to display them and to manage their interactions. In Cocoa, you will find a class of window controllers that manage windows. If your application has multiple windows, it will normally have multiple window controllers.

View Hierarchies

Hierarchies of views function as they do in any framework— they let you create groups of views that may contain others. Note that the run-time view hierarchy is not the inheritance hierarchy of object-oriented programming. A superview is not a superclass.

The hierarchy of views is logical and not related to their physical locations. In other words, a view that contains another view simply contains it; its location is irrelevant to the containment. In fact, the list of contained views may be ordered in a way that is totally different from their visual representations.

Each view may have one or more subviews that are contained within it (both physically on the imaging device and logically within the object). A view may also have a superview in which it is contained. The topmost view in a window hierarchy is the content view. The content view has no superview; it is contained within its window, and the window has a specific reference to its content view. From the content view's subviews (and their subviews) you can reach all of the views within a window.

View Geometry

You normally size and shape views in Interface Builder. Although they are often resized during program execution, this resizing is commonly in response to user actions, and you don't get involved.

As in most frameworks, each view has its own coordinate system. In the framework, the (0,0) point is typically the lower-left corner of the view. You can flip the view's coordinate system so that the vertical axis increases from top to bottom and the (0,0) point is at the top left. Each view has conversion routines that let it convert points and rectangles from other views' coordinate systems to its own.

One difference from some other frameworks is that views can be rotated. They need not always appear with their "vertical" dimension pointing up.

Two rectangles are important for views:

1. A view's *frame* identifies its location in the coordinates of its superview. The frame determines the view's size and shape. It contains the Aqua interface shadow drawn around controls and windows.

2. A view's *layoutRect* is the view's frame without the shadow.

You can use Interface Builder's Info window to set view bounds and frames as shown in Figure 20-1.

Figure 20-1. Setting a Frame in Interface Builder

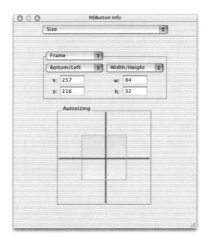

The size pane provides a pop-up menu that lets you switch between the frame and layoutRect values. Below that, two pop-up menus and associated text entry fields let you specify coordinates and size for the view.

You can use any pair of coordinates that you want. Mac OS 9 and earlier (including Carbon) relies on a coordinate system with 0,0 at the upper left of the display (this is where the CRT electron scanning gun starts on old video monitors). Cocoa uses an origin of 0,0 at the lower left. This makes the upper right of four quadrants the primary location for screen display. This is consistent with the general use of two-dimensional coordinate systems in which the positive quadrant (upper right) gets most of the attention.

Whatever view you have selected in your interface is reflected in the Info window. You can resize and move views in their enclosing window and the coordinates in the Info window will change.

Note that in the right-side (size) pop-up menu, a Default item is available. Interface Builder will size the selected object as well as it can.

Resizing Views   The behavior of views when their superview is resized is not a simple issue. Both size and location come into play. For example:

- When a window is resized, buttons within it are normally not resized: Buttons are often of a standard size.

- When a window is resized, buttons that are located in specific locations are often moved relative to the edge of the view (that is, the OK button is usually a fixed distance in from the lower-right corner of the view).

- The frame of a view within a resized window is often resized directly with the window: Making the window one inch wider normally increases the size of its content by one inch.

- The information within a frame (text or graphics—the contents of an embedded view's bounds rectangle) is normally unaffected, although the change in the embedded view's frame may make more or less of the content visible.

If you want to handle this programmatically, the framework provides two sets of three constants that you can OR together to control the resizing behavior of a view when its superview is resized. For width, the three constants are as follows:

1. `NSViewMinXMargin` allows the left (min) horizontal margin to vary.

2. `NSViewMaxXMargin` allows the right (max) horizontal margin to vary.

3. `NSViewWidthSizable` allows the view itself to be resized.

Three similar constants are provided for YMargin and the height.

With Interface Builder, you can use the Info window's Size pane to manipulate these values. Figure 20-2 shows the basic controls.

Figure 20-2. Setting Sizing Behavior in Interface Builder

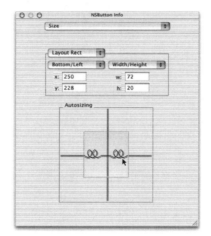

The schematic diagram at the bottom of the Size pane represents a view (the inner square) within its superview (often a window). You can click on the horizontal or vertical springs and struts to switch between keeping the selected view a constant size (struts) in that dimension as the superview is resized or resizing it proportionately (springs).

In Figure 20-2, the horizontal dimension is set to resize proportionately as the superview changes; the vertical dimension is set to a constant value.

You can use the parts of the axes outside the inner view to indicate its behavior with regard to location. In Figure 20-3, the inner view is set to be a constant distance from the left margin of its superview, while its top moves proportionately to the resizing of its superview.

Use the Interface Builder Test Interface command in its File menu to see how setting these options changes your view behavior.

Figure 20-3. Setting Moving Values in Interface Builder

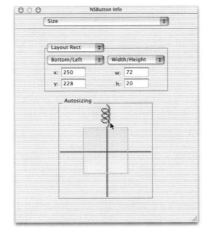

Drawing

There really are only two methods that you need to worry about when it comes to drawing views: `drawRect` and `setNeedsDisplay`. In addition, if you need to draw on demand (that is, draw something like a graph or diagram based on changing data rather than drawing an object such as a button or text field), you will probably need to use the NSBezierPath class.

drawRect Actual drawing within a view is done by `drawRect`. If you use standard views (buttons, text fields, and the like), Cocoa does all the drawing for you. If you implement a custom view class, you must implement `drawRect`; otherwise, nothing will be drawn.

Before your `drawRect` method is called, all the coordinate conversion and focusing are done for you. You can draw starting at your view's 0,0 coordinate (its lower left), and you can know that everything will appear properly in the window no matter where the view and the window are located on the display.

A single parameter—an NSRect—is passed in to `drawRect`. You can use it to optimize your code. It represents the smallest rectangle within your view that needs redrawing. If your view is very complex, this can be a major efficiency. If drawing the view is not particularly burdensome, the extra programming and processing to analyze the part that needs redrawing may not be worth the effort.

Remember that you need to implement `drawRect` only for your custom views. Even if you override a standard Cocoa view object, its `drawRect` method may still be satisfactory for your purposes.

```
public void drawRect(NSRect aRect); //Java
- (void)drawRect:(NSRect)aRect; //Objective-C
```

setNeedsDisplay You call `setNeedsDisplay` frequently: It is what causes Cocoa to redraw your view by calling its `drawRect` method. You never call `drawRect` directly, because Cocoa needs to have the opportunity to focus, set up coordinates, and otherwise prepare for drawing.

Two versions of `setNeedsDisplay` exist:

1. You can specify that the entire view needs (or does not need) redrawing by passing in a boolean.

2. You can specify the rectangle within the view that needs redrawing.

Using the rectangle makes for greater efficiency, but—as with the case of drawing—can make code more complicated.

Below are the headers for both versions of `setNeedsDisplay` along with a snippet of code from Sketch. This is a very common type of drawing code. The custom view (of which this is a method) contains a variety of graphic objects. The custom view has a method called `invalidateGraphic` (shown here) that invalidates a specific object that is passed in as a parameter. All it does is to call `setNeedsDisplay` passing in the object's bounds. (Diary does not use this sort of code because its drawing is confined to controls, not user-created objects that can be of irregular shapes and sizes.)

If your view contains objects whose size and location you do not know, you could use the other version of `setNeedsDisplay`, and just pass in a value of TRUE so that the entire view is redrawn.

Java:

```java
public void setNeedsDisplay(NSRect invalidRect);
public void setNeedsDisplay(boolean aFlag);

public void invalidateGraphic(SKTGraphic graphic)
  {
  setNeedsDisplay(graphic.drawingBounds());
  ...
}
```

Objective-C:

```objc
- (void)setNeedsDisplayInRect:
  (NSRect)invalidRect;
- (void)setNeedsDisplay:(BOOL)flag;
```

```
- (void)invalidateGraphic:(SKTGraphic *)graphic {
  [self setNeedsDisplayInRect:[graphic drawing-
  Bounds]];

  ...

}
```

NSBezierPath   This is the core of the drawing mechanism in Cocoa. It is based on the cubic equation developed by Pierre Bézier for CAD/CAM systems in the 1970s, which later became the basis for Adobe's PostScript model.

A path is an ordered sequence of data points. The lines and curves that join them may form a recognizable shape (line, rectangle, or circle), and convenience methods help you create such shapes. A path may be closed; if it is, its enclosed area can be shaded and otherwise manipulated.

NSBezierPath contains most of the drawing tools that you need. You can specify arrows for the ends of line segments, line dashing, and width for lines.

In addition to the drawing tools, NSBezierPath manages hit detection: It can report if a given point is contained in itself.

If you are used to programming in PostScript, you will be right at home in the NSBezierPath class. If you are used to the QuickDraw routines in Mac OS 9 and earlier, you also will find NSBezierPath familiar. (On Mac OS X, Quartz implements much of the functionality that QuickDraw did on Mac OS 9 and earlier; however, you get to many of the basic drawing routines through NSBezierPath.)

If you need to draw images on the fly, look at the documentation of NSBezierPath (search for it by name using Cocoa Help from Project Builder). However, before doing this, consider whether you really need to draw in this way. All of your interface elements are drawn automatically by Cocoa; in addition, text in NSTextField or NSTextView objects is drawn automatically. A great many Cocoa programs require absolutely no custom drawing.

Events, Mouse Handling, and Scrolling

Views are responders, and the handle events including mouse tracking and mouse clicks. The default behavior of Cocoa views is usually satisfactory; in fact, modifying it typically breaks the user interface. Despite the fact that these subjects are critically important and require a great deal of code to be properly implemented, Cocoa takes care of them and implements them, so you rarely need to worry about them.

The only attention you need to give to these items is to use the Info window in Interface Builder to enable (or not) the views in your interface.

Identifying Views

Views in Interface Builder are easily manipulated by pointing and clicking. If you need to manipulate views programmatically, you need to be able to identify them.

If one of your objects needs to access a view—either to set or retrieve data from it, to enable/disable it, or to remove it or move it around—it needs to be able to identify it easily. The simplest way to handle this is to make the view in question an outlet of your object.

Adding Views

Two sections of code from the examples show how you can add views dynamically. `addPage` is used in TextEdit to add a new page of text when the user is using the Wrap to Page command in the Format menu. `makeScalePopupButton` is also used in the page wrap view; it is the small pop-up in the scroll bar at the bottom of the window that lets you scale the window's contents.

Each of these methods is standard code, and each demonstrates common issues that arise when you add views.

addPage There are three steps involved in dynamically adding a view:

1. Get a reference to the view into which it is to be placed.

2. Create the new view.

3. Add it.

The relevant lines of code are underlined in the following code snippets. The only item that needs to be pointed out is that it is common in finding a reference to the view to be added to that it may need to be fished through some intermediate views. In this case, the object that is adding the page has a reference to a scroll view, and it needs to retrieve a document view object from that one.

Java:

```
public void addPage() {
  int numberOfPages = numberOfPages();
  MultiplePageView pagesView =
    (MultiplePageView) scrollView.documentView();
  NSSize textSize =
    pagesView.documentSizeInPage();
  NSTextContainer textContainer =
    new NSTextContainer(textSize);

  pagesView.setNumberOfPages(numberOfPages + 1);

  NSTextView textView = new NSTextView(
    pagesView.documentRectForPageNumber
      (numberOfPages),
    textContainer);
  textView.setHorizontallyResizable(false);
  textView.setVerticallyResizable(false);

  pagesView.addSubview(textView);
  layoutManager().addTextContainer(textContainer);
  }
```

Objective-C:

```
- (void)addPage {
  unsigned numberOfPages = [self numberOfPages];
  MultiplePageView *pagesView =
    [scrollView documentView];
  NSSize textSize = [pagesView documentSizeInPage];
  NSTextContainer *textContainer =
    [[NSTextContainer alloc]
    initWithContainerSize:textSize];

  [pagesView setNumberOfPages:numberOfPages + 1];

  NSTextView *textView;
  textView = [[NSTextView alloc]
    initWithFrame:[pagesView
    documentRectForPageNumber:numberOfPages]
    textContainer:textContainer];
  [textView setHorizontallyResizable:NO];
  [textView setVerticallyResizable:NO];

  [pagesView addSubview:textView];
  [[self layoutManager] addTextContainer:
      textContainer];
  [textView release];
  [textContainer release];
}
```

makeScalePopUpButton Adding the scale pop-up menu is much the same, but it has some additional features. This method is a method of the view, so there is no need to find a reference to it. In the first underlined section of code, the pop-up menu is created. (The complete code to fill the button with values is shown here, as it can be modified for other purposes.)

At the bottom, the newly created button refuses to ever be the first responder. It is still enabled, and it still responds to users' mouse clicks, but it is out of the responder chain, and events other than mouse clicks do not go to it.

Finally, it is added to the view as before.

Java:

```
protected void makeScalePopUpButton () {
  if (_scalePopUpButton == null) {
    /* Create the pop up button. */
    _scalePopUpButton = new NSPopUpButton(
      new NSRect(0f, 0f, 1f, 1f), false);
    _scalePopUpButton.setBezelStyle(
      NSButtonCell.RegularSquareBezelStyle);

    /* Fill it with the scales. */
    int numberOfDefaultItems = MenuLabels.length;
    for (int i=0; i<numberOfDefaultItems; i++) {
      String label =
        NSBundle.localizedString(MenuLabels[i]);
      _scalePopUpButton.addItem(label);

      NSMenuItem item = (NSMenuItem)
        _scalePopUpButton.itemAtIndex(i);

      if (ScaleFactors[i] != 0f) {
       Number factor = new Float(ScaleFactors[i]);
       item.setRepresentedObject(factor);
       }
    }

    _scalePopUpButton.selectItemAtIndex
      (DefaultSelectedItem);

    /* Hook it up. */
    _scalePopUpButton.setTarget(this);
    _scalePopUpButton.setAction(new NSSelector(
      "scalePopUpAction",
      new Class[] {getClass()})
    );

    /* Pick a suitable font. */
    _scalePopUpButton.setFont
      (NSFont.toolTipsFontOfSize(10f));
```

```
      /* Make sure the pop-up is big enough to
        fit the cells. */
      _scalePopUpButton.sizeToFit();

      /* Don't ever let it become the first
        responder. */
      _scalePopUpButton.
        setRefusesFirstResponder(true);

      /* Put it in the scroll view. */
      addSubview( scalePopUpButton);
    }
}
```

Objective-C:

```
- (void)makeScalePopUpButton {
  if (_scalePopUpButton == nil) {
  unsigned cnt, numberOfDefaultItems =
    (sizeof(_NSDefaultScaleMenuLabels) /
    sizeof(NSString *));
  NSButtonCell *curItem;

  // create it
  _scalePopUpButton = [[NSPopUpButton alloc]
    initWithFrame:NSMakeRect(0.0, 0.0, 1.0, 1.0)
    pullsDown:NO];
  [[_scalePopUpButton cell]
    setBezelStyle:NSShadowlessSquareBezelStyle];
  [[_scalePopUpButton cell]
    setArrowPosition:NSPopUpArrowAtBottom];

  // fill it
  for (cnt = 0; cnt < numberOfDefaultItems; cnt++) {
    [_scalePopUpButton
      addItemWithTitle:NSLocalizedStringFromTable
      (_NSDefaultScaleMenuLabels[cnt],
      @"ZoomValues",
      nil)];
    curItem = [_scalePopUpButton itemAtIndex:cnt];
```

```
      if (_NSDefaultScaleMenuFactors[cnt] != 0.0) {
        [curItem setRepresentedObject:
          [NSNumber numberWithFloat:
            _NSDefaultScaleMenuFactors[cnt]]];
      }
    }
    [_scalePopUpButton
      selectItemAtIndex:
        _NSDefaultScaleMenuSelectedItemIndex];

    // hook it up
    [_scalePopUpButton setTarget:self];
    [_scalePopUpButton
        setAction:@selector(scalePopUpAction:)];

    // set a suitable font
    [_scalePopUpButton
        setFont:
          [NSFont toolTipsFontOfSize
            :_NSScaleMenuFontSize]];

    // Make sure the pop-up is big enough to fit the
cells.
    [_scalePopUpButton sizeToFit];

    // don't let it become first responder
    [ scalePopUpButton
      setRefusesFirstResponder:YES];

    // put it in the scroll view
    [self addSubview: scalePopUpButton];
    [_scalePopUpButton release];
    }
}
```

Adding Views from Outlets You can create a view hierarchy in Interface Builder by dragging views into the nib window (they do not have to be in their own windows). If you create an outlet in your object, you can connect such a windowless view to that outlet. You then can use addSubView to add that view when you need it.

See the next section for information on adding views to windows.

Removing Views   You sometimes need to remove a view from its hierarchy. The `removeFromSuperview` method does that. Note that this is the method of the view that you are removing: Cocoa takes care of fixing up the superview's hierarchy, responder chain, and the like.

```
public void removeFromSuperview(); //Java
- (void)removeFromSuperview; //Objective-C
```

Using Windows

Cocoa windows are much lighter-weight objects than you may be used to working with. In the first place, they are not descendants of the view class, so they do not bring with them a whole host of methods that are frequently overridden to remove view functionality from windows.

In the second place, window controller objects (NSWindow-Controller) manage loading, titling, and closing the window. Window controllers normally work with nib-based windows that you create in Interface Builder. There is usually one window controller per window.

Because windows are not views, and because window controllers handle their creation, windows have four primary roles to play:

1. They manage the display of the view hierarchy within them.

2. They manage event dispatching to those views.

3. They manage a text field editor that is shared among all of their text views.

4. They have a delegate that responds to events that affect the window (resizing and zooming).

Very much like views, windows are critical and pervasive objects in the framework—but they are overridden even less often than view objects. Windows, after all, not only display their views' data, but also are responsible for interacting with the Window Server and managing events and menus. Changing their appearance or behavior is often a mistake.

Occasionally, it is appropriate to add functionality to windows (rather than changing default behavior). You can do this easily by adding a delegate to the window—and this is common, easy to implement, and quite appropriate.

Window Delegate Methods

Rather than override an NSWindow, you typically add a delegate to the window. For example, a window delegate can implement `windowWillClose` in order to do special processing as a window is about to close.

The window delegate methods are listed at the bottom of NSWindow.h.

Window Notifications

Window notifications let you know when something will or has happened to a window. They are listed at the bottom of NSWindow.h along with the delegate methods. An object can register to receive a given window's `WindowWillCloseNotification` to do special processing at that time.

Geometry

Figure 20-4 shows the Interface Builder Size pane in the Info window for a window. You will note that in addition to the values you can set for views, there are other fields that you can use to set the minimum and maximum sizes of a window. You also can specify how it can be moved on the desktop.

Figure 20-4. Window Sizing in Interface Builder

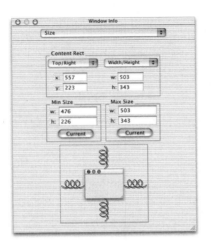

Window Controllers

Each window loaded from a nib file normally has a window controller. A variety of window controller methods are called as the window is created, and you can override them to set its title and otherwise manipulate the window just before it is shown.

Customizing the window title is frequently needed when a window displays the contents of a document. As a result, hooks in NSDocument let you access the controller during the load process, and you can generally avoid overriding NSWindowController.

One reason to override a window controller is when you have subsidiary nib files containing their own objects. The window controller can take responsibility for freeing the objects in the nib file when the window is closed and they are no longer needed. You can install your window controller as a delegate (implementing `windowWillClose`) or register for a notification (`WindowWillCloseNotification`) to do this.

If you do override NSWindowController, you normally override the following methods. You rarely call window controller methods (either original or overridden); Cocoa's default window loading and manipulation code works just fine.

Java:

```
public void windowDidLoad();
public void windowWillLoad();
public string windowTitleForDocumentDisplayName (
  String displayName);
```

Objective-C:

```
- (void)windowDidLoad;
- (void)windowWillLoad;
- (NSString *)windowTitleForDocumentDisplayName:(
  NSString *)displayName;
```

Creating and Loading Windows

The most basic (and frequent) use of windows is to have them open automatically from your main nib file along with the views and controls that you have placed there using Interface Builder. The second most basic and frequent use relies on a document; whenever a new document is created or an old one is opened, a window is opened to display the contents of the document. Both of these scenarios are implemented as templates in Interface Builder.

There are some more advanced and sophisticated issues that need to be addressed:

• Interrupting the loading of nib files to modify data in the window

• Setting position and responder status

• Programmatically adding views to a window

Working with Nib Files in Documents Two methods of NS-Document (windowControllerWillLoadNib and windowControllerDidLoadNib) are called as the document object loads its nib and prepares to open the window. Overriding `windowControllerDidLoadNib` is the right time to set values in the window. (If you override `windowControllerlerWillLoadNib`, the views and controls in the window are not yet there; however, you may do this is you need to prepare something that does not require them.)

Here is a method from Diary that overrides `windowControllerDidLoadNib` in order to fill the window's fields with data. Sketch does a similar process.

Several points about overriding `windowControllerDidLoadNib` are worth noting:

- Although it is a method of NSDocument, it provides you with access to the window controller (its argument) as well as to the window itself (via the controller's `window` accessor). If you need to store references to either one in your document, you can do so here.

- Toolbars, which are totally dynamic objects, need to be added to windows after they are created and just before they are displayed. This is the right hook to do that.

Java:

```
public void windowControllerDidLoadNib(
  NSWindowController aController) {

  super.windowControllerDidLoadNib(aController);

  this.loadFieldsFromDiaryData ();

  ...
  (aController.window()).setToolbar (theToolbar);
};
```

Objective-C:

```
- (void)windowControllerDidLoadNib:(
  NSWindowController *)windowController {
```

```
NSToolbar* toolbar;

[super windowControllerDidLoadNib:
  windowController];

[self loadFieldsFromDiaryData];

  ...

[[windowController window]setToolbar:toolbar];
}
```

Setting Position and Responder Window placement and activation is handled in most cases in response to a mouse click. However, sometimes when you open a window, you want to set them up manually. Again, windowControllerDidLoadNib (for NSDocument objects) or one of the window delegate or notifications is the right place to do this. The relevant methods you might call are:

Java:

```
public void makeKeyAndOrderFront(Object anObject);
public boolean makeFirstResponder
  (NSResponder aResponder);
```

Objective-C:

```
- (void)makeKeyAndOrderFront:(id)sender;
- (BOOL)makeFirstResponder:
  (NSResponder *)aResponder;
```

The first method, makeKeyAndOrderFront, makes the window the key and places it in the front. The parameter is the sender (an Object in Java, an id in Objective-C). In most usage, the sender is irrelevant and is set to null.

The second method, makeFirstResponder, is used to set a specific view (usually a control) to the head of the window's responder chain. (If the window is the key window, the window itself is at the front of the responder chain.) To use this method, you must have an identifier for the view to be made the first responder. It must be linked to an outlet, or it must have a tag that you can use to find it.

If you have saved window positions, you can restore them here. See "Saving Window Positions" on page 389.

Setting Subviews   Sometimes all or part of the window's content view is created separately—either dynamically or as a separate hierarchy in Interface Builder. If you need to set a window's view, use `setContentView`.

Working with Images

The biggest difference between imaging in this framework and imaging in other frameworks is the coordinate system that is used. In both cases, the horizontal axis running from left to right starts at zero and goes up. In the case of Mac OS 9 and earlier, however, the value of zero on the vertical access is at the top of the screen; in Cocoa, it is at the bottom. As a result, Mac OS objects were often located on the screen (or in a view) by means of their top-left point; in Cocoa, it is often the lower-left point.

Drawing normally takes place within views. Images are lightweight objects that you can draw without using a view. The image thus drawn can then be quickly moved to a view for display or printing.

Images can be in various formats; a single image may contain multiple representations of the same image using different formats. Each representation is an instance of a descendant of NSImageRep.

If you are coming from another framework, you can realize the efficiencies that images offer you: You have very little overhead and you don't have to worry about the representation.

NSImage

NSImage is responsible for managing all of its representations and for selecting (and drawing) the appropriate one for a given device. For convenience, images may be named.

Each NSImage may have a delegate that implements `image-DidNotDraw` (aRect—NSRect). This method is called only if NSImage was unable to draw the image. It returns an NSImage*—which could be an alternative image to draw. If it returns nil, NSImage no longer tries to draw the image, assuming either that the delegate has done so or that no image should be drawn.

NSImageRep

The image representation is what actually does the work for the image object. NSImageReps are created from raw images in files, on the pasteboard, and data objects in memory. The NSImage class maintains a registry of the image types that it can handle and the subclasses of NSImageRep that should be created for each one. Filtering services that may be present on a given system can expand the range of image types that are handled; NSImageRep provides methods for including or excluding filtering service conversions.

If you are not adding a new type of image representation, you can probably ignore this section: NSImage manages the process for you. The most probable case where you may need to be involved is one in which your application relies on specific filtering services.

Implementing Toolbars

Toolbars, one of the most useful and distinctive aspects of the Aqua interface, are totally dynamic objects. You may think of them as views and controls, but in reality, they usually are not. They are built at run time, and doing so brings together a number of the concepts discussed in this chapter and the previous ones.

Here are the steps in using a toolbar:

1. Declare names for the toolbar items.

2. Set default toolbar items.

3. Set allowable toolbar items (for all toolbars, but necessary for customizable toolbars).

4. Create the toolbar when the window is about to open.

5. Return NSToolbarItem objects on demand; they dispatch the appropriate methods in response to user clicks on the images in the toolbar.

Declare Toolbar Item Names

The Diary toolbar contains five icons:

1. New

2. Delete

3. Next

4. Back

5. Drawer

Note that each of these items corresponds to a method in the application. Furthermore, each of those methods can also be invoked from the menu bar. Because a toolbar is visible or not at the user's option, you must provide an alternative way of getting to its functionality.

Each toolbar item has a string identifying it; these are not the strings that appear if the users select the option to use names and icons. (See "Create Toolbar Items for Response to User Clicks" on page 447 for those strings.)

Java:

```
private static final String NewToolbarItem =
  "New";
private static final String DeleteToolbarItem =
  "Delete";
private static final String NextToolbarItem =
  "Next";
private static final String PreviousToolbarItem =
  "Back";
private static final String DrawerToolbarItem =
  "Drawer";
```

Objective-C:

```
NSString *NewToolbarItem = @"New";
NSString *DeleteToolbarItem = @"Delete";
NSString *NextToolbarItem = @"Next";
NSString *PreviousToolbarItem = @"Back";
NSString *DrawerToolbarItem = @"Drawer";
```

Set Default Toolbar Items

You must set a delegate for your toolbar (in Diary and many other applications it is the main document object, because that is guaranteed to be overridden—NSWindow is usually not overridden, nor is NSApplication.) The delegate must implement all of the NSToolbar delegate methods. If it does not, the `setDelegate` method will fail and display an error message on the console in Project Builder (in debug mode).

If your toolbar does not appear, check the console, and check the delegates.

This is boilerplate code. First, you create a mutable array that will be returned as the result of the function. Then, you add the string constants you declared to the array. Finally, you return the array which, at this point, consists merely of an array of String objects (Java) or NSString* objects (Objective-C).

Java:

```
public NSArray toolbarDefaultItemIdentifiers
  (NSToolbar toolbar) {
  NSMutableArray toolbarIdentifiers =
    new NSMutableArray ();

  toolbarIdentifiers.addObject
    (PreviousToolbarItem);
  toolbarIdentifiers.addObject
    (NextToolbarItem);
  toolbarIdentifiers.addObject
    (NewToolbarItem);
  toolbarIdentifiers.addObject
    (DeleteToolbarItem);
  toolbarIdentifiers.addObject
    (DrawerToolbarItem);

  return toolbarIdentifiers;
}
```

Objective-C:

```
- (NSArray *)toolbarDefaultItemIdentifiers:(
  NSToolbar*)toolbar
  {
    NSMutableArray* itemIdentifiers =
      [[[NSMutableArray alloc]init] autorelease];

    [itemIdentifiers addObject:
      NewToolbarItem];

    [itemIdentifiers addObject:
      DeleteToolbarItem];

    [itemIdentifiers addObject:
      NextToolbarItem];
```

```
    [itemIdentifiers addObject:
      PreviousToolbarItem];

    [itemIdentifiers addObject:
      DrawerToolbarItem];

  return itemIdentifiers;
}
```

Set Allowed Toolbar Items

You need a similar array of strings representing the allowed toolbar items. The only difference in Diary is the name of the method. (In customizable toolbars, the default array is usually smaller than the allowed array.)

Java:

```java
public NSArray toolbarAllowedItemIdentifiers
  (NSToolbar toolbar) {
  NSMutableArray toolbarIdentifiers =
    new NSMutableArray ();
  toolbarIdentifiers.addObject
    (NewToolbarItem);
  toolbarIdentifiers.addObject
    (DeleteToolbarItem);
  toolbarIdentifiers.addObject
    (NextToolbarItem);
  toolbarIdentifiers.addObject
    (PreviousToolbarItem);
  toolbarIdentifiers.addObject
    (DrawerToolbarItem);

  return toolbarIdentifiers;
}
```

Objective-C:

```objc
- (NSArray *)toolbarAllowedItemIdentifiers:(
NSToolbar*)toolbar
  {
    NSMutableArray* itemIdentifiers =
      [[[NSMutableArray alloc]init] autorelease];
```

```
    [itemIdentifiers addObject:
      NewToolbarItem];

    [itemIdentifiers addObject:
      DeleteToolbarItem];

    [itemIdentifiers addObject:
      NextToolbarItem];

    [itemIdentifiers addObject:
      PreviousToolbarItem];

    [itemIdentifiers addObject:
      DrawerToolbarItem];

  return itemIdentifiers;
}
```

Create the Toolbar

When the window is created and about to open, you need to create the toolbar. Here is the code to do that; all you do is change the names of the toolbar elements.

Java:

```
public void windowControllerDidLoadNib(
  NSWindowController aController) {

  super.windowControllerDidLoadNib(aController);
  this.loadFieldsFromDiaryData ();

  //notifications removed for clarity

  NSToolbar theToolbar = new NSToolbar
    ("DiaryToolbar");
  theToolbar.setVisible (true);
  theToolbar.setDelegate (this);
  theToolbar.setDisplayMode (DisplayModeDefault);

  theToolbar.insertItemWithItemIdentifierAtIndex
    (NewToolbarItem, 0);
  theToolbar.insertItemWithItemIdentifierAtIndex
```

```
        (DeleteToolbarItem, 1);
    theToolbar.insertItemWithItemIdentifierAtIndex
        (NextToolbarItem, 2);
    theToolbar.insertItemWithItemIdentifierAtIndex
        (PreviousToolbarItem, 3);
    theToolbar.insertItemWithItemIdentifierAtIndex
        (DrawerToolbarItem, 4);

    theToolbar.allowsUserCustomization ();
    (aController.window()).setToolbar (theToolbar);
}
```

Objective-C:

```
- (void)windowControllerDidLoadNib:(
  NSWindowController *)windowController {
    NSToolbar* toolbar;

    [super windowControllerDidLoadNib:
        windowController];
    [self loadFieldsFromDiaryData];

    //notifications removed for clarity

    toolbar = [[NSToolbar alloc] initWithIdentifier:
        @"Diary Toolbar"];
    [toolbar setVisible:true];
    [toolbar setDelegate:self];
    [toolbar setDisplayMode:DisplayModeDefault];

    [toolbar insertItemWithItemIdentifier:
        NewToolbarItem atIndex:0];
    [toolbar insertItemWithItemIdentifier:
        DeleteToolbarItem atIndex:1];
    [toolbar insertItemWithItemIdentifier:
        NextToolbarItem atIndex:2];
    [toolbar insertItemWithItemIdentifier:
        PreviousToolbarItem atIndex:3];
    [toolbar insertItemWithItemIdentifier:
        DrawerToolbarItem atIndex:4];
```

```
    [[windowController window]setToolbar:toolbar];
}
```

Create Toolbar Items for Response to User Clicks

The delegate's `toolbarItemForItemIdentifier` method is called to actually set up the toolbar. This, too, is boilerplate code. There is a subtle difference in the Java and Objective-C code that follows: The target for the item can be set in each clause of the `if` statement or embedded in an additional `if` statement at the bottom. You can do it either way in either language.

For each of your potential toolbar icons, do the following:

1. Create an NSToolbarItem object.

2. Check whether the item clicked (`itemIdentifier`) matches a specific toolbar item name that you set using the constants in step 1.

3. Set a label to appear under the icon (if the toolbar display mode is set to do so—here the default is used, and it does display a label).

4. Provide a tool tip.

5. Set the item's action—you create a selector for the method to be linked to the icon.

6. Set the image for the icon.

Note that for customizable toolbars, there are additional values you can set.

Java:

```
public NSToolbarItem toolbarItemForItemIdentifier
    (NSToolbar toolbar, String itemIdentifier,
        boolean willInsert) {
```

```java
NSToolbarItem item =
  new NSToolbarItem(itemIdentifier);

if (itemIdentifier.equals(NextToolbarItem)) {
  item.setLabel ("Next");
  item.setToolTip ("Next");
  item.setAction (
    new NSSelector ("stepEntryForward",
      new Class[]{DiaryDocument.class}));
  item.setImage (NSImage.imageNamed("Next"));
} else
if (itemIdentifier.equals(PreviousToolbarItem))
{
  item.setLabel ("Back");
  item.setToolTip ("Back");
  item.setAction (
   new NSSelector ("stepEntryBackward",
     new Class[]{DiaryDocument.class}));
  item.setImage (NSImage.imageNamed("Back"));
} else
if (itemIdentifier.equals(NewToolbarItem))
{
  item.setLabel ("New");
  item.setToolTip ("New");
  item.setAction (
    new NSSelector ("addEntry",
      new Class[]{DiaryDocument.class}));
  item.setImage (NSImage.imageNamed("New"));
} else
if (itemIdentifier.equals(DeleteToolbarItem)) {
  item.setLabel ("Delete");
  item.setToolTip ("Delete");
  item.setAction (
    new NSSelector ("deleteEntry",
      new Class[]{DiaryDocument.class}));
  item.setImage (NSImage.imageNamed("Delete"));
} else
if (itemIdentifier.equals(DrawerToolbarItem)) {
  item.setLabel ("Drawer");
  item.setToolTip ("Drawer");
```

```
    item.setAction (
      new NSSelector ("toggleDrawer",
        new Class[]{DiaryDocument.class}));
    item.setImage (NSImage.imageNamed("Drawer"));
  } else
  {
    item = null;
  };
  if (item != null)
    {
    item.setTarget (this);
    item.setEnabled (true);
    };
  return item;
}
```

Objective-C:

```
- (NSToolbarItem *) toolbar: (NSToolbar *)toolbar
    itemForItemIdentifier: (NSString *) itemIdent
    willBeInsertedIntoToolbar:
      (BOOL) willBeInserted
  {
  NSToolbarItem *toolbarItem =
    [[[NSToolbarItem alloc]
      initWithItemIdentifier: itemIdent]
      autorelease];

    if ([itemIdent isEqual: NextToolbarItem]) {
      [toolbarItem setLabel: @"Next"];
      [toolbarItem setToolTip: @"Next"];
      [toolbarItem setImage:
        [NSImage imageNamed: @"Next"]];
      [toolbarItem setTarget: self];
      [toolbarItem setAction:
        @selector(stepEntryForward:)];
    } else
    if ([itemIdent isEqual: BackToolbarItem]) {
      [toolbarItem setLabel: @"Back"];
      [toolbarItem setToolTip: @"Back"];
      [toolbarItem setImage:
        [NSImage imageNamed: @"Back"]];
```

```
            [toolbarItem setTarget: self];
            [toolbarItem setAction:
              @selector(stepEntryBackward:)];
        } else
    if ([itemIdent isEqual: NewToolbarItem]) {
            [toolbarItem setLabel: @"New"];
            [toolbarItem setToolTip: @"New"];
            [toolbarItem setImage:
              [NSImage imageNamed: @"New"]];
            [toolbarItem setTarget: self];
            [toolbarItem setAction:
              @selector(addEntry:)];
        } else
    if ([itemIdent isEqual: DeleteToolbarItem]) {
            [toolbarItem setLabel: @"Delete"];
            [toolbarItem setToolTip: @"Delete"];
            [toolbarItem setImage:
              [NSImage imageNamed: @"Delete"]];
            [toolbarItem setTarget: self];
            [toolbarItem setAction:
              @selector(deleteEntry:)];
        } else
    if ([itemIdent isEqual: DrawerToolbarItem]) {
            [toolbarItem setLabel: @"Drawer"];
            [toolbarItem setToolTip: @"Drawer"];
            [toolbarItem setImage:
              [NSImage imageNamed: @"Drawer"]];
            [toolbarItem setTarget: self];
            [toolbarItem setAction:
              @selector(toggleDrawer:)];
        } else
      else
        {
        toolbarItem = nil;
        }
      return toolbarItem;
}
```

Drawers

Unlike toolbars, drawers are actual view and window objects. In fact, they are a trio of objects: a window, a drawer object that provides the functionality, and a content view that is placed within the drawer.

You can create them dynamically in Interface Builder. A palette item provides all three when you drag it into a nib. The only additional piece of functionality that you need is the ability to open and close the drawer in response to user actions.

1. Declare an outlet in your object for the drawer:

```
private NSDrawer drawer; //Java
IBOutlet NSDrawer *drawer; //Objective-C
```

2. Link the drawer to an outlet in your object using Interface Builder.

3. As needed, call the NSDrawer object's `toggleDraw-er` method:

Java:

```
public void toggleDrawer (Object Sender) {
        ((NSDrawer)drawer).toggle(this);
}
```

Objective-C:

```
- (IBAction)toggleDrawer:(id)sender
{
    [drawer toggle: self];
}
```

Summary

This chapter has provided you with an overview of the main Aqua interface elements, views, and windows, along with two of the more interesting additions to the developer's set of tools—toolbars and drawers. Compared to other frameworks, there is less overriding in Cocoa: You focus in on what you want to do, and accomplish it using techniques such as delegation.

In fact, there is even more to visualization—special views to manage scrolling and text, for example. They are similar to objects in other frameworks, and you generally use them in Interface Builder without modifying them.

The next chapter—which deals with controls—also touches on features that are common to other frameworks. It, though, is more specialized than this chapter. Interface Builder and the ability to wire objects together easily using a graphical user interface (for the programmer!) make the deployment and programming of controls much easier in the Cocoa environment.

Chapter 21
Interface Design and Controls

Except for command line tools and services, almost every Mac OS X application has a graphical user interface. The design of that interface is up to the application developer, but Apple provides an abundance of guidance, assistance, and resources to help you develop the interface. The reason for this assistance is twofold:

- *Apple wants to help developers produce software that, in turn, drives sales of its products.*

- *The overall look and feel of a computer running Mac OS X is more consistent and satisfying to users when all applications adhere to standards.*

If you are using Cocoa, MacApp, or PowerPlant, you have taken a large step toward consistency and standards. The buttons, text fields, sliders, and other controls that you implement are drawn by the respective frameworks and they implement Apple's interface guidelines.

This chapter addresses the general issue of guidelines and standards and explains why they are important for your application. It then walks through each of the interface elements that you can use in Interface Builder, providing you with the terminology, human interface guidelines, and relevant programming topics for each one. These interface elements are grouped into three categories:

- *Action controls such as buttons that users employ to initiate (or stop) processing.*

- *Interface elements that allow users to enter data—text, choices, and the like.*

- *Output elements that provide information to users from the program.*

The focus of this chapter is on the Aqua interface, which can be implemented both in Cocoa and in Carbon. You can use Interface Builder in both environments, although if you have a Carbon application that does not use nib files, it is not particularly productive to do so.

The Role of Guidelines and Standards

From its start in 1984, the Macintosh computer has led the way for the industry in hardware and software design. Because design has been a key component of the Macintosh, Apple has promulgated its design guidelines and standards to developers so that all Macintosh applications can look and behave as similarly as possible. Consistency of interface design means that the learning curve for a new application is much less challenging for users.

The behavior of interface elements is even more critical than their appearance. The disclosure triangle that lets you expand lists and dialogs is now widely recognized by users, as is the sort order triangle that appears at the top of columns in list views. Both are shown in Figure 21-1.

Figure 21-1. Disclosure Triangles and Sort Buttons

**Disclosure   Sort Button
Triangles**

When you think about it, these interface elements (*widgets*, to some) are extraordinarily complex. Their behaviors are simple: disclosing or hiding details and sorting a list. However, what they do depends on their context. A triangle pointing down or to the right and located in the margin of a list is a disclosure triangle; one pointing up or down and located in the title of a column in a list view is a sort button.

Yet, having used such interface elements once, most users understand what they are and have no problem using them in other environments. Even a somewhat different use of a disclosure triangle (in the Save sheet shown in Figure 21-2) is usually not a mystery to users who see it for the first time.

Remember that most people are totally uninterested in learning how to use your program's interface: They are interested in doing what your program lets them do. Whenever someone focuses on a tool rather than the task, something is wrong.

Figure 21-2. Disclosure Button in a Save Sheet

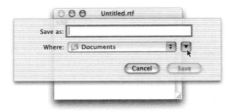

It is very important to Apple's ease-of-use reputation that all of the applications running on the Macintosh adhere to the guidelines. Your creativity should be focused on the substance of your application, and not on inventing new interface widgets.

If you need a new interface functionality, try to use existing interface elements in a new *and consistent* manner. For example, it would probably be a poor choice to decide that a triangle could function as a zoom button. That is somewhat similar to its normal behavior of showing and hiding information, but the fact that zooming involves resizing the image is sufficient to argue that it is not the same and a different element should be used.

Interface functionality that applies (or could apply) to a variety of applications should use the standard elements if at all possible. If you need changes or extensions that others might want to use, check the Apple Developer Connection mailing lists and forums to see what may be in the works.

When it comes to domain-specific functionality for your own application, feel free to invent consistent and logical interface elements that reflect the world of gene splicing, money supply management, and the like. Apple is not going to have widgets for you, so there is no point looking.

In short:

1. Use the standard interface elements.

2. Do not redefine them.

3. Implement new interface elements that are specific to your application and its world.

Apple's User Experience Web page (http://developer.apple.com/ue/) contains a host of documentation as well as references to sample code. In particular, the *Aqua Human Interface Guidelines* (downloadable in a PDF file) are essential to any developer. During the development of Mac OS X, this publication has been revised several times, so make certain that you have the current version. (Sizes of interface elements changed fairly late in the development process.)

Note that many of the controls in this chapter use the System font. That is 13-point Lucida Grande for United States/Roman systems. In other locations, it may vary, and you should check the actual font. By default, Interface Builder does the right thing if your development location is set properly while you are laying out the interface.

User Actions

Actions are initiated for the most part by buttons and toolbar icons. A mouse click—sometimes modified with a keyboard modifier—causes an immediate action to occur. Sometimes the immediate action is the cessation of a process—as in the case of a Stop button for a copy command.

There are six types of controls that can cause immediate actions; four of them are buttons.

1. Rounded bevel button

2. Square button

3. Round button

4. Push button

5. Checkbox

6. Radio button

There are two basic pieces of information the designer has to convey to a user when it comes to user action controls:

1. You can click on this item.

2. An action—which must be made clear—will occur immediately.

This may seem self-evident, but look objectively at software—even some of the best software—and you will see interface mysteries galore. Often in the specious name of "design" people eliminate the subliminal clues that guide users. Clickable items are normally bordered—that's a clue. How many times have you found yourself looking at an interface or Web site and wondering what is hot? How many times have you spent an inordinate amount of time searching for something only to discover that clicking on an apparently dead image (a corporate logo?) will do the trick?

If there is any ambiguity about whether something is clickable, use the Help pane in the Info window in Interface Builder to add a tool tip. The presence of the tool tip—almost without regard to its content—will tell the user a mouse click is appropriate.

Remember that context is important in the interface. Users of the Aqua interface have come to know and love the toolbar. There are usually no standard buttons in the toolbar; there are normally no borders (unless they are part of an icon). Users have had no trouble learning that any image in the toolbar is clickable. This means that you must learn the converse: No unclickable (i.e., decorative) elements can go in a toolbar.

As you will see in the Info window in Interface Builder, you can set a variety of attributes for each button, including the following:

- A title (such as OK or Cancel).

- An icon.

- A keyboard equivalent.

- A sound to play when the button is clicked. The Sounds tab in your nib file contains a variety of sounds (you can add others by dragging them in). Type the name of a sound into the Sound field in the Info window and it will play in response to the mouse click.

- Feedback behavior—a momentary change or light of the button; toggle, change from on to off; and so forth.

- You can choose between normal and small sizes for most of these buttons. Small sizes are useful for palettes and less important interface elements.

To explore these and other attributes, drag a button from the palette into a view, change the settings, and use the Test Interface (COMMAND-R) command to see what happens.

Not all of these buttons accept all of the attributes.

Push Buttons

This is the most basic button. Users recognize it from its extensive use in the interface to Mac OS X. You cannot place an icon in this button, and you should use the System font for the text. A small size is available.

Round Buttons

A round button can contain an icon; if it does, its title is normally included in the graphic. A small size is available.

Rounded Bevel Buttons

Rounded bevel buttons can contain icons. They may or may not have text in them. You can use bevel buttons with icons in them as data input devices; the immediate action consists of setting a programmatic value (such as paper orientation in Page Setup). There is no small size, but you can resize the button as you see fit.

Square Buttons

Except for the border, this is the same as a rounded bevel button in its appearance and behavior.

Radio Buttons and Checkboxes

These can be used as action controls, but normally they are considered to be user input controls, setting values that will be acted upon later when the user clicks OK (or some other control). They are discussed later in this chapter in "User Input" starting on page 461.

Steppers

This control, originally part of the Classic Mac environment, is used for small adjustments to numerical information (such as the hour or minutes in setting the time). It also is used in contexts like that for changing text (AM/PM, in the time). Using Interface Builder, you can set its low and high values, decide whether it wraps around, and set the increment. If you attach a stepper to an outlet, you can access it programmatically from within Cocoa and set these values dynamically. Usually, a stepper control is placed next to a text field in which the results of its stepping can be seen.

User Input

There are four basic types of user input:

1. Text

2. Images

3. Multiple choices

4. Continuous choices

Text Fields

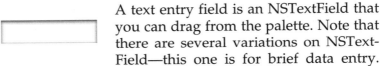

A text entry field is an NSTextField that you can drag from the palette. Note that there are several variations on NSText-Field—this one is for brief data entry. You select the font and other text attributes by selecting the field in your window and using the Format menu in Interface Builder.

Remember the imagination and creativity of users: There are critical clues to indicate that this interface element is designed to be typed in. Cocoa automatically handles tabbing among data entry fields in a view. The tabbing proceeds from the upper left to the bottom right, stopping at each entry field along the way. When ready for keystrokes, a focus ring appears around a text entry field indicating to the user that is the destination of keystrokes.

Spacing within and among text fields is critically important so that they look good and so that users can read them. The guidelines in Interface Builder help you adjust the spacing appropriately. (Note that guidelines appear for text baselines, which helps you make different-sized or different-font labels match up with data entry text.)

Field1:

Field2:

It is useful to have a composite object containing labeled fields that you can use as a starting point for developing a data entry interface. Interface Builder provides such an object. It is a group of two text entry fields and two static text label fields.

You can expand this object as necessary. If you need to do so, first select it in Interface Builder. Then, ungroup the objects using the Layout menu. Add more text fields (or select and copy these) until you have the right number. Adjust the labels and regroup.

Text Views

The text view object comes complete with its own text editing environment and a scroller that contains it. You use fields such as those shown in the previous section for small amounts of data entry (one line or less); a text view is intended to hold larger amounts of text, offer more editing functionality, and provide the ability to add images. You can control all of this from the Attributes pane in the Info window for a text view.

Text views (like text fields) support the clipboard, so users can enter text by using the Paste command or from the keyboard.

Because this view in the Interface Builder palette comes complete with its containing scroller, you have very little work to do to implement sophisticated text manipulation of large amounts of text.

Image Input

Text input comes primarily from the keyboard. Image input comes through the clipboard or through drag-and-drop. (You can implement your own drawing and image manipulation routines as is the case in the Sketch example, but they are not part of the Cocoa objects. In other words, there is no NSDrawingImage view complete with menu and palette commands.)

In addition to setting the size of an image view, you can set its scaling characteristics. This is important not only when the user resizes the window, but also when the image that the user pastes into the image view is not the same size.

Color Well

A color well object lets users store colors for use in their applications. Clicking a color well brings up the Color Picker. Selecting a color from the Color Picker then places that color in the color well.

Although the image input and color well objects as shown here look quite similar, they are not identical. Notice the difference in the borders between the two. Also, in practice, they are used at very different sizes. The color well is usually the size shown here (after all, it merely contains a swatch of color). The image input object is normally substantially bigger. Also, the color well normally appears in a palette or with other tools, and the image input object appears in the context of user data.

Choices

In addition to text and image input, users are often requested to provide choices from discrete or continuous objects.

Checkboxes Checkboxes let users choose yes or no from one or more elements. The choices need not be mutually exclusive. A small version of the checkbox is available. Checkboxes are sometimes used to launch actions, but users typically do not expect them to do so.

One very common use of a checkbox to launch an action is a checkbox that, when clicked, causes changes to the interface. For example, if you click a checkbox labeled "Collate Pages," subsidiary checkboxes or radio buttons might let you choose forward- or reverse-collating. (But remember that users like to control the interface, and any such changes that may appear mysterious can irritate users who then are frustrated in trying to get back to data entry elements that they just saw a moment ago—and that subsequently vanished into thin air.)

Checkboxes often are grouped together (see "Groupings" on page 468) into logically related items.

Radio Buttons A set of checkboxes presents independent choices to users; radio buttons let users choose among mutually exclusive choices. Because the set of choices is important, radio buttons are normally grouped in a box or otherwise set aside so that two sets of radio buttons do not confuse users.

Radio buttons are available in small sizes. Like checkboxes, they can initiate actions; however, the same caveats apply to using radio buttons to launch actions as apply to checkboxes in the same situation.

Pop-up Menus Radio buttons allow mutually exclusive choices, all of which are visible to the user at one time (subject to window scrolling). However, a set of more than about 4–7 at the most is confusing to users. A pop-up menu provides a simple way of handling a set of mutually exclusive choices that range from that number up to about 12. The choices are all visible at one time, but only when the user has clicked on the pop-up menu.

Placing more than about a dozen items in a pop-up menu produces a scrolling list that is unmanageable. The government of Canada had this in mind when setting up the country's 10 provinces and 3 territories: A pop-up menu is fine for selecting one of them in an address. The 50 states of the United States are eminently unsuited for a pop-up menu, but that has not stopped interface designers from using them. (See Combo boxes, in the next section, for ideas about dealing with the states.)

The problems with long pop-up menu lists include the fact that it is hard to navigate with the mouse down to the right choice and the fact that the long list often zooms off the top or bottom of the display.

A pop-up menu appears with the current choice centered on the control. That is, the menu can extend both above and below the control itself, depending on where the choice is. A pull-down menu extends below the control when the mouse is clicked on it. A pull-down menu is distinguished from a pop-up menu by a single down arrow at the right rather than the pair of up and down arrows shown here. You can select between the two in Interface Builder.

Pop-up and pull-down menus (the controls that users see and that are described in documentation) are implemented with the NSPopUpButton class.

Combo Boxes A combo box combines a text entry field with a pop-up menu. Users can use one of the predefined choices or they can type in their own. A particularly useful feature is the Completes attribute (set in the Attributes pane of the Info window). If a user starts to type in the text field, Cocoa will pick an entry from the pop-up menu that matches the keys processed so far.

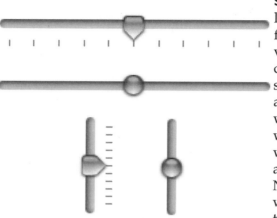

Sliders Sliders let users select from a range of values. Both vertical and horizontal sliders are available; each comes with versions with markers and without. In fact, all of these are NSSlider objects with various attributes shown (each of the four is separately shown on the Interface Builder palette).

Placards Placards allow user input using pop-up menus, buttons, or other controls. They appear in windows—often in scroll bars as shown here.

They are usually set programmatically and can contain any control (or even explanatory information). The example code for TextEdit was described in the previous chapter (see the section "makeScalePopUpButton" on page 429).

Providing Information to the User

In addition to allowing users to start actions and to enter data, interface elements display information to the user. Sometimes these roles merge. For example, users frequently can change the information that is presented to them.

Displaying Text

Informational Text

Message Text

The same text field object that is used for data entry can also be used for displaying unmodifiable text. The Interface Builder palette has two such objects that you can use. After you drag one of them into your window, you click the text field to enter text, and you use the Format menu to format it.

You can enable such a text field. That way, if a user clicks on it, something will happen. In almost all cases, that is a mistake. Users normally do not click on text that is not editable (the absence of a border and focus ring and the inability to select text are clues that this is not editable text).

Displaying Progress

A progress bar can show a user that something is happening. Feedback is important for letting a user feel in control. Progress bars can be indeterminate (such as this one), or they can be determinate—you change the attribute in the Info window. Wherever possible, determinate progress bars are better, because the user can get a sense of how much time is left. Sometimes, however, it is impossible to calculate the duration of a task.

If you are programming something that may take quite a while, do everything you can to provide a range of feedback so that the user does not give up and force the application to quit. One example of good user feedback for determinate and indeterminate processes is the Installer. At all times, a list of the tasks is visible at the left of the window. When each task is performed, a progress bar of some kind is usually displayed. Thus, even if the user does not know how much time is left in a given step, the status of the entire process is understandable.

Organizing
Information

Five ways of organizing information are available in Interface Builder. The simplest is the ability to group interface elements; the others allow formatted and controlled displays of large amounts of organized data.

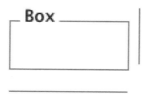

Groupings A box can contain any number of controls. You can drag them into it—or you can select them and choose the Group In submenu from the Layout menu. (You can group items into a custom view, a scroller, or a box.)

The box can be named, but it also can simply consist of lines. You can use boxes to organize controls in a complex window. However, remember that some of your controls will group themselves. If you have a set of three radio buttons in a window—and only that one set of three radio buttons—you do not need to box them. If you have a set of three radio buttons and another set of four, boxes are likely to be a good idea.

Tab View If you find yourself grouping too many objects with boxes, consider rearranging your window so that not all of them are visible at one time.

A tab view lets you place several views into a window. (System Preferences uses tab views extensively.)

For all practical purposes, six tabs are about as many as you can expect to put into a window; more than that means that the tab titles start to merge. However, if you consider that a tab view effectively allows you to make a window up to six times larger, it can be a very effective space-saver.

In organizing tabs, make their names descriptive and simple. Tab 1 and Tab 2 (or Step 1 and Step 2) are not good names. To edit tab views in Interface Builder, click the tabs to type in new names. You can also add new controls to the individual views. (See "Tab Views" on page 267 for help on doing this.)

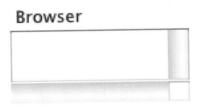

Browser A browser is a very sophisticated way of displaying rows and columns of data. It is used extensively throughout Mac OS X (in the Finder columns view, for example), and users understand its functionality. (Users learn very sophisticated interfaces if there is a consistent logic to them—and if they appear frequently.)

The definitive source for the browser is Tech. Note 2009 (located on Apple's developer Web site at http://developer.apple.com/technotes/tn/tn2009.html). The definitive example is SimpleBrowser, which implements the Finder columns view.

Browsers always have a horizontal scroll bar. Each panel has a vertical scroll bar. Any of these may be disabled if the window is big enough or the volume of data is small enough.

You set up browsers with descriptions of the data: element IDs for the rows and property IDs for the columns. You then provide callback routines for the browser to use: It will request whatever data is required when it is needed. Everything that is involved with navigation is handled automatically by the browser itself. All you do is provide the data.

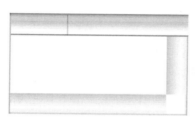

Table View A table view implements a basic table or spreadsheet, and it manages column resizing, selection, and editing for you.

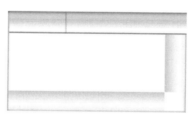

Outline View Outline views, a subclass of table views, are similar to the Finder's list view. They consist of entries which can be opened or closed with disclosure triangles.

Like the browser, an outline view relies on you to describe and later to provide the data.

Small Control Variants

Most controls have variants that are smaller versions of themselves. The small variants are not just scaled: They may use different font sizes for their text, for example. You can use Interface Builder's Show Info window to select the small variants. They are useful for toolbars and for other subsidiary purposes in windows.

Summary

This chapter provided an overview of the Aqua interface controls you can use in both Cocoa and Carbon. They fall into three groups: user action controls that allow the user to do something with a mouse click, user input controls that allow input of data (usually via the keyboard or clipboard), and user information controls that display data to the user.

Each control has been named and identified. Using interface elements consistently (and consistently with the Apple human interface guidelines) makes your application easier to learn and use—it also makes it look like (and be) a true Mac OS X application.

In most cases, your application will appear next to other applications: Macintosh users have always used a number of applications at the same time because of the similarity of their interfaces. In a shared environment like this, not only is it important to make your application fit in visually, but you also have to be a good neighbor, sharing the computer's resources properly. That idea is explored in the following chapter.

Chapter 22
Living in a Shared Environment

"Sharing" is used in its broadest sense in this chapter. It refers to the sharing of computer resources and of data over time and space. You may think of sharing as something that doesn't affect you or your applications—you are resolutely single-user and single-machine in your design. But sharing affects almost every user and every application.

You share the processor and all of the computer resources with the operating system; when you copy data from one application to another, you are sharing it via the clipboard; and when you open a document that you created yesterday, you are sharing the data that was stored then. Beyond that, if your computer has two or more processors, they share the responsibility for running your application (and

473

any other work that they may happen to be doing). Within your application, you may choose to use several threads that can process more or less simultaneously as the operating system optimizes the sharing of its resources; and within your application—even if it is single-threaded—your objects may share themselves and data elements.

Cocoa provides the tools to do all this at a very basic level—so basic that you may not even be aware of what it's doing all the time. Your awareness and implementation of sharing are limited to implementing a few class-specific methods and calling some memory management methods—if you need to do so.

All of the classes and methods in this chapter are widely used. Archiving and unarchiving objects are the essence of Interface Builder (you create the interface objects, it builds them, then archives them in a nib file). The coding methods and protocol are used both for archiving and for clipboard and services support. The locking protocol and methods are used for synchronism throughout the system. NSThread, of course, is the heart of multithreaded applications.

Archiving, Serialization, and Distribution

All object-oriented programming languages make it very easy to create objects at run time—nothing could be simpler. However, as soon as it is necessary to store that object on disk or to move it to a different address space or run-time environment, problems crop up.

The archiving and distribution architecture is described in this section. The sophisticated handling of moving graphs of objects to and from memory is done for you by the framework; even the work of managing small graphs of objects (the views of a window, for instance) is done by standard objects (such as NSView). You don't have to worry about how it happens. ("Graph" in this sense refers to the structured collections of objects that may relate to one another, such as the controls within a view that in turn is located within a window.)

Terminology

Archiving is the process of taking objects from memory and storing them on disk (it actually includes both archiving and serialization—the distinction will be made shortly). *Distribution* is the process of taking objects from your application's address space and preparing them for transfer to another address space dynamically. Both archiving and distribution are based on the abstract superclass NSCoder and on the NSCoding protocol. NSObject adopts the NSCoding protocol and has specific methods to support NSCoder and the NSCoding protocol. As a result, all NSObjects have the basic ability to be archived and distributed (although not all implement the protocol).

Archiving is the general process of moving objects from memory to disk, and vice versa. Where a distinction needs to be made in the direction, *unarchiving* is used. It is noted in the text that archiving refers only to the to-disk direction. Otherwise, archiving is used without regard to direction.

Coding is the process of converting an object to a format that can be shared—either on disk in a file or with another process on the same machine or elsewhere on the network. NSCoder objects are passed around in various NSObject methods as objects are being encoded and decoded. In practice, the objects that are passed around are descendants of NSCoder: NSArchiver and NSUnarchiver for files, and NSPortCoder for passing objects to another process or another machine on the network.

Archiving

Archivers use NSData objects to store their data; those objects are then read to or written from disk. Archiving works with full-fledged objects. The result of an unarchive method is an NSData type that can be immediately coerced to the type that you know it is.

Archiving   As the following code snippets from Diary show, you can archive an object by passing it to the `archived-DataWithRootObject` method of NSArchiver class. Once you have an NSData object, you can place it in a dictionary with a key—`entryImageKey`, in this case.

You will notice that the dictionary is built up directly with the `_ID` and `_title` objects. Dictionaries can only contain a limited number of types of objects. NSData is among them, but NSImageRep is not. Therefore, you need to convert the NSImageRep object to an NSData object before processing it in the dictionary. This is such a common occurrence—converting a Cocoa object to an NSData object—that the underlined code to archive and unarchive the image is boilerplate code. Just change the name of the variable with the object to be archived.

Java:

```
public NSMutableDictionary
  propertyListRepresentation() {
  NSMutableDictionary dict =
    new NSMutableDictionary();

  dict.setObjectForKey(_ID,entryIDKey);
  dict.setObjectForKey(_title,entryTitleKey);
  ...

  if (_image != null) {
    dict.setObjectForKey(
      NSArchiver.archivedDataWithRootObject
        (image), entryImageKey);
  }
  return dict;
}
```

Objective-C:

```
- (NSDictionary*) propertyListRepresentation
{
  NSMutableDictionary *dict =
    [NSMutableDictionary dictionary];
```

```
[dict setObject:_ID forKey:entryIDKey];
[dict setObject:_title forKey:entryTitleKey];
 ...

if (_image) {
  [dict setObject:
    [NSArchiver
      archivedDataWithRootObject: image
      forKey:entryImageKey]];
  }
 return dict;
}
```

Unarchiving Unarchiving is similarly easy. You do need to check that you actually have found an NSData object with the right key in the dictionary. Once you have it, you can safely unarchive it and coerce it to the type that you know it is.

Java:

```
public void loadPropertyListRepresentation (NSDic-
  tionary dict) {
  Object obj;

  _ID = (String)dict.objectForKey(entryIDKey);
  _title = (String)dict.objectForKey
    (entryTitleKey);

  obj = dict.objectForKey(entryImageKey);
  if (obj != null) {
    _image = (NSImage)
      NSUnarchiver.unarchiveObjectWithData
        ((NSData)obj);
  }
}
```

Objective-C:

```
- (void)loadPropertyListRepresentation:
    (NSDictionary *)dict {

  id obj;
```

```
_ID = (NSString *)[dict objectForKey:entryIDKey];
_title = (NSString *)
  [dict objectForKey:entryTitleKey];

obj = [dict objectForKey:entryImageKey];
if (obj) {
  _image = (NSImage *)
  [NSUnarchiver unarchiveObjectWithData:obj];
 }
}
```

Serializing

Archiving preserves class information. As a result, when you unarchive an object, it is reconstituted as a class, and you can use it. (You may have to coerce it from a generic NSObject to the object of your type—see the underlined code in the previous snippets.)

Serializing writes out the information within an object so that it can be restored later. The methods in the previous section (`propertyListRepresentation` and `loadPropertyListRepresentation`) serialize the contents of their object. This distinction is particularly notable in the case of dearchiving and deserializing. You call the class method `NSUnarchiver.unarchiveObjectWithData` to unarchive an object; it returns an NSData object. When deserializing an object, you create the object first and then call that object's `loadPropertyListRepresentation` method (or whatever you choose to call the comparable method) to fill the newly created object with its data.

As the code in this section shows, you can combine archiving and serializing.

Creating Objects from Serialized Data

You can dynamically create objects from serialized data. As with all the code in this section, the following snippets are boilerplate. Simply insert your class name and the names of its variables; also, declare dictionary keys for its class name and the variables.

There are two parts to this process. First, store the name of the class in addition to the data. In the underlined code of `prop-ertyListRepresentation`, the name of your object's class is retrieved and stored in the dictionary that will serialize the object's data.

On retrieval, convert the class name string to an actual class. Then create an instance of this class. (The two necessary lines of code are underlined.) Note that in Java, you need to coerce the NSObject result of `newInstance` to your own class.

This recipe is from the Sketch example, and its use there is typical. In Sketch, the SKTGraphic object is an abstract class from which SKTRectangle, SKTTextArea, and others descend. The abstract class method `graphicWithPropertyLis-tRepresentation` creates instances of the appropriate descendants. Because the class name is stored, it is the descendant that is instantiated. (This sort of code does not appear in Diary because none of the classes has variations of itself as subclasses.)

Java:

```
public NSMutableDictionary
  propertyListRepresentation() {
    Object obj, obj2;
    NSMutableDictionary dict =
      new NSMutableDictionary();

    String className = this.getClass().getName();
    dict.setObjectForKey(className,ClassKey);

    ...
  return dict;
}

public static Object
  graphicWithPropertyListRepresentation
  (NSDictionary dict) {

  Class theClass;
```

```java
SKTGraphic theGraphic = null;

try {
  theClass = Class.forName(
    (String)dict.objectForKey(ClassKey));
  } catch (ClassNotFoundException e) {
    theClass = null;
}

if (theClass != null) {
  try {
    theGraphic =
      (SKTGraphic)theClass.newInstance();
  } catch (InstantiationException e) {
    theGraphic = null;
  } catch (IllegalAccessException e) {
    theGraphic = null;
  }

  if (theGraphic != null) {
    theGraphic.
      loadPropertyListRepresentation(dict);
  }
}
  return theGraphic;
}
```

Objective-C:

```objc
- (NSMutableDictionary *)
 propertyListRepresentation {
 NSMutableDictionary *dict =
   [NSMutableDictionary dictionary];

 NSString *className =
   NSStringFromClass([self class]);
 NSRange sktRange =
   [className rangeOfString:@"SKT
   options:NSAnchoredSearch];

 [dict setObject:className forKey:SKTClassKey];
```

```
    ...

    return dict;
}

+ (id)graphicWithPropertyListRepresentation:(NS-
  Dictionary *)dict {
  Class theClass = NSClassFromString(
    [dict objectForKey:SKTClassKey]);
  id theGraphic = nil;

  if (theClass) {
    theGraphic =
      [[[theClass alloc] init] autorelease];
    if (theGraphic) {
      [theGraphic
        loadPropertyListRepresentation:dict];
    }
  }
  return theGraphic;
}
```

For many objects, this is all that needs to be done. For some objects (such as NSTextArea), additional data needs to be handled. If you use this architecture, you simply override `propertyListRepresentation` and `loadPropertyListRepresentation` to handle that additional data. Below is the code from SKTTextArea. You have seen this code before in various guises. When extending a super object's serialization methods, remember to call the inherited method (that code is underlined). Note that the only data the SKTTextArea object adds to the SKTGraphic object is its text area; this is a standard Cocoa object, and it needs to be archived into an NSData object before being placed in the dictionary. If the descendant object has simple data to store (integers or boolean preferences, for example), they do not have to be archived before being placed in the dictionary.

Note that the highest-level implementation of methods such as this create the dictionary and return it. Thus, in SKTGraphic (the root of this class of objects), the dictionary to be used is created. In the descendant, it is used. Also, note that the names of these methods are commonly used, but you can name them whatever you want.

Java:

```java
public NSMutableDictionary propertyListRepresenta-
  tion() {
  NSMutableDictionary dict =
    super.propertyListRepresentation();
  dict.setObjectForKey
    (NSArchiver.archivedDataWithRootObject(
      this.contents()),TextAreaContentsKey);
  return dict;
}

public void loadPropertyListRepresentation(NSDic-
  tionary dict) {
  Object obj;

  super.loadPropertyListRepresentation(dict);

  obj = dict.objectForKey(TextAreaContentsKey);
   if (obj != null) {
     this.setContents((NSAttributedString)
       NSUnarchiver.unarchiveObjectWithData((NSDa-
  ta) obj));
   }
}
```

Objective-C:

```objc
- (NSMutableDictionary *)propertyListRepresenta-
  tion {
  NSMutableDictionary *dict =
    [super propertyListRepresentation];
  [dict setObject:
  [NSArchiver archivedDataWithRootObject:
  [self contents]] forKey:SKTTextAreaContentsKey];
  return dict;
}
```

```
-  (void) loadPropertyListRepresentation:
   (NSDictionary *)dict {
   id obj;

   [super loadPropertyListRepresentation:dict];

   obj = [dict objectForKey:
     SKTTextAreaContentsKey];
   if (obj) {
     [self setContents:
       [NSUnarchiver unarchiveObjectWithData:obj]];
   }
}
```

Distribution

Distribution is a similar process. It relies on ports and connections between ports (see "Tasks" on page 491) so that you can transfer objects among processes.

Copying

Among the most basic programming tools needed to implement sharing is some ability to copy objects. Copying objects (cloning them, in some terminologies) is not quite so simple as you might imagine. Objects often contain instance variables that refer to other objects or to complex data structures. A copy of an object needs to handle these embedded objects appropriately; often they need to be copied themselves and references to the new objects stored in the copied object.

There is a distinction between shallow copying (cloning) and deep copying (cloning). A shallow copy is simply a copy of the object's bit structure in memory; references to objects in both the copy and the original point to the same objects. Deep copying makes copies of embedded objects where necessary. A shallow copy's references point back to the same objects as the original does, so a change to either the original or the copy has the same effect on the embedded objects. The NSMutable-

Copying protocol produces such shallow copies; NSCopying produces deep copies.

In some circumstances, you may decide that the single NSCopying protocol is appropriate to use and that it should produce shallow copies. Note also that the distinction between a shallow and a deep copy is clear conceptually, but may not be so hard and fast in reality. Nothing prevents a copy having some fields that are deep copies and others that are shallow copies. If this is the result of carelessness, it's obviously wrong; however, if the situation justifies it (and it is documented), there is nothing wrong with it.

Copying

Copying is implemented with protocols—NSCopying and NSMutableCopying. Objects are created by both protocols and may (or may not) be modified by others. These new objects are not autorelease objects: You must manage their disposal yourself.

Copying needs to be implemented based on your object's data structures. A reference to a font, a string, or a dictionary may well not need to be copied; references to subviews of a view usually do need to be reinstantiated and copied.

The challenge is actually not particularly daunting if your application is well structured; call the superclass's method first to allow it to do its own work. You probably will have relatively few instance variables that need to be copied.

On a case-by-case basis you will need to decide what to do about copying state variables. For example, is a copy of a view to have the same location and selection as the original? Should its location be slightly offset? Should its location be as it would be for a newly created view and should its selection be nil? These are your decisions to make.

Using the clipboard to share information often takes advantage of printing routines to put PDF versions there. As a result, the clipboard is covered later in this book—see "PDF and

Clipboard Support" starting on page 532 as well as Chapter 27 for more on that topic.

Synchronism

You may never have given much thought to synchronism—the processing of several chores at once. Synchronism didn't exist on the early personal computers, and even today it is fairly rare. Multiprocessing, multitasking, and multithreading are all aspects of synchronism: They allow several things to go on at the same time. When a computer has more than one processor and has network connections and peripherals that have their own processors, it makes little sense to hold everything hostage to a model that handles one thing at a time.

Kinds of Synchronism

Synchronism has four principal aspects:

- A hardware environment in which several things can be done at once.

- An operating system that is designed to manage multiple processes.

- Application software that takes advantage of the hardware and operating system.

- Perceptual synchronism which refers to the structuring of an application's interface so that although nothing actually moves faster, it appears to do so for the user. (The display of progressive GIFs on Web pages is one such example.)

Cocoa implements the first two. Your concern is with the third condition: software that takes advantage of all of this. Old-time programmers who wrestled with mainframes know the enormous performance improvements that you may be able to achieve when you use synchronism properly.

Hardware Synchronism   Hardware-based synchronism takes advantage of the fact that a computer (even with a single processor) is often waiting for disk reads to complete, printing jobs to finish, network connections to work, etc. Having hardware components that can work simultaneously is a necessary precondition for implementing any kind of synchronism. If you have only a single processor and no peripherals, nothing can be done on that computer that is not done by the processor: Synchronism is impossible in this case.

Today's computers, of course, present multiple opportunities for synchronism. Multiple processors within a single computer (not to mention networked computers that can share processing chores) allow a high level of synchronism; peripherals with their own processors and buffers (such as modern printers) allow the main processor not to have to wait for slower devices.

Unless you are writing a very time-critical application that is intimately tied to a specific hardware configuration, as an application developer you are unlikely to be closely involved with hardware synchronism. However, the strategies that you take in implementing application synchronism rely on there being some form of hardware synchronism (you just don't know what specifically exists).

Core OS Synchronism   The Darwin code (based on the Mach kernel) implements as much synchronism as possible.

Application Synchronism   You come in at this level. By doing nothing in your application, you can take advantage of the Mac OS X kernel's efficiencies. However, a range of opportunities presents itself to you if you want to make your application as ready as possible to take advantage of these modern features.

Perceptual Synchronism   There are many tricks that can increase the perceived responsiveness of an application. One of the most common is embodied in progressive GIFs: Start the response to a command as soon as possible, rather than waiting until all (invisible) processing is complete. Another technique—proven in much research—is to provide the user with the ability to control (and terminate) actions that take time. A user who feels in control of a process will swear that it takes less time than a process that cannot be controlled.

Opportunities for Synchronism

Here are some strategies for taking advantage of synchronism.

Take Advantage of Hardware and OS Synchronism Possibilities

You can increase your application's throughput by interleaving communications calls with your application's code, rather than doing all of your processing and then transmitting everything. This means that your total elapsed time of using the network is longer than if you had waited to handle all of your communications at once, but as long as the protocol and networking software allow sharing, you don't degrade anyone else's performance. And because at least a certain amount of the network processing is dependent on remote events, your computer's processor is likely to be waiting for a significant amount of time during communications processing. This strategy is available to you on many operating systems, not just Mac OS X.

Use Multiple Threads Because Mac OS X provides support for threading, you can create multiple threads within your application. If each thread does standard (or at least similar) processing involving computation, memory accesses, disk accesses, etc., chances are that each thread will periodically wait for processor, memory, or disk. By having several threads, you increase the likelihood that one thread's wait state will coincide with another thread's performance. (You can also give threads separate priorities so that a less important thread chugs along slowly but surely while your higher-priority main thread does its critical processing as quickly as possible.)

Threads all share your task's globals. If you are going to use threads, you will need to consider using locks to protect these globals from corruption (see "Locking" later on this page). Because they share your task's globals, the task cannot terminate until its last thread terminates.

Use Multiple Tasks   You can spin off an additional task to do processing that is more independent than that of a thread. Each task has its own memory space and its own globals. As a result, you don't have to worry about locking shared resources, but you also don't have the advantage of easily being able to share data. Tasks can be fired off to perform processes that the originating task no longer cares about (imaging to a file, communications, etc.).

If you are planning a system for an environment that may grow in the future, tasks can also position you very well to work in a multiprocessing environment. Because tasks are independent, you can distribute them across a network of computers. Even if this is not your environment today, the architecture presents few problems in the present—and may provide significant opportunities in the future.

Whatever you do—with tasks or threads—you have to banish the notion (if you still have it) that a single application program is in charge of everything.

Locking

As soon as you move out of the single-processing model, you need to manage interactions among processes. In multiuser databases on mainframes, this has been an issue for decades. You can take advantage of that experience in designing your application.

The simplest case is illustrated by what happens when you see an unusual lamp in an antique store that you cannot live without but which you suspect (fear? hope?) will not work its magic on your spouse, partner, or family. If you run home and drag the appropriate people back to the antique store, the lamp may have been sold to another sucker. You can prevent this by asking the dealer to hold the lamp—but that puts the dealer in the rather tricky position of possibly turning down a sale just so that you can come back and say no.

A lock is basically a hold on all processing—except for that of one thread. In the lamp example, if you could convince the dealer to place a lock on the lamp, no one else can buy it until you release your lock. (Databases use sophisticated locks, as do antique dealers—your agreement may be that the dealer can't sell the lamp, but that it can be shown without commitment to prospective buyers.)

Locks are whatever you say they are. Although locks are often associated with resources (printers, for example) and with data (a customer record, for example), the Cocoa lock mechanism has no intrinsic meaning. You can lock a method, which you might do if you know that a call to that method will make heavy demands on the computer's resources. Although you allow users to have many windows open at the same time and to work with many images, perhaps you will lock the method that does heavy image manipulation so that if a user decided to reimage several images at the same time, the imaging code would be locked to prevent crippling the system.

Note that locks are implemented in the next higher system level from their callers. Thus, if two threads within a task use a lock to manage shared resources, the lock and presumably the shared resources are owned by the task. Similarly, if two tasks within the OS share a locked resource, the lock and the resource reside in the OS.

NSLock The heart of the locking mechanism is the NSLock object. You create lock objects fairly early in your application—certainly before you spin off threads. (If you don't spin off threads, you have no reason to create locks.)

NSConditionLock A descendant of NSLock is NSConditionLock. This is a more sophisticated lock: It has a condition value (an int) that you can set. You can request that the lock be granted if that condition has a certain value. By defining constants with meaningful (to you) values, you can add a great deal of sophistication to your locks.

You normally set the lock's condition value by using `init-WithCondition` or using `unlockWithCondition`. If the condition value changes dynamically (between initialization and unlocking), you can override the condition method.

Beware of getting too sophisticated with your conditions if you are not experienced in this area. In particular, conditions that themselves involve other locks can bring you to grief. A thread that requests a lock is blocked from further execution until that lock is granted, which means that you can easily get yourself locked out from everything.

In the cases where you do need to request multiple locks within a single thread, use NSRecursiveLock.

NSRecursiveLock   A thread is blocked when it requests a lock until that lock is granted (unless it uses the timeout feature in `lockBeforeDate`). If methods within your thread might attempt to acquire a lock that your thread has already acquired, you might be in the position of nesting your locks—and the second lock will never be granted and your thread will be blocked from further execution because the first lock cannot be released. In this case, use NSRecursiveLock rather than NSLock. It brings a little more overhead with it, but it prevents you from accidentally locking yourself out. (These rules about locks apply to individual locks. If your thread acquires five separate locks—five separate instantiations of NSLock—you don't have to worry about locking yourself out.)

NSLocking   The NSLocking protocol defines lock and unlock methods that you use to manipulate NSLock objects. As noted previously, the lock method of the protocol blocks your thread from further execution until the lock is granted. You are almost always better off to use the NSLock `lockBefore-Date` method.

For unlocking, however, the `unlock` method is used in all cases (except for when you need to set a condition for an NSConditionalLock).

Threading

Each task starts off with a single thread. If you want to create additional threads, you use the NSThread object. Threads share your task's global variables. If you are going to be creating locks for data or processing, create them in your task's first thread before creating additional threads.

Tasks

Tasks have more independence than threads; they live in their own address space and function independently. You don't use locks if you are sharing resources among tasks, because locks need to be in a common address space. A task runs in its own environment: a directory, which includes standard input, output, and error files; and other implementation-specific variables. When you create a task, it inherits your own task's environment unless you explicitly change its environment in whole or in part. This must be done before the task is started; thereafter, it is responsible for making any changes in its environment.

Connections

NSConnection lets you share objects between threads or tasks whether on the same machine or on different hosts.

A connection consists of two NSConnection objects, one in each thread that is communicating with the other. Each connection has a send and receive port; they mirror one another in the two threads (that is, the send port in the NSConnection of one thread is the receive port in the NSConnection of the other thread).

This is the implementation of the Mach messaging architecture. It is one of the most powerful features of Darwin. Sharing messages and data in a world of multiple processors and processes is not easily accomplished with traditional operating systems.

You can use NSConnection to share distributed objects between threads and to send messages back and forth. From your point of view, the connection's root object is what is seen by others; the connection's root proxy is what you see at the other end of the connection.

Summary

The shared environment of Mac OS X processing allows you to take full advantage of the modern OS and of sophisticated contemporary hardware with multiple processors and peripherals with their own processors and memory. If you come from the hoary mainframe world, this is second nature to you. If you have lived all of your life on a personal computer, however, you may not realize the power of these features. There is no doubt that the future will bring more processors, more connectivity—and more opportunities for applications that are prepared to live in this world.

Nothing requires you to use tasks and threads, but becoming familiar with them and using them where appropriate prepares you for the most sophisticated system designs of the future.

This chapter has explored various aspects of sharing of data, including sharing it over time and space with archiving, serialization, and distribution. Synchronism involves sharing resources—particularly memory—and it, too, has been covered here.

These are relatively low-level concerns. That is, you use the methods shown in this chapter, but you rarely do more than reimplement them as boilerplate code. Instead, you focus at the next highest level of data: documents and files. They are covered in the next chapter.

Chapter 23
Documents and Files

Most computer users work with files on a routine basis. Whether they are word processing documents, image files, or spreadsheets, the basic paradigm of the personal computer remains very much document-centric.

Recently the Internet and local area networks have created a new breed of user who does not focus on documents. For this user, email messages, Web sites, and databases supplant paper surrogates. Still, a lot of work (and play) depends on a user entering data, modifying it, saving it, and then opening it at another time or sending it on to someone else.

Cocoa supports a robust document model. Like the frameworks of Carbon, the document model handles much of the work for you. In any of these environments, you may never need to execute read *or* write *statements.*

This chapter provides an overview of document handling on Mac OS X and Cocoa. In particular, you will find sections on:

- *Working with document-based architectures*

- *Implementing documents and views*

- *Saving and restoring documents*

- *Managing changed documents (using Undo and Dirty)*

Document-Based Architectures

The advent of the personal computer and its widespread use in offices gave birth to the document-based architecture that is so common today. Before then, computers had worked primarily with data files located on various storage devices (mostly of a magnetic nature). By the 1970s, databases started to replace the flat files, but not much else changed. Typical batch processing on mainframes consisted of two types of operations:

1. Reading a record from an input file, doing something, and then writing it out to the same or a different file.

2. Reading a lot of records from one or more input files, doing something, and then writing out a summary or synthesis to a printer of another file. (Payroll and invoicing programs are examples.)

On personal computers, the model is very different: The entire contents of a document are read into memory, things happen, and then everything is written back out. On mainframes, the concept of reading everything into memory before working on it would be considered absurd.

The consequence of this is that the normal processing for a document-based application consists of three tasks:

1. Reading a document and displaying it

2. Allowing the user to do something with it

3. Writing it out

Document support in Cocoa addresses all three of these tasks. While the first and third are obvious, it is not always clear that the document supports the second task. Undo and keeping track of when a document needs to be saved are tasks that the document needs to provide in a Cocoa application; therefore, the document is heavily involved in all three of these tasks.

Some people find the model-view-controller architecture useful in helping them plan and design applications. A variation on that architecture is helpful to other people. In it, the two basic components—models (data and processing logic) and views (visualization and interface)—are used. Rather than identify a third component (controllers), the concept of controllers is used to identify objects and/or methods of views and models that provide bridges to other controllers and thus from models to views, and vice versa.

This revision to the model-view-controller architecture is helpful in looking at documents, since it maps absolutely to documents as they are used in Cocoa (and most other frameworks). Think of a document as a model object; it uses controller objects and has its own controller methods. It is those controller objects and classes that can communicate with the view that displays it.

Likewise, a view object uses controller objects and has its own controller methods, which it uses to communicate with document (model) controller objects.

Whatever your feeling about architectures and theories such as these, remember that their purpose is to help you understand code that you read and to help you write better code. The architecture, paradigm, or theory is a tool to help you, not a goal in and of itself.

This idea is discussed at this point because the classic model-view-controller architecture has trouble accommodating documents, as they logically fall into two categories (models and controllers).

Implementing Documents and Views

As with so much of Cocoa, implementing documents and views consists of a great deal of boilerplate code. The general outlines are provided in this section.

There are three sections of code:

1. Document headers: the source code basics you need to declare

2. Constructors: creating the document

3. Window controllers: displaying the document

Document Headers

The start of the Diary header files is presented here. The Project Builder templates produce similar code, but you need to insert your own variables.

The standard import commands for the AppKit and Foundation frameworks are always required. If you are implementing a document-based application, you must subclass NSDocument; the Project Builder template does this for you.

Note that Project Builder creates a class and appropriate files using MyDocument. If you are going to change this—and you should—change it before you do anything else. Compile and run the template file both before and after this change to make certain that all is well. Note that the template does not include code to save your document, but do not worry about that. This chapter will help you fix it.

Next, declare your Interface Builder outlets. Note that in Java they are private; in Objective-C they are identified as IBOutlets. The list of outlets here must match the list in Interface Builder to which you have attached interface elements. Furthermore, the types should match (i.e., your NSTextField in your code must be attached to an NSTextField or descendant thereof in Interface Builder).

Declare variables that you use. As described previously, you may wind up fishing data through a variety of subsidiary objects. In the Diary example, a single data member belongs to the document class: a DiaryData object (underlined). That single object has its own data (such as `title`), and an array of DiaryEntry objects. Accessors let you fish down to the actual data through each level.

Finally, declare strings that you may need for notifications, dictionary support, and the like. In Java, there is only one file, and these strings are declared there. In Objective-C, the strings are declared at the top of the .m file (the other headers are in the .h file).

Java:

```
// DiaryDocument.java

import com.apple.cocoa.application.*;
import com.apple.cocoa.foundation.*;
```

```java
public class DiaryDocument extends NSDocument {

  //Interface Builder outlets
  private NSTextField diaryTitleField;
  private NSTextField diaryOwnerField;
  ...

  //Data
  private DiaryData theDiary;

  //Dictionary keys
  private static final String
    PrintInfoKey = "PrintInfo";

  public static final String DiaryDocumentType =
    "DiaryDocumentType";
  private static final String
    DiaryDocumentVersionKey =
    "DiaryDocumentVersion";
  private static final
    String CurrentDiaryDocumentVersion = "1";

  //Toolbar strings
  ...
```

Objective-C:

```objc
// DiaryData.h
#import <Cocoa/Cocoa.h>

@interface MyDocument : NSDocument
{

  IBOutlet NSTextField *diaryOwnerField;
  IBOutlet NSTextField *diaryTitleField;
  ...

  @private DiaryData *theDiary;

}
```

```
//DiaryData .m

#import "MyDocument.h"

@implementation MyDocument

NSString *PrintInfoKey = @"PrintInfo";
NSString *DiaryDocumentType =
  @"DiaryDocumentType";
NSString *MyDocumentType = @"MyDocumentType";
NSString *CurrentMyDocumentVersion = @"1";
NSString *CurrentMyDocumentVersionKey =
  @"MyDocumentVersionKey";
```

Constructors

You must provide constructors for your document object. You do not call them, but they must be ready to be called by Cocoa at appropriate times. In Java, constructors are not inherited, and you need a constructor for each way in which your document can be created (as a blank document, with a file name, and from a URL).

Objective-C does not require this; your single `init` method is called in all cases. But in Objective-C, you do have to worry about memory management. In Java, the `new` function creates a subsidiary object (DiaryData). In Objective-C you use `alloc` to create an instance of DiaryData. Because you have allocated it, you need to provide a `dealloc` method to deallocate it (and any other objects you have allocated).

All of these methods are called automatically, but you must implement each of them for yourself. Also, note that the inherited method is called in every case.

Java:
```
public DiaryDocument() {
  super();
  theDiary = new DiaryData();
}
```

```
public DiaryDocument(String fileName,
  String fileType) {
    super(fileName, fileType);
    theDiary = new DiaryData();
}

public DiaryDocument(java.net.URL url,
  String type) {
    super(url, type);
    theDiary = new DiaryData();
}
```

Objective-C:

```
- (id)init {
  self = [super init];
  if (self) {
    theDiary = [[DiaryData alloc] init];
  }
  return self;
}

- (void)dealloc {
  [[NSNotificationCenter defaultCenter]
    removeObserver:self];

  [super dealloc];
}
```

Along with constructors, you need to provide the framework with the name of the nib file to be loaded with your document. Following are the methods. If you change the name of your nib file (and you might prefer not to have the generic Project Builder MyDocument default), you must change the under-lined code.

Java:

```
public String windowNibName() {
  return "DiaryDocument";
}
```

Objective-C:

```
- (NSString *)windowNibName {
    return @"MyDocument";
}
```

Window Controllers

If you have any initialization to do (such as setting fields in the view of your document), you do it in an override of `win-dowControllerDidLoadNib`. In Diary, the `loadFields-FromDiaryData` method is called. In the examples, in-line code sets the fields in many cases.

You almost always override this method. Even if you start off by not doing so, you should put an override in because you will probably need it as your project grows.

Java:

```
public void windowControllerDidLoadNib
    (NSWindowController  aController) {
    super.windowControllerDidLoadNib(aController);
    this.loadFieldsFromDiaryData();
    ...
```

Objective-C:

```
- (void)windowControllerDidLoadNib:
    (NSWindowController *)windowController {
    NSToolbar* toolbar;

    [super windowControllerDidLoadNib:
        windowController];
    [self loadFieldsFromDiaryData];
    ...
```

Saving and Restoring Data

The methods shown here need to be overridden to implement saving and restoring data. The code here is from Diary and is based on Sketch; rather than use in-line accessors, methods are called to load and unload the data.

The architecture involves taking your document's data and converting it into an NSData object. You can do this in any way that you want—archiving, serializing, or some other manner. The methods that you write (called `loadDiaryTo-Dictionary` and `unloadFromDictionary` are mirror images of one another. Do anything you want, and use the rest of the code as is.

Saving Documents

You override `dataRepresentationOfType` to create an NSData object that contains your data. It can be any type of object that you want (here it is a dictionary).

As you can see, from `dataRepresentationOfType`, `diaryDocumentData` is called. You implement any method that you want, but it must return an NSData object which, in turn will be returned through `dataRepresentationOfType`. `diaryDocumentData` then turns around and calls `create-DiaryDictionary`.

This is where most of your work occurs. It should be familiar, however, given that it has been described many times:

1. Create a dictionary.

2. Set keys and values for basic information (a version number and an archived PrintInfo object).

3. Call a method to move data from your interface to internal variables.

4. Pass the dictionary into a method that loads the internal values into it and returns it.

Depending on your application's design, step 3—moving data from the interface to internal variables—may be performed elsewhere. It often makes sense to make the moving of data the last step of a previous process rather than an intermediate step in the data writing process.

Java:

```java
public NSData dataRepresentationOfType(String
  type) {
  if (type.equals (DiaryDocumentType)) {
    return this.diaryDocumentData();
  }
  else
    return null;
}


public NSData diaryDocumentData() {
  NSDictionary dict = createDiaryDictionary();
  String plistStr =
    NSPropertyListSerialization.
      stringFromPropertyList(dict);
  NSMutableStringReference mutStrRef =
    new NSMutableStringReference();

  NSData data;
  mutStrRef.setString(plistStr);
  data = mutStrRef.dataUsingEncoding
    (NSStringReference.ASCIIStringEncoding,
  false);

  return data;
}


public NSMutableDictionary createDiaryDictionary()
  {
  NSMutableDictionary dict =
    new NSMutableDictionary();
  dict.setObjectForKey
    (CurrentDiaryDocumentVersion,
    DiaryDocumentVersionKey);
  dict.setObjectForKey
    (NSArchiver.archivedDataWithRootObject
    (printInfo()),
    PrintInfoKey);
```

```
        //move data from fields to variables
        this.moveFieldsToDiaryData ();

        theDiary.loadDiaryToDictionary (dict);

        return dict;
}
```

Objective-C:

```objc
- (NSData *)dataRepresentationOfType:(NSString
  *)aType {
  return [self diaryDocumentData];
}

- (NSData *)DiaryDocumentData {
    NSDictionary *dict =
      [self createDiaryDictionary];
    NSString *string = [dict description];
    return
      [string
        dataUsingEncoding:NSASCIIStringEncoding];
}

- (NSDictionary *)createDiaryDictionary{
    NSMutableDictionary *dict =
      [NSMutableDictionary dictionary];

    [dict setObject:DiaryDocumentVersion
      forKey:DiaryDocumentVersionKey];
    [dict setObject:[NSArchiver
      archivedDataWithRootObject:[self printInfo]]
      forKey:PrintInfoKey];

    [self moveFieldsToDiaryData:nil];

    [theDiary loadDiaryToDictionary:dict];

    return dict;
}
```

Restoring Data   NSDocument automatically sets up the architecture to manage multiple document types. This is handled with data representations. Each data representation is identified with a string, and depending on which one is presented, you provide the appropriate data.

You override `loadDataRepresentation` to read your data. If you handle multiple types of data, you can create an `if` statement so as to branch on the type parameter that is passed in. The code shown here is from Diary, is based on the Sketch example, and is boilerplate code that works in most cases. You need to rewrite the two underlined lines of code to create an instance of your own data object, and to load it.

The PrintInfo object and the undo manager object are common in document-based applications. If you do not support printing or undo, leave them out (and shame on you).

Note that you may not create your own data object such as the Diary. If the amount of data in your document is small, you may simply park it in a local variable in your document object.

Java:

```
public boolean loadDataRepresentation(NSData data,
  String type) {
  NSDictionary dict = this.diaryDictionaryFromDa-
ta(data);

  theDiary = new DiaryData();
  theDiary.unloadFromDictionary
    ((NSMutableDictionary)dict);

  data = (NSData)dict.objectForKey(PrintInfoKey);
  if (data != null) {
    NSPrintInfo printInfo =
      (NSPrintInfo)NSUnarchiver.
      unarchiveObjectWithData(data);
```

```
        if (printInfo != null) {
          this.setPrintInfo(printInfo);
          }
        }

        if (this.undoManager() != null) {
          this.undoManager().removeAllActions();
        }

        return true;
  }
```

Objective-C:

```
- (BOOL)loadDataRepresentation:(NSData *)data
    ofType:(NSString *)aType {
  NSMutableDictionary *dict =
    [self diaryDictionaryFromData:data];

  theDiary = [[DiaryData alloc] init];
  [theDiary unloadFromDictionary:dict];

  data = [dict objectForKey:PrintInfoKey];
  if (data) {
  NSPrintInfo *printInfo =
    [NSUnarchiver unarchiveObjectWithData:data];
  if (printInfo) {
    [self setPrintInfo:printInfo];
    }
  }

  [[self undoManager] removeAllActions];

  return YES;
}
```

As you can see from the underlined code, the DiaryData object is created, and then its `unloadFromDictionary` method is called. It contains a very standard code: It unloads two simple variables (Diary owner and title), and then it creates an array filled with objects—the individual Diary entries. Here is that code:

Java:

```java
public NSMutableDictionary unloadFromDictionary
  (NSMutableDictionary dict) {
  _diaryOwner =
    (String)dict.objectForKey(diaryOwnerKey);
  _diaryTitle =
    (String)dict.objectForKey(diaryTitleKey);

  NSArray entryDicts =
    (NSArray) dict.objectForKey(entriesListKey);
  if (_entries != null) {
    _entries.removeAllObjects();
  }
  else
    _entries = new NSMutableArray();

    currentEntryIndex = -1;

  if (entryDicts != null) {
    int i, c = entryDicts.count();
      for (i=0; i<c; i++) {
        _entries.addObject
          (DiaryEntry.
           entryFromPropertyListRepresentation
           ((NSDictionary)entryDicts.
            objectAtIndex(i)));
        currentEntryIndex ++;
      }
  }

  return dict;
}
```

Objective-C:

```objc
- (NSMutableDictionary *)unloadFromDictionary:
  (NSMutableDictionary *)dict
{
  NSArray *entryDicts;
```

```
_diaryOwner = [dict objectForKey:diaryOwnerKey];
_diaryTitle = [dict objectForKey:diaryTitleKey];

entryDicts = [dict objectForKey:entriesListKey];
if (_entries)
  {
    [_entries removeAllObjects];
  }
else
  {
    _entries = [NSMutableArray  alloc] init]];
  }

currentEntryIndex = -1;
if (entryDicts) {
  int i, c = [entryDicts count];
  for (i=0; i< c; i++) {
    [_entries addObject:(DiaryEntry*)
      [DiaryEntry
      entryFromPropertyListRepresentation:
      [entryDicts objectAtIndex:i]]];
    currentEntryIndex ++;
  }
}

return dict;

}
```

Undo and Dirty Documents

If you use the default undo mechanism in Cocoa, your documents are automatically dirtied for you. The dot appears in the center of the close button to indicate unsaved changes, and if the user tries to close the document, a sheet prompting for saving is displayed.

While you can implement undo/redo in very complex ways (and you can also implement dirtying of documents yourself), the process is very simple if you use standard code. The heart of the code consists of the snippets shown here. When a variable's value is changed, it is called. It assumes that the object in which this code resides has a method that returns an undo manager. NSDocument has such a method, so your document will have it, too. If this code is called from another object, it will need a reference either to your document or to its own undo manager.

If you use the two-step architecture of accessors (which do not dirty documents and cannot be undone) and changers (which do dirty documents and can be undone), the logical place for this code is in the changers that change your variables. If you expose them as actions, you can link them to interface elements in Interface Builder. This is the issue that was alluded to earlier with regard to when to move data:

- You can leave data in interface elements and move it into internal variables only when you need to reuse the interface elements or dispose of the data.

- You can immediately move the data into internal variables as soon as editing is complete (that is, when another interface element is clicked).

The second mechanism makes it very easy to implement undo/redo for individual elements. The second mechanism is a very elegant way of producing a single event to Undo or Redo. Depending on your application and the nature of the data, you can choose one or the other. You can also group undo/redo actions to have the best of both worlds.

This section gives the Diary example code that registers the undo for changing an entry title. There are three steps to the process:

1. Create the basic actions.

2. Register the undo actions.

3. Clear the undo stack when you are done.

Create the Basic Actions

This is an example of a changer from Diary. It changes the DiaryEntry title; it is the action that is connected to the interface title field. Note that it checks whether the value of that field is equal to the current value of the title; if not, it calls a second method. By convention in Diary, change...byScript methods are changers that can be invoked from the user interface—as here—or via AppleScript. Thus, the check for the interface value is omitted.

Java:

```java
public void changeEntryTitle (Object Sender){
  if (!(titleField.stringValue().equals
    (theDiary.entryTitle()))) {
      this.changeEntryTitleByScript
        (titleField.stringValue());
  };
}
```

Objective-C:

```objc
- (void)changeEntryTitle:(id)sender {
  if (![[titleField stringValue] isEqualToString:
    [theDiary entryTitle]])
      [self changeEntryTitleByScript:
        [titleField stringValue]];
}
```

Register the Undo Actions

When you perform an undoable action, you need to register the undo method and value with the undo manager. If the user chooses Undo from the Edit menu, the method and value you have registered will be used.

Java:

```java
public void changeEntryTitleByScript (String the-
  NewTitle){
  if (undoManager() != null) {
    String theTitle = theDiary.entryTitle();
    Class arrClass[] = {String.class};
```

```
    Object args [] = {theTitle};
    undoManager().
      registerUndoWithTargetAndArguments
      (this,
       new NSSelector
         ("changeEntryTitleByScript",
          arrClass),
        args);
    undoManager().
      setActionName ("Change Entry Title");
  }

  theDiary.setEntryTitle (theNewTitle);
  NSNotificationCenter.defaultCenter().
    postNotification (
      DiaryEntryDidChangeNotification, this);
}
```

Objective-C:

```
- (void)changeEntryTitleByScript:
  (NSString*)theNewTitle {
  NSString* theTitle = [theDiary entryTitle];
  [[self undoManager] registerUndoWithTarget:self
    selector:@selector(changeEntryTitleByScript:)
    object:nil];
  [[self undoManager] setActionName:
    "Change Entry Title"];

  [theDiary setEntryTitle: theNewTitle];
  [[NSNotificationCenter defaultCenter]
    postNotificationName:
      DiaryEntryDidChangeNotification
    object: self];
}
```

In Objective-C, you can also use prepareWithInvocation-Target. This is a two-step process as shown in the following code. You pass the same target as before (often yourself) and the actual method invocation that you want to be used. In the code here, if the action is to be undone, you want the con-tentsCopy method to be called by using contentsCopy (that is, the before image of the data). This method is particularly useful when there are multiple arguments to be passed in the callback method and when non-objects are involved.

Here is the same method using `prepareWithInvocation-Target`:

```
- (void)changeEntryTitleByScript:(NSString*)
  theNewTitle {
  [[[self undoManager]
    prepareWithInvocationTarget:self]
    changeEntryTitleByScript:
    [theDiary entryTitle]];
  [[self undoManager] setActionName:
    "Change Entry Title"];

  [theDiary setEntryTitle: theNewTitle];
  [[NSNotificationCenter defaultCenter]
    postNotificationName:
      DiaryEntryDidChangeNotification
      object: self];
}
```

Clear the Undo Stack

At an appropriate moment (such as when the document is saved), you clear the undo stack.

Java:

```
public void updateChangeCount(int changeType) {
  super.updateChangeCount(changeType);
  if (changeType == NSDocument.ChangeCleared) {
    if (this.undoManager() != null) {
      this.undoManager().removeAllActions();
    }
  }
}
```

Objective-C:

```
- (void)updateChangeCount:(int)changeType {
  [super updateChangeCount: changeType];
  if (changeType == [NSDocument ChangeCleared])
    [undoManager removeAllActions];
}
```

Dirtying Documents

You need to update the document's change count when it is dirtied and then again when it is saved. NSDocument itself does most of the processing for you. You can override update-ChangeCount if you want to do additional processing at that time, as shown in the previous section.

Summary

With documents and files, you can save and restore data between different executions of your program. The process involves not only reading and writing them, but also flattening and then restoring the objects they contain. Furthermore, you need to implement support for dirtying documents and undoing (or redoing) commands that change them.

The end of the development process is in sight: Menu commands are one of the last parts of the graphical user interface that you need to implement.

Chapter 24
Managing Menus

Menus are one of the most basic parts of the graphical user interface. In Cocoa, they are easy to set up; in MacApp Carbon-based applications, they are nearly as easy.

The Aqua Human Interface Guidelines (available on Apple's Web site via a link on http://developer.apple.com/ue/) provides the last word on menu styling and placement. In short, the guidelines request that you keep your menu items short, absolutely clear, and organized in a logical manner. Long-standing arguments about the proper use of menus have simmered down, and the consensus is that menus should be short (a dozen items is plenty), and that hierarchical menus (submenus) can be overused with extraordinary ease.

This chapter is brief in part because menus are so easy to implement in Cocoa, but also because menus no longer have the role they used to have in the interface.

Menus and Other Interface Elements

The original Macintosh (and other graphical user interface systems) consisted of relatively small screens. The routine for users was simple: Select something in the active window, then choose the menu command to act on it. With small screens and smaller windows, this was about the extent of the interface.

With the advent of larger screens and more powerful processors, windows began to accumulate additional controls. If you compare screen shots of modern software with that from 10 or 15 years ago, you will be struck by the proliferation of controls everywhere: in windows, tucked into corners of scroll bars (placards), in palettes, and now in Mac OS X in toolbars and drawers.

What this means is that the controls and commands that a user needs to use are located as close as possible to the focus of attention. For most users, the focus of attention is rarely at that menu bar at the top of the screen.

If you are designing applications in the old style, think about changing your point of view. Although it is not part of Apple's guidelines, you can consider menu commands as second-class commands, used only when the right command is not available. They also function as a useful backup mechanism for users who do not know where all the close commands are located (or even that certain interface elements hide commands).

Naturally, all of the standard menu commands must be implemented (Cocoa does this for you). In addition, all of your application's primary functionality should be exposed in the menu bar. But it is no longer necessary for every bell and whistle to have its own menu command: Your array of interface choices is much greater than it was before.

So not only should you keep your menu commands terse and clear, but you should also not clutter your menu bar with commands that people will not use. Watch how you use your Macintosh, and you may be surprised. For most people, the experience of using menu commands with the mouse is getting less and less frequent. Keyboard equivalent-driven menu commands, however, remain at least as popular as ever.

One of the consequences of this proliferation of controls is that menu commands are present in many places and in many configurations. For example, a placard in a scroll bar might let you adjust a view's zoom factor (as in TextEdit). You might also be able to access the zoom factor via a hierarchical menu in the menu bar and in a contextual menu. In each location, the adjacent controls are different; this allows the application designer to have several logical groups of the same commands.

The Dock and the Finder toolbar are perfect examples of this. You can put a folder or document into the Dock as well as into the toolbar; when you want to return to Current Projects, you can get there with one click depending on which context is most convenient at that moment.

This is what users expect today. The menu bar as the sole source of commands—much less organized the way the developer wants—is not the only game in town.

Contextual Menus

Contextual menus appear when a user CONTROL-clicks on an interface element to which such a menu has been attached.

You create each contextual menu by itself in Interface Builder, and you attach it to an interface element's menu outlet. Each view (and thus each interface element) has its own menu outlet.

Contextual menu commands should be named with the same names as menu bar commands. Although the Finder implements a special Show Package Contents command in the contextual menu for packages, such an interface choice is unusual.

Remember, too, that contextual menus appear just that way—in a context. Half a dozen particularly relevant menu commands are sufficient. Users know the menu bar is there if they need more.

Dock Menus

The icons in the Dock support pop-up menus that are similar to contextual menus. These menus contain a combination of commands from the application that is running and from the Finder.

Application
Dock Menu
Commands

You can place commands from your application in the Dock menu that pops up when a user holds the mouse down over your Dock tile. These commands appear at the top of the menu (the standard Finder commands are below them).

Note that your application must be running in order for these menu commands to be visible. You may decide to launch a small faceless application at startup in order to place your menu commands in the Dock. When one is chosen, you can launch your full application.

There are three steps involved in implementing application Dock menus:

1. Create the menu using Interface Builder.

2. Connect it to your NSApplication object.

3. Add it to your application's info.plist.

Creating the Menu   Like most interface elements, you can use Interface Builder to create your Dock menu and place it in a nib file. In view of the fact that the Dock menu may be accessed in very different ways from your standard application menus (such as when your application is in the background), it is best to create a new nib file for your Dock menu.

Create the nib file in Interface Builder. Save the nib file, and add it to your project. If you have launched Interface Builder from Project Builder with your project open in Project Builder, you will be prompted to do so. If not, you must manually add the file to the project using Add File in the Project menu.

Connecting It to Your Application   Use the Inspector in Interface Builder to change File's Owner to NSApplication. Then, create a menu just as you normally would. Connect File's Owner to the menu, selecting the dockMenu outlet in NSApplication.

Adding It to the info.plist   With Project Builder, add the nib file to the info.plist. In the Targets pane, select your application, then choose the Application Settings tab. Click the Expert button, and then add a sibling to the property list. It should be named AppleDockMenu, and its value is the name of your Dock nib file (without the .nib suffix). (There is more detail about updating the info.plist in "Property List Settings" starting on page 553.)

You can also add an NSApplication delegate that implements `applicationDockMenu`. This method should return an NS-

Menu* object which is the application's Dock menu. If you use this method, you can dynamically change the items in the Dock menu.

Finder Dock Menu Commands

From the bottom up, these are the Dock menu commands.

Quit   If an application is running, its Quit command is the bottom command in a Dock menu. If the user OPTION-clicks on the Dock icon and the application is running, this changes to Force Quit.

You can use this little tidbit in your documentation and on-screen assistance. It is much better for a user to know that if there is a problem the one application can be stopped than to use a three-key combination to bring up a Force Quit window in which a different application could accidentally be terminated.

Show in Finder   This command opens a Finder window and locates the application or document that the Dock icon represents. It is available for all Dock icons.

Keep in Dock   When an application is running, the Keep in Dock command is added to the menu. All running applications have icons in the Dock, and it is frequently convenient for users to request that they remain there for future use.

You cannot "help" the user out and force your application's icon to remain in the Dock.

Windows   For running applications, the open windows that have been added to the bottom of the application's Window menu are listed. The other Window menu commands are not shown.

Summary

This chapter is short because so much of menu command processing is done for you. In Cocoa, you declare the action methods that will implement menu commands, and just link them to the commands themselves in Interface Builder.

Carbon is almost as easy to use, but you do have to handle the connections yourself within your code. Of course, if you use a Carbon framework such as MacApp or PowerPlant, that is done for you automatically in most cases.

The last general function for most applications is printing—the topic of the next chapter.

Chapter 25
Printing

Printing in Cocoa (as in MacApp and most other frameworks) is a simple operation for you to implement. At its most basic, you take a view that is displayed and pass it to a method that redraws it for the selected printer. The standard page setup and page layout settings are managed by the framework.

This works for small views where a simple copy of the screen image is sufficient. It breaks down when you want the printed version to be different (with timestamps, for example, or headers and footers that do not appear on the screen). In that case, you create a separate view just for printing and place your data into it. If you have set up your application well, the data (model) and the view are as distinct as pos-

sible; as a result, it should be a simple matter to redraw the objects in a new view.

Mac OS X supports PDF print previews. When these are required, you can implement them with a special override if needed.

Although the standard page setup and printing dialogs are usually satisfactory, you can also extend them.

Basic Printing

Printing is handled by the NSPrintOperation object. You are responsible for creating it, associating a view with it, and running it.

Using the Displayed View

The simplest form of printing involves overriding the print method of a view. If you do so, printing will just work for that view. Here is the code:

Java:

```
public void print {
  (NSPrintOperation.
    printOperationWithView (this)).runOperation();
}
```

Objective-C:

```
- (void)print:sender {
  [[NSPrintOperation printOperationWithView:self]
    runOperation];
}
```

Of course, most of the time, you do not want to print a single view. Rather, you want to print the contents of a window. Because printing starts from a single view and proceeds through its subviews, you will soon realize that if you place a view at the back of each of your windows (possibly containing a background pattern), you will have the view that you need for printing.

If you have a document-based application, you override the NSDocument `printShowingPrintPanel` method in your override of NSDocument. You create a print operation based on a view and then run it. The method is called with a flag indicating whether you should request the print panel be shown in a sheet. Normally, you do so for a document-based view. (If you are printing a simple view, as in the previous case, you might not want to do so. The print panel allows users to select a printer—usually a good idea—but it also lets them choose a page range, which is irrelevant in some cases.)

Java:

```java
public void printShowingPrintPanel(boolean flag) {
    NSPrintOperation op = NSPrintOperation.
      printOperationWithView(diaryView, printInfo);
    op.setShowPanels(flag);
    op.runOperation();
}
```

Objective-C:

```objc
- (void)printDocumentUsingPrintPanel:(BOOL)flag {
    NSPrintOperation *op =
      [NSPrintOperation printOperationWithView:
          diaryView
        printInfo:[self printInfo]];
    [op setShowPanels:flag];
    [op runOperation];
}
```

If your view contains scrollers, the results of printing it may be surprising. You actually do not want to print the scroller in many cases; rather, you want to print the entire contents of the view contained within it—no matter how long it is.

One way of handling that is to implement a per-page view in your application (TextEdit does this). Another way is to reformat the contents for your printing view.

Using a Special View

If you want to remove scrollers from your view so that variable-length text views can be printed, or if you want to add headers or footers, you need to create a special view for printing.

In the case of variable-length text fields, the problem is not particularly difficult, because at the moment you are printing the view, the field is not variable length. You know exactly how big it is. You can create a view (or resize one) to be exactly the size that you need for printing.

The Sketch example creates a view for printing its objects using the following code. If you need to do this, you need only do two things:

1. Create a rectangle the size of the view to be printed. What this size is and how it is calculated are up to you.

2. Create an instance of your own view and initialize it according to your own application's code. You may add other objects to it; you also might subclass your normal view to automatically add objects for printing.

In the Java example, these two steps are done in two lines of code; in Objective-C, they are done in one line. You can use either structure in either language. Then (unless you have changed variable names), this code will work for you.

Java:

```
public void printShowingPrintPanel(boolean flag){
  NSSize paperSize = this.documentSize();

  NSRect tempRect = new NSRect (0.0f, 0.0f, paper-
Size.width(),
    paperSize.height());
```

```
SKTRenderingView view = new SKTRenderingView(tem-
pRect,
  this.graphics());
NSWindow tempWnd = new NSWindow(tempRect,
  NSWindow.BorderlessWindowMask,
  NSWindow.NonRetained,
  false);
tempWnd.contentView().addSubview(view);

NSPrintOperation printOp = NSPrintOperation.
  printOperationWithView(view, printInfo());
NSWindow docWindow = this.
  appropriateWindowForDocModalOperations();
printOp.setShowPanels(flag);
printOp.setCanSpawnSeparateThread(true);
if (docWindow != null) {
  printOp.runModalOperation(docWindow, null,
    null, null);
} else {
  printOp.runOperation();
}
}
```

Objective-C:

```
- (void)printShowingPrintPanel:(BOOL)flag {
    NSSize paperSize = [self documentSize];
    SKTRenderingView *view =
      [[SKTRenderingView alloc]
      initWithFrame:NSMakeRect(0.0, 0.0,
        paperSize.width,
      paperSize.height) graphics:[self graphics]];
    NSWindow *window = [[NSWindow alloc]
      initWithContentRect:NSMakeRect(0.0, 0.0,
      paperSize.width, paperSize.height)
      styleMask:NSBorderlessWindowMask
      backing:NSBackingStoreNonretained defer:NO];
    NSPrintInfo *printInfo = [self printInfo];
    NSPrintOperation *printOp;
```

```
NSWindow *docWindow =
  [self
    appropriateWindowForDocModalOperations];;

[[window contentView] addSubview:view];
[view release];
printOp = [NSPrintOperation
  printOperationWithView:view
    printInfo:printInfo];
[printOp setShowPanels:flag];
[printOp setCanSpawnSeparateThread:YES];

if (docWindow) {
  (void)[printOp
    runOperationModalForWindow:docWindow
    delegate:nil didRunSelector:NULL
    contextInfo:NULL];
} else {
    (void)[printOp runOperation];
}

[window release];
}
```

Print Panels

Print panels are the sheets that let you choose a printer, select a page range, and cancel the whole operation. They are displayed by the print operation object that you create and run.

Normally, the default panels are just fine. However, if you need to extend the print panel, create a view and add it to the bottom of the default print panel. You do so with the following code:

Java:

```
public void setAccessoryView(NSView aView);
```

Objective-C:

```
- (void)setAccessoryView:(NSView *)aView;
```

You also can set your own print pane within the print panel. This is preferred, because the basic look of the print panel will be preserved.

Print Info

Print info is the collection of data that is set using the Page Setup command. Your application has a print info object that it uses for its printing.

You can use the `printInfo` and `setPrintInfo` accessors to get the object. If you save data for your application (whether in a document or not), you should get the print info object and save it as shown here:

Java:

```
dict.setObjectForKey
  (NSArchiver.archivedDataWithRootObject
    (printInfo()),
  PrintInfoKey);
```

Objective-C:

```
[dict setObject [NSArchiver
  archivedDataWithRootObject:
    printinfo]
    forKey: PrintInfoKey];
```

This is the methodology described in Chapter 23. There are other ways to store the print info object, but all that matters is that it is stored.

Setting the print info object is also possible, but it has to be done carefully. You may prefer to add to the default print info dialog by calling the `setAccessoryView` method of NSLayout. Once you have done this, your application's print info object will have the data that you have specified in your view (and that your user has selected).

Java:

```
public void setAccessoryView(NSView aView;
```

Objective-C:

```
- (void)setAccessoryView:(NSView *)aView;
```

PDF and Clipboard Support

It is often the case that you need to produce a PDF version of your view. PDFOperationWithViewInsideRect creates a print operation that you can then run to transform a view into PDF and returns it in an NSMutableData object. You can then place that on the clipboard as you will see in next section. Here is the basic code to generate the PDF:

Java:

```
public static NSPrintOperation
  PDFOperationWithViewInsideRect
    (NSView aView,
     NSRect rect,
     NSMutableData data,
     NSPrintInfo aPrintInfo)
```

Objective-C:

```
+ (NSPrintOperation *)
  PDFOperationWithView:(NSView *)aView
  insideRect:(NSRect)rect
  toData:(NSMutableData *)data
  printInfo:(NSPrintInfo *)aPrintInfo;
```

Using that `print` operation, you can then produce a PDF image that you can place on the clipboard or use as a print preview. Here is how Sketch does it.

Java:

```
public void copy(Object sender) {
  NSArray orderedSelection =
    orderedSelectedGraphics();
  if (orderedSelection.count() > 0) {
    SKTDrawDocument document = drawDocument();
    NSPasteboard pboard =
      NSPasteboard.generalPasteboard();
    Object arrObjects [] =
      {SKTDrawDocument.DrawDocumentType,
      NSPasteboard.TIFFPboardType,
      NSPasteboard.PDFPboardType};
    pboard.declareTypes
      (new NSArray(arrObjects), null);

    pboard.setDataForType(document.
      drawDocumentDataForGraphics
        (orderedSelection),
        SKTDrawDocument.DrawDocumentType);
    pboard.setDataForType(document.
      TIFFRepresentationForGraphics
      (orderedSelection),
      NSPasteboard.TIFFPboardType);
    pboard.setDataForType(document.
      PDFRepresentationForGraphics
      (orderedSelection),
      NSPasteboard.PDFPboardType);
    _pasteboardChangeCount = pboard.changeCount();
    _pasteCascadeNumber = 1;
    _pasteCascadeDelta = new NSMutablePoint
      (DefaultPasteCascadeDelta,
      DefaultPasteCascadeDelta);
  }
}
```

```
public NSData PDFRepresentationForGraphics
  (NSArray graphics) {
  NSRect bounds =
    drawingBoundsForGraphics(graphics);

  SKTRenderingView view = new SKTRenderingView(
    new NSRect (0.0f, 0.0f, bounds.maxX(),
    bounds.maxY()), graphics);
  NSWindow tempWnd = new NSWindow
    (new NSRect (0.0f, 0.0f,
    bounds.maxX(), bounds.maxY()),
    NSWindow.BorderlessWindowMask,
    NSWindow.NonRetained, false);

  NSPrintInfo printInfo = printInfo();
  NSMutableData pdfData = new NSMutableData();
  NSPrintOperation printOp;

  tempWnd.contentView().addSubview(view);
  printOp =
    NSPrintOperation.
      PDFOperationWithViewInsideRect
      (view, bounds, pdfData, printInfo);
  printOp.setShowPanels(false);

  if (printOp.runOperation()) {
    } else {
      pdfData = null;
    }

  return pdfData;
}
```

Objective-C:

```
- (IBAction)copy:(id)sender {
  NSArray *orderedSelection =
    [self orderedSelectedGraphics];
  if ([orderedSelection count] > 0) {
    SKTDrawDocument *document =
    [self drawDocument];
  NSPasteboard *pboard =
```

```
  [NSPasteboard generalPasteboard];

[pboard declareTypes:[NSArray
  arrayWithObjects:SKTDrawDocumentType,
  NSTIFFPboardType,
  NSPDFPboardType, nil] owner:nil];
[pboard setData:
  [document drawDocumentDataForGraphics:
  orderedSelection]
  forType:SKTDrawDocumentType];
[pboard setData:
  [document TIFFRepresentationForGraphics:
  orderedSelection] forType:NSTIFFPboardType];
[pboard setData:
  [document PDFRepresentationForGraphics:
  orderedSelection] forType:NSPDFPboardType];
_pasteboardChangeCount = [pboard changeCount];
_pasteCascadeNumber = 1;
_pasteCascadeDelta = NSMakePoint
  (SKTDefaultPasteCascadeDelta,
  SKTDefaultPasteCascadeDelta);
  }
}

- (NSData *)PDFRepresentationForGraphics:
  (NSArray *)graphics {
    NSRect bounds =
      [self drawingBoundsForGraphics:graphics];
    SKTRenderingView *view =
      [[SKTRenderingView alloc]
      initWithFrame:NSMakeRect(0.0, 0.0,
      NSMaxX(bounds),
      NSMaxY(bounds)) graphics:graphics];
    NSWindow *window =
      [[NSWindow alloc]
      initWithContentRect:NSMakeRect(0.0, 0.0,
      NSMaxX(bounds), NSMaxY(bounds))
      styleMask:NSBorderlessWindowMask backing:
      NSBackingStoreNonretained defer:NO];
    NSPrintInfo *printInfo = [self printInfo];
    NSMutableData *pdfData =
      [[NSMutableData alloc] init];
```

```
NSPrintOperation *printOp;

[[window contentView] addSubview:view];
[view release];
printOp = [NSPrintOperation
  PDFOperationWithView:view
  insideRect:bounds toData:pdfData
  printInfo:printInfo];
[printOp setShowPanels:NO];

if ([printOp runOperation]) {
    [pdfData autorelease];
} else {
    [pdfData release];
    pdfData = nil;
}
[window release];

return pdfData;
}
```

Summary

In Mac OS X, the print architecture supports not just printing but also PDF generation. Printing is the last general-purpose application technology described in this book. The remaining chapters deal with specialized features of Mac OS X that you may or may not use.

For starters, the following chapter deals with human interface devices such as those used in games.

Chapter 26
Action! Games and Multimedia

This chapter contains essential information for game developers, but its subject matter goes far beyond games. Imagine for a moment a game in which you can use your computer to manipulate a wide range of devices whose controls and behavior you see on the screen. Perhaps you decide to try gene splicing or building DNA in a biology simulator game.

The only problem with this scenario is that it is not a game. Computers are constantly used to manipulate mechanical devices, and they receive input not only from the mouse and the keyboard, but also from a variety of control and graphical inputs—joysticks, dials, and the like.

The Macintosh computer has always been prominent in research—particularly in biomedical research and in space. In large part, this is because many research projects require scientists to combine computer programming skills with other, domain-based skills. The Macintosh has always provided advanced programming tools, and it continues to do so with Mac OS X.

Managing the human interface devices that run games and scientific experiments requires interacting with the basic hardware governed by the kernel. This chapter shows you the highlights of the Human Interface Device (HID) manager, which will be your constant companion.

Also in this chapter, you will find information about NSMovie and NSMovieView. These are the Cocoa classes that let you play and manipulate QuickTime movies.

Finally, the correct way to handle immersive interfaces using the full screen is described.

Human Interface Device (HID) Manager

One of the key features of Mac OS X and its kernel design is that you are insulated from the hardware. That is all well and good until you actually need to communicate directly with hardware. The key to this on the Mac OS X side is the communication concept of a Mach port in the kernel; on the device side, it is the USB standard that comes into play.

USB devices are categorized into a variety of classes, including hubs, mass storage (disks), monitors, printers, power devices, and human interface devices. This last category includes everything from keyboards, trackballs, and writing tablets to joysticks, knobs, switches, throttles, and steering wheels.

These devices are used to control games as well as equipment connected to the computer. They are also used for standard and adaptive input to applications and the operating system itself.

Human interface devices for USB are specified thoroughly on the USB site. See http://www.usb.org/developer for more information. For more information on the HID Manager, see the kernel documentation page—http://gemma.apple.com/techpubs/macosx/Kernel/kernel.html. The code in this section is based on the full code in "Working with HID Class Device Interfaces" references on that site.

Each HID device contains usage information that is defined for all USB HID devices in usage tables that you can download from http://www.usb.org/developers/hidpage.html. A device (such as a keyboard or trackball) can be defined by a combination of a usage page and usage number, which forms a unique value.

Interacting with HID devices is easy with the HID Manager. A detailed example is given in the kernel documentation mentioned above. Here is the summary of key steps in the process.

The code in this section is C++ Carbon code. The initial implementation of the HID Manager on Mac OS X is in that environment.

Create a Mach Port

Mach ports are an abstraction of the communication channels for your devices. You can get a Mach port by calling the following function:

```
IOReturn ioReturnValue  kIOReturnSuccess;
mach_port_t masterPort = NULL;

ioReturnValue = IOMasterport (bootstrap_port,
  &masterPort);
```

You will use `masterPort` throughout your program.

Find All Devices on the Port

The following code is not particularly simple, but it is called every time you want to find HID devices on the port. You do not have to vary it.

The heart of the device search is a call to `IOServiceGet-MatchingServices`. Located in IOKitLib.h, this method takes a dictionary that specifies the services you are searching for. It returns an iterator that you can later use to loop through those services.

You construct the dictionary to find all HID devices with this code:

```
hidMatchDictionary = IOServiceMatching
  (kIOHIDDeviceKey);
```

You then call `IOServiceGetMatchingServices`:

```
ioReturnValue=IOServiceGetMatchingServices
  (masterPort, hidMatchDictionary,
   hidObjectIterator);
```

If the iterator is not `NULL` on return, and if `ioReturnValue` is `kIOReturnSuccess`, you use the iterator to loop through the devices to find one that you are interested in.

Create an Interface to a Device

When you have found a device in which you are interested, you create an interface to it in order to use it. To do this, you run the iterator that was returned in the previous step:

```
io_name_t className;
IOCFPlugInInterface **plugInInterface =NULL;
HRESULT plugInResult =S_OK;
SInt32 score =0;
IOReturn ioReturnValue =kIOReturnSuccess;

while ((hidDevice = IOIteratorNext (
  hidObjectIterator)))
{
  … do your test…
```

```
if (deviceWanted)
{
ioReturnValue =IOObjectGetClass(
  hidDevice,className);

ioReturnValue =
  IOCreatePlugInInterfaceForService(hidDevice,
  kIOHIDDeviceUserClientTypeID,
  kIOCFPlugInInterfaceID,
  &plugInInterface,
  &score);

if (ioReturnValue ==kIOReturnSuccess)
{
  plugInResult =(*plugInInterface)->
    QueryInterface(plugInInterface,
    CFUUIDGetUUIDBytes(kIOHIDDeviceInterfaceID),
    (LPVOID)hidDeviceInterface);
  (*plugInInterface)->Release(plugInInterface);
}
}
```

You use this same code in all cases. The only customization is the test to see if you want to use a specific device. If you do, you need to create a hidDeviceInterface for each one (the variable is underlined in the code snippet). If you are developing an application in which multiple devices can be used (a game, for example), you will need to structure this code so that the body is located in a function which can be called repeatedly, and from which you can store hidDeviceInterface in an array or other data structure.

On the other hand, if you are searching for a single device, you can use the in-line code as it is here.

Open the Device

Once you have a device (or an array of devices), you open it (or them):

```
ioReturnValue =(*hidDeviceInterface)->
  open(hidDeviceInterface,0);
```

The name of your device interface needs to be passed in twice as shown in the underlined code. If you use a different name, change this.

Communicate

Use `getElementValue` to get the value of any element in the device.

```
result =(*hidDeviceInterface)->getElementValue
    (hidDeviceInterface, gXAxisCookie,&hidEvent);
```

The two keys to this are the constant identifying which element you are interested in and the `hidEvent`. This is used throughout the HID Manager and is defined as follows:

```
struct IOHIDEventStruct
{
    IOHIDElementTypetype;
    IOHIDElementCookieelementCookie;
    SInt32value;
    AbsoluteTimetimestamp;
    UInt32longValueSize;
    void *longValue;
};

typedef struct IOHIDEventStruct IOHIDEventStruct;
```

HID events are element values associated with a time. The element values are stored in the cookie within the event itself.

You can use the HID Manager to retrieve such events. You also can use it to create queues into which streams of events are placed.

At this point, you have the mechanism in place to access any HID device on a USB port and to get any of its data using the `getElementValue` method.

Close the Device

When you are finished, close the device and release the interface:

```
ioReturnValue =(*hidDeviceInterface)->
```

```
close(hidDeviceInterface);
(*hidDeviceInterface)->
  Release(hidDeviceInterface);
```

Free the Mach Port

Make sure to call the following function:

```
mach_port_deallocate (mach_task_self(),
  masterPort);
```

Identifying Devices

Although the data structures for HID devices include space for serial numbers, these rarely are used. As a result, apparently identical devices can appear.

Beecause you can plug and play USB devices, it is possible for a user to unplug a joystick or other HID device, plug it in again, and discover it will—or will not—appear as a new device.

The IO kit uses the following rule in this case. A device that appears on the USB bus in the same location as an apparently identical device (same model, manufacturer, name) is the same. Any difference causes the IO kit to think it is a different device. Thus, if your joystick is not responding properly and you unplug it, blow on the connector, and then plug it back in (a typically useless operation), it will appear as the same device. If you plug it into the USB hub on your display when it had been plugged directly into the computer's USB port, it will appear as a different device (although it is actually the same).

NSMovie and NSMovieView

NSMovie wraps a QuickTime movie. It is not a wrapper for all of QuickTime, but some of the QuickTime code is located here.

NSMovie

NSMovie is the wrapper for the movie itself. Note that the constructors in Java and Objective-C are slightly different. Also, in Objective-C, you can get a reference to the QuickTime movie itself on which you can use the QuickTime calls directly. That reference is not available from Java.

The constructors and inits create a movie in one of three ways:

1. An empty movie (Java) or a movie from a QuickTime movie pointer (Objective-C).

2. A movie from the clipboard (pasteboard).

3. A movie from a URL. For now, that URL must be local (e.g., file:///users/jfeiler/movies/cat.mov). The by-Ref argument determines how the movie will be archived if you choose to do that. If byRef is true, the URL (not the movie) will be archived. If it is false, the movie (not the URL) will be archived.

Java:

```
public NSMovie();
public NSMovie(NSPasteboard aPasteboard);
public NSMovie(java.net.URL anURL, boolean byRef);
```

Objective-C:

```
- (id)initWithMovie:(void*)movie;
- (id)initWithPasteboard:
  (NSPasteboard*)pasteboard;
- (id)initWithURL:(NSURL*)url
  byReference:(BOOL)byRef;

- (void*)QTMovie;
```

NSMovieView

NSMovieView is a standard view in Interface Builder. It includes the most common commands that you need for a movie:

- `goToBeginning`
- `goToEnd`
- `showController`
- `isPlaying`
- `cut`, `copy`, `paste`, `clear`

Note that the movie controller itself is normally used for navigation, so you rarely need to use `goToBeginning` and such. What is important to note is that NSMovieView supports the clipboard so that users can copy and paste movies into and out of your application's NSMovieView objects.

Immersive Applications

Games typically take control of the entire display, banishing menu bars, the desktop, and all other elements. Movies also sometimes have full-screen interfaces.

You do not write to the screen buffer on Mac OS X. To capture the full screen, you use a pair of methods in Carbon. (You must include the QuickTime framework in your project.)

The first method takes a host of arguments, but you can pass `NULL` and zero for many of them.

```
OSErr BeginFullScreen (Ptr *restoreState,
  GDHandle whichGD,
  SInt16 *desiredWidth,
  SInt16 *desiredHeight,
  WindowRef *newWindow,
  RGBColor *eraseColor,
  SInt32 flags );
```

Here is a typical use of `BeginFullScreen`:

```
WindowRef fullScreenWindow;
PtrstateToRestore;

BeginFullScreen(&stateToRestore,nil,0,0,
  &fullScreenWindow,0,fullScreenAllowEvents);
```

The WindowRef (`fullScreenWindow`) is created and returned by the method call; you can use it elsewhere in your program. For example, if you receive an application deactivate event, you should hide the window with

```
HideWindow (fullScreenWindow);
```

The pointer (`stateToRestore`) is a pointer to any data structure (or `NULL`) that you want. It is returned to you when you call `EndFullScreen`. Nothing is done to it in the meantime.

The last argument in the example shown here is a constant defined in QuickTime. Here is its definition:

```
enum { fullScreenHideCursor = 1,
  fullScreenAllowEvents = 2,
  fullScreenDontChangeMenuBar = 4,
  fullScreenPreflightSize = 8 };
```

Finally, you end full-screen mode with a call to the following method:

```
OSErr EndFullScreen (Ptr fullState, SInt32 flags);
```

As noted previously, you get your own pointer back with whatever information you placed in it. The second parameter can be nil (and often is).

Summary

The range of HID devices is vast. While many are used today for gaming, a quick glimpse at the header files will show you that telephone, set-top boxes, and a wide array of devices not yet deployed can be supported with these interfaces. Mac OS X is ready.

Chapter 27
Writing and Using Services

Services are one of the most useful features of Mac OS X. They move the concept of the shared clipboard far beyond its simple cut-and-paste stage. They can expose small (or large) pieces of an application's functionality to the world. This matters to you whether your application is destined to become a client or a server of a service. For example, if your application occasionally needs to perform some rather routine operation, you can rely on a service to provide that functionality and not write it yourself.

On the other hand, you may have an application that does one thing very cleverly; you can package your particular expertise as a service and let people incorporate it into other applications. Far too many great ideas for software have foundered when their developers have realized that to bring them to market they need to implement and re-implement a host of surround features that they have no interest in.

For all this, services are remarkably easy to implement in Cocoa. Note that services rely on the object that is known to users as the clipboard and to programmers as the pasteboard. As its programmatic name is NSPasteboard, that terminology is used in this chapter. In describing it to users, you should refer to the clipboard.

How Services Work

When you copy data to or from the clipboard, its type (text, picture, and so forth) has always been copied with it. Applications have been able to check whether they can handle clipboard types before copying information from it. In this way, applications can copy and paste their own data types in addition to the system data types.

The Basic Service Structure

Services rely on this mechanism, but they extend it. A service can be thought of as a round-trip to the clipboard from within an application. Typically, here is what happens:

1. You select something (such as text) in your application.

2. You choose a service from the Services submenu of the application menu.

3. The data is copied onto the pasteboard from your application.

4. The application providing the service is launched, if necessary, by the operating system.

5. That application receives the data from the pasteboard.

6. It does something to the data, and places it back on the pasteboard.

7. The data is returned to your application, where it replaces the selected data from step 1.

In this way, a sentence can be capitalized by a service, or a word can have its spelling replaced (the systemwide spell checking is implemented by a system service in Mac OS X).

Once you have set up a service, all of this happens automatically. If you use Cocoa, you already are a client of services where appropriate (for example, services involving text are available when you click in a text field or text view).

Other Types of Services

That pattern has variations that lead to two other types of services:

Output-Only Services Some services take no input. They only return data. They are enabled when your active target accepts the kind of data that the service provides. For example, Grab provides a service: It captures a screen shot and returns it as a TIFF image. If you are working in an object that accepts the pasting of a TIFF image, the Grab service is enabled automatically in the Services menu.

Input-Only Services Stickies are an example of such a service, as is Mail. In each case, you highlight some text. When you choose the service, it is copied to a new sticky or placed in the address or text of a new mail message. Nothing happens to the selected text in your own document.

How It Happens

Mac OS X uses the information you provide in your application's property list to set up the Services menu (that information is described in "Property List Settings" on page 553). It scans that information for all applications in standard locations to build the menu when you log in.

Standard locations are defined as the Applications folders at your computer's root, in your home directory, and in the Network domain. If your application is not located in one of those folders, it will not be scanned and will not be available as a service no matter what you do. Remember this when you test your application: You will have to move it to your Applications folder to test it.

This scanning happens at log in time. That means that you have to log out and log in again to see your service in the Services menu. You can make modifications to its code once it is in the menu without logging in again.

Business Models for Services

It is interesting to note that users and many developers really are intrigued with the idea of small, special-purpose applications. At the same time, what is on the market tends to be large, monolithic applications. Users want them, too. (You have only to look at the Project Builder mailing lists at Apple to see how many new features are requested for that application.)

Services offer a way to eat this particular cake and have it, too. Because the business model of commercial software changes at a glacial rate, many of the opportunities for services are within organizations such as corporations and schools. Because services can be so narrowly focused on a particular task, they can be small. Designed to be plugged into a variety of applications, they need not be particularly complicated to write. They should also be relatively inexpensive, and the combination of low cost to produce and low price to sell should still allow for a profit. (At least that is the theory.)

Many services (like much software in general) are provided as shareware and even freeware. Because services are focused so tightly on one task, it can be less risky to use them than other software from sources you may not normally deal with. Remember that a service is using a copy of your data: You are not entrusting your data to an application that will store it in a proprietary format that you cannot get to.

Setting Up a Service

Setting up a service requires making some entries in the property list (info.plist) for your application in Project Builder and then writing some code.

Property List Settings

Start by going to the Expert button in the Application Settings of the Target pane for your application as shown in Figure 27-1.

Figure 27-1. Expert Button in Application Settings

In the scrolling list at the bottom, select any item, and then click the Create Sibling button to create a new entry at that level. Name it NSServices as shown in the figure.

The pop-up menu to the right of the name is initially set to indicate that the new entry is a string. You must change it to an array to work with it further. As Figure 27-2 shows, once you have set it to an array, a disclosure triangle appears to the left of the name, and you can open the array.

Figure 27-2. Setting a Property to Be an Array

At the same time, the New Sibling button changes to New Child. You create one new child to begin with. Once you have done so, you select it and use the New Sibling button to create other second-level values. In practice, this turns out to be very simple, and it is logical, but you may need to get used to the interface.

The first entry in the NSServices array is numbered 0—you do not change the number. You can add additional services, but it is usually easiest to start with one to make certain that it works properly.

Go through the process again: Select the 0 entry, change its type to a dictionary with the pop-up menu, and then use the New Child button to create a subentry. Selecting that subentry, you can use the New Sibling button to add more as shown in Figure 27-3.

Figure 27-3. The NSServices Array

To rename any entry, just double-click on its default name and change the name. All of the property names (at the left in the figures shown here) are required. The ones at the right are not. Here is what the various properties mean:

NSMenuItem   This is the text that will appear in the Services menu for all applications. It is grayed out if your service is not applicable (based on the current selection and the items that the current object can receive by way of pasted values).

NSMessage   This is the name of the method in the services provider object of your application that will be called. (You will create this method in the next section.) It is not the name of an existing method in your application before you have added services. It may call an existing method, but it is a new one just created to handle services.

NSPortName   This is your application's name.

NSReturnTypes   This is an array of one or more types that your service will return. It can include standard Cocoa pasteboard types, or it can hold types specific to your application—or a mixture. For input-only services, the array is empty.

NSSendTypes   This is the companion array of types that can be sent to your service. For output-only services, it is empty.

NSUserData   This is a string that is passed into your service provider's method. You can use it for dispatching code so that one method provides several services. You could also use it to identify the requester of the service. This could be part of a security implementation. Remember, though, that the string is constant—it is specified in the property list, so you cannot modify it when the service is requested. NSUserData is optional.

Writing the Code

Services are managed by a service provider object. You create this object (as a descendat of Object in Java or NSObject in Objective-C), and you implement methods in it to handle each of the service requests. (If you use the optional NSUserData property, a single method can handle multiple service requests with the dispatching controlled by the NSUserData string that is passed in from the property list.) At run time, you instantiate this object and set it as the application's service provider.

Creating the Service Provider   Create a new class in your application: Go to the New File command in the File menu and choose Java Class or Objective-C class.

In Diary, an input-only service is provided. If you select some text in an application, you can choose New Diary Entry from the Services menu: A new Diary entry will be created with that text as the main text, with a title that consists of the date and time, and with a subtitle reading "Created by a Mac OS XService." (The user presumably will change these.) This is a simple way to quickly add a Diary entry from any text that you find in an email, a document you read, or a Web site.

The service provider class can have any structure that you want. In this case, it needs to be instantiated with a reference to the DiaryDocument object itself so that the service can use the reference to create a new entry. Here is the shell of the service provider code:

Java:

```java
import com.apple.cocoa.foundation.*;
import com.apple.cocoa.application.*;

public class DiaryService extends Object {
  private DiaryDocument theDiary;

  public DiaryService(DiaryDocument aDiary) {
    super();
    theDiary = aDiary;

  public void newEntryForService
    (NSPasteboard pboard,
    String userData,
    String error) {

    ...
  };
}
```

Objective-C:

```objc
#import <Cocoa/Cocoa.h>
#import "DiaryDocument.h"
```

```
@interface DiaryService : NSObject {
  DiaryDocument* theDiary;
}

- (void)init;

- (void)newDiaryEntryForService:
  (NSPasteboard *)pboard
  userData:(NSString *)data
  error:(NSString **)error;

@end
```

You create an instance of this class and then install it as a service as soon as your application starts up. In the Diary application, the service class is called DiaryService. Here is the instantiation and installation code. Because it needs the reference to DiaryDocument, it is located at the end of the constructor for DiaryDocument in Diary.

Java:

```
DiaryService theService = new DiaryService(this);
NSApplication.sharedApplication().
  setServicesProvider (theService);
```

Objective-C:

```
DiaryService *theService =
  [[DiaryService alloc] init:self];
[[NSApplication sharedApplication]
  setServiceProvider:theService];
```

You will note that the constructor and initializer of this object take a reference to this/self. At this point, that is the document object. This reference allows the service to access the document data that it will need).

Implementing the Service Provider Next, you write the code for your service provider. You can do whatever you want within it, but you must implement each method you have identified in the NSMessage property item for each of your services. Each of these methods has three arguments:

1. A pasteboard from which you can take data and to which you may return data.

2. A string which is the string (if any) you specified in the NSUserData property.

3. A string containing an error message that you can return.

In the `newEntryForService` method, you need to retrieve the text from the service request; you the create a Diary entry. The procedure for retrieving the text is common to many services. In fact, the underlined code in these snippets is the boilerplate code you use to retrieve any data from the clipboard (pasteboard). The calls to create the Diary entry are not boilerplate, but they are analogous to the calls you make to implement your own services. Note that this code contains no error checking, and the literal string used would normally be declared as a constant.

Java:

```
public void newEntryForService
{
   String pboardString;
   String newString;
   NSArray  types;

   types = pboard.types ();
   pboardString = stringForType
     (NSPasteboard.StringPboardType);

   theDiary.addEntry (null);
   theDiary.setEntryTitle (
     (String)new NSDate().toString(););
   theDiary.setEntrySubtitle (
     "Created by a Mac OS X Service");
   theDiary.setEntryEntry (pboardString);
```

```
    return;

}
```

Objective-C:

```
- (void)newEntryForService:
  (NSPasteboard *)pboard
 userData:(NSString *)data
 error:(NSString **)error
 {
    NSString *pboardString;
    NSString *newString;
    NSArray *types;

    types = [pboard types];

    pboardString =
      [pboard stringForType:NSStringPboardType]));

    [theDiary addEntry:null];
    [theDiary setEntryTitle:
        [NSCalendarDate date]];
    [theDiary setEntrySubtitle: @"Entry Created
        by Mac OS X Service"];
    [theDiary setEntryEntry: pboardString];

    return;
 }
```

Summary

Services provide a long-wanted facility to share applications' functionality. You can incorporate them into your applications and workflows as well as provide them to others. They are an important new feature of Mac OS X that helps you to create your own custom solutions.Also available in Mac OS X is AppleScript: the user programming language that your application can support. It is the topic of the next chapter.

Chapter 28
Scripting in Mac OS X

AppleScript has been one of the most popular features of the Mac OS since its debut in System 7. On Mac OS X, it is available in the Carbon and Cocoa frameworks. The implementation on Cocoa is different from that on Carbon in a number of significant ways that reflect the Cocoa architecture.

Mac OS X provides users with a vast array of ways to do things, and that includes going about the tasks of running programs and doing the work (and play) that they want to do. Continuing Apple's tradition of user-centric computing, users now have the ability to do the same thing with the keyboard and mouse, from the command line, from scripts—and with the integration of services. The developer's job is to create the functionality and package it in as many of these formats as possible so that the user can find it and take advantage of it in the easiest way possible.

Because of its importance, AppleScript is documented well on Apple's developer Web site. There are many constants defined for use in the grammar files. This chapter walks you through a very simple grammar to show you how to get started.

AppleScript Overview

The intensely interactive point-and-click/typing interface was a welcome breath of fresh air to computer users who were tired of typing obscure commands into their computers. For certain tasks (among them, content creation—that is, writing, drawing, and multimedia editing), this interactivity cannot be beat.

Yet for other tasks—intensely repetitive and boring tasks such as reformatting scores of images from TIFF files to JPEG files—the interactivity is a pain. It does not matter that the command line was gibberish: Typing in one line of gibberish and then going home for the night while the computer works may be worth it.

Early automation tools for the interactive interface focused on simulating mouse and keyboard processing. These scripts and macros worked well once they were developed, but they were prone to problems caused by any change in the environment. If a dialog box moved a fraction of a hair on the screen, the preprogrammed mouse click went awry.

It is in this context that Apple started to develop Apple events and AppleScript: projects that would make an application's objects and functionality programmable by users. AppleScript is a language with syntax that is not hard for advanced users to master. Furthermore, it was designed from the start to be used with a variety of dialects—pro and novice as well as French and Chinese.

Classes and Commands

There are two parts to AppleScript: classes and commands. You may implement either of them, but normally both are implemented in one way or another. You define classes to represent your application's data objects. Internally, you can write a variety of functions to support the translation from Apple-Script to object: People are used to writing about the fifth object, the first, or the last, and you must support that. (With interactive applications, you do not worry about this issue because the user clicks on whichever object is to be acted on.)

Scripting Functionality and Interface

The commands that you define represent your application's functionality. They may also represent its interface. Apple-Script in Cocoa is supported at both the AppKit and Foundation levels. In architectural terms, it is implemented in your model (data) classes as well as in your view (interface) classes. The reason for this is that users do not make the distinctions that developers make. Some scripts are designed to automate tasks that appear logical and integrated to a user but not to a developer.

Take as an example a real-life set of instructions to a personal assistant. These might include opening the mail and preparing a cup of morning coffee—clearly substantive tasks. The instructions might also include an instruction to tilt the window blinds in a certain way—surely an interface type of task. Yet, to the user, all are of equal importance: When they are completed, work can begin.

Uses of Scripting

Scripting is used in a variety of ways to make users' and developers' lives easier.

Automation of Test Suites   You can use scripting yourself to run your application through its paces in order to test it. The advantage of automated test suites of any sort is that you can accumulate all sorts of interesting combinations and run through them overnight or during a weekend. The repeatability of an automated test suite makes it an ideal tool for quality assurance.

Demonstrations AppleScript is used to drive demonstrations. You can build scripts that run your application over and over, but you can also build them to stop at given points.

Solutions and Integration AppleScript is used extensively in solutions that involve integration of several products (a database, for example, and a page layout program). AppleScript consultants write solutions from your building blocks—if they are scriptable. If they are not, they may go elsewhere. The users of AppleScript are a very vocal group in the Macintosh community!

Training You can write scripts that run to a certain point and then stop, allowing the user to continue if possible.

Setups You can also write scripts that revert an environment back to a known condition. These are popular in computer labs as well as in training environments where the script has run to a certain point, and then stopped to allow the user to continue—but the user doesn't have a clue and just walks away leaving the computer in a befuddled mess. A setup script can restore everything to a known state.

Making Your Application Scriptable

If your application is scriptable, it recognizes AppleScript commands that users write. In addition, users can open its dictionary from the Script Editor Open Dictionary command in its File menu to find out what scripting commands they can use.

The dictionary, shown in Figure 28-1, reflects your Apple-Script syntax. It is formatted by Script Editor from your scripting resources. Because it is formatted from these resources, it always matches the syntax. Also, because no additional coding on your part is required, the dictionary is always available.

Figure 28-1. Script Editor Dictionary

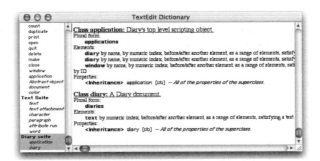

To display your application's dictionary and to make it scriptable, you must add NSAppleScriptEnabled to your property list in Project Builder. In the Targets pane, select your project. Then, click the Application Settings tab, followed by the Expert button as shown in Figure 28-2.

Unless NSAppleScriptEnabled is in the property list already, click New Sibling to add it. Make certain that its type is String, and type YES for its value.

Next, you build your grammar.

Figure 28-2. Making Your Application Scriptable in Project Builder

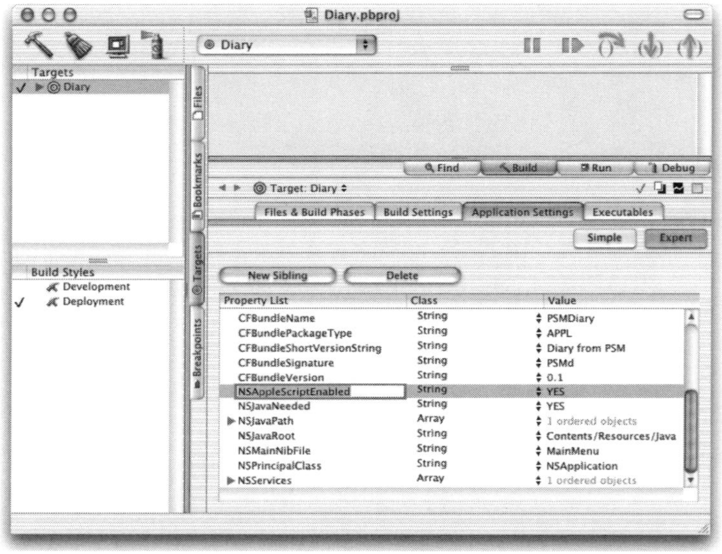

Building the Grammar

You build your grammar in two parts: The script suite is the programmer's view of your AppleScript support, and the terminology file is the localized version. You have one script suite file and as many terminology files as languages that you support.

The script suite file should be placed at the top level of your Resources folder in your project and on disk. The terminology files should be placed in the appropriate lproj folders on disk (English.lproj, Dutch.lproj, or whatever). They will automatically appear in the Project Builder hierarchy organized together.

Figure 28-3 shows the Project Builder hierarchy; Figure 28-4 shows the Finder hierarchy. (Remember to use the Add File command from the Project menu to add the files to your project after you have placed them properly on disk.

Figure 28-3. Project Builder AppleScript File Structure

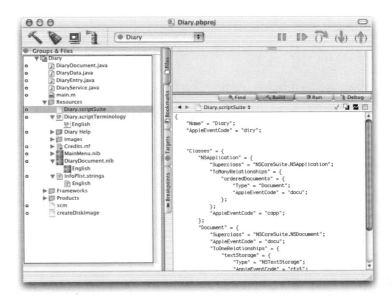

Figure 28-4. Finder AppleScript File Structure

Implementing the Grammar

The script suite and terminology files have a similar structure. Stripped of all the actual code, here is what the `scriptsuite-file` looks like:

```
{
    "Name" = "Diary";
    "AppleEventCode" = "diry";

    "Classes" = {
    };
    "Commands" = {
    };
}
```

Likewise, here is what the terminology file looks like:

```
{
    "Name" = "Diary suite";
    "Description" = "Diary specific classes.";

    "Classes" = {
    };
```

```
"Commands" = {
};


}
```

These files quickly get quite lengthy, so it helps to know your way around them. Note that if you do not have classes or commands, those sections do not appear at all.

Classes

To implement support for classes, you need to write code in the script suite, the terminology file, and your application.

Implementing the Script Suite The Classes section of Diary.scriptSuite is shown here. You can see its logical structure represented in the dictionary shown in Figure 28-1.

Note that for each class your application responds to, you must provide its superclass as well as an event code. You may also provide details of its internal structure using `ToManyRelationship`, `ToOneRelationship` or whatever other relationships are needed.

```
"Classes" = {
    "NSApplication" = {
        "Superclass" = "NSCoreSuite.
          NSApplication";
        "ToManyRelationships" = {
            "orderedDocuments" = {
                "Type" = "Document";
                "AppleEventCode" = "docu";
            };
        };
        "AppleEventCode" = "capp";
    };
    "DiaryEntry" = {
        "Superclass" = "NSCoreSuite.
          AbstractObject";
        "AppleEventCode" = "dent";
    };
    "DiaryDocument" = {
      "Superclass" = "NSCoreSuite.NSDocument";
```

```
                    "AppleEventCode" = "docu";
                    "ToManyeRelationships" = {
                        "entries" = {
                            "Type" = "DiaryEntry";
                            "AppleEventCode" = "dent";
                        };
                    };
                };
            };
```

This code defines three classes: NSApplication, DiaryEntry, and DiaryDocument. Within the NSApplication class, one key is defined: `orderedDocuments`. Within DiaryDocument, another key is defined: `entries`. These will be used in your application code.

Implementing the Terminology File The terminology file maps your AppleScript terminology to an individual language. Here is the terminology file for the script suite:

```
"Classes" = {
    "NSApplication" = {
        "Name" = "application";
        "PluralName" = "applications";
        "Description" = "Diary's top level
            scripting object.";
    };
    "DiaryDocument" = {
        "Name" = "diary";
        "PluralName" = "diaries";
        "Description" = "A Diary document.";
    };
    "DiaryEntry" = {
        "Name" = "entry";
        "PluralName" = "entries";
        "Description" = "An individual
            diary entry.";
    };
```

The file is fairly self-explanatory. For each class defined in the script suite, natural language names and a description are provided. These are what show up in the Script Editor dictionary.

Application Support You can implement a number of methods that help AppleScript run through objects to find the third word of the fifth paragraph and so forth. At a minimum, you should implement accessors for the keys that you defined in the script suite. These have the standard naming convention: `setKey` and `key` for setters and getters, respectively.

Commands

Handling commands is similar to classes. You define them in the script suite file, set their terminology, and then implement them in your application.

Summary

This chapter harks back to the question posed in this book's introduction: "Who is a programmer?" By making your application scriptable, you provide the raw material for the end user as programmer. That person, in turn, can take your work and combine it with other work products to create something new and undreamed-of.

The last chapter of this book pursues this paradigm one more step as it explores the possibilities for writing reusable code for programmers.

Chapter 29
Writing Reusable
Components

If you refer back to the diagrams in Chapter 2 that describe the evolution of Mac OS X, you will see that the operating system and its application programs have grown from a monolithic blob of code custom-written for every task to a sophisticated collection of interacting components, most of which are used and reused. Users, too, are coming to understand and appreciate this architecture. Instead of the mysterious blob of "the system" and its extensions, control panels, plug-ins, and the like, today's Mac OS X users can see that their computers run dozens of programs at a time.

The benefits of componentized software are well known; the problem has always been implementing components in the real world. With Mac OS X, users can see the individual components at work (using

Process Viewer), and they can use them and assemble them into customized solutions using the command line in Terminal, AppleScript, and Services.

You automatically reap the benefits of componentized software when you use an object-oriented framework such as Cocoa, MacApp, or PowerPlant. But there is yet another type of component reuse available to you through the use of reusable code that you assemble.

This chapter provides an overview of the two main strategies for reusing code across applications: frameworks and palettes. As with so much of the Mac OS X architecture, it just works. In addition, it is a very powerful architecture. So you might as well use it.

Frameworks

Frameworks on Mac OS X are dynamic linked libraries that are packaged in a versioned bundle. Note that this usage of "framework" is different from its usage in the sense of an object-oriented framework such as Cocoa, MacApp, or PowerPlant. Frameworks as dynamic linked libraries in Mac OS X need not be object-oriented, although they frequently are.

Why Use a Framework?

A framework encapsulates code that can stand more or less by itself. At one extreme, it can be common code that is used by many applications. At another extreme, it can be very esoteric code that is used by few applications—but you may not want its source code modified or even viewed by the programmers who use it.

A framework also can be an effective way of combining programming languages. Using the Java bridge, you can expose Objective-C objects to Java programmers, and vice versa.

Finally, frameworks can be a very good way of splitting a programming project into independent components that separate programmers or teams of programmers can work on.

Once you have created a framework in Project Builder, you go about programming it just as you would any other code: You declare objects, variables, and methods, and write normally. You can add files to the framework just as you always do.

Frameworks cannot run on their own. As a result, if you are building a framework, you normally build a companion project to incorporate it and run it so that you can test it.

How Frameworks Run

Frameworks are dynamically linked shared libraries. This means that when a program runs, it is linked to a single copy of the library to which other programs may also be linked. Only one copy of the library code runs. This can improve efficiency (each of the application programs is smaller, because the shared code is in the single library).

Dynamic Linking Dynamic linking happens at the last possible moment. (The alternative is static linking, which happens at the end of the compilation process.) Only those parts of the framework that are needed are linked.

Because symbol resolution (the process of linking) is done on an as-needed basis and at the lowest possible level, you should be careful that you plan for it. Related methods and objects should be in the same module if they will be used together; the module will be linked and all will be available. On the other hand, if some related code is used frequently and other equally related code is used infrequently, you may want to attempt to separate them so that the less frequently used code is not linked unnecessarily.

Frameworks may contain multiple versions of themselves. Mac OS X takes care of linking to the appropriate one, providing that you have set the version properly (see "Versioning the Framework" on page 576).

Reentrant Because a single library may be shared by many programs at the same time, the code must be reentrant. That is, any process that is linked to it must be able to use it without coming into conflict with another process. This applies at the low level of code as well as at the higher level of architecture: If the library stores any information in a common variable (or on disk), that information must not be specific to a client unless it is so identified.

Where Frameworks Live When you deploy frameworks, they are normally placed in the Frameworks folder within a Library folder. Library folders exist in a user's home directory, at the system level, and at the network domain. When a dynamic linked library needs to be loaded, Mac OS X looks in these places (in that order).

Creating a Framework

You create frameworks in Project Builder by using the New Project command from the File menu. Choose the appropriate item from the list. Project Builder will automatically set up the files and build settings for you.

Inside the framework, you write code that you will want to use from other applications. In those applications, you use a framework by choosing Add Framework (not Add File) from the Project menu. Project Builder will import it properly.

Versioning the Framework

Use the Target button in the project structure pane of Project Builder to go to Build Settings. Set FRAMEWORK_VERSION to the current version of your framework. By default, this variable starts with A.

Palettes

Palettes often are used with frameworks. They are components that can be added to Interface Builder so that your new interface elements can be used and reused.

The same reasons for using frameworks apply to palettes: They encapsulate functionality that you do not want to have to reimplement each time you use it.

You create a new palette in Interface Builder by choosing IB Palette from the list of choices in the Starting Point. Your palette can be a combination of existing Interface Builder objects (in a customized window, for example, that you will want to use in many applications for your organization). More often, however, it involves custom objects (including custom views) that you want to reuse.

If you have custom objects in your palette, you match the palette up with a framework that provides the code for the objects. You need to write three sets of code for your palette objects:

1. You write the functional code that you would always write to support an object—outlets and actions.

2. You override IBPalette to implement the object's functionality within Interface Builder (such as the setting of connections using the Info window).

3. You override IBInspector to provide other information.

If you are building a framework to support a palette, you include InterfaceBuilder.framework.

Sample palette and framework files are part of the examples for Interface Builder and Project Builder. They approach the issues in different ways, so it can be useful to compare BusyPalette with ProgressViewPalette to see where they differ.

The Object Itself   This is the object that is instantiated at run time in the final application. The palette objects are normally subclasses of NS-

View (or of other view objects). You implement the same basic functionality that you would write in Project Builder if you were coding the object directly.

You must make certain to override coding methods so that the object can be read and written. If it contains any data (such as values the user may have set in Interface Builder), this step is required. If it uses only default values, you do not have to do this.

Here are the shells of the methods you implement:

```
- (id)initWithCoder:(NSCoder *)decoder
{
  self = [super initWithCoder:decoder];
  ...
  return self;
}

- (void)encodeWithCoder:(NSCoder *)coder
{
  [super encodeWithCoder:coder];
  ...
}
```

IBPalette

This is the object that you manipulate in Interface Builder as you build your interface. Create a descendant of IBPalette for your palette object. Depending on the object, you may need to allocate (and deallocate) variables as it is created. You may override finishInstantiate to do processing when an object is first created. You always override inspectorClass-Name; it returns the name of the IBInspector class that is described in the next section.

```
- (NSString *)inspectorClassName
{
  return @"YourPaletteInspector";
}
```

IBInspector

You override IBInspector to implement the functionality your object displays in the Info window (formerly called the Inspector window—hence the name).

You also may provide a nib with interface elements that will appear in the Info window's Attributes pane to let users set your object's values. If so, you must load this nib in your IBInspector `init` method.

You always override the methods that complete actions in the Info window—`ok` and `revert`. If your object has data values (titles or labels, for example), you move them from the view into the variables that will be stored.

Summary

Perhaps the most important thought for developers to take away from the world of Mac OS X is that programming in that environment starts from a much more sophisticated level than in most other environments. Core Foundation and Cocoa's Foundation framework wrap simple concepts in powerful classes and class wrappers; Apple Class Suites bring such classes to C++ along with sophisticated error checking.

The Carbon and Cocoa frameworks handle interface and event dispatching quickly and with very little need for custom-written code. What code you do write can be provided to users and other developers for further use with AppleScript and through frameworks and palettes you create.

In short, from a developer's point of view, Mac OS X is a font of productivity tools that you can use and create for others to use. It also is a sophisticated and elegant user experience with its Aqua interface, and the frameworks help you take advantage of and adhere to the interface guidelines.

Mac OS X is missing one important feature: your imagination. Whether it is sophisticated business logic, imaginative media authoring tools, or as-yet-unheard-of ideas, Apple has done its part. The rest is up to you.

Index

O

X

About the Author

JESSE FEILER is the author of a number of Mac OS X books including *Mac OS X: The Complete Reference* and *Java Programming on Mac OS X*. He is also the author of *WebObjects 5 Developer's Guide*, as well as many books on the Web-based enterprise (such as *Database-Driven Web Sites* and *Managing the Web-Based Enterprise)*, the Y2K problem, home offices, databases, and FileMaker. His books on Open-Doc, Cyberdog, Apple Guide, and Rhapsody are now collector's items.

He has worked as a developer and manager for companies such as the Federal Reserve Bank of New York (monetary policy and bank supervision), Prodigy (early Web browser), Apple (information systems), New York State Department of Health (rabies and lead poisoning), The Johnson Company (office management), and Young & Rubicam (media planning and new product development).

His interests in new forms of technical training have led him to MediaSchool (http://www.mediaschool.com), for which he has authored several Mac OS X courses available over the Internet, as well as to Geek Cruises' Mac Mania cruise to Alaska. He is also the first author of a technical book to be published both on paper and on an e-book.

Active in the community, he is President of the Mid-Hudson Library System, Chair of the Philmont Comprehensive Plan Board, founder of the Philmont Main Street Committee, and Treasurer of the HB Playwrights Foundation.

He lives 100 miles north of New York City in the Village of Philmont with a rescued greyhound and a cat. His research into iMovie, iDVD, and Image Capture has earned him the sobriquet "The Digital Scourge of Philmont."